IN THE SHADE OF
THE QUR'ĀN

In the name of God, the Compassionate, the Merciful

Sayyid Quṭb

❧

IN THE SHADE OF
THE QUR'ĀN

Fī Ẓilāl al-Qur'ān

VOLUME IX

❧

SŪRAHS 10–11

Yūnus – Hūd

❧

Translated and Edited by
Adil Salahi

❧

THE ISLAMIC FOUNDATION
AND
ISLAMONLINE.NET

Published by

THE ISLAMIC FOUNDATION,

Markfield Conference Centre,
Ratby Lane, Markfield, Leicestershire LE67 9SY, United Kingdom
Tel: (01530) 244944, Fax: (01530) 244946
E-mail: i.foundation@islamic-foundation.org.uk
Website: www.islamic-foundation.org.uk

Quran House, PO Box 30611, Nairobi, Kenya

PMB 3193, Kano, Nigeria

ISLAMONLINE.NET,
PO Box 22212, Doha, Qatar
E-mail: webmaster@islam-online.net
Website: www.islamonline.net

British Library Cataloguing-in-Publication Data
Qutb, Sayyid, 1903–1966
    In the shade of the Qur'an: Fi zilal al-Qur'an,
    Vol. 9: Surah 10–11: Yunus–Hud
    1. Koran – Commentaries
    I. Title   II. Salahi, M.A.   III. Islamic Foundation
    IV. Fi zilal al-Qur'an
    297.1'227

ISBN 0 86037 329 0
ISBN 0 86037 334 7 pbk

Typeset by: N.A.Qaddoura
Cover design by: Imtiaze A. Manjra
Printed and bound in Great Britain by
Antony Rowe Ltd., Chippenham, Wiltshire

Contents

Transliteration Table

Consonants. Arabic

initial: unexpressed medial and final:

ء	’	د	d	ض	ḍ	ك	k
ب	b	ذ	dh	ط	ṭ	ل	l
ت	t	ر	r	ظ	ẓ	م	m
ث	th	ز	z	ع	‘	ن	n
ج	j	س	s	غ	gh	هـ	h
ح	ḥ	ش	sh	ف	f	و	w
خ	kh	ص	ṣ	ق	q	ي	y

Vowels, diphthongs, etc.

Short: ـَ a   ـِ i   ـُ u

long: ـَا ā   ـِي ī   ـُو ū

diphthongs: ـَوْ aw

ـَىْ ay

viii

Violence in Sayyid Qutb's Perspective

Perhaps Sayyid Qutb was at his best when he wrote about those parts of the Qur'ān that were revealed in Makkah, during the first 13 years of the Prophet's message. These dealt mainly with the basics of faith, the beliefs a Muslim must accept, the principles applicable in human life and the moral values that must be upheld. The parts that were revealed later, in Madinah, outline legislation that must be applied in any Muslim society and comment on events that involved the Muslim community. While both are contained within the same book that organizes human life in the Islamic way, there are marked differences in style and approach.

The present volume includes two *sūrahs* of medium length, both of which were revealed in Makkah. Both demonstrate Sayyid Qutb's superb presentation of the divine discourse in a way that shows its immediate relevance to human life, here and now, and indeed at all times and places. He portrays the complementarity of the two *sūrahs*, which may not be readily apparent, as their subject matter and thematic sequence give each *sūrah* its distinct character.

Primarily, the Makkan parts of the Qur'ān address the moulding of the Muslim community so as to provide a living example of Islam in practice. Hence they are closely related to our own situation whereby the advocates of Islam aim to bring about the rebirth of the Muslim community that implements Islam in all fields of life. Sayyid Qutb dwells at length on every aspect they tackle as such rebirth was his main preoccupation. Hence, he considered a clear understanding of these parts of the Qur'ān, an understanding that remains free of ambiguity and short-term preoccupations, to be a main prerequisite for the success of Islamic revival. He saw his main task as making such understanding possible through a clear presentation of the meaning of the Qur'ān, drawing on the same line adopted by the first Muslim generation which brought about the first and most shining example of Islamic life.

To Sayyid Quṭb, and indeed to all Muslims who properly understand the far-reaching significance of the declaration that everyone must make before they are considered Muslim, following the Prophet's example is an essential part of the Islamic faith. This does not merely apply to the principles of faith and the major Islamic beliefs, but also to the line of action he followed and the methodology he put in place to determine the attitudes of the Muslim community to different situations. Unless we follow the Prophet's example, we are liable to err, and our errors could have detrimental consequences for our own community and for the success of the Islamic message.

This does not imply any rigidity in our approach to dealing with the problems that we may face. No one denies the fact that life presents different problems in different communities and at different times. No two problems or two human situations are the same. Hence, to suggest that we must have the same practical solutions for all problems at all times and in all localities betrays a serious flaw. Instead, what we are speaking about when we emphasize the need to follow the Prophet's example is the overall approach that determines our standpoint. When this is clear in our minds we can deal with practical realities as we deem fit, taking into consideration all factors that influence our situation and the likely outcome of the measures we take. This means that the approach is the same, but the practical steps we take are totally different.

The large number of military takeovers in Arab countries, resulting in an immediate change of regime, and bringing into power different philosophies and political programmes, inevitably influenced the thinking of Islamic revivalists. Many thought that a military takeover would be the shortest route to bring back Islam into the lives of the Muslim peoples of these countries. Such thoughts were reinforced when different groups advocating Islamic revival were subjected to brutal persecution, long imprisonment, torture, killings and a denial of their basic human rights. Being the largest revivalist movement in the Arab world, the Muslim Brotherhood suffered most, particularly in Egypt where the Nasser regime was determined to ruthlessly crush any real or perceived opposition to its rule. It is no wonder that many victims of the Nasser dictatorship should think of a 'quick' solution; namely, a military *coup*. After all, Nasser himself had come to power through such means, followed by a series of mini-plots against colleagues and rivals. Giving Nasser a taste of his own medicine appealed to many. It is then pertinent to ask: what was Sayyid Quṭb's reaction to such ideas?

When the Egyptian army staged its takeover that ended the monarchy in Egypt in 1952, Sayyid Quṭb was a strong supporter. In fact, he was the first to call it a 'revolution' in his press articles. Prior to that, the phrase used by the media and the new junta themselves to refer to the *coup* was 'the army's action'. He personally knew a number of the military officers who became members of the Revolutionary Command Council, and he was close to Nasser himself. But his support was based on assurances that the ultimate objective of the takeover was to serve the cause of Islam, and to give back to Egypt its Islamic character. He was even offered positions high up in the new hierarchy, but he declined. At the outset, when he still trusted the new rulers, his reason was that he wanted to remain free, untied to the government, so that his advice could be better received. Even when he was invited to join the government as a minister, he declined, preferring to wait until the new regime had established its character.

It did not, however, take long for that character to crystallize, with the regime speedily moving away from Islam, and Nasser establishing one of the most brutal dictatorships of the twentieth century. While Sayyid Quṭb was mightily disappointed, considering this to be a terrible setback, the shift, or the deception involved, made him realize that the desired change could never come about through a quick takeover, particularly a military one. Thereafter, he distanced himself from the regime, but the regime continued to try to lure him with offers of high position. His answer though was always the same: "If the government aims to serve Islam, I am a strong supporter with all my power. If it has a different agenda, my way is totally different."

Events moved fast, and the military regime felt it could not gain absolute control of Egypt until the Muslim Brotherhood, the only opposition organization enjoying strong popular support, was smashed. A stage-managed attempt on Nasser's life was used to justify the arrest of tens of thousands of Islamic advocates, the large majority of whom belonged to the Brotherhood. Sayyid Quṭb was among them and, like most of them, was brutally tortured.

In prison, Sayyid Quṭb reflected deeply on what had happened to the Brotherhood, a movement dedicated to Islamic revival. However, he was not so much troubled by the fact that a military dictatorship should try to smash such a movement, kill its leaders, imprison and torture its rank and file. To him, this was in the nature of things: Islam stood for the freedom of mankind from all forms of tyranny, at all levels, within the family, tribe or society, by individuals, groups, or governments. Hence, a military dictatorship was bound to be on a collision course with an Islamic revivalist movement. What troubled him most though was the fact that those who were ready to compromise with the government, or to declare their regret for taking a stand in opposition to it, were numerous as compared with those who remained steadfast. All were aware that the Brotherhood did not take any action to overthrow Nasser's government, and that the charges against its leaders and general membership were false. Yet they were prepared to accept them as true, apologize for such misdeeds, and declare their firm support for the government.

Most people would argue that taking such a position was understandable. If it could bring about the release of innocent people from prison, then it would be a small price to pay. It did not commit those people to anything more than keeping a low profile, showing that they no longer had any interest in politics. After all, such people had not committed any crime in the first place. They were unjustly imprisoned. Hence, to obtain their release by declaring support of the government did not amount to much. They could still maintain their religious stance and continue to worship privately in peace.

To Sayyid Quṭb, and indeed to any Islamic scholar aspiring for Islamic revival, this was unacceptable for any advocate of Islam. Such advocates should provide the practical example of the change Islam produces in human life. If they were to hide within the confines of their homes, or their immediate social circle and suppress their beliefs, what chance would be left for people to learn the true nature of Islam and the social order it wants to put in place? Besides, *jihād*, or the struggle for God's cause, is an essential principle of Islam, which is required of all Muslims. If those who are the vanguard of the movement aiming to bring about Islamic reawakening sit at home, abandoning all interest in the life of the community, what chance do they leave for such a reawakening?

To understand what sort of response should be taken by those who were in Nasser's prisons for no reason other than their advocacy of Islam, Sayyid Quṭb looked for guidance in the only infallible sources: the Qur'ān and the Prophet. He looked at the situation the Prophet and his Companions faced from the Quraysh persecution in Makkah. They were subjected to imprisonmewt, torture, economic and social boycott, as well as a barrage of false accusations. The Prophet himself was the target of several assassination attempts. At no time did God or the Prophet permit those who were suffering such brutal persecution to apologize or retract the advocacy of their cause. On the contrary, they always advised them to persevere in the face of adversity, making clear to them that such perseverance is a prerequisite for their eventual victory. Moreover, they were required not to retaliate. Although some of them at least could have caused their persecutors some trouble, they were told to stay their hands.

Under such duress, some of the early Muslims complained to the Prophet asking: "Would you not pray to God on our behalf? Would you not request His help against our enemies?" The Prophet's reply was to tell them of the trials earlier advocates of the divine faith had to put up with, and to reassure them of the eventual triumph. He said: "Some of those before you were cut in half, with a saw, from the head downwards; and some endured torture with combs made of iron tearing the flesh off their bones but they never wavered. By God Almighty, He will accomplish this matter of ours until a lone traveller can move in peace from Ṣanaʿāʾ to Ḥaḍramawt, fearing none other than God and that the wolf might attack his sheep. But you are hasty."

In this and similar reports Sayyid Quṭb discerned clear guidance that advocates of Islam must never seek a 'quick' solution, or precipitate the normal development of their mission. He felt this was confirmed in several Qur'ānic verses, such as: "*Are you not aware of those who have been told, 'Hold back your hands [from fighting], and attend regularly to prayer, and pay your* zakāt*? When, at length, the order for fighting was issued to them, some of them stood in awe of men as one should stand in awe of God – or even greater awe."* (4: 77) He saw that a situation may arise when refraining from fighting back against aggression and injustice by tyrannical authorities could be the best that the advocates of Islam could do to further their cause. Conversely, if they were to precipitate the natural development of their task, they could easily lose all.

The only exception being granted to one who is tortured beyond the limits of human tolerance in an attempt to force him to renounce his faith altogether. In this case only, such a person is permitted to declare to his tormentors that he has abandoned Islam, provided that deep inside he remains a firm believer. Some of us might think that this concession applied to members of the Muslim Brotherhood as they endured brutal torture and struggled for survival in Nasser's prisons. It certainly could be the case. However, the concession applies to individuals, not to the message of Islam as a whole. And then, only when a person suffering unbearable torture tries to pacify his tormentors by saying to them what they want to hear, but he himself must remain, in reality, committed to Islam. He may not be able to continue with any public advocacy of Islam, but his commitment to Islam and rejection of whatever is contrary to it must never be in doubt.

It was not a case of such forced retraction that Sayyid Quṭb rejected. It was the changing of sides, and the backing of a dictatorship even when it continued to suppress the Islamic message. To him, the compromise many prisoners sought or accepted was a sell out and this he could not condone. For how can an advocate of Islam support tyranny that seeks to reduce Islam to a set of rituals that has no bearing on the life of either the individual or the community?

What this state of affairs meant was that the movement that sought Islamic revival needed to go back to basics. He felt that there was a serious flaw in its policy and strategy. Since there could be no flaw in the message it advocated, because the message is given by God, the flaw must be the line determined by human beings. The main task then was to put in place a programme that remedied such a flaw. Such a programme could only be one of education so that those who wished to join the most noble task in human life, which is the advocacy of the divine message as undertaken by the Prophet Muḥammad, would know what was required and expected of them in all situations. They would not be surprised by a military junta's deception, or by having to endure persecution at the hands of the enemies of Islam.

Such education must be based on the Qur'ān and the *Sunnah*, with the parts of the Qur'ān revealed in Makkah forming the core ingredient. These are explained and illustrated by the practical example provided by the Prophet and his Companions during the 13 years of Islamic advocacy in Makkah. Hence, it is not surprising that these parts of the Qur'ān, including the two *sūrahs* in this volume, should receive very careful attention in his commentary, as they address a situation that is not dissimilar to the one the advocates of Islam face today. He considered that the global Islamic movement, consisting of all organizations working for the revival of Islam, wherever they happened to be and regardless of what conditions they functioned under, were at the same stage that the Prophet and his Companions were in during the Makkan period. Hence, they had no option other than to follow in the Prophet's footsteps, addressing their message to other people while they themselves continued to learn, through study and practical struggle, what Islamic advocacy really meant and what sort of society Islam would bring about. As they went about their task, they would inevitably face stiff opposition from different quarters, just as did the Prophet and his Companions, as well as earlier prophets and their followers. They had no option but to struggle for their cause, without compromising their beliefs and principles, and without falling for the temptation of a 'quick fix'.

This education and moulding stage could take any length of time. It was not a question of a course of study ending with an exam requiring a certain pass mark. It was rather a matter of absorbing certain principles and beliefs in such a way that they became the starting point in one's thinking. Thus, they would come to influence one's attitude in all situations, and shape one's whole thinking. This could take 13 years as it did at the time of the Prophet, or it could take much longer. The length of this stage was immaterial to the advocates of Islam, because what concerned them was the attainment of such a degree of faith that made them worthy of being trusted with God's message and its implementation in human life.

This comes out very clearly in Sayyid Quṭb's writings, particularly in *In the Shade of the Qur'ān* and in *Milestones*. He repeatedly insists that advocates of Islam must have no objective other than that of doing their duty of delivering God's message to other people. They should entertain no goal to be achieved in this life, not even the triumph of the Islamic message at their hands. They would receive their reward from God on the Day of Resurrection. When they have done their best, God will do with them and His message whatever He wills. They cannot question this. Thus, all thoughts of hastily overthrowing an existing regime in order to replace it with an Islamic one are wrong and must not be entertained by Islamic advocates.

Time and again Sayyid Quṭb explains that Islamic advocacy must be pure of any ulterior motive. Only when the advocates of Islam have shown themselves to be worthy of shouldering the heavy task of implementing Islam will God entrust it to them. They demonstrate this by enduring the most difficult of tests, always remaining steadfast. When there are sufficient numbers of them who thus prove themselves, then it may be God's will to hand them the task of establishing an Islamic state in which they achieve no personal gain whatsoever. This is the course followed by Islam during the lifetime of its first advocate, the Prophet Muḥammad (peace be upon him), and it is the course to be followed every time its followers want to put it back in place.

This approach is far removed from any hasty attempt to seize power whether by a military takeover or popular uprising. Sayyid Quṭb's view being: who will implement Islam if those who gain power have not yet developed a proper understanding of its main principles? Will they not then be more interested in maintaining their power, rather than actually implementing Islam? Once they try to hold on to power, they soon move into the realm of being dictators themselves. The only difference is that they rule in the name of Islam, putting at its doorstep the blame for all their misdeeds. To Sayyid Quṭb, all dictators and dictatorships are the same, be they Roman, Persian, Western or Eastern. He asserts time and again that Islam has no interest in replacing a Roman or Persian tyranny with an Arab one. Mankind must be liberated from all types of tyranny. All people must be free and must exercise their freedom, particularly in the choice of their beliefs. He defines Islam as "a declaration for the liberation of man, all mankind, on earth, all earth, from subjugation by any being other than God Almighty."

The answer is not to stage a *coup* to remove tyranny by force. This often leads to a new dictatorship. To Sayyid Quṭb there is no such thing as a 'quick fix' because true freedom comes only through Islam, when a community decides to implement its principles and values, conducting all its affairs on their basis. To achieve this, it is imperative that sufficient numbers of believers who are totally committed to the Islamic cause, and who prove that through struggle and sacrifice, i.e. *jihād*, come together to establish their Muslim community. Commitment to Islam should be total and free of any personal ambition, including that of being the medium through which Islamic victory is achieved. Hence, the task of the Islamic revivalist movement is, to Sayyid Quṭb, education which could take many different forms. For example, education of the advocates themselves so that they could develop an unshakeable belief in the truth of Islam, be aware of their advocacy task and be ready to give any sacrifice they are called on to make for the cause of Islam. It also includes educating the general public in order to make them fully aware of what it really means to be Muslim, and how they can bring their lifestyles into line with Islam. When such a process of transformation is set in motion, it develops naturally and brings about the desired change. It may involve great sacrifices for the advocates of Islam, but this is in the nature of the divine message, throughout history, as the author clearly explains in commenting on the histories of earlier prophets given in the two *sūrahs* included in this volume.

Sayyid Quṭb not only made these ideas crystal clear in his writings, particularly in *In the Shade of the Qur'ān* and *Milestones*, he also put them into practice. When he was released from prison in 1964, he was approached by a group of young men who had started to form organizations on the lines of the Muslim Brotherhood. They wanted him to take over their leadership and merge them into one movement. They tried hard to persuade him to do so but he was not short of sincere advice that he should not. Such advice was not based on the risks involved in leading a secret Islamic revivalist movement, because that would not have been important to him. Work for Islam is a duty and he never shrank from such a duty. However, someone very close to him said: "Since you have not founded this organization on your own understanding, and since you have not imbibed your method into it from the first day, it is bound to have much that needs correction. It is very difficult to achieve such correction in the present environment, which maintains a very hostile and strict watch over all Islamic activities. It would be much better for everyone that, if you want to work through an organization, you should be the founder and it should have no connection to any movement, past or present."

This advice contained much sense, because if he were to start a new organization, it would be joined only by those who agreed with its programme based on education. However, Sayyid Quṭb felt that the new groups which wanted to give him their leadership were composed of such sincere young men and women who were genuinely committed to Islam. They needed to have the right approach, so that they would be spared the pitfalls that lay ahead. Such pitfalls could lead to a new wave of suppression accompanied by much suffering and persecution. Sayyid Quṭb hoped to steer them away from such pitfalls and spare them much hardship, provided that they accept the change of course he desired.

In the discussions that followed between Sayyid Quṭb and the leaders of these new groups, he asked them about their immediate and long-term objectives. One of their primary objectives was "revenge for the injustice perpetrated by the Nasser regime on the Brotherhood in 1954". He insisted that they must put all such thoughts out of their minds. This though was not easy for them to accept. Nonetheless, he argued with them at length, saying that all that they would succeed in doing would be to assassinate Nasser or some of his assistants. He would then be replaced by yet another dictator. Even if the new ruler were less brutal, he would still be someone who would not allow the cause of Islam to gain any ground. The degree of suppression might be less, but the message of Islam would still be suppressed. The nature of the regime would remain the same, even if it moved away from being an outright military dictatorship. He further argued that even if the new regime moved towards democracy, allowing free elections, it would still be hostile to Islamic revival and try to prevent it with all its might. It would also come under strong pressure from different quarters, including Zionist and Imperialist ones, which are extremely hostile to

Islam. As such, no success in avenging the injustice of 1954 would make any difference to the overall objective of Islamic revival.

Sayyid Quṭb insisted that these young leaders not only broaden their vision, but also never lose sight of their ultimate objective. The only way to achieve that objective was to follow the Prophet's guidance as he went about advocating Islam in Makkah and then established the first Muslim state in Madinah. He never sought revenge for any aspect of the brutal persecution the Quraysh piled on his followers. Instead, he counselled his followers not to be hasty. In the circumstances that prevailed in Egypt, nothing reflected hastiness more than seeking revenge for 1954.

The long discussions that followed yielded the fruits he desired and the young leaders accepted his argument. They now drew up plans to disseminate this basic standpoint to the rank and file of their organization, with a programme of study taking shape. Not only so, but earlier steps were reversed. The leaders of the new organization had arranged for arms to be smuggled into Egypt in preparation for the time when they would be ready to commence their revenge operations. They now agreed to Sayyid Quṭb's order for all such arms to be diverted, and that no thought of their use ever be entertained.

Hence, when a year later the existence of this new movement was uncovered by the Egyptian authorities, they could find no evidence of any takeover attempt or indeed preparations for such. Nonetheless, a new round of mass arrests took place and the detainees were subjected to torture on an unprecedented scale. Confessions were sought in every possible way. One of Sayyid Quṭb's nephews, a young man of 22, died at the hands of his jailers, lasting no more than a week after his arrest. Many indeed were those who died as a result of such brutality. Yet, when a specially constituted military court sat to try Sayyid Quṭb and his group, little evidence of any plot of any sort was produced. He and six others were sentenced to death but it is hard to find any plausible reason for any sentence.[1] In fact, young people were sentenced to 10 and 15 years imprisonment for nothing other than reading Sayyid Quṭb's *Milestones*.

---

1. Sayyid Quṭb, Muhammad Yusuf Hawwash and Abd al-Fattah Ismaʿil were executed in August 1966, while the other four death sentences were commuted to life imprisonment.

Today, nearly 40 years after these events, we see how everything Sayyid Quṭb said to those who at the time represented a new generation of Islamic advocates came true. The wave of persecution that started in 1965 had no justification other than the mere existence of an organization that aimed to advocate the message of Islam peacefully and educate people in how to follow the Prophet's guidance. Events that followed between those advocating Islam in one way or another and the regimes that followed Nasser bear out all that he said to those men who sought to work under his leadership. Yet haste remains a weakness among many of the advocates of Islam. It was haste that the Prophet warned his Companions against. Following the Prophet's example, Sayyid Quṭb also warned against it.

Yet today, the war against Islam waged by the Zionists and Neo-Imperialists tries to describe Sayyid Quṭb as the philosopher of Islamic terror. This is by no means surprising. Their predecessors of old described the Prophet as a sorcerer and a madman. These were the most sophisticated labels they could attach to him at the time. In our modern era, it is terrorism that the hostile camp tries to attach to Islam and its advocates. Futile will their efforts be, for, by the nature of things and by God's design, the truth will triumph.

London   **Adil Salahi**
Ramaḍān, 1424
November, 2003

SŪRAH 10

Yūnus

(Jonah)

Prologue

In this *sūrah*, we return to those parts of the Qur'ān revealed in Makkah, the two preceding *sūrahs* both being Madinan revelations. Although the Makkan revelations share the common Qur'ānic features and the uniqueness that separates the Qur'ān, in subject, style and mode of expression, from any human discourse, they also have their own ambience.[1] This is generated by their subject matter and the way in which it is tackled. The *sūrahs* revealed in Makkah mainly concentrate on the nature of Godhead, servitude, and relations between God and man; providing a full understanding of who the true Lord is so that people may worship and submit to Him alone implementing His law; purging the true faith of all deviation and confusion, and charting the way for people to return to the true faith based on self-surrender to God alone. The way these themes are tackled in Makkan revelations is especially inspiring, adding as they do effective rhythms, powerful speech, and even sound effects. These we explained in the Prologue to *Sūrah* 6,[2] and we will make further reference to them throughout the present *sūrah*.

---

1. For further discussion, reference may be made to the Introduction to Volume I, and to the Prologue to *Sūrah* 3 in Volume II.
2. See the Prologues to *Sūrahs* 6 and 7 in Volumes V and VI respectively.

1

The last Makkan revelations discussed in this work were *Sūrahs* 6 and 7, Cattle and The Heights. Although these two *sūrahs* are placed together in their Qur'ānic order, they did not have the same sequence in the chronological order of revelation. They are followed in the Qur'ān by *Sūrahs* 8 and 9, The Spoils of War and The Repentance, which feature the special characteristics and themes of the later part of the Qur'ān revealed in Madinah. Now, however, we have two Makkan *Sūrahs*, Jonah and Hūd, which have the same sequence in both chronological order and Qur'ānic arrangement. We note a remarkable similarity between the two earlier Makkan *sūrahs* and the two present ones, both in subject matter and presentation. *Sūrah* 6, Cattle, concentrates on the essence of faith, confronting the unbelievers with it and refuting all erring beliefs and practices. *Sūrah* 7, The Heights, on the other hand, speaks about the practical implementation of faith in human life and its confrontation with *jāhiliyyah* during different periods of history. The same is true of the two *sūrahs* in this volume, Jonah and Hūd. However, *Sūrah* 6 is distinguished from *Sūrah* 10 by its very powerful rhythm, quick pulse and sophistication of scene and movement. *Sūrah* 10, on the other hand, has a more relaxed rhythm and easy flow of scene and movement. *Sūrahs* 7 and 11, The Heights and Hūd display great similarity in theme, presentation and rhythm. Nevertheless, every *sūrah* in the Qur'ān has its own character, special features and distinctive properties.

Sūrah 10 follows its own distinctive approach to the subject matter of the Makkan revelations, and this reflects its character and features. In this Prologue we will do no more than provide a brief introduction to the themes the *sūrah* tackles.

- It first addresses the idolaters' attitude to the fact that the Prophet received revelations from on high, and to the Qur'ān itself. It makes clear that there is nothing to wonder about with regard to revelation. It further asserts that the Qur'ān could not have been invented by anyone who might have then attributed it to God.

    These are verses of the divine book, full of wisdom. Does it seem strange to people that We have inspired a man from their own midst: 'Warn all mankind, and give those who believe the glad tidings that they are on a sound footing with their Lord?' The unbelievers say: 'This is plainly a skilled enchanter.' (Verses 1–2)

When Our revelations are recited to them in all their clarity, those who have no hope of meeting Us say: 'Bring us a discourse other than this Qur'ān, or else alter it.' Say: 'It is not for me to alter it of my own accord. I only follow what is revealed to me. I dread the torment of an awesome day if I should disobey my Lord!' Say: 'Had God so willed, I would not have recited it to you, nor would He have brought it to your knowledge. I spent a whole lifetime among you before it [was revealed to me]. Will you not, then, use your reason?' Who is more wicked than one who attributes his lying inventions to God or denies His revelations? Indeed those who are guilty shall not be successful. (Verses 15–17)

This Qur'ān could not have been devised by anyone other than God. It is a confirmation of [revelations] that went before it, and a full explanation of God's Book, about which there is no doubt. It certainly comes from the Lord of all the worlds. If they say: 'He has invented it,' say: 'Produce, then, one sūrah like it, and call for help on all you can other than God, if what you say is true.' Indeed they disbelieve what they cannot grasp, particularly since its inner meaning has not become clear to them. Likewise did those who lived before them disbelieve. But see what happened in the end to those wrongdoers. (Verses 37–39)

- It also addresses the unbelievers' demand to be shown some supernatural sign – other than the Qur'ān – and their suggestion to hasten the fulfilment of the Qur'ānic warnings. The *sūrah* makes clear to them that the basic evidence of the truth of the Islamic faith is the Qur'ān itself which embodies, through its superior qualities, evidence of its divine nature. Hence, the challenge to all unbelievers to produce a single *sūrah* similar to the Qur'ān. It also explains that signs and evidence are given by God and subject to His will. The time when they receive their

3

reward is determined by God alone. The Prophet has no say in this, as he is only a servant of God, like the rest of God's creation. All this contributes to the expostulation on the Islamic concept of Godhead and people's submission to Him.

> *Indeed, We destroyed generations before your time when they persisted in their wrongdoing. The messengers sent to them brought them veritable evidence of the truth, but they would not believe. Thus do We reward the guilty. Then We made you their successors on earth, so that We might see how you behave.* (Verses 13–14)

> *They ask: 'Why has no sign been sent down to him by his Lord?' Say: 'God's alone is the knowledge of what is beyond the reach of human perception. Wait, then, if you will: I too am waiting.'* (Verse 20)

> *To every community was sent a messenger. It is when their messenger had come to them that judgement is passed on them in all fairness; and never are they wronged. They say: 'When will this promise be fulfilled, if you are truthful?' Say: 'I have no control over any harm or benefit to myself, except as God may please. For every community a term has been appointed. When their time arrives, they can neither delay it by a single moment, nor indeed hasten it.' Say: 'Do but consider. Should His punishment befall you by night or by day, what could there be in it that the guilty ones should wish to hasten?' 'Is it, then, when it has come to pass that you will believe in it? Is it now, while so far you have been asking for it to come speedily?'* (Verses 47–51)

• The *sūrah* also addresses the unbelievers' confused ideas about God and people's relation to Him. This is essentially what the Prophet talked to them about, but they denied the truth of revelation, expressed doubts about it, demanding at times that the Prophet should produce a different Qur'ān, and at other times that he should produce a physical miracle. Meanwhile they continued to worship things that they claimed to be God's

4

partners, things which would cause them neither benefit nor harm. They falsely claimed that such alleged partners could intercede with God on their behalf. They also falsely claimed that God had a son. The *sūrah* explains to them the attributes of God, the true Lord of the universe, and how His power is manifested in the universe, and within themselves, as well as in a multitude of universal phenomena. It reminds them of how they appeal to Him alone when things go wrong and they find themselves powerless in the face of danger. This is the central issue which takes up large portions of the *sūrah* and leads to its other themes. (Verses 3–6; 18; 22–23; 31–36; 66–70)

Your Lord is God who created the heavens and the earth in six days, and established Himself on the Throne, regulating and governing all that exists. There is none who may intercede with Him unless He first grants leave for that. That is God, your Lord: so worship Him alone. Will you not then keep this in mind? To Him you shall all return. This is, in truth, God's promise. He originates all His creation, and then brings them all back to life so that He may reward, with equity, those who have believed and done good deeds. As for the unbelievers, they shall have a scalding drink and a grievous suffering for their unbelief. He it is who made the sun a source of radiant light and the moon a light [reflected], and determined her phases so that you may know how to compute the years and measure [time]. God has not created this otherwise than in accordance with the truth. He makes plain His revelations to people of knowledge. Indeed in the alternating of night and day, and in all that God has created in the heavens and the earth, there are signs for people who are God-fearing. (Verses 3–6)

They worship, side by side with God, what can neither harm nor benefit them, and say: 'These will intercede for us with God.' Say: 'Do you presume to inform God of something in the heavens or on earth that He does not know? Limitless is He in His glory, and exalted above whatever they may associate with Him.' (Verse 18)

He it is who enables you to travel on land and sea. Then when they are on board ships, and sailing along in a favourable wind, they feel happy with it, but then a stormy wind comes upon them and waves surge towards them from all sides, so that they believe they are encompassed [by death]. [At that point] they appeal to God, in complete sincerity of faith in Him alone: 'If You will save us from this, we shall certainly be most grateful.' Yet when He has saved them, they transgress in the land, offending against all right. Mankind, it is against your own souls that your offences rebound. [You care only for] the enjoyment of this present life, but in the end you will return to Us when We will tell you the truth of what you were doing [in this life]. (Verses 22–23)

Say: 'Who is it that provides for you from heaven and earth? Or, who is it that has power over hearing and sight? Who brings forth the living out of that which is dead, and brings forth the dead out of that which is alive? Who regulates all affairs?' They will say: 'God.' Say, then: 'Will you not, then, fear Him?' 'Such is God, your true Lord. Apart from the truth, what is left but error? How is it, then, that you turn away?' Thus is the word of your Lord proved true with regard to those who do evil: they will not believe. Say: 'Does any of your partners [whom you associate with God] originate creation, and then bring it back [to life] again?' Say: 'It is God alone who originates creation and then brings it back [to life] again. How is it, then, that you are so misled?' Say: 'Does any of your partners [whom you associate with God] guide to the truth?' Say: 'God alone guides to the truth. Who is more worthy to be followed: He that guides to the truth, or he who cannot find the right way unless he is guided? What is then amiss with you? How do you judge?' Most of them follow nothing but mere conjecture. But conjecture can in no way be a substitute for truth. God has full knowledge of all that they do. (Verses 31–36)

Indeed, to God belong all those who are in the heavens and earth. Those who invoke other beings beside God do not follow any real partners with Him. They follow mere conjecture, and they utter nothing but falsehood. It is He who has made the night for you, so that you may have rest, and the day, so that you may see. In this there are certainly signs for those who listen. They say: 'God has taken unto Himself a son.' Limitless is He in His glory. Self-sufficient is He. To Him belongs all that is in the heavens and earth. No evidence whatever have you for this. Would you say about God something which you do not know? Say: 'Those who invent falsehood about God shall not be successful. They may have a brief enjoyment in this world, but then to Us they must return, and We will then make them suffer severe torment for their unbelief.' (Verses 66–70)

- The *sūrah* also illustrates for the unbelievers God's presence in all that has a bearing on human life, and in all that people themselves do. This fills us with awe and keeps us on our guard. To give but one example of this we may quote: *"In whatever business you may be engaged, and whatever part you may recite of the Qur'ān, and whatever deed you [mankind] may do, We will be your witnesses from the moment you are engaged with it. Not even an atom's weight [of anything whatsoever] on earth or in heaven escapes your Lord, nor is there anything smaller or larger than that, but is recorded in a clear book."* (Verse 61)

- A sense that God's punishment may come at any moment is imparted to people in order to help them shake off the false sense of security that results from enjoying an abundance of riches and luxuries.

  This present life may be compared to rain which We send down from the sky, and which is then absorbed by the plants of the earth from which men and animals eat. Then, when the earth has been clad with its fine adornments and well embellished, and its people believe that they have full mastery over it, Our command comes down upon it, by night or by day, and We make it like a field that has been mowed down, as if it did not blossom but yesterday. Thus do We spell out Our revelations to people who think. (Verse 24)

Say: 'Do but consider. Should His punishment befall you by night or by day, what could there be in it that the guilty ones should wish to hasten?' 'Is it, then, when it has come to pass that you will believe in it? Is it now, while so far you have been asking for it to come speedily?' (Verses 50–51)

- Furthermore, the *sūrah* points out that the unbelievers often have a false sense of security in this life, overlooking the hereafter and denying man's inevitable meeting with God on the Day of Judgement. It warns them against such indulgence, showing them that it is a raw deal that they choose for themselves when they neglect the life to come in preference for this life and its enjoyments. It explains to them that this present life is only a test and the outcome is determined on the Day of Resurrection. It adds a number of scenes of that day, particularly in relation to the alleged partners of God who will disown those who worship them. It also makes clear that no offering will be accepted from anyone on the Day of Judgement to release them from their deserved punishment.

> *Those who entertain no hope of meeting Us, but are content with the life of this world, and feel well at ease about it, and those who pay no heed to Our revelation, shall have the Fire as their abode in requital for what they used to do. Those who believe and do righteous deeds will be guided aright by their Lord by means of their faith. Running waters will flow at their feet in the gardens of bliss. There they will call out: 'Limitless are You in Your glory, God,' and their greeting will be, 'Peace!' Their call will conclude with the words: 'All praise is due to God, the Lord of all the worlds!'* (Verses 7–10)
>
> *Indeed, We destroyed generations before your time when they persisted in their wrongdoing. The messengers sent to them brought them veritable evidence of the truth, but they would not believe. Thus do We reward the guilty. Then We made you their successors on earth, so that We might see how you behave.* (Verses 13–14)

8

God calls to the abode of peace, and guides him that wills to a straight path. For those who do good there is a good reward, and more besides. Neither darkness nor any disgrace will overcast their faces. These are destined for paradise, where they will abide. As for those who have done evil, an evil deed is rewarded with its like. Ignominy will overshadow them – for they will have none to protect them from God – as if their faces have been covered with patches of the night's own darkness. Such are destined for the fire, where they will abide. One day We shall gather them all together, and then We shall say to those who associated partners with God: 'Keep to your places, you and those you associated with God as partners.' We will then separate them from one another. Then those whom they associated as partners with God will say: 'It was not us that you worshipped.' 'God is sufficient as a witness between us and you. We were, for certain, unaware of your worshipping us.' There and then every soul will realize what it had done in the past; and all will be brought back to God, their true Lord Supreme. All their invented falsehood will have forsaken them. (Verses 25–30)

On the Day when He will gather them together, [it will seem to them] as though they had not sojourned in this world more than an hour of a day, getting to know one another. Lost indeed will be those who [in their lifetime] disbelieved in meeting God and did not follow the right guidance. (Verse 45)

Should every wrongdoer possess all that the earth contains, he will gladly offer it all as ransom. They will harbour feelings of remorse when they see the suffering. Judgement will be passed on them in all fairness; and they will not be wronged. (Verse 54)

• The *sūrah* deals with the consequences of the unbelievers' confused concept of Godhead, denial of the resurrection and the life to come, and also their denial of divine revelations and disbelief of the Prophet's warnings. Such confusion led them to claim for themselves some of God's attributes, such as the authority to legislate for themselves, making things lawful or forbidden just as their pagan beliefs allowed them to do. Thus, they allocated certain things to their deities which they claimed to be God's partners. Such allocations included priests issuing decrees of prohibition and permissibility as they deemed fit. The priests then take for themselves what they claimed to be allocated to God: *"Say: 'Do but consider all the means of sustenance that God has bestowed on you! Some of it you then made unlawful, and some lawful.' Say: 'Has God given you leave to do so, or do you fabricate lies against God?' But what will they think, those who invent lies against God, on the Day of Resurrection? God is truly bountiful to mankind, but most of them are ungrateful."* (Verses 59–60)

In order to present and establish such facts and ensure their proper effect on the hearts and minds of its audience, the *sūrah* employs a wide variety of special effects that are characteristic of the Qur'ānic style. Profound and moving as these inspiring effects are, they are of a type that suits the special nature of this *sūrah*. For example:

- The *sūrah* portrays a variety of universal scenes that impress on our minds the truth of Godhead, His elaborate planning of the universe and conducting of its affairs. These scenes highlight the fact that a multitude of factors need to come together in perfect balance so as to allow for the emergence of life and the support of human life in particular. The Qur'ān presents the basic theme of Godhead in such an inspiring fashion, without resort to any philosophical argument or logical treatise. God knows that it is sufficient to direct human nature to contemplate the universe and its visible aspects in order to awaken its receptive faculties and interact with them. Hence, the Qur'ān employs this particular address to human nature in a language it readily understands. Here are some such inspiring examples:

    Your Lord is God who created the heavens and the earth in six days, and established Himself on the Throne, regulating and governing all that exists. There is none who may intercede with Him unless He first grants leave for that. That is God, your Lord: so worship Him alone. Will you not then keep this in mind? (Verse 3)

He it is who made the sun a source of radiant light and the moon a light [reflected], and determined her phases so that you may know how to compute the years and measure [time]. God has not created this otherwise than in accordance with the truth. He makes plain His revelations to people of knowledge. Indeed in the alternating of night and day, and in all that God has created in the heavens and the earth, there are signs for people who are God-fearing. (Verses 5–6)

Say: 'Who is it that provides for you from heaven and earth? Or, who is it that has power over hearing and sight? Who brings forth the living out of that which is dead, and brings forth the dead out of that which is alive? Who regulates all affairs?' They will say: 'God.' Say, then: 'Will you not, then, fear Him?' 'Such is God, your true Lord. Apart from the truth, what is left but error? How is it, then, that you turn away?' (Verses 31–32)

It is He who has made the night for you, so that you may have rest, and the day, so that you may see. In this there are certainly signs for those who listen. (Verse 67)

Say: 'Consider all that there is in the heavens and the earth.' But of what benefit could all signs and warnings be to people who will not believe? (Verse 101)

• This *sūrah* is full of scenes portraying events that people witness and participate in, even though they remain unaware of their full significance and elaborate planning. The Qur'ān presents them with pictures of their own lives as these develop. It raises a mirror before people's eyes so that they can see themselves for what they truly are. A couple of examples follow:

When affliction befalls man, he appeals to Us, whether he be lying on his side, sitting, or standing, but as soon as We relieve his affliction, he goes on as though he had never appealed to Us to save him from the affliction that befell him. Thus do their deeds seem fair to those who are given to excesses. (Verse 12)

Whenever We let people taste grace after some hardship has afflicted them, they turn to scheme against Our revelations.

11

Say: 'More swift is God's scheming. Our messengers are recording all that you may devise.' He it is who enables you to travel on land and sea. Then when you are on board ships, and sailing along in a favourable wind, they feel happy with it, but then a stormy wind comes upon them and waves surge towards them from all sides, so that they believe they are encompassed [by death]. [At that point] they appeal to God, in complete sincerity of faith in Him alone: 'If You will save us from this, we shall certainly be most grateful.' Yet when He has saved them, they transgress in the land, offending against all right. Mankind, it is against your own souls that your offences rebound. [You care only for] the enjoyment of this present life, but in the end you will return to Us when We will tell you the truth of what you were doing [in this life]. (Verses 21–23)

• The *sūrah* includes a host of information about the fate suffered by earlier communities. At times this is given in the form of a report, while at others an account of the history of earlier messengers is given. Such information portrays a very powerful picture of the destruction of those who denied the truth in the past. Thus, it gives a warning against suffering a similar fate. People must not be deluded by the comforts of this present life, for it is merely a brief test, lasting no more than an hour in which people get to know one another before reaching their final abode, either in long-lasting suffering or in eternal bliss.

Indeed, We destroyed generations before your time when they persisted in their wrongdoing. The messengers sent to them brought them veritable evidence of the truth, but they would not believe. Thus do We reward the guilty. Then We made you their successors on earth, so that We might see how you behave. (Verses 13–14)

Relate to them the story of Noah. He said to his people: 'My people! If my presence among you and my reminders to you of God's revelations are repugnant to you – well, in God have I placed my trust. Decide, then, what you are going to do, and [seek the help of] those whom you associate as partners with

God. Be clear about your course of action, leaving no room for uncertainty, then carry out against me whatever you may have decided and give me no respite. But if you turn away, [remember that] I have asked of you no reward whatsoever. My reward rests with none but God. I have been commanded to be one of those who surrender themselves to Him.' But they disbelieved him. So We saved him and all those who joined him in the ark, and made them inherit the earth. And We drowned the others who denied Our revelations. Reflect on the fate of those who were forewarned. (Verses 71–73)

Then after those [prophets] We sent Moses and Aaron with Our signs to Pharaoh and his nobles, but they persisted in their arrogance, for they were hardened offenders. When the truth came to them from Us, they said: 'This is clearly nothing but sorcery.' Moses replied: 'Do you say this to the truth when it has come to you? Can this be sorcery? But sorcerers will never be successful.' (Verses 75–77)

And We brought the Children of Israel across the sea; but Pharaoh and his legions pursued them with tyranny and aggression. But as he was about to drown, Pharaoh said: 'I have come to believe that there is no deity other than Him in whom the Children of Israel believe, and to Him I surrender myself.' [But God said:] 'Only now? But before this you were rebelling [against Us], and you spread corruption in the land. But today We shall save only your body, so that you may become a sign to those who will come after you; for a great many people do not heed Our signs.' (Verses 90–92)

What are they waiting for except a repetition of the days [of calamity] experienced by those who have gone before them? Say: 'Wait, then, if you will. I am also waiting.' Thereupon, We save Our messengers and those who believe. Thus have We willed it upon Ourselves: We save those who believe. (Verses 102–103)

- The *sūrah* also portrays scenes of the Day of Resurrection when both unbelievers and believers will receive their wages for their deeds in this life. The presentation here is effectively animated, leaving a profound effect on our hearts. Along with the scenes of destruction that overwhelms the guilty ones and the salvation of the believers, we are presented with two contrasting scenes of life in the hereafter, and two more of the beginning and the end:

For those who do good there is a good reward, and more besides. Neither darkness nor any disgrace will overcast their faces. These are destined for paradise, where they will abide. As for those who have done evil, an evil deed is rewarded with its like. Ignominy will overshadow them – for they will have none to protect them from God – as if their faces have been covered with patches of the night's own darkness. Such are destined for the fire, where they will abide. (Verses 26–27)

One day We shall gather them all together, and then We shall say to those who associated partners with God: 'Keep to your places, you and those you associated with God as partners.' We will then separate them from one another. Then those whom they associated as partners with God will say: 'It was not us that you worshipped.' 'God is sufficient as a witness between us and you. We were, for certain, unaware of your worshipping us.' There and then every soul will realize what it had done in the past; and all will be brought back to God, their true Lord Supreme. All their invented falsehood will have forsaken them. (Verses 28–30)

Should every wrongdoer possess all that the earth contains, he will gladly offer it all as ransom. They will harbour feelings of remorse when they see the suffering. Judgement will be passed on them in all fairness; and they will not be wronged. (Verse 54)

- Another special effect is that of challenging the unbelievers who denied the very idea of revelation to produce a single *sūrah* like the Qur'ān. When the challenge is made, the Prophet is instructed to leave them to their fate, which is the same as that of earlier wrongdoers. He should follow his own way, paying no attention

14

to what may happen to them. The whole sequence of the challenge followed by the Prophet leaving them and carrying on with his mission is bound to impress on them the fact that he was absolutely certain of the truth of his message, and assured of the care he was promised by his Lord. Such confidence was bound to shake them violently.

This Qur'ān could not have been devised by anyone other than God. It is a confirmation of [revelations] that went before it, and a full explanation of God's Book, about which there is no doubt. It certainly comes from the Lord of all the worlds. If they say: 'He has invented it,' say: 'Produce, then, one sūrah like it, and call for help on all you can other than God, if what you say is true.' Indeed they disbelieve what they cannot grasp, particularly since its inner meaning has not become clear to them. Likewise did those who lived before them disbelieve. But see what happened in the end to those wrongdoers. (Verses 37–39)

Say: 'Mankind, if you are still in doubt as to what my faith is, then [know that] I do not worship those whom you worship beside God, but I worship God alone who will cause all of you to die. I have been commanded to be one of those who believe. And adhere exclusively and sincerely to the true faith, and do not be one of those who associate partners with God. Do not invoke, instead of God, anything that can neither benefit nor harm you. For if you do, you will surely be among the wrongdoers.' Should God afflict you with any hardship, none other than He can remove it; and if He wills any good for you, none can withhold His bounty. He bestows it on whomsoever He wills. He is truly Forgiving, truly Merciful. Say: 'Mankind, the truth has come to you from your Lord. Whoever chooses to follow the true guidance, does so for his own good; and whoever chooses to go astray, does so at his own peril. I am not responsible for your conduct.' Follow whatever is revealed to you, and be patient in adversity, until God shall give His judgement. He is the best of all judges. (Verses 104–109)

With such clarity, the *sūrah* is concluded.

Error and Challenge

This *sūrah*, number 10, was revealed after *Sūrah* 17, The Night Journey, at a time when the unbelievers were engaged in a heated debate concerning the truth of revelation, the Qur'ān and its denunciation of their erroneous beliefs and ignorant practices. The Qur'ān exposed the fundamental contradictions in their beliefs. From the old divine religion of Abraham and Ishmael, the Arabs retained the belief that God was the Creator, Sustainer, who gives life and causes death, and who has power over all things. In stark contradiction to these, they claimed that God had children and that the angels were His daughters, representing them as idols and appealing to them to intercede with God on their behalf. Needless to say this confusion in beliefs had far-reaching effects on their life, most important among which was the authority claimed by their chiefs and monks to pronounce certain types of cattle and fruits as lawful and others as forbidden. They also allocated a portion of these to God, and another portion to their false deities.

They countered the Qur'ānic criticism of their absurd beliefs and contradictory concepts by rejecting the Prophet, his message and revelations, and by accusing him of being a sorcerer. They demanded that he should show them some miracle to prove that he received revelations from on high. They made different demands, as related in *Sūrah* 17, in which God says: "*They say: 'We shall not believe in you till you cause a spring to gush forth for us from the earth, or [till] you have a garden of date trees and vines, and you cause rivers to flow through it, or till you cause the sky to fall upon us in pieces, as you have threatened, or till you bring God and the angels face to face before us, or till you have a house of gold, or you ascend to heaven. Indeed we shall not believe in your ascent to heaven until you bring us a book for us to read.' Say, 'All glory belongs to my Lord. Surely I am only a man and a messenger.' Nothing has ever prevented people from believing [in God] whenever guidance has come to them except for their saying: 'Can it be that God has sent a human being as His messenger?'*" (17: 90–95) Also in this *sūrah*, God says: "*They ask: 'Why has no sign been sent down to him by his Lord?' Say: 'God's alone is the knowledge of what is beyond the reach of human perception. Wait, then, if you will: I too am waiting.'*" (Verse 20)

They also demanded that the Prophet bring them a different Qur'ān which contained no criticism of their idols, beliefs and practices. They promised that they would then believe in him. The *surah* states: "*When Our revelations are recited to them in all their clarity, those who have no hope of meeting Us say: 'Bring us a discourse other than this Qur'ān, or else alter it.' Say: 'It is not for me to alter it of my own accord. I only follow what is revealed to me. I dread the torment of an awesome day if I should disobey my Lord!' Say: 'Had God so willed, I would not have recited it to you, nor would He have brought it to your knowledge. I spent a whole lifetime among you before it [was revealed to me]. Will you not, then, use your reason?' Who is more wicked than one who attributes his lying inventions to God or denies His revelations? Indeed those who are guilty shall not be successful.*" (Verses 15–17)

It was in such an atmosphere that the *surah* was revealed. It is clearly apparent from its flow that it is all a single unit. In fact it is difficult to try to divide it into sections and passages. This disproves the argument that verses 40 and 94–96 were revealed later in Madinah. These verses are closely linked to the rest of the *surah*. Indeed, if we were to leave out any verse, we cause a disruption in the flow of the *surah*.

The unity of purpose in the *surah* is clearly apparent as we see when we compare its opening and its end. It opens with the verses saying: "*Alif. Lām. Rā. These are verses of the divine book, full of wisdom. Does it seem strange to people that We have inspired a man from their own midst: 'Warn all mankind, and give those who believe the glad tidings that they are on a sound footing with their Lord?' The unbelievers say: 'This is plainly a skilled enchanter.'*" (Verses 1–2) Its final verse reads: "*Follow whatever is revealed to you, and be patient in adversity, until God shall give His judgement. He is the best of all judges.*" (Verse 109) Thus, the theme of revelation is brought up at the beginning and the end, as it is frequently highlighted throughout the *surah*.

The same unity is noticed in the different special effects employed in the *surah*. For example, the unbelievers who opposed the Prophet Muḥammad (peace be upon him) try to hasten the punishment they have been warned against. But they are told here that such punishment occurs suddenly, when no repentance or declaration of acceptance of the true faith will be of any avail. When historical accounts are later

17

given in the *sūrah* we see the same scene as it took place in earlier communities and their sudden punishment.

In answer to their request to speed up their punishment, the *sūrah* has the following to say: "*They say: 'When will this promise be fulfilled, if you are truthful?' Say: 'I have no control over any harm or benefit to myself, except as God may please. For every community a term has been appointed. When their time arrives, they can neither delay it by a single moment, nor indeed hasten it.' Say: 'Do but consider. Should His punishment befall you by night or by day, what could there be in it that the guilty ones should wish to hasten?' 'Is it, then, when it has come to pass that you will believe in it? Is it now, while so far you have been asking for it to come speedily?' Then it will be said to the wrongdoers: 'Taste the long-lasting torment. Is this requital anything other than the just due for what you used to do?'*" (Verses 48–52)

When the story of Moses and his encounter with Pharaoh is given later in the *sūrah*, it concludes with a scene that may be taken as the physical implementation of the earlier warning: "*And We brought the Children of Israel across the sea; but Pharaoh and his legions pursued them with tyranny and aggression. But as he was about to drown, Pharaoh said: 'I have come to believe that there is no deity other than Him in whom the Children of Israel believe, and to Him I surrender myself.' [But God said:] 'Only now? But before this you were rebelling [against Us], and you spread corruption in the land. But today We shall save only your body, so that you may become a sign to those who will come after you; for a great many people do not heed Our signs.'*" (Verses 90–92)

Throughout the *sūrah* we are given several scenes of how communities which stubbornly denied the truth were taken unawares as God's punishment overwhelmed them. All this provides clear links between themes, scenes and modes of expression.

Similarly, at the beginning of the *sūrah* the unbelievers' accusation against the Prophet is reported: "*This is plainly a skilled enchanter.*" (Verse 2) When the encounter between Moses and his opponents is told later, we read: "*When the truth came to them from Us, they said: 'This is clearly nothing but sorcery.'*"[3] (Verse 76)

---

3. Although different words, 'enchanter' and 'sorcery', are used in translation, the same word is used in the original Arabic text. The translation tries to capture the particular connotations emphasized in each instance. – Editor's note.

Although the *sūrah* is named after the Prophet Jonah, there is no more than a very brief reference to Jonah and his people as follows: *"Had it believed, every community would have profited by its faith. It was so only with Jonah's people. When they believed, We lifted from them the suffering of disgrace in this life, and allowed them to enjoy things for a while."* (Verse 98) The case of Jonah's people is the only clear example of a community which saved themselves before being overwhelmed by God's punishment. They believed in God when there was still time for them to do so. Moreover, they provided the only instance among those receiving God's messages of an entire community accepting the faith after having first given a negative response. Hence, they were saved from the punishment their Prophet warned them against.

All these examples demonstrate the *sūrah's* complete unity. It is a single unit which is difficult to divide into sections.

Human Dignity and Divine Faith

It is clear from the texts we have quoted in this Prologue that the main issue the *sūrah* centres around is that of explaining the true concepts of Godhead and people's position in relation to God, and how these influence human life. The other themes in the *sūrah*, such as revelation, the hereafter, and earlier divine messages, are used to illustrate the main issue and to explain its influence on people's lives, beliefs, worship and action.

In fact, this is the central issue of the Qur'ān as a whole, particularly those parts revealed in Makkah. Defining God and His position as the Lord, the Sovereign who controls all, and the meaning of being a servant of God and the limitations of that position, so as to make people submit to Him alone, acknowledging His Lordship and sovereignty is indeed what the Qur'ān is all about. Whatever else is given by way of emphasis, illustration, and re-emphasis.

When carefully considered, this fundamental issue of Godhead deserves such profound explanation. It equally deserves that God should send all His messengers to advocate it, and that all His messages explain it: *"Before your time We never sent a messenger without having revealed to him that there is no deity other than Me. Therefore, you shall worship Me alone."* (21: 25)

19

Human life on earth will not be set on the right track unless this fundamental truth is absolutely clear in people's minds, and finds its full implementation in their lives.

Without this fundamental truth, human life will not take its rightful position in relation to the universe we live in and interact with. When people are confused about this issue they begin to ascribe divinity to animate and inanimate objects, and indeed to ghosts and fantasies. They enslave themselves in a ludicrous, but miserable way to these false deities. On the instigation of clerics and con men who will always try to deceive people for their own personal gain, they make offerings to their false deities, sacrificing some of their earnings given to them by God, their only Lord and Sustainer. Yet these things and beings have no power whatsoever; they cannot cause people any harm or benefit. They live either in fear of these false deities, or try to curry favour with them, when like them, these beings are subject to God's power. This is how God describes their situation:

> Out of the produce and the cattle He has created, they assign a portion to God, saying: 'This is for God' – or so they pretend – 'and this is for the partners we associate [with Him].' Whatever they assign to their partners never reaches God, but that which is assigned to God does reach their partners. How ill they judge! Thus have the partners they associate [with God] made the killing of their own children seem goodly to many idolaters, seeking to bring them to ruin and to confuse them in their faith. Had God willed otherwise, they would not have done so. Leave them, then, to their false inventions. They say: 'Such cattle and crops are forbidden. None may eat of them save those whom we permit' – so they falsely claim. Other cattle they declare to be forbidden to burden their backs; and there are cattle over which they do not pronounce God's name, inventing [in all this] a lie against Him. He will surely requite them for their inventions. They also say: 'That which is in the wombs of these cattle is reserved to our males and forbidden to our women.' But if it be stillborn, they all partake of it. He will requite them for all their false assertions. He is Wise, All-knowing. Losers indeed are those who, in their ignorance, foolishly kill their children and declare as forbidden what God has provided for them as sustenance, falsely

attributing such prohibitions to God. They have gone astray and they have no guidance.[4] (6: 136–140)

These are merely some examples of serving deities other than God with property and children being made offerings for some creatures, without any sanction granted by God.

Similarly, human life will not be set straight in the way people deal with each other unless they hold the right concepts of God and man, and until they reflect these in their practices and general code of living. Man will not maintain his full dignity and realize complete freedom under any system that does not assign all Lordship and sovereignty to God alone. Such a system must be based on the belief that life, both in this world and in the life to come, in public and private, is subject to God who alone has the authority to legislate.

This is a fact borne out by human history. Every time people deviated from the true faith that required them to submit themselves to God alone in belief and practice, law-making and worship, they suffered the loss of their humanity, dignity and freedom.

The Islamic reading of history attributes the humiliation of the masses by tyranny to the basic factor of deviation by the masses from the divine faith based on attributing Godhead, Lordship, sovereignty and all authority to God alone. Speaking of Pharaoh and his people, God says: "*Pharaoh issued a call to his people, saying: 'My people! Does not the dominion over Egypt belong to me, since all these running waters flow at my feet? Can you not see? Am I not better than this contemptible man who can hardly make his meaning clear? And then, why have no golden armlets been given to him, and why have no angels come together with him?' Thus he incited his people to levity, and they obeyed him; for they were a community of transgressors.*" (43: 51–54) Thus the fact that Pharaoh was able to incite his people and get his way with them is attributed to the fact that they were transgressors. No tyrant can get his people to do his bidding and incite them to do what is frivolous if they truly believe in God alone, acknowledging no Lordship or sovereignty to anyone else.

---

4. For a full explanation of these verses, see Volume V, pp. 331–341.

What happened with those who rebelled against submission to God alone, allowing some of their numbers to rule over them implementing a law other than God's law, is that they ended up enduring the misery of submission to others. Such submission, however, squanders away their dignity and freedom, regardless of the type of government, even though they may think that some forms of government ensures such dignity and freedom.

When Europe rebelled against a Church that tyrannized under the false guise of religion, it tried to run away from God. People in Europe thought that they could best preserve their freedom, dignity and humanity under democratic government. They pinned their hopes on the guarantees provided by democratic constitutions, parliamentary systems, a free press, judicial and legal checks, majority rule, and similar ideals. But what happened in practice? Capitalism managed to exercise tyrannical power reducing all checks and institutions into little more than slogans or myths. The great majority of the people became subservient to the powerful minority that owned the capital which enabled it to control the parliamentary majority, the constitution, the press and all other checks and balances that people imagined would guarantee their freedom and other rights.

Certain groups turned away from individualistic or democratic systems which usher in a tyranny of capital or class and established 'collective' systems. But what has this meant in practice? They simply replaced subservience to the capitalist class with subservience to the working class. Or we may say, they replaced subservience to capitalists and big companies with subservience to the state which controlled capital and enjoyed total power. This made the tyranny of the state an even worse tyranny.

In every situation or regime where some people are subservient to others, a heavy tax is paid to different deities, in cash and kind. Submission is inevitable. If it is not made to God, then it is made to others. When submission is purely to God, it sets people free, and preserves their dignity and honour. By contrast, submission to other beings destroys people's humanity, dignity, freedom and all their good qualities, wastes their money and ruins their material interests.

Hence, the central issue of Godhead and people's relation with Him is given such careful and detailed attention in all divine messages and

Scriptures. This *sūrah* is an example of this care. The basic issue here is not concerned with the worship of statues in the ignorant societies of the ancient past; its concerns are man throughout all generations, and all forms of *jāhiliyyah*, past and present. Indeed, all *jāhiliyyah* systems are based on making people subservient to others.

This is the reason why the central issue in all divine Scriptures is to make clear that all Godhead and Lordship belong to God alone: *"Before your time We never sent a messenger without having revealed to him that there is no deity other than Me. Therefore, you shall worship Me alone."* (21: 25)

Hence, the conclusion of this *sūrah* runs as follows: *"Say: 'Mankind, if you are still in doubt as to what my faith is, then [know that] I do not worship those whom you worship beside God, but I worship God alone who will cause all of you to die. I have been commanded to be one of those who believe. And adhere exclusively and sincerely to the true faith, and do not be one of those who associate partners with God. Do not invoke, instead of God, anything that can neither benefit nor harm you. For if you do, you will surely be among the wrongdoers. Should God afflict you with any hardship, none other than He can remove it; and if He wills any good for you, none can withhold His bounty. He bestows it on whomsoever He wills. He is truly Forgiving, truly Merciful.' Say: 'Mankind, the truth has come to you from your Lord. Whoever chooses to follow the true guidance, does so for his own good; and whoever chooses to go astray, does so at his own peril. I am not responsible for your conduct.' Follow whatever is revealed to you, and be patient in adversity, until God shall give His judgement. He is the best of all judges."* (Verses 104–109)

I

A Book Full of Wisdom

Yūnus (Jonah)

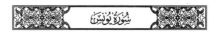

In the Name of God, the Merciful, the Beneficent

Alif. Lām. Rā. These are verses of the divine book, full of wisdom. (1)

Does it seem strange to people that We have inspired a man from their own midst: Warn all mankind, and give those who believe the glad tidings that they are on a sound footing with their Lord? The unbelievers say: 'This is plainly a skilled enchanter.' (2)

Your Lord is God who created the heavens and the earth in six days, and established Himself on the Throne, regulating and governing all that exists. There is none who may intercede with Him unless He first grants leave for that. That is God, your Lord: so worship Him alone. Will you not then keep this in mind? (3)

إِلَّا مِنۢ بَعْدِ إِذْنِهِۦۚ ذَٰلِكُمُ ٱللَّهُ رَبُّكُمْ فَٱعْبُدُوهُۚ أَفَلَا تَذَكَّرُونَ ٣

To Him you shall all return. This is, in truth, God's promise. He originates all His creation, and then brings them all back to life so that He may reward, with equity, those who have believed and done good deeds. As for the unbelievers, they shall have a scalding drink and a grievous suffering for their unbelief. (4)

إِلَيْهِ مَرْجِعُكُمْ جَمِيعًاۖ وَعْدَ ٱللَّهِ حَقًّاۚ إِنَّهُۥ يَبْدَؤُاْ ٱلْخَلْقَ ثُمَّ يُعِيدُهُۥ لِيَجْزِيَ ٱلَّذِينَ ءَامَنُواْ وَعَمِلُواْ ٱلصَّٰلِحَٰتِ بِٱلْقِسْطِۚ وَٱلَّذِينَ كَفَرُواْ لَهُمْ شَرَابٌ مِّنْ حَمِيمٍ وَعَذَابٌ أَلِيمٌۢ بِمَا كَانُواْ يَكْفُرُونَ ٤

He it is who made the sun a source of radiant light and the moon a light [reflected], and determined her phases so that you may know how to compute the years and measure [time]. God has not created this otherwise than in accordance with the truth. He makes plain His revelations to people of knowledge. (5)

هُوَ ٱلَّذِي جَعَلَ ٱلشَّمْسَ ضِيَآءً وَٱلْقَمَرَ نُورًا وَقَدَّرَهُۥ مَنَازِلَ لِتَعْلَمُواْ عَدَدَ ٱلسِّنِينَ وَٱلْحِسَابَۚ مَا خَلَقَ ٱللَّهُ ذَٰلِكَ إِلَّا بِٱلْحَقِّۚ يُفَصِّلُ ٱلْءَايَٰتِ لِقَوْمٍ يَعْلَمُونَ ٥

Indeed in the alternating of night and day, and in all that God has created in the heavens and the earth, there are signs for people who are God-fearing. (6)

إِنَّ فِي ٱخْتِلَٰفِ ٱلَّيْلِ وَٱلنَّهَارِ وَمَا خَلَقَ ٱللَّهُ فِي ٱلسَّمَٰوَٰتِ وَٱلْأَرْضِ لَءَايَٰتٍ لِّقَوْمٍ يَتَّقُونَ ٦

Those who entertain no hope of meeting Us, but are content with the life of this world, and feel well at ease about it, and those who pay no heed to Our revelation, (7)

إِنَّ ٱلَّذِينَ لَا يَرْجُونَ لِقَآءَنَا وَرَضُواْ بِٱلْحَيَوٰةِ ٱلدُّنْيَا وَٱطْمَأَنُّواْ بِهَا وَٱلَّذِينَ هُمْ عَنْ ءَايَـٰتِنَا غَـٰفِلُونَ ۝

shall have the Fire as their abode in requital for what they used to do. (8)

أُوْلَـٰٓئِكَ مَأْوَىٰهُمُ ٱلنَّارُ بِمَا كَانُواْ يَكْسِبُونَ ۝

Those who believe and do righteous deeds will be guided aright by their Lord by means of their faith. Running waters will flow at their feet in the gardens of bliss. (9)

إِنَّ ٱلَّذِينَ ءَامَنُواْ وَعَمِلُواْ ٱلصَّـٰلِحَـٰتِ يَهْدِيهِمْ رَبُّهُم بِإِيمَـٰنِهِمْ تَجْرِى مِن تَحْتِهِمُ ٱلْأَنْهَـٰرُ فِى جَنَّـٰتِ ٱلنَّعِيمِ ۝

There they will call out: 'Limitless are You in Your glory, God,' and their greeting will be, 'Peace!' Their call will conclude with the words: 'All praise is due to God, the Lord of all the worlds!' (10)

دَعْوَىٰهُمْ فِيهَا سُبْحَـٰنَكَ ٱللَّهُمَّ وَتَحِيَّتُهُمْ فِيهَا سَلَـٰمٌ وَءَاخِرُ دَعْوَىٰهُمْ أَنِ ٱلْحَمْدُ لِلَّهِ رَبِّ ٱلْعَـٰلَمِينَ ۝

If God were to hasten for mankind the ill [they have earned] as they would hasten the good, their end would indeed come forthwith. But We leave those who have no hope of meeting Us in their overweening arrogance, blindly stumbling to and fro. (11)

وَلَوْ يُعَجِّلُ ٱللَّهُ لِلنَّاسِ ٱلشَّرَّ ٱسْتِعْجَالَهُم بِٱلْخَيْرِ لَقُضِىَ إِلَيْهِمْ أَجَلُهُمْ فَنَذَرُ ٱلَّذِينَ لَا يَرْجُونَ لِقَآءَنَا فِى طُغْيَـٰنِهِمْ يَعْمَهُونَ ۝

When affliction befalls man, he appeals to Us, whether he be lying on his side, sitting, or standing, but as soon as We relieve his affliction, he goes on as though he had never appealed to Us to save him from the affliction that befell him. Thus do their deeds seem fair to those who are given to excesses. (12)

وَإِذَا مَسَّ ٱلْإِنسَٰنَ ٱلضُّرُّ دَعَانَا لِجَنۢبِهِۦٓ أَوْ قَاعِدًا أَوْ قَآئِمًا فَلَمَّا كَشَفْنَا عَنْهُ ضُرَّهُۥ مَرَّ كَأَن لَّمْ يَدْعُنَآ إِلَىٰ ضُرٍّ مَّسَّهُۥ كَذَٰلِكَ زُيِّنَ لِلْمُسْرِفِينَ مَا كَانُوا۟ يَعْمَلُونَ ۝

Indeed, We destroyed generations before your time when they persisted in their wrongdoing. The messengers sent to them brought them veritable evidence of the truth, but they would not believe. Thus do We reward the guilty. (13)

وَلَقَدْ أَهْلَكْنَا ٱلْقُرُونَ مِن قَبْلِكُمْ لَمَّا ظَلَمُوا۟ وَجَآءَتْهُمْ رُسُلُهُم بِٱلْبَيِّنَٰتِ وَمَا كَانُوا۟ لِيُؤْمِنُوا۟ كَذَٰلِكَ نَجْزِى ٱلْقَوْمَ ٱلْمُجْرِمِينَ ۝

Then We made you their successors on earth, so that We might see how you behave. (14)

ثُمَّ جَعَلْنَٰكُمْ خَلَٰٓئِفَ فِى ٱلْأَرْضِ مِنۢ بَعْدِهِمْ لِنَنظُرَ كَيْفَ تَعْمَلُونَ ۝

When Our revelations are recited to them in all their clarity, those who have no hope of meeting Us say: 'Bring us a discourse other than this Qur'ān, or else alter it.' Say: 'It is not for me to alter it of my own accord. I only follow what is revealed to me. I dread the torment of an awesome day if I should disobey my Lord!' (15)

وَإِذَا تُتْلَىٰ عَلَيْهِمْ ءَايَاتُنَا بَيِّنَٰتٍ قَالَ ٱلَّذِينَ لَا يَرْجُونَ لِقَآءَنَا ٱئْتِ بِقُرْءَانٍ غَيْرِ هَٰذَآ أَوْ بَدِّلْهُ قُلْ مَا يَكُونُ لِىٓ أَنْ أُبَدِّلَهُۥ مِن تِلْقَآئِ نَفْسِىٓ إِنْ أَتَّبِعُ إِلَّا مَا يُوحَىٰٓ إِلَىَّ إِنِّىٓ أَخَافُ إِنْ عَصَيْتُ رَبِّى عَذَابَ يَوْمٍ عَظِيمٍ ۝

Say: 'Had God so willed, I would not have recited it to you, nor would He have brought it to your knowledge. I spent a whole lifetime among you before it [was revealed to me]. Will you not, then, use your reason?' (16)

قُل لَّوۡ شَآءَ ٱللَّهُ مَا تَلَوۡتُهُۥ عَلَيۡكُمۡ وَلَآ أَدۡرَىٰكُم بِهِۦ فَقَدۡ لَبِثۡتُ فِيكُمۡ عُمُرٗا مِّن قَبۡلِهِۦٓ أَفَلَا تَعۡقِلُونَ ۝

Who is more wicked than one who attributes his lying inventions to God or denies His revelations? Indeed those who are guilty shall not be successful. (17)

فَمَنۡ أَظۡلَمُ مِمَّنِ ٱفۡتَرَىٰ عَلَى ٱللَّهِ كَذِبًا أَوۡ كَذَّبَ بِـَٔايَٰتِهِۦٓ إِنَّهُۥ لَا يُفۡلِحُ ٱلۡمُجۡرِمُونَ ۝

They worship, side by side with God, what can neither harm nor benefit them, and say: 'These will intercede for us with God.' Say: 'Do you presume to inform God of something in the heavens or on earth that He does not know? Limitless is He in His glory, and exalted above whatever they may associate with Him.' (18)

وَيَعۡبُدُونَ مِن دُونِ ٱللَّهِ مَا لَا يَضُرُّهُمۡ وَلَا يَنفَعُهُمۡ وَيَقُولُونَ هَٰٓؤُلَآءِ شُفَعَٰٓؤُنَا عِندَ ٱللَّهِ قُلۡ أَتُنَبِّـُٔونَ ٱللَّهَ بِمَا لَا يَعۡلَمُ فِي ٱلسَّمَٰوَٰتِ وَلَا فِي ٱلۡأَرۡضِ سُبۡحَٰنَهُۥ وَتَعَٰلَىٰ عَمَّا يُشۡرِكُونَ ۝

All mankind were once but one single community, and then they disagreed among themselves. Had it not been for a decree from your Lord that had already gone forth, all their differences would have been resolved. (19)

وَمَا كَانَ ٱلنَّاسُ إِلَّآ أُمَّةٗ وَٰحِدَةٗ فَٱخۡتَلَفُواْ وَلَوۡلَا كَلِمَةٞ سَبَقَتۡ مِن رَّبِّكَ لَقُضِيَ بَيۡنَهُمۡ فِيمَا فِيهِ يَخۡتَلِفُونَ ۝

29

They ask: 'Why has no sign been sent down to him by his Lord?' Say: 'God's alone is the knowledge of what is beyond the reach of human perception. Wait, then, if you will: I too am waiting.' (20)

وَيَقُولُونَ لَوْلَا أُنزِلَ عَلَيْهِ ءَايَةٌ مِّن رَّبِّهِ فَقُلْ إِنَّمَا ٱلْغَيْبُ لِلَّهِ فَٱنتَظِرُوٓا إِنِّي مَعَكُم مِّنَ ٱلْمُنتَظِرِينَ ﴿٢٠﴾

Whenever We let people taste grace after some hardship has afflicted them, they turn to scheme against Our revelations. Say: 'More swift is God's scheming. Our messengers are recording all that you may devise.' (21)

وَإِذَآ أَذَقْنَا ٱلنَّاسَ رَحْمَةً مِّنۢ بَعْدِ ضَرَّآءَ مَسَّتْهُمْ إِذَا لَهُم مَّكْرٌ فِىٓ ءَايَاتِنَا قُلِ ٱللَّهُ أَسْرَعُ مَكْرًا إِنَّ رُسُلَنَا يَكْتُبُونَ مَا تَمْكُرُونَ ﴿٢١﴾

He it is who enables you to travel on land and sea. Then when you are on board ships, and sailing along in a favourable wind, they feel happy with it, but then a stormy wind comes upon them and waves surge towards them from all sides, so that they believe they are encompassed [by death]. [At that point] they appeal to God, in complete sincerity of faith in Him alone: 'If You will save us from this, we shall certainly be most grateful.' (22)

هُوَ ٱلَّذِى يُسَيِّرُكُمْ فِى ٱلْبَرِّ وَٱلْبَحْرِ حَتَّىٰ إِذَا كُنتُمْ فِى ٱلْفُلْكِ وَجَرَيْنَ بِهِم بِرِيحٍ طَيِّبَةٍ وَفَرِحُوا بِهَا جَآءَتْهَا رِيحٌ عَاصِفٌ وَجَآءَهُمُ ٱلْمَوْجُ مِن كُلِّ مَكَانٍ وَظَنُّوٓا أَنَّهُمْ أُحِيطَ بِهِمْ دَعَوُا ٱللَّهَ مُخْلِصِينَ لَهُ ٱلدِّينَ لَئِنْ أَنجَيْتَنَا مِنْ هَٰذِهِ لَنَكُونَنَّ مِنَ ٱلشَّٰكِرِينَ ﴿٢٢﴾

Yet when He has saved them, they transgress in the land, offending against all right. Mankind, it is against your own souls that your offences rebound. [You care only for] the enjoyment of this present life, but in the end you will return to Us when We will tell you the truth of what you were doing [in this life]. (23)

فَلَمَّآ أَنجَىٰهُمْ إِذَا هُمْ يَبْغُونَ فِى ٱلْأَرْضِ بِغَيْرِ ٱلْحَقِّ يَٰٓأَيُّهَا ٱلنَّاسُ إِنَّمَا بَغْيُكُمْ عَلَىٰٓ أَنفُسِكُم مَّتَٰعَ ٱلْحَيَوٰةِ ٱلدُّنْيَا ثُمَّ إِلَيْنَا مَرْجِعُكُمْ فَنُنَبِّئُكُم بِمَا كُنتُمْ تَعْمَلُونَ ٢٣

This present life may be compared to rain which We send down from the sky, and which is then absorbed by the plants of the earth from which men and animals eat. Then, when the earth has been clad with its fine adornments and well embellished, and its people believe that they have full mastery over it, Our command comes down upon it, by night or by day, and We make it like a field that has been mowed down, as if it did not blossom but yesterday. Thus do We spell out Our revelations to people who think. (24)

إِنَّمَا مَثَلُ ٱلْحَيَوٰةِ ٱلدُّنْيَا كَمَآءٍ أَنزَلْنَٰهُ مِنَ ٱلسَّمَآءِ فَٱخْتَلَطَ بِهِۦ نَبَاتُ ٱلْأَرْضِ مِمَّا يَأْكُلُ ٱلنَّاسُ وَٱلْأَنْعَٰمُ حَتَّىٰٓ إِذَآ أَخَذَتِ ٱلْأَرْضُ زُخْرُفَهَا وَٱزَّيَّنَتْ وَظَنَّ أَهْلُهَآ أَنَّهُمْ قَٰدِرُونَ عَلَيْهَآ أَتَىٰهَآ أَمْرُنَا لَيْلًا أَوْ نَهَارًا فَجَعَلْنَٰهَا حَصِيدًا كَأَن لَّمْ تَغْنَ بِٱلْأَمْسِ كَذَٰلِكَ نُفَصِّلُ ٱلْءَايَٰتِ لِقَوْمٍ يَتَفَكَّرُونَ ٢٤

God calls to the abode of peace, and guides him that wills to a straight path. (25)

وَٱللَّهُ يَدْعُوٓا۟ إِلَىٰ دَارِ ٱلسَّلَٰمِ وَيَهْدِى مَن يَشَآءُ إِلَىٰ صِرَٰطٍ مُّسْتَقِيمٍ ٢٥

Preview

This *sūrah* is a single unit, difficult to divide into sections and sub-units. In this respect it is similar to *Sūrah* 6, Cattle, which takes up Volume V of this work. However, each of the two *sūrahs* has its own distinctive character. This *sūrah* also flows in successive waves to inspire our hearts, choosing various rhythms for its address. It wonders at the outset how the unbelievers received the Qur'ān, the new revelation from on high, and follows this with scenes of the universe which reflect the truth of God's creation and His control of the universe. This is followed with scenes of the Day of Judgement. It reflects on how people react to the events they witness and on the fate of earlier communities. Its other themes have already been referred to in the Prologue.

If we have to divide the *sūrah* into sections, then the first one occupies more than its first half and this flows with perfect ease. This is followed by a short account of the Prophet Noah and his mission, and a brief reference to the prophets sent after him, before giving an account of the history of the Prophet Moses and a reference to the Prophet Jonah and his community. These accounts and references form another section. The final verses in the *sūrah* form a section of their own.

In view of the nature of this *sūrah*, we will attempt to discuss it in groups of waves addressing related themes.

This first section begins with three individual letters, *Alif, Lām, Rā,* in the same way as *Sūrahs* 2, 3 and 7 discussed in Volumes I, II and VI respectively. We explained in our commentary on these earlier *sūrahs* our view about why these *sūrahs* begin with such individual letters.[1] To recap, from a linguistic point of view, these three individual letters

---

1. It is useful to summarize our view here: these individual letters are simply an implicit reference to the fact that this divine revelation, the Qur'ān, is composed of letters of the same nature as those which some *sūrahs* open with. They are the same letters of the language of the Arabs, the first community to be addressed by the Qur'ān. Yet they form this Book which is of a miraculous nature. Those Arabs, masters of eloquence and poetic description, cannot produce a single *sūrah* similar to the Qur'ān. This miraculous excellence appears clearly in everything God makes. The earth is composed of particles of different elements with well-known characteristics, but the utmost that people can make of them is a brick, a tool, a machine, etc. On the other hand, from these very particles and elements God makes life, which no one else can do. From these letters and sounds, people make words and sentences in prose or verse, but God makes of them the Qur'ān which provides the infallible criterion to distinguish the truth from falsehood. The difference between people's language and the Qur'ān is the same as the difference between a lifeless object and a creature full of life. – Editor's note.

32

form a subject while the predicate is the sentence that follows: '*These are verses of the divine book, full of wisdom.*' (Verse 1)

The *sūrah* then refers to a number of things which reflect the wisdom to which reference is made in the description of this book, the Qur'ān. These start with a revelation to God's Messenger so that he could warn all people and deliver a piece of happy news to the believers. It refutes the objection voiced by some people that God has chosen a human being to be the recipient of His revelations. It also refers to the creation of the heavens and the earth and how their affairs are conducted and regulated, as well as making the sun a source of bright light while the moon reflects light. Mention is also made of the stages the moon goes through and how people use these to calculate the years and measure time. The alternation of the night and day is also mentioned by way of reference to the wisdom involved in such alternation.

After presenting these scenes, the *sūrah* moves on to speak of those who do not reflect on such miracles and who do not expect to meet with their Lord, who creates and regulates all things. It refers to the black end that awaits those who choose to remain unaware of the import of God's creation and, by contrast, the perfect happiness that is in store for believers. The *sūrah* also refers to the wisdom behind delaying the punishment till its appointed day. Had God decided to speed up the awful result of their work, they would immediately face their end.

The *sūrah* then reflects on the attitude of human beings to good and evil. It shows how they appeal earnestly to God to lift their suffering, and how they forget Him after He has responded to their appeals: they unhesitatingly go back to their old, errant ways. In short, they take no lesson from what happened to earlier communities who met their doom.

Although the fate of those communities was clear to the Arabs whom the Prophet Muḥammad addressed, calling on them to accept God's message, the unbelievers asked the Prophet to bring them a different Qur'ān or change parts of it. They would not consider that the Qur'ān was revealed by God, and as such admits no change or modification. They worshipped idols which could bring them no benefit and cause them no harm, and they relied on no sound proof to support their beliefs. At the same time they denied God in spite of the revelations they received from on high supporting the call to believe in Him alone.

Furthermore, they demanded miracles, ignoring the clearly miraculous nature of the Qur'ān itself, and turning a blind eye to all signs scattered in the world around them confirming that God is the Lord of the universe.

This first passage then portrays a vivid example of how people receive God's grace and how they react when hardship or disaster befalls them. This is given in a scene that is full of life, with people boarding ships that go easily in the sea before they face a raging storm that brings them into contact with ferocious waves from every direction.

This passage then draws another scene which describes the deceptive fleeting nature of this life, and how all its glitter vanishes in an instant, while people are dazzled by its brightness, unaware of the impending doom. At the same time, God calls on them to seek the life of peace, security and reassurance which does not end suddenly, like the present life. He states that all these signs are explained for a definite purpose: '*Thus do We spell out Our revelations to people who think.*' (Verse 24) It is such people who understand God's wisdom in His creation and the way He conducts and regulates all matters.

Something to Marvel at

'*Alif. Lām. Rā. These are verses of the divine book, full of wisdom.*' (Verse 1) These are three letters of the Arabic alphabet from which all the verses of this divine book that is full of wisdom are composed. The unbelievers deny that God revealed this book to His Messenger. Furthermore, whilst they realize that these are the letters of their language, they are unable to produce a single verse similar to what the Qur'ān contains. In fact the *sūrah* includes a challenge to them to do so. Yet their inability to take up that challenge does not lead them to reflect that the thing which God's Messenger has and they lack is the revelation he receives from on high. Had it not been for revelation, he would have had the same difficulty, and would have been unable to compose out of these letters that are available to all a single verse like the Qur'ān.

'*These are verses of the divine book, full of wisdom.*' (Verse 1) It is indeed a wise book which addresses human beings with what suits human nature. It portrays in the present *sūrah* some aspects that are always true of human nature, reflected across every generation. In its wisdom it calls on those who remain unaware to wake up and reflect on the signs they see all around them in the wide universe, in the heavens and the earth, in the sun and the moon, in the night and day, in the fate of earlier communities and how they had responded to the appeals of their messengers, and in everything that points to the great power that conducts and regulates all existence.

"Does it seem strange to people that We have inspired a man from their own midst: 'Warn all mankind, and give those who believe the glad tidings that they are on a sound footing with their Lord?' The unbelievers say: 'This is plainly a skilled enchanter.'" (Verse 2) This is a rhetorical question which wonders at the attitude which considers the very concept of revelation strange.

Every one of God's messengers was received with the same disbelieving question: *'Has God sent a human being as His messenger?'* (17: 94) This question stems from the fact that people do not appreciate the value of 'humanity' which they themselves represent. They find it hard to believe that a human being could be chosen as God's messenger and that God sends down to him revelations, commanding him to make the way of guidance for others clear. They imagine that God would send an angel or some other creature belonging to a category superior to mankind. They do not realize how God has honoured man, and part of that honour is that man is well qualified to bear God's message, and that God chooses certain human beings with whom He has this special relationship.

At the time of the Prophet Muḥammad (peace be upon him), this was the main point of contention among the unbelievers who refused to believe in his message. The same was true of the unbelievers of earlier generations and communities. In this modern age of ours, some people invent a similarly absurd doubt. They wonder: how does contact happen between a human being with his limited physical nature and God who is totally unlike everything else and whose nature is unlike the nature of everything He has created?

Such a question cannot be asked except by one who fully comprehends the nature of God Himself with all its aspects, and who also understands all the characteristics God has given to man. No one in his right mind, aware of the limitations of his reason, would make

35

such a claim. Such a person knows that the characteristics of human nature are still being discovered today, and that scientific discovery has not come to an end. Beyond the reach of human perception and understanding there will always remain worlds unknown to man.

What this means is that human beings have latent potential known only to God. God certainly knows best to whom to assign His message. Knowing this ability is beyond all people and it may even be unknown to the person who is chosen for the task, until that choice is made. God, who has breathed of His soul into man knows every little detail of every nature. He can endow any human being with the ability to undertake this unique contact and bond in a way which can be appreciated only by those who experience it.

A number of contemporary commentators on the Qur'ān have endeavoured to prove the fact of revelation through scientific means so as to make it easier to understand. We however object to this approach. Science has its own scope and domain, and it has certain tools to suit its domain and to move within its scope. Science has not even claimed to have arrived at any certainty with regard to the spirit and human soul, because it is well beyond its domain. The spirit is not subject to the sort of material experiment which science can make. Therefore, those scientific disciplines that work within recognized scientific principles have avoided discussion of anything relating to the spirit. So-called 'spiritual studies' are merely attempts that have doubtful methods and very suspicious aims. The only way to arrive at any certainty in this area is to refer to the only sources of certainty which we have, namely, the Qur'ān and the *Ḥadīth*. We take any statement in these two sources at its face value, without adding anything to it or modifying it in any way and without drawing any conclusion on the basis of analogy. Addition, modification and analogy are all mental processes, but in this area the human mind is outside of its domain, and has no suitable tools to work with.

"Does it seem strange to people that We have inspired a man from their own midst: Warn all mankind, and give those who believe the glad tidings that they are on a sound footing with their Lord?" (Verse 2) This is in a nutshell the purpose of revelation: to warn people of the consequences of their disobedience and to deliver happy news to the believers as to the outcome of their obedience. This inevitably

includes an outline of the duties that are to be fulfilled and the prohibitions to be avoided. The warning is addressed to all mankind, because it should be conveyed to all people, who must be made aware of the consequences of their actions. The happy news though is given only to the believers.

Indeed all human beings need to be warned so that they are aware of what may happen to them when they reject God's message and refuse to follow His guidance. On the other hand, only the believers receive the happy news of reassurance and of being on firm ground. The connotations generated here by the Arabic text all point to a general atmosphere of warning. The believers are 'on a sound footing' which means that they are sure of their steps, unhesitating, unshakeable even during the most worrying of times. They are 'on a sound footing with their Lord,' in a presence where believers find reassurance and safety while others worry as they contemplate their impending doom.

Why a Human Messenger?

God's wisdom is clearly apparent in choosing to send down His revelations to a man from among themselves and one whom they knew well. Thus they could give and take from him without difficulty or embarrassment. His wisdom in sending messengers is even clearer. By his very nature, man can accept and follow good or evil. His tool to distinguish between the two is his reason. This reason needs to have an accurate criterion to which it can refer whenever things become doubtful and unclear, or whenever temptations or immediate interests affect his judgement. He needs a measure which is totally unaffected by anything that influences the human body, mentality or temperament, so as to give him the right answer concerning any uncertainty. This measure and criterion is nothing other than God's guidance and His law.

This requires that divine faith should provide a firm basis to which the human mind refers all its concepts and ideas in order to determine which of them are correct and which are false. To say, by contrast, that divine faith always reflects how people conceive this faith which is, consequently, liable to evolve and develop, is to make this basis subject to influence by human concepts and logic. This undermines the whole basis and leaves no proper measure or criterion to evaluate human concepts.

Such a view is not much different from saying that religion is of human making. The ultimate result is the same. The risk is too strong and the trap is very dangerous. Hence it is imperative that we always be on our guard against its short and long term results.

Although the question of revelation is so clear, the unbelievers receive it as though it is very strange: "*The unbelievers say: 'This is plainly a skilled enchanter.'*" (Verse 2) They describe him as an enchanter or a sorcerer because what he says is beyond the power of human beings. Yet they should acknowledge the fact of revelation on account of this, because sorcery is incapable of including statements about universal facts or of delivering a complete code of living, laws and moral principles which make for a highly civilized society. They tended to confuse revelation with sorcery because in all pagan beliefs, sorcery was a part of religion. They did not have the clarity that a Muslim possesses with regard to the nature of divine faith. This realization saves Muslims from all the legends and superstitions of pagan beliefs.

> *Your Lord is God who created the heavens and the earth in six days, and established Himself on the Throne, regulating and governing all that exists. There is none who may intercede with Him unless He first grants leave for that. That is God, your Lord: so worship Him alone. Will you not then keep this in mind? To Him you shall all return. This is, in truth, God's promise. He originates all His creation, and then brings them all back to life so that He may reward, with equity, those who have believed and done good deeds. As for the unbelievers, they shall have a scalding drink and a grievous suffering for their unbelief. He it is who made the sun a source of radiant light and the moon a light [reflected], and determined her phases so that you may know how to compute the years and measure [time]. God has not created this otherwise than in accordance with the truth. He makes plain His revelations to people of knowledge. Indeed in the alternating of night and day, and in all that God has created in the heavens and the earth, there are signs for people who are God-fearing. (Verses 3–6)*

This, the question of Lordship, is the main issue of faith. The unbelievers did not seriously deny the concept of Godhead. They acknowledged God's existence – for human nature cannot entirely reject the basic concept of God except in few highly unusual cases – but they associated other deities with Him and to these they addressed their worship. In some cases, the unbelievers considered their false deities to be intermediaries who could bring them closer to God. Others thought they could give themselves certain powers which belong to God alone, thereby enacting legislation which God had not sanctioned.

The Qur'ān does not enter into any cold philosophical argument, of the type introduced in Muslim cultural circles by the influence of Greek philosophy, concerning the questions of Godhead and Lordship. Instead it resorts to the simple, straightforward logic of human nature. It states that God is the One who created the heavens and the earth and everything in them. He is the One who has made the sun a source of radiant light and given the moon its quality to reflect light, determining its stages. He also made the day and night alternate. All these natural phenomena can awaken man's heart and mind if he would only contemplate them and reflect on the power that controls them. God who has created all this and controls its movement is the One who deserves to be the Lord to whom people address their worship, assigning to Him no partners from among His creation. This is a simple logical conclusion which does not need any long argumentative debate based on cold deductive reasoning that touches no heart and awakens no mind.

This vast universe, with its heavens and earth, sun and moon, night and day, and all that is created in the heavens and the earth and lives in them of plants, birds, animals and other communities, follow the laws of nature God has set in operation.

The deep dark night with its still silence, disturbed only by the movement of phantoms; the dawn that opens up into it like a smiling, happy babe; the movement that the early breath of the morning brings to start a new day full of life; the calm shades that seem still to the beholder when they are in fact moving along gently; the birds that hop and fly here and there in never ending movement; the emerging plants that look forward to continued growth; the countless creatures that come and go everywhere; the unending cycle of birth and death;

and the life that continues along its way determined by God, are all countless images, forms, types, movements that start and finish; cycles that take people to old age or to start young lives, to invigoration and fading away, to birth and death, and so on through a continuous life cycle that never stops. All this calls on every sense and atom in human beings to pause and reflect. It only takes an alert mind and an open heart to contemplate such signs as are everywhere in the universe. The Qur'ān directly awakens hearts and minds so that man can so reflect.

The Lord to Be Worshipped

"Your Lord is God who created the heavens and the earth in six days." (Verse 3) Your Lord who deserves to be worshipped alone is the Creator of all that is. It is He who created the heavens and the earth according to an elaborate plan of creation and to wise purpose. He did all this *'in six days'.* We will not delve into any argument about these six days, for they are mentioned here only to point to the wisdom behind the elaborate planning of creation and how the affairs of the universe are conducted so as to suit God's purpose. Anyway, these six days belong to the realm that God has kept to Himself. We cannot find what they are unless He chooses to inform us. Hence, we do not go beyond what is stated about them in the Qur'ān.

'And established Himself on the Throne.' (Verse 3) This expression indicates a position of a firm, overall authority exercised by a higher being. It gives a physical image in the inimitable style of the Qur'ān. The conjunction, 'and', is used in the Arabic text in the form of 'then', but it does not indicate any chronological order. It only indicates a mental dimension. Time has no significance in this context. There is simply no state or form applicable to God which came into existence after it was not there. Limitless is God in His glory. He is not subject to an event taking place, and all that events entail of time and location. Hence we emphatically say that 'and', in the present context, indicates a mental dimension.

'Regulating and governing all that exists.' (Verse 3) He determines the beginning and the end, the shape and the form, the preliminaries and the conclusions, and chooses the laws that govern its stages and its final place.

'There is none who may intercede with Him unless He first grants leave for that.' (Verse 3) All decisions and judgements belong to Him alone. There are no intercessors who may bring anyone closer to Him. No one of His creatures may intercede with Him unless He grants him permission to do so, in accordance with His wise planning. Intercession may be earned through firm belief and good deeds, not by appealing to false intercessors. This answers what the Arabs used to say about the angels: that statues of them which they worshipped enjoyed an inalienable right of intercession. How absurd!

What all this means is that the Creator has the absolute authority to govern and regulate all matters, and no one may intercede without His permission. *'That is God, your Lord'* who is worthy of having His Lordship acknowledged by all. *'So worship Him alone.'* (Verse 3) For He is the One to whom all submission should be addressed. *'Will you not then keep this in mind?'* (Verse 3) The whole thing is so clear and so firmly established that it only requires a mere admonition for the truth to be well engraved in people's minds.

We need to pause a little to reflect on the statement that follows all the universal phenomena pointing to God and His Lordship: *'That is God, your Lord: so worship Him alone.'* (Verse 3) As we have already said, the unbelievers among the Arabs did not seriously deny the existence of God. They acknowledged that He is the Creator who gives sustenance, initiates life, causes death, regulates all matters and is able to do whatever He wills. This acknowledgement though was not followed by its logical consequence of acknowledging His Lordship over their lives. That would have been reflected by submitting to Him alone in all matters, addressing all worship rituals to Him and accepting His rule in all their affairs. That is precisely the meaning of the statement: *'That is God, your Lord: so worship Him alone.'* Worship means submission, obedience and acknowledging all these attributes as belonging to God alone.

In all structures based on *jāhiliyyah*[2] the concept of Godhead is drastically narrowed down. People begin to think that by merely

---

2. *Jāhiliyyah* is an Islamic term that refers in the first instance to the state of affairs that prevailed in Arabia in the period immediately before the advent of Islam. The word is derived from a root that signifies 'ignorance'. In its broader usage it refers to any situation that is not based on belief in God's oneness, implying that such a situation is generated by, or based on, a state of ignorance. – Editor's note.

acknowledging the existence of God, they have attained to faith, and that once people make that acknowledgement they have then done all that is required of them. They thus avoid the natural consequence of that acknowledgement, which requires submission to God alone, who is the overall Sovereign and ruler, and against whom no one has any authority unless it comes from Him.

Similarly the meaning of 'worship' is seriously curtailed in any *jāhiliyyah* society. It becomes synonymous with offering worship rituals. People then think that once they address these rituals to God, they are worshipping Him alone. The fact is that the term 'worship', *'ibādah* in Arabic, is derived from the root *'abada* which signifies submission. Worship rituals are only one aspect of submission, which remains much wider in import.

Jāhiliyyah is not a period of history or a particular stage of development. It is a state characterized by the curtailment of the concepts of Godhead and worship on the above lines. Such curtailment leads people to associate partners with God while they imagine that they are following His faith, as is the case today in all parts of the world. This includes those countries whose populations have Muslim names and address their worship to God, but who have Lords other than God. Yet the Lord is the One whose authority over us all should be acknowledged, whose law should be implemented, to whom we should submit, carry out His orders and refrain from what He forbids, and whom we should obey in all matters. This is how the Prophet explained worship to his companion, 'Adiy ibn Ḥātim, as he told him: 'They obeyed their [rabbis and monks who legislated for them as they pleased], and that is how they worshipped them.'[3]

Justice for All

To emphasize this meaning of worship, a later verse in this *sūrah* states: "*Say: 'Do but consider all the means of sustenance that God has bestowed on you! Some of it you then made unlawful, and some lawful.' Say: 'Has God given you leave to do so, or do you fabricate lies against God?'*" (Verse 59) Our situation today is not at all different from what

---

3. A full treatment of this *ḥadīth* is given in Volume VIII, pp. 136–139. – Editor's note.

prevailed during that period of ignorance and to whose people God clearly states: '*That is God, your Lord: so worship Him alone. Will you not then keep this in mind?*' (Verse 3) So, worship Him, associating no partners with Him. For to Him you shall return to face the reckoning when He gives each one, believer or unbeliever, his or her fitting reward: '*To Him you shall all return. This is, in truth, God's promise.*' (Verse 4) You return to none of the partners or the intercessors you claim. He has promised that you will return to Him and His promise is certain to be fulfilled. For resurrection is the completion of creation.

"He originates all His creation, and then brings them all back to life so that He may reward, with equity, those who have believed and done good deeds. As for the unbelievers, they shall have a scalding drink and a grievous suffering for their unbelief." (Verse 4) Administering justice to all is in itself one of the aims of original creation and bringing all creatures back to life. Similarly, giving pure happiness and enjoyment without any unwelcome consequences to spoil its effects is another aim of the process of creation and resurrection. This is the utmost point of perfection which humanity can reach. Such a zenith cannot be attained in this life on earth which is always mixed with worry and distress. No happy experience in this life is free of a hiccup or an unwelcome aftermath, except perhaps for pure spiritual happiness which is very rarely experienced by human beings.

Had the inevitable termination of the happiness of this world been the only feeling people acknowledge, it would have been enough to make it imperfect and incomplete. In this life, humanity does not attain its highest potential, which implies getting rid of its weaknesses, shortcomings, and their consequences, as well as an enjoyment that is free of fear, worry, and apprehension of quick termination. Such happiness, graphically described in the Qur'ān, is attained in heaven. As such, it is only proper that one of the aims of creation and resurrection is to enable those human beings who follow divine guidance, implementing the right code of living, to attain the highest standard of humanity.

The unbelievers have put the divine code of living aside and have chosen not to move along the way that leads to the attainment of human perfection. According to the laws of nature that never fail, their deviation keeps them well short of that level of perfection. As

Shaikh Rashīd Riḍā' says, they will have to suffer the consequences of their errant ways just like one who violates the rules of health: he suffers disease and debility and they suffer distress after distress. The end result will be unmitigated misery, in contrast to the pure happiness the believers enjoy: 'As for the unbelievers, they shall have a scalding drink and a grievous suffering for their persistent disbelief.' (Verse 4)

The *sūrah* then highlights some of the cosmic phenomena which are next to the creation of the heavens and the earth in their magnificence: "*He it is who made the sun a source of radiant light and the moon a light [reflected], and determined her phases so that you may know how to compute the years and measure [time]. God has not created this otherwise than in accordance with the truth. He makes plain His revelations to people of knowledge.*" (Verse 5) These are two very clear scenes which we take for granted because of our long familiarity with them and their continuous repetition. Who could imagine the awesome feelings of majesty and magnificence of a person who sees the sun rising and setting for the first time, or the full moon making its first appearance followed by its first setting? The Qur'ān reminds us of these two very familiar scenes so as to bring them back to us anew. It awakens in our hearts a desire to look and reflect over such great phenomena.

The Qur'ān draws our attention to the elaborate design clearly seen in their creation: '*He it is who made the sun a source of radiant light.*' (Verse 5) We feel that it is almost ablaze. '*And the moon a light [reflected].*' It shines and illuminates. '*And determined her phases.*' (Verse 5) It stands every night in a new position which gives it a corresponding shape. This is seen by all of us when we look at the moon, night after night. We do not need to have any specialized knowledge of astronomy to realize this. The purpose is clear: '*so that you may know how to compute the years and measure time.*' (Verse 5) Today, we all still calculate time on the basis of the sun and the moon's movements.

Is all this a pastime, a coincidence or something false? Certainly not. Such an elaborate system, providing such perfect harmony and accuracy which never fail, could not be without purpose. It is neither false nor a coincidence: '*God has not created this otherwise than in accordance with the truth.*' (Verse 5) The truth is its tool, substance and objective. The truth is constant and firmly rooted, and these phenomena which point to the truth are also clear, constant and permanent. '*He makes His revelations plain to people of knowledge.*' (Verse 5) Knowledge and learning are needed to understand the elaborate planning behind these magnificent scenes.

The heavens, the earth, the blazing sun, and the illuminating moon combine to produce the succession of day and night. This is a telling phenomenon which inspires anyone who opens his heart and mind to the messages contained in the universe: "*Indeed in the alternating of night and day, and in all that God has created in the heavens and the earth, there are signs for people who are God-fearing.*" (Verse 6) The Arabic term used for the 'alternating of night and day' refers both to their succession and their varying length. Both are well-known aspects which lose their significance with familiarity, except in those moments when man's soul and conscience are awakened and he begins to contemplate the rise and setting of different stars and planets like a man reborn, responding to every aspect and every phenomenon. Only in such moments does man truly live, shaking away the rust of familiarity and repetition which becloud his vision and blunt his responses.

"*And in all that God has created in the heavens and the earth.*" (Verse 6) If man just stood for a moment watching what '*God has created in the heavens and the earth*' and looked at the countless number of species, forms, situations and material conditions, he would have sufficient material for a life of reflection and contemplation. For in all this, '*there are signs for people who are God-fearing.*' (Verse 6)

It is only such people who have a conscience, sharpened by their fear of God, who are alert and responsive to the evidence of God's great might. For it is all clearly apparent in the perfection of His creation.

Addressing Human Nature

To appeal to human nature is a central part of the Qur'ānic approach. The Qur'ān utilizes the signs that are seen everywhere around us in the universe to point to God as the Lord Creator. God knows that these address human nature in a clear and telling way. The Qur'ān does not employ the argumentative style of later philosophers, for God knows that this does not appeal to people's hearts. It remains instead within its area of cold reasoning which neither generates motivation nor contributes to building human life.

The proofs presented by the Qur'ān remain the most convincing to hearts and minds alike. The very existence of the universe, its harmonious movement, and whatever changes and transformations that take place in it – according to laws that were set in operation long before they were discovered by man – cannot be explained without acknowledging the existence of an able hand that controls it all. Those who dispute this fact do not offer any plausible alternative. They merely say that the universe has long existed with its operative laws, and that its existence does not need any explanation. Anyone who finds such argument acceptable or reasonable may please himself.

Such arguments were made in Europe when breaking away from the tyranny of the Church led people to deny God altogether. Now they are also said in our countries as a means of getting away from the practical implications of belief in God. Most people in the unbelieving communities of times gone by acknowledged God's existence, but disputed His Lordship, as was the case in Arabian *jāhiliyyah*, where the Qur'ān made its first address to mankind. The Qur'ānic proof refuted their belief in God's existence and His attributes, and demanded that they should take their beliefs to their natural conclusion and so acknowledge God's Lordship. In other words the Qur'ān demanded that they submit to Him alone in laws and worship alike. The state of ignorance that prevails in our own time tries to rid itself of this powerful logic by denying God's existence altogether.

What is strange is that even in countries claiming to be Islamic, this is promoted in a variety of ways under the guise of science. Thus we hear that what is 'metaphysical' has no place in 'scientific' methodology. Everything that is related to God is thus considered 'metaphysical'. Those running away from God try to use this back door, only because they fear and try to deceive others. As for fear of God, this is a quality of which they are devoid.

Nevertheless, the very existence of the universe and its meticulously accurate and harmonious systems remains a proof too strong for the unbelievers to face. Human nature, in heart, mind and soul, responds to this proof. The Qur'ānic approach addresses human nature as a whole in the broadest and most direct way.

Two Different Destinies

Those who see this perfect universal system and who do not realize that it means that this life, in which human perfection cannot be attained, is not the ultimate one, will never be in heaven which is reserved for the righteous. Such people do not expect to meet with God. They see perfection in creation yet they do not reflect on the message it presents. Heaven is preserved for those who believe and do righteous deeds. In heaven they will be relieved from the burdens of this world and they will glorify God in an atmosphere of unmingled happiness that never ends: "*Those who entertain no hope of meeting Us, but are content with the life of this world, and feel well at ease about it, and those who pay no heed to Our revelation, shall have the fire as their abode in requital for what they used to do. Those who believe and do righteous deeds will be guided aright by their Lord by means of their faith. Running waters will flow at their feet in the gardens of bliss. There they will call out: 'Limitless are You in Your glory, God,' and their greeting will be, 'Peace!' Their call will conclude with the words: 'All praise is due to God, the Lord of all the worlds!'*" (Verses 7–10)

The whole universal system clearly points to the fact that it has been created by an all-powerful Creator. Those who do not reflect on its various aspects cannot realize that resurrection, reckoning and judgement are essential elements of this system, so that justice is done and humanity is allowed to attain perfection. They have no expectation of meeting God. Hence, they limit their aspirations to this present life, with all its shortcomings, and are content with its pleasures. They do not see its imperfections. Nor do they realize that it cannot be the ultimate end, although they depart from it without having had their full reward for the good or evil they have done, or attained the heights to which they can aspire by virtue of their being human.

When people limit their aspirations to what this life offers and are content with this, they sink lower and lower, because they have no sublime height to aspire to, and no horizon to reach. They have, by necessity, to look down to this life on earth, oblivious of the signs in the universe which awaken hearts, sharpen feelings and provide the motivation necessary to seek the sublime. Hence, they '*shall have the fire for their abode in requital for what they used to do.'* (Verse 8) This is a fitting end.

The believers by contrast realize that there is something much superior to this present life. Their deeds are righteous because their faith motivates them to obey God's commands and expect His generous reward in the hereafter. These are the ones who *'will be guided aright by their Lord by means of their faith.'* (Verse 9) Having faith establishes a relationship between them and God who guides them to do what is right. As a result of this guidance, their hearts are alive, fully aware of the straight path they have to follow. Their conscience is alert, directing them always to do what is good and what earns God's pleasure. These are the ones who are admitted into heaven where *'running waters will flow at their feet.'* (Verse 9) The reference here to running waters in heaven is at the same time a reference to water generally which is always associated with growth, fertility and life.

What are their preoccupations once in heaven? What do they wish for? They have no need for wealth, position, or personal gain. What God gives them is far better than any such concern which is in any case now behind them. Instead, their preoccupation, their top priority, is described as their 'appeal' or 'call' to glorify God in the beginning and praise Him in the end. In between times they greet one another and are greeted by the angels: *"There they will call out: 'Limitless are You in Your glory, God,' and their greeting will be, 'Peace!' Their call will conclude with the words: 'All praise is due to God, the Lord of all the worlds!'"* (Verse 10)

All the concerns and worries of this life are over. Its needs are no longer of any value. They enjoy an atmosphere of perfect bliss where God is praised and glorified. This is when man attains perfection.

Man's Changing Attitude

The *sūrah* then picks up the challenge posed by the pagan Arabs to God's Messenger, whereby they required him to deliver forthwith the punishment he warned them against. They are told that postponing such punishment to a specified time is an aspect of God's mercy. A scene is then drawn to demonstrate how they behave when they suffer some affliction. At that moment, their nature returns to its purity and they appeal to God, their Lord. When the affliction is relieved, those who habitually go beyond the limits revert to their erring ways. They are then reminded of the fate of earlier communities who also transgressed. This serves as a warning to stop them exceeding their limits. After all, this present life is a test which determines their destiny.

> *If God were to hasten for mankind the ill [they have earned] as they would hasten the good, their end would indeed come forthwith. But We leave those who have no hope of meeting Us in their overweening arrogance, blindly stumbling to and fro. When affliction befalls man, he appeals to Us, whether he be lying on his side, sitting, or standing, but as soon as We relieve his affliction, he goes on as though he had never appealed to Us to save him from the affliction that befell him. Thus do their deeds seem fair to those who are given to excesses. Indeed, We destroyed generations before your time when they persisted in their wrongdoing. The messengers sent to them brought them veritable evidence of the truth, but they would not believe. Thus do We reward the guilty. Then We made you their successors on earth, so that We might see how you behave.* (Verses 11–14)

The pagan Arabs used to challenge the Prophet, asking him to immediately deliver God's punishment. They asked him to do so in different ways. For example, in this *sūrah* it is stated: "*They say: 'When will this promise be fulfilled, if you are truthful?*'" (Verse 48) In another *sūrah*: "*They challenge you to hasten evil rather than good, although exemplary punishments have come to pass before their time.*" (13: 6). Or in similar vein, they say: "*God, if this be indeed Your revealed truth, then rain down upon us stones from the skies, or inflict grievous suffering on us.*" (8: 32)

All this describes their stubborn attitude to God's guidance. In His wisdom, God chose not to inflict a collective punishment on them as He did with earlier communities. Instead, He knew that the great majority of them would eventually accept the faith and that they would work to establish its roots firmly in the land. This took place after Makkah had fallen to the Prophet. At the time they made their ignorant challenge, it was not conceivable that such a change would come to pass. But this was the real good which God wanted for them, which was infinitely better than the type they wanted to experience quickly. He also warns them against ignoring His purpose behind delaying their fate. Yet those who entertain no expectation of meeting with God continue in their arrogance until they eventually meet their fate.

In connection with the challenge to hasten evil, the *sūrah* portrays the situation of those who suffer affliction. Here we have a clear case of contradiction with people asking for evil to be brought forthwith when they are unable to endure modest affliction. Yet when such affliction is removed, they revert to those practices which caused the affliction in the first place: "*When affliction befalls man, he appeals to Us, whether he be lying on his side, sitting, or standing, but as soon as We relieve his affliction, he goes on as though he had never appealed to Us to save him from the affliction that befell him. Thus do their deeds seem fair to those who are given to excesses.*" (Verse 12)

It is an ingeniously drawn picture of a frequently occurring situation. Man may move along in life, committing all types of sin and excess. He pays little attention to what is permissible and what is not, as long as he is in good health and enjoying comfortable conditions. Only those who are conscious of God remember in such a situation, that after health and strength there will be illness and weakness. Affluence makes people forget and power leads to excess. But when affliction overtakes man he is worried, vulnerable and helpless. He appeals earnestly to God, unable to endure the hardship, eager to have his affliction replaced with comfort. When his appeal is granted and the affliction removed, he does not reflect on the lessons of this experience. Instead, he reverts to his old ways, heedless of the consequences.

The *sūrah* co-ordinates this image with the psychological condition it describes and the type of person it delineates. Thus the affliction is shown to last a long time. '*When affliction befalls man, he appeals to Us, whether he be lying on his side, sitting, or standing.*' (Verse 12) All such situations are described so that we have a feeling of how man stops when the energy he derives from his health, wealth or power is cut off. It is just like something moving by impetus suddenly hitting a block. When the block is removed, it dashes along. Here we have the verb, 'goes on', describing man's violent movement which leaves no time for reflection, learning or gratitude: '*As soon as We relieve his affliction, he goes on as though he had never appealed to Us to save him from the affliction that befell him.'* (Verse 12)

It is this kind of nature – i.e. remembering God when suffering affliction, but not once it is removed – which makes those people who exceed their limits think that their excesses are only normal and fair. *'Thus do their deeds seem fair to those who are given to excesses.'* (Verse 12)

It is only right that people should reflect on what happened in the past to those who indulged in excesses: *'Indeed, We destroyed generations before your time when they persisted in their wrongdoing. The messengers sent to them brought them veritable evidence of the truth, but they would not believe. Thus do We reward the guilty.'* (Verse 13) Their transgression beyond the limits, which is another way of describing their disbelief in God's oneness and their association of partners with Him, led to their ruin. Their fate was clear for the Arabs to see in those areas which were once inhabited by the ʿĀd and the Thamūd and in Sodom and Gomorra where the people of Lot dwelt. Their fate should be a sufficient lesson to all people.

Having been shown the fate of those who turned away from God's guidance after it had been explained to them by their prophets, the unbelievers are reminded that they are now their successors, having power in the land so that they can show themselves worthy of God's trust: *"Then We made you their successors on earth, so that We might see how you behave."* (Verse 14) This is a powerful statement. They now enjoy something that once belonged to others but from whom it was removed. They too will leave it after their test is over, and they will be rewarded in accordance with what they do.

Thus Islam shows man the facts as they are so that he is not deceived by appearances. This creates in the human heart an alertness based on consciousness and fear of God. This alertness works as a safety valve for both the individual and the community. When man realizes that he is being tested in this earthly life and that everything he possesses or enjoys during this life is a part of this test, such realization gives him immunity against arrogance and delusion. He no longer seeks abundance of enjoyment at any cost, because he realizes that he will have to account for what he enjoys. There is, in essence, a constant feeling of being watched. This is clear in God's statement: *'so that We might see how you behave.*' (Verse 14) This should make man extra careful, keen to do well, and pass his test.

Here we have the basic difference between the way Islam nurtures a believer's mind and philosophies which give no place to God's watchfulness over man or reckoning in the hereafter. A believer in Islam and a follower of any philosophy will never share common ground in respect of their views, morality, or lifestyle.

A Demand to Change the Qur'ān

Once they have been made aware that they are the successors to earlier guilty communities, the *sūrah* then provides examples of their deeds: "*When Our revelations are recited to them in all their clarity, those who have no hope of meeting Us say: 'Bring us a discourse other than this Qur'ān, or else alter it.' Say: 'It is not for me to alter it of my own accord. I only follow what is revealed to me. I dread the torment of an awesome day if I should disobey my Lord!' Say: 'Had God so willed, I would not have recited it to you, nor would He have brought it to your knowledge. I spent a whole lifetime among you before it [was revealed to me]. Will you not, then, use your reason?' Who is more wicked than one who attributes his lying inventions to God or denies His revelations? Indeed those who are guilty shall not be successful. They worship, side by side with God, what can neither harm nor benefit them, and say: 'These will intercede for us with God.' Say: 'Do you presume to inform God of something in the heavens or on earth that He does not know? Limitless is He in His glory, and exalted above whatever they may associate with Him.' All mankind were once but one single community, and then they disagreed among themselves. Had it not been for a decree from your Lord that had already gone forth, all their differences would have been resolved. They ask: 'Why has no sign been sent down to him by his Lord?' Say: 'God's alone is the knowledge of what is beyond the reach of human perception. Wait, then, if you will: I too am waiting.'*" (Verses 15–20)

Such was their attitude to God's Messenger, the Prophet Muḥammad (peace be upon him), when they were given power in the land. "*When Our revelations are recited to them in all their clarity, those who have no hope of meeting Us say: 'Bring us a discourse other than this Qur'ān, or else alter it.'"* (Verse 15) This is a very strange request which betrays a lack of seriousness and a total ignorance of the role of the Qur'ān in human life and the reason for its revelation. Those who expect to meet God would never entertain such a request.

The Qur'ān is a complete constitution for human life. It is so well formulated that it satisfies all human needs at both individual and community levels. It takes human life along the road to perfection, in as much as man can achieve this in this world, then to complete perfection in the life to come. Those who realize the nature of the Qur'ān would not even think of asking for a different one let alone changing some of it.

Most probably those who did not have any expectation of meeting God tried to be too clever. They looked on the matter as a kind of literary challenge. All that Muḥammad needed to do was to accept the challenge and compose a different discourse, or to replace some parts of it. Here he receives clear instructions: *"Say: 'It is not for me to alter it of my own accord. I only follow what is revealed to me. I dread the torment of an awesome day if I should disobey my Lord!'"* (Verse 15) The matter is not one of a competition, demonstrating skills or poetic talent. The Qur'ān is a constitution outlining a complete code of living devised by the One who controls the whole universe. He is the One who has created man and knows what suits him best. The Prophet cannot alter it on his own initiative. He only conveys God's message and follows what is revealed to him. Any change in the Qur'ān represents a very serious act of disobedience to God, and such a person is liable to severe punishment on the Day of Judgement. That is indeed a prospect to dread.

> *Say: 'Had God so willed, I would not have recited it to you, nor would He have brought it to your knowledge. I spent a whole lifetime among you before it [was revealed to me]. Will you not, then, use your reason?'* (Verse 16)

The Qur'ān is a revelation given by God. That it must be conveyed to you is also an order issued by God, and one which must be obeyed. Had God willed that the Prophet not recite it to you, he would not have done so, and had He willed not to bring it to your knowledge,

He would have kept it from you. Its revelation and recitation to people so that they become aware of its message are all matters decided by God alone. The Prophet is commanded to say all this to people and to further say that he had spent a lifetime among them, forty full years, without ever telling them anything about the Qur'ān, because it had not yet been bestowed to him from on high. Had it been within his power to produce something similar to it, or even like some parts of it, why would he have waited a whole lifetime to do so? It again boils down to the fact that the Qur'ān is God's revelation. The role of the Prophet is simply to convey it to mankind.

The Prophet is further instructed to make it clear that he would never have invented a lie and attributed it to God. Far be it from him to do anything of the kind. He would never have claimed to have received revelations unless that were absolutely true. For the one who attributes a fabrication to God and the one who denies His revelations go too far in the wrong: *"Who is more wicked than one who attributes his lying inventions to God or denies His revelations?"* (Verse 17) As the Prophet warns them strongly against committing the second of these two very grave wrongs, he himself would not even commit the first by inventing fabrications and attributing them to God. *"Indeed, those who are guilty shall not be successful."* (Verse 17)

Knowing Something Unknown to God

The *sūrah* continues with its account of what they said and did after they had succeeded earlier communities. So what comes after their absurd request for a new Qur'ān? *"They worship, side by side with God, what can neither harm nor benefit them, and say: 'These will intercede for us with God.' Say: 'Do you presume to inform God of something in the heavens or on earth that He does not know? Limitless is He in His glory, and exalted above whatever they may associate with Him.'"* (Verse 18)

When people deviate from the truth, there is no end to their absurdity. The numerous deities to whom they address their worship can neither harm nor benefit them in any way. Nevertheless, they think they have a role to play, claiming that they *'will intercede for us with God.'* (Verse 18)

In reply, the Prophet is instructed to say to them: "*Do you presume to inform God of something in the heavens or on earth that He does not know?*" (Verse 18) God does not know anyone who can intercede with Him. Do you then presume to know what is unknown to God Himself? Are you, by implication, informing Him of the existence, in the heavens or on earth, of beings He is unaware of? Here the Qur'ān adopts sarcasm as the means to best counter their unrivalled absurdity. But this is followed with a statement of God's glorification which makes it clear that all their claims are absolutely false: "*Limitless is He in His glory, and exalted above whatever they may associate with Him.*" (Verse 18)

Thereafter, the Qur'ān clarifies that the claim that God has partners is an incidental development. Originally, human nature believed in God's oneness. Only later did people begin to disagree about this: "*All mankind were once but one single community, and then they disagreed among themselves.*" (Verse 19) In His wisdom, God has determined to let all of them be until their appointed time. His will is done, and His purpose is accomplished: "*Had it not been for a decree from your Lord that had already gone forth, all their differences would have been resolved.*" (Verse 19)

Then the account of what those new generations given power on earth said is continued: "*They ask: 'Why has no sign been sent down to him by his Lord?' Say: 'God's alone is the knowledge of what is beyond the reach of human perception. Wait, then, if you will: I too am waiting.'*" (Verse 20) All the signs that this great revelation includes do not seem to be enough for them. Nor are they satisfied with all the signs that they see in the universe. They appeal for a miracle like the ones shown to earlier communities. Their request shows them to be totally oblivious to the nature of the Prophet's message and its own great miracle. That is not a temporary miracle which is over and done with once a community has seen it. It is the Qur'ān, a permanent miracle which addresses our hearts and minds from one generation to another.

In reply to this request, God directs His Messenger to refer them to Him, for He alone knows what He has in store, and He alone will determine whether He shows them some miracle or not: "*Say: 'God's alone is the knowledge of what is beyond the reach of human perception. Wait, then, if you will: I too am waiting.'*" (Verse 20) This reply implies a delay and a warning. It also provides, by implication, an outline of the limitations of God's servants. Muḥammad (peace be upon him), who was the greatest of all God's prophets and messengers, had no knowledge of what God chose to keep to Himself. He had no influence over what would happen to people, for that is determined by God alone. Thus the distinction between God and His servants is clearly delineated.

When All Are Powerless

Now the *sūrah* goes on to speak of human nature when people are shown God's grace after having experienced misfortune and hardship. It gives them an example of what actually takes place in real life. The scene so depicted is vivid and powerful.

> *Whenever We let people taste grace after some hardship has afflicted them, they turn to scheme against Our revelations. Say: 'More swift is God's scheming. Our messengers are recording all that you may devise.' He it is who enables you to travel on land and sea. Then when you are on board ships, and sailing along in a favourable wind, they feel happy with it, but then a stormy wind comes upon them and waves surge towards them from all sides, so that they believe they are encompassed [by death]. [At that point] they appeal to God, in complete sincerity of faith in Him alone: 'If You will save us from this, we shall certainly be most grateful.' Yet when He has saved them, they transgress in the land, offending against all right. Mankind, it is against your own souls that your offences rebound. [You care only for] the enjoyment of this present life, but in the end you will return to Us when We will tell you the truth of what you were doing [in this life]. (Verses 21–23)*

Strange indeed is this human creature, for he does not remember God except in times of hardship and affliction. He does not remove from his nature all the bad influences that distort it, bringing it back to its purity, except when he feels the pressure of misfortune weighing heavily upon him. But when he feels safe and secure, he either forgets or transgresses. The only exceptions are those who follow God's guidance. Their nature remains pure and responsive all the time. It enjoys the purity of faith which keeps it clean and shining.

"*Whenever We let people taste grace after some hardship has afflicted them they turn to scheme against Our revelations.*" (Verse 21) Thus did Pharaoh's people with Moses. Whenever they were overwhelmed by God's punishment, they cried out, sending their earnest appeals for its lifting, and promising to change and mend their ways. Once they were shown God's mercy, they started to scheme against God's revelations, giving them wrong interpretations. They even claimed different reasons for the lifting of their afflictions. The Quraysh, the Arab tribe living in Makkah at the Prophet's time, did the same. When they experienced drought and feared for their lives, they came to the Prophet, appealing to him by their ties of kinship, to pray to God on their behalf. He did and God answered his prayers, sending rain in abundance. But the Quraysh did not fulfil their pledges. They schemed against God's revelations and persisted in their erring ways. Indeed this is a constant phenomenon, unless man accepts the divine faith and follows God's guidance.

"*Say: 'More swift is God's scheming. Our messengers are recording all that you may devise.'*" (Verse 21) God is certainly more able to plan and make their scheming ineffective. All that which they scheme is laid open before Him. When their scheming is known in advance, it is very easy to foil. "*Our messengers are recording all that you may devise.*" Nothing of it is overlooked or forgotten. As for the identity of those messengers and how they record and write, all we know is that which we can glean from statements like the present one. We accept these statements as they are, without trying to interpret them further.

Then we are given a very vivid scene which is portrayed as if it is happening before our eyes. We react to it with feeling and emotion. It begins with establishing the fact of God's power that controls both what is moving and what is motionless: "*He it is who enables you to travel on land and sea.*" (Verse 22) The whole *sūrah* emphasizes the fact of God's limitless power which controls the whole universe and the destiny of all creatures that live in it.

The full scene then unfolds before us: "*Then when you are on board ships...*" (Verse 22) As we look we see the ships moving on their way: "*and sailing along in a favourable wind...*" (Verse 22) We also learn about the feelings of those who are on board: "*they feel happy with it...*" (Verse 22) In the midst of this atmosphere of complete serenity, and the happiness that it spreads, everyone is suddenly jolted: "*a stormy wind comes upon them...*" (Verse 22) What a calamity! "*And waves surge towards them from all sides...*" (Verse 22) The ships start to shake violently, and the waves hit against them time and again, and they spin like a feather in the air. Those on board are overtaken with fear, feeling that there is no escape: "*and they believe they are encompassed [by death]...*" (Verse 22) There is simply nowhere to turn.

At that moment, and in the midst of all this furore, their nature sheds all the filth it accumulated, blunting its reactions. Their minds rid themselves of all erring thoughts. Their nature reverts to its original condition, undistorted. It acknowledges God as the only Lord in the universe and submits to Him alone: "*[At that point] they appeal to God, in complete sincerity of faith in Him alone: 'If You will save us from this, we shall certainly be most grateful.'*" (Verse 22)

Then the winds subside, and the waves die down. The people on board begin to catch their breath, and their pounding hearts slow down. Soon the ships reach the shore, and the people feel secure. When they step on land, feeling its firmness, they are sure that they are not about to perish. They have their lives ahead of them. Then what?

A Description of Life in This World

"*Yet when He has saved them, they transgress in the land, offending against all right.*" (Verse 23) This also comes as a complete surprise.

This in itself is a whole scene, and we miss none of its totality and fine detail. Nor do we miss any feeling or reaction it induces. In essence we are given a picture of a real event, but it is also a mental scene describing the nature of many people regardless of the generation they were born into. Hence the *sūrah* follows it with comments addressed to mankind throughout history.

"*Mankind, it is against your own souls that your offences rebound.*" (Verse 23) Whether these offences are committed against oneself, by sending it on the way to perdition, letting it indulge in disobedience that is certain to make it the loser, or offences against all humanity since humanity represents one soul, the offenders will suffer the consequences. These consequences will also be shared by those who allow them to offend.

The worst type of offence is that which represents an aggression against God Himself, usurping His Lordship and sovereignty, claiming these for the usurpers themselves. When people are guilty of this type of offence, they suffer its wretched consequences in this present life before they endure its punishment in the hereafter. These consequences are manifested in corruption that spreads into the whole life. All mankind are miserable because of it. No human dignity, freedom or virtue is left untouched by it.

The basic point here is that people should submit themselves purely to God, or else they will find themselves submitting to tyrants who try to impose their authority on them. The struggle to establish the principle of God's oneness in human life and to acknowledge God as the only Lord is a struggle for human dignity, freedom and morality, and indeed for every value which helps man to break his shackles, and lift himself to the high standards that befit him.

"*Mankind, it is against your own souls that your offences rebound. [You care only for] the enjoyment of this present life.*" (Verse 23) That then is all that you will have. "*In the end you will return to Us when We will tell you the truth of what you were doing [in this life].*" (Verse 23) That is the reckoning and reward that take place in the hereafter, when all the misery and suffering of this life is clearly over.

So how much are the pleasures of this life worth? What is the reality of their enjoyment? This is described in the *sūrah* in a Qur'ānic scene that portrays aspects of everyday activity, but to which most people pay little attention: "*This present life may be compared to rain which We send down from the sky, and which is then absorbed by the plants of the earth from which men and animals eat. Then, when the earth has been clad with its fine adornments and well embellished, and its people believe that they have full mastery over it, Our command comes down upon it, by night or by day, and We make it like a field that has been mowed down, as if it did not blossom but yesterday. Thus do We spell out Our revelations to people who think. God calls to the abode of peace, and guides him that wills to a straight path.*" (Verses 24–25)

This is the reality of the life of this world, where people have only its pleasures which they are content with, seeking no higher aspiration and hoping for no better abode. Rain comes down from the sky and is soon absorbed by plants which grow and blossom. The earth takes on its finest adornments, as if she were a bride preparing for her happiest night. People take pleasure in looking on, feeling that its fine appearance is the result of their own efforts. In the back of their minds they think they control everything on earth and that nothing can change this.

Yet in the midst of all this pleasure and fine celebration, their confidence is suddenly shattered. What has happened? The answer is simple: "*Our command comes down upon it, by night or by day, and We make it like a field that has been mowed down, as if it did not blossom but yesterday.*" (Verse 24) It all happens in a moment. It is all expressed in a sentence. Such mode of expression is a deliberate contrast to the detailed description which paints the land's fertility and beauty, as well as people's pleasure and confidence.

Such is the life of this world which some people regard as their utmost aspiration, and for the pleasures of which they sacrifice their future life. It is a life in which there is no settlement or security. People's control over it is very limited indeed. The *sūrah* then contrasts this image with the other world: "*God calls to the abode of peace, and guides him that wills to a straight path.*" (Verse 25) The contrast is remarkable. In one place there is no security. Even the most perfect of enjoyments can be replaced with complete misery in a matter of seconds. The other is the home of peace to which God invites people. It is reserved for those who keep their hearts and minds receptive of God's guidance and who endeavour to attain the happiness of the life to come, which is indeed the life of peace.

2

Addressing the Human Mind

For those who do good there is a good reward, and more besides. Neither darkness nor any disgrace will overcast their faces. These are destined for paradise, where they will abide. (26)

لِّلَّذِينَ أَحْسَنُوا الْحُسْنَى وَزِيَادَةٌ وَلَا يَرْهَقُ وُجُوهَهُمْ قَتَرٌ وَلَا ذِلَّةٌ أُوْلَٰئِكَ أَصْحَٰبُ الْجَنَّةِ هُمْ فِيهَا خَٰلِدُونَ ۝

As for those who have done evil, an evil deed is rewarded with its like. Ignominy will overshadow them – for they will have none to protect them from God – as if their faces have been covered with patches of the night's own darkness. Such are destined for the fire, where they will abide. (27)

وَالَّذِينَ كَسَبُوا السَّيِّئَاتِ جَزَاءُ سَيِّئَةٍ بِمِثْلِهَا وَتَرْهَقُهُمْ ذِلَّةٌ مَّا لَهُم مِّنَ اللَّهِ مِنْ عَاصِمٍ كَأَنَّمَا أُغْشِيَتْ وُجُوهُهُمْ قِطَعًا مِّنَ الَّيْلِ مُظْلِمًا أُوْلَٰئِكَ أَصْحَٰبُ النَّارِ هُمْ فِيهَا خَٰلِدُونَ ۝

One day We shall gather them all together, and then We shall say to those who associated partners with God: 'Keep to your places, you and those you associated with God as partners.' We will then separate them from one another. Then those whom they associated as partners with God will say: 'It was not us that you worshipped. (28)

وَيَوْمَ نَحْشُرُهُمْ جَمِيعًا ثُمَّ نَقُولُ لِلَّذِينَ أَشْرَكُوا مَكَانَكُمْ أَنتُمْ وَشُرَكَاؤُكُمْ فَزَيَّلْنَا بَيْنَهُمْ وَقَالَ شُرَكَاؤُهُم مَّا كُنتُمْ إِيَّانَا تَعْبُدُونَ ۝

God is sufficient as a witness between us and you. We were, for certain, unaware of your worshipping us.' (29)

فَكَفَىٰ بِٱللَّهِ شَهِيدًۢا بَيْنَنَا وَبَيْنَكُمْ إِن كُنَّا عَنْ عِبَادَتِكُمْ لَغَٰفِلِينَ ﴿٢٩﴾

There and then every soul will realize what it had done in the past; and all will be brought back to God, their true Lord Supreme. All their invented falsehood will have forsaken them. (30)

هُنَالِكَ تَبْلُوا۟ كُلُّ نَفْسٍ مَّآ أَسْلَفَتْ وَرُدُّوٓا۟ إِلَى ٱللَّهِ مَوْلَىٰهُمُ ٱلْحَقِّ وَضَلَّ عَنْهُم مَّا كَانُوا۟ يَفْتَرُونَ ﴿٣٠﴾

Say: 'Who is it that provides for you from heaven and earth? Or, who is it that has power over hearing and sight? Who brings forth the living out of that which is dead, and brings forth the dead out of that which is alive? Who regulates all affairs?' They will say: 'God.' Say, then: 'Will you not, then, fear Him?' (31)

قُلْ مَن يَرْزُقُكُم مِّنَ ٱلسَّمَآءِ وَٱلْأَرْضِ أَمَّن يَمْلِكُ ٱلسَّمْعَ وَٱلْأَبْصَٰرَ وَمَن يُخْرِجُ ٱلْحَىَّ مِنَ ٱلْمَيِّتِ وَيُخْرِجُ ٱلْمَيِّتَ مِنَ ٱلْحَىِّ وَمَن يُدَبِّرُ ٱلْأَمْرَ فَسَيَقُولُونَ ٱللَّهُ فَقُلْ أَفَلَا تَتَّقُونَ ﴿٣١﴾

Such is God, your true Lord. Apart from the truth, what is left but error? How is it, then, that you turn away? (32)

فَذَٰلِكُمُ ٱللَّهُ رَبُّكُمُ ٱلْحَقُّ فَمَاذَا بَعْدَ ٱلْحَقِّ إِلَّا ٱلضَّلَٰلُ فَأَنَّىٰ تُصْرَفُونَ ﴿٣٢﴾

Thus is the word of your Lord proved true with regard to those who do evil: they will not believe. (33)

كَذَٰلِكَ حَقَّتْ كَلِمَتُ رَبِّكَ عَلَى ٱلَّذِينَ فَسَقُوٓا۟ أَنَّهُمْ لَا يُؤْمِنُونَ ﴿٣٣﴾

Say: 'Does any of your partners [whom you associate with God] originate creation, and then bring it back [to life] again?' Say: 'It is God alone who originates creation and then brings it back [to life] again. How is it, then, that you are so misled?' (34)

قُلْ هَلْ مِن شُرَكَآبِكُم مَّن يَبْدَؤُا۟ ٱلْخَلْقَ ثُمَّ يُعِيدُهُۥ قُلِ ٱللَّهُ يَبْدَؤُا۟ ٱلْخَلْقَ ثُمَّ يُعِيدُهُۥ فَأَنَّىٰ تُؤْفَكُونَ ﴿٣٤﴾

Say: 'Does any of your partners [whom you associate with God] guide to the truth?' Say: 'God alone guides to the truth. Who is more worthy to be followed: He that guides to the truth, or he who cannot find the right way unless he is guided? What is then amiss with you? How do you judge?' (35)

قُلْ هَلْ مِن شُرَكَآبِكُم مَّن يَهْدِىٓ إِلَى ٱلْحَقِّ قُلِ ٱللَّهُ يَهْدِى لِلْحَقِّ أَفَمَن يَهْدِىٓ إِلَى ٱلْحَقِّ أَحَقُّ أَن يُتَّبَعَ أَمَّن لَّا يَهِدِّىٓ إِلَّآ أَن يُهْدَىٰ فَمَا لَكُمْ كَيْفَ تَحْكُمُونَ ﴿٣٥﴾

Most of them follow nothing but mere conjecture. But conjecture can in no way be a substitute for truth. God has full knowledge of all that they do. (36)

وَمَا يَتَّبِعُ أَكْثَرُهُمْ إِلَّا ظَنًّا إِنَّ ٱلظَّنَّ لَا يُغْنِى مِنَ ٱلْحَقِّ شَيْئًا إِنَّ ٱللَّهَ عَلِيمٌۢ بِمَا يَفْعَلُونَ ﴿٣٦﴾

This Qur'ān could not have been devised by anyone other than God. It is a confirmation of [revelations] that went before it, and a full explanation of God's Book, about which there is no doubt. It certainly comes from the Lord of all the worlds. (37)

وَمَا كَانَ هَٰذَا ٱلْقُرْءَانُ أَن يُفْتَرَىٰ مِن دُونِ ٱللَّهِ وَلَٰكِن تَصْدِيقَ ٱلَّذِى بَيْنَ يَدَيْهِ وَتَفْصِيلَ ٱلْكِتَٰبِ لَا رَيْبَ فِيهِ مِن رَّبِّ ٱلْعَٰلَمِينَ ﴿٣٧﴾

If they say: 'He has invented it,' say: 'Produce, then, one *surah* like it, and call for help on all you can other than God, if what you say is true.' (38)

أَمْ يَقُولُونَ ٱفْتَرَىٰهُ قُلْ فَأْتُوا بِسُورَةٍ مِّثْلِهِۦ وَٱدْعُوا مَنِ ٱسْتَطَعْتُم مِّن دُونِ ٱللَّهِ إِن كُنتُمْ صَٰدِقِينَ ۝

Indeed they disbelieve what they cannot grasp, particularly since its inner meaning has not become clear to them. Likewise did those who lived before them disbelieve. But see what happened in the end to those wrongdoers. (39)

بَلْ كَذَّبُوا بِمَا لَمْ يُحِيطُوا بِعِلْمِهِۦ وَلَمَّا يَأْتِهِمْ تَأْوِيلُهُۥ كَذَٰلِكَ كَذَّبَ ٱلَّذِينَ مِن قَبْلِهِمْ فَٱنظُرْ كَيْفَ كَانَ عَٰقِبَةُ ٱلظَّٰلِمِينَ ۝

Some of them do believe in it, while others do not. But your Lord is fully aware of those who spread corruption. (40)

وَمِنْهُم مَّن يُؤْمِنُ بِهِۦ وَمِنْهُم مَّن لَّا يُؤْمِنُ بِهِۦ وَرَبُّكَ أَعْلَمُ بِٱلْمُفْسِدِينَ ۝

If they disbelieve you, then say: 'I shall bear the consequences of my deeds, and you your deeds. You are not accountable for what I do and I am not accountable for your doings.' (41)

وَإِن كَذَّبُوكَ فَقُل لِّي عَمَلِي وَلَكُمْ عَمَلُكُمْ أَنتُم بَرِيٓـُٔونَ مِمَّآ أَعْمَلُ وَأَنَا۠ بَرِيٓءٌ مِّمَّا تَعْمَلُونَ ۝

Yet some of them [pretend to] listen to you; but can you make the deaf hear you, incapable as they are of using their reason? (42)

وَمِنْهُم مَّن يَسْتَمِعُونَ إِلَيْكَ أَفَأَنتَ تُسْمِعُ ٱلصُّمَّ وَلَوْ كَانُوا لَا يَعْقِلُونَ ۝

And some of them [pretend to] look towards you; but can you show the way to the blind, bereft of sight as they are? (43)

وَمِنْهُم مَّن يَنظُرُ إِلَيْكَ أَفَأَنتَ تَهْدِي ٱلْعُمْيَ وَلَوْ كَانُوا لَا يُبْصِرُونَ ۝

Indeed, God does not do the least wrong to mankind, but it is men who wrong themselves. (44)

إِنَّ ٱللَّهَ لَا يَظْلِمُ ٱلنَّاسَ شَيْئًا وَلَكِنَّ ٱلنَّاسَ أَنفُسَهُمْ يَظْلِمُونَ ﴿٤٤﴾

On the Day when He will gather them together, [it will seem to them] as though they had not sojourned in this world more than an hour of a day, getting to know one another. Lost indeed will be those who [in their lifetime] disbelieved in meeting God and did not follow the right guidance. (45)

وَيَوْمَ يَحْشُرُهُمْ كَأَن لَّمْ يَلْبَثُوٓاْ إِلَّا سَاعَةً مِّنَ ٱلنَّهَارِ يَتَعَارَفُونَ بَيْنَهُمْ قَدْ خَسِرَ ٱلَّذِينَ كَذَّبُواْ بِلِقَآءِ ٱللَّهِ وَمَا كَانُواْ مُهْتَدِينَ ﴿٤٥﴾

Whether We show you some of what We have promised them or We cause you to die, it is to Us that they shall return. God is witness of all that they do. (46)

وَإِمَّا نُرِيَنَّكَ بَعْضَ ٱلَّذِى نَعِدُهُمْ أَوْ نَتَوَفَّيَنَّكَ فَإِلَيْنَا مَرْجِعُهُمْ ثُمَّ ٱللَّهُ شَهِيدٌ عَلَى مَا يَفْعَلُونَ ﴿٤٦﴾

To every community was sent a messenger. It is when their messenger had come to them that judgement was passed on them in all fairness; and never are they wronged. (47)

وَلِكُلِّ أُمَّةٍ رَّسُولٌ فَإِذَا جَآءَ رَسُولُهُمْ قُضِىَ بَيْنَهُم بِٱلْقِسْطِ وَهُمْ لَا يُظْلَمُونَ ﴿٤٧﴾

They say: 'When will this promise be fulfilled, if you are truthful?' (48)

وَيَقُولُونَ مَتَىٰ هَٰذَا ٱلْوَعْدُ إِن كُنتُمْ صَٰدِقِينَ ﴿٤٨﴾

Say: 'I have no control over any harm or benefit to myself, except as God may please. For every community a term has been appointed. When their time arrives, they can neither delay it by a single moment, nor indeed hasten it.' (49)

قُل لَّآ أَمْلِكُ لِنَفْسِي ضَرًّا وَلَا نَفْعًا إِلَّا مَا شَآءَ ٱللَّهُ لِكُلِّ أُمَّةٍ أَجَلٌ إِذَا جَآءَ أَجَلُهُمْ فَلَا يَسْتَـْٔخِرُونَ سَاعَةً وَلَا يَسْتَقْدِمُونَ ﴿٤٩﴾

Say: 'Do but consider. Should His punishment befall you by night or by day, what could there be in it that the guilty ones should wish to hasten? (50)

قُلْ أَرَءَيْتُمْ إِنْ أَتَىٰكُمْ عَذَابُهُۥ بَيَٰتًا أَوْ نَهَارًا مَّاذَا يَسْتَعْجِلُ مِنْهُ ٱلْمُجْرِمُونَ ﴿٥٠﴾

Is it, then, when it has come to pass that you will believe in it? Is it now, while so far you have been asking for it to come speedily?' (51)

أَثُمَّ إِذَا مَا وَقَعَ ءَامَنتُم بِهِۦٓ ءَآلْـَٔنَ وَقَدْ كُنتُم بِهِۦ تَسْتَعْجِلُونَ ﴿٥١﴾

Then it will be said to the wrongdoers: 'Taste the long-lasting torment. Is this requital anything other than the just due for what you used to do?' (52)

ثُمَّ قِيلَ لِلَّذِينَ ظَلَمُوا۟ ذُوقُوا۟ عَذَابَ ٱلْخُلْدِ هَلْ تُجْزَوْنَ إِلَّا بِمَا كُنتُمْ تَكْسِبُونَ ﴿٥٢﴾

They will ask you: 'Is all this true?' Say: 'Yes, by my Lord. It is most certainly true, and you will never be beyond God's reach.' (53)

وَيَسْتَنۢبِـُٔونَكَ أَحَقٌّ هُوَ قُلْ إِي وَرَبِّىٓ إِنَّهُۥ لَحَقٌّ وَمَآ أَنتُم بِمُعْجِزِينَ ﴿٥٣﴾

Should every wrongdoer possess all that the earth contains, he will gladly offer it all as ransom. They will harbour feelings of remorse when they see the suffering. Judgement will be passed on them in all fairness; and they will not be wronged. (54)

 وَلَوْ أَنَّ لِكُلِّ نَفْسٍ ظَلَمَتْ مَا فِي ٱلْأَرْضِ لَٱفْتَدَتْ بِهِۦ وَأَسَرُّوا۟ ٱلنَّدَامَةَ لَمَّا رَأَوُا۟ ٱلْعَذَابَ وَقُضِيَ بَيْنَهُم بِٱلْقِسْطِ وَهُمْ لَا يُظْلَمُونَ ﴿٥٤﴾

Indeed, to God belongs all that is in the heavens and earth. God's promise always comes true, but most of them do not know it. (55)

أَلَا إِنَّ لِلَّهِ مَا فِي ٱلسَّمَٰوَٰتِ وَٱلْأَرْضِ أَلَا إِنَّ وَعْدَ ٱللَّهِ حَقٌّ وَلَٰكِنَّ أَكْثَرَهُمْ لَا يَعْلَمُونَ ﴿٥٥﴾

He alone gives life and causes death, and to Him you shall all return. (56)

هُوَ يُحْيِۦ وَيُمِيتُ وَإِلَيْهِ تُرْجَعُونَ ﴿٥٦﴾

Mankind, there has come to you an admonition from your Lord, a cure for all that may be in your hearts, and guidance and grace for all believers. (57)

يَٰٓأَيُّهَا ٱلنَّاسُ قَدْ جَآءَتْكُم مَّوْعِظَةٌ مِّن رَّبِّكُمْ وَشِفَآءٌ لِّمَا فِي ٱلصُّدُورِ وَهُدًى وَرَحْمَةٌ لِّلْمُؤْمِنِينَ ﴿٥٧﴾

Say: 'In God's bounty and grace, in this let them rejoice; for this is better than all that they may amass.' (58)

قُلْ بِفَضْلِ ٱللَّهِ وَبِرَحْمَتِهِۦ فَبِذَٰلِكَ فَلْيَفْرَحُوا۟ هُوَ خَيْرٌ مِّمَّا يَجْمَعُونَ ﴿٥٨﴾

Say: 'Do but consider all the means of sustenance that God has bestowed on you! Some of it you then made unlawful, and some lawful.' Say: 'Has God given you leave to do so, or do you fabricate lies against God?' (59)

قُلْ أَرَأَيْتُم مَّآ أَنزَلَ ٱللَّهُ لَكُم مِّن رِّزْقٍ فَجَعَلْتُم مِّنْهُ حَرَامًا وَحَلَٰلًا قُلْ ءَآللَّهُ أَذِنَ لَكُمْ أَمْ عَلَى ٱللَّهِ تَفْتَرُونَ ﴿٥٩﴾

But what will they think, those who invent lies against God, on the Day of Resurrection? God is truly bountiful to mankind, but most of them are ungrateful. (60)

وَمَا ظَنُّ ٱلَّذِينَ يَفْتَرُونَ عَلَى ٱللَّهِ ٱلْكَذِبَ يَوْمَ ٱلْقِيَامَةِ إِنَّ ٱللَّهَ لَذُو فَضْلٍ عَلَى ٱلنَّاسِ وَلَٰكِنَّ أَكْثَرَهُمْ لَا يَشْكُرُونَ ۝٦٠

In whatever business you may be engaged, and whatever part you may recite of the Qur'ān, and whatever deed you [mankind] may do, We will be your witnesses from the moment you are engaged with it. Not even an atom's weight [of anything whatsoever] on earth or in heaven escapes your Lord, nor is there anything smaller or larger than that, but is recorded in a clear book. (61)

وَمَا تَكُونُ فِي شَأْنٍ وَمَا تَتْلُواْ مِنْهُ مِن قُرْءَانٍ وَلَا تَعْمَلُونَ مِنْ عَمَلٍ إِلَّا كُنَّا عَلَيْكُمْ شُهُودًا إِذْ تُفِيضُونَ فِيهِ وَمَا يَعْزُبُ عَن رَّبِّكَ مِن مِّثْقَالِ ذَرَّةٍ فِي ٱلْأَرْضِ وَلَا فِي ٱلسَّمَاءِ وَلَا أَصْغَرَ مِن ذَٰلِكَ وَلَا أَكْبَرَ إِلَّا فِي كِتَٰبٍ مُّبِينٍ ۝٦١

For certain, those who are close to God have nothing to fear, nor shall they grieve; (62)

أَلَا إِنَّ أَوْلِيَاءَ ٱللَّهِ لَا خَوْفٌ عَلَيْهِمْ وَلَا هُمْ يَحْزَنُونَ ۝٦٢

for they do believe and remain God-fearing. (63)

ٱلَّذِينَ ءَامَنُواْ وَكَانُواْ يَتَّقُونَ ۝٦٣

Theirs are the glad tidings in the life of this world and in the life to come: there is no changing the word of God. This is the supreme triumph. (64)

لَهُمُ ٱلْبُشْرَىٰ فِي ٱلْحَيَوٰةِ ٱلدُّنْيَا وَفِي ٱلْأَخِرَةِ لَا تَبْدِيلَ لِكَلِمَٰتِ ٱللَّهِ ذَٰلِكَ هُوَ ٱلْفَوْزُ ٱلْعَظِيمُ ۝٦٤

Be not grieved by what they say. All might and glory belong to God alone. He alone hears all and knows all. (65)

وَلَا يَحْزُنكَ قَوْلُهُمْ إِنَّ ٱلْعِزَّةَ لِلَّهِ جَمِيعًا هُوَ ٱلسَّمِيعُ ٱلْعَلِيمُ ۝٦٥

Indeed, to God belong all those who are in the heavens and earth. Those who invoke other beings beside God do not follow any real partners with Him. They follow mere conjecture, and they utter nothing but falsehood. (66)

أَلَا إِنَّ لِلَّهِ مَن فِي ٱلسَّمَـوَٰتِ وَمَن فِي ٱلْأَرْضِ وَمَا يَتَّبِعُ ٱلَّذِينَ يَدْعُونَ مِن دُونِ ٱللَّهِ شُرَكَآءَ إِن يَتَّبِعُونَ إِلَّا ٱلظَّنَّ وَإِنْ هُمْ إِلَّا يَخْرُصُونَ ٦٦

It is He who has made the night for you, so that you may have rest, and the day, so that you may see. In this there are certainly signs for those who listen. (67)

هُوَ ٱلَّذِي جَعَلَ لَكُمُ ٱلَّيْلَ لِتَسْكُنُوا۟ فِيهِ وَٱلنَّهَارَ مُبْصِرًا إِنَّ فِي ذَٰلِكَ لَآيَـٰتٍ لِّقَوْمٍ يَسْمَعُونَ ٦٧

They say: 'God has taken unto Himself a son.' Limitless is He in His glory. Self-sufficient is He. To Him belongs all that is in the heavens and earth. No evidence whatever have you for this. Would you say about God something which you do not know? (68)

قَالُوا۟ ٱتَّخَذَ ٱللَّهُ وَلَدًا سُبْحَـٰنَهُۥ هُوَ ٱلْغَنِيُّ لَهُۥ مَا فِي ٱلسَّمَـٰوَٰتِ وَمَا فِي ٱلْأَرْضِ إِنْ عِندَكُم مِّن سُلْطَـٰنٍ بِهَـٰذَآ أَتَقُولُونَ عَلَى ٱللَّهِ مَا لَا تَعْلَمُونَ ٦٨

Say: 'Those who invent false-hood about God shall not be successful. (69)

قُلْ إِنَّ ٱلَّذِينَ يَفْتَرُونَ عَلَى ٱللَّهِ ٱلْكَذِبَ لَا يُفْلِحُونَ ٦٩

They may have a brief enjoyment in this world, but then to Us they must return, and We will then make them suffer severe torment for their unbelief.' (70)

مَتَـٰعٌ فِي ٱلدُّنْيَا ثُمَّ إِلَيْنَا مَرْجِعُهُمْ ثُمَّ نُذِيقُهُمُ ٱلْعَذَابَ ٱلشَّدِيدَ بِمَا كَانُوا۟ يَكْفُرُونَ ٧٠

Preview

This new passage touches the human conscience with a flow of observations that aim to put human nature face to face with clear evidence of God's oneness, the truthful address of His Messenger and the concept of the Day of Judgement, the reckoning and justice that are certain to be administered to all on that day. These touches work on the whole of the human soul, taking it on a grand tour of the universe, opening up for it the broad horizons of its own world. It moves from ancient times to the present, and from this life to the real one beyond. The previous passage contained similar aspects, discussed in Chapter 1, but the present ones are clearer, certain to receive the right response from any person with an uncorrupted nature. The unbelievers genuinely feared that the Qur'ān would weaken them considerably. Hence they urged one another not to listen to it because they wanted to continue with their erring beliefs and practices.

When Deities Quarrel with Their Worshippers

For those who do good there is a good reward, and more besides. Neither darkness nor any disgrace will overcast their faces. These are destined for paradise, where they will abide. As for those who have done evil, an evil deed is rewarded with its like. Ignominy will overshadow them – for they will have none to protect them from God – as if their faces have been covered with patches of the night's own darkness. Such are destined for the fire, where they will abide. (Verses 26–27)

The last verse in the preceding passage said: "*God calls to the abode of peace, and guides him that wills to a straight path.*" (Verse 25) Here we have an outline of the rules that determine the reward of those who follow God's guidance and those who turn away from it. It shows God's grace, mercy, fairness and justice in both types of reward.

Those who do well in their choice of belief and practice, recognizing the right path and understanding the universal law which leads to the 'abode of peace' will have a goodly reward which is the fair outcome of what they do. But they will also have something more of God's unlimited bounty: '*For those who do good there is a good reward, and more besides.*' (Verse 26) They will be spared the misery of the Day of Resurrection, and the stress experienced by others before judgement is passed on all creatures: "*Neither darkness nor any disgrace will overcast their faces.*" (Verse 26) The Arabic phrase incorporates two words for darkness and disgrace. The first denotes dust, darkness and a pale colour that comes as a result of unhappiness or distress. The other denotes humiliation, shame and subjection to insults. They are free of all this. The verse portrays a dense crowd, afflicted with misery, fear, and humiliation, as evidenced by the marks on people's faces. To be spared all this is a great gain, an act of grace which is added to the expected reward.

Such people who enjoy this high position "*are destined for paradise.*" (Verse 26) They are its owners and dwellers, and there "*they will abide.*" (Verse 26)

"*As for those who have done evil.*" (Verse 27) A more literal translation of this phrase would be 'those who have earned evil'. The earnings they have made out of the transaction of this life are simply evil. They will have their fair reward, which means that they will not have their punishment increased or doubled. They are simply given their reward, like for like. "*An evil deed is rewarded with its like.*" (Verse 27) They are the ones to endure humiliation which weighs down heavily on them: "*Ignominy will overshadow them – for they will have none to protect them from God.*" (Verse 27) There is simply no one to provide them with protection against the inevitable workings of divine law which metes out punishment to those who choose the path of evil.

The *sūrah* then paints an image of the mental darkness that overshadows them and leaves its impact on their terrified faces. They look '*just as if their faces have been covered with patches of the night's own darkness.*' (Verse 27) The whole atmosphere is dark, causing much fear and apprehension. People's faces are made to look as if they are wearing the cover of the dark night.

Those who are abandoned in the midst of all this darkness '*are destined for the fire.*' (Verse 27) They are its owners and dwellers, and there '*they will abide.*' (Verse 27)

But where are those whom they claimed to be God's partners and the ones they thought would intercede on their behalf? How come they could not provide them with any protection? What is happening to them on this fearful Day of Resurrection: "*One day We shall gather them all together, and then We shall say to those who associated partners with God: 'Keep to your places, you and those you associated with God as partners.' We will then separate them from one another. Then those whom they associated as partners with God will say: 'It was not us that you worshipped. God is sufficient as a witness between us and you. We were, for certain, unaware of your worshipping us.' There and then every soul will realize what it had done in the past; and all will be brought back to God, their true Lord Supreme. All their invented falsehood will have forsaken them.*" (Verses 28–30)

What we have here is a scene depicting one aspect of the Day of Judgement. It is painted in such a way that makes it far more effective than a clear statement to the effect that the partners they associate with God and their intercessors will not protect their worshippers against God, and can avail them of nothing. They are all brought together: the unbelievers and the false deities they associated as partners with God. The Qur'ān describes the latter as 'their partners' in a sarcastic manner which also denotes that they are of their own invention, and hence never partners with God.

To all these, unbelievers and partners, an order is given: "*Keep to your places, you and those you associated with God as partners.*" (Verse 28) Stop where you are. That is the order. They must stand still the moment the order is issued, for an order given on that day is complied with immediately, without question. Then one group is set apart from the other: "*We will then separate them from one another.*" (Verse 28)

At this point the unbelievers do not speak. It is their claimed partners that speak to exonerate themselves from the crime committed by the unbelievers when they worshipped them in place of God, or in association with Him. They speak to make it clear that they were totally unaware of their being worshipped. As such, they have had no role in the crime. They appeal to God to be their witness: "*Then those whom they associated as partners with God will say: 'It was not us that you worshipped. God is sufficient as a witness between us and you. We were, for certain, unaware of your worshipping us.'*" (Verse 29)

Thus is the status of those who were worshipped. They are weak, appealing to be exonerated of the sinful practices of their worshippers.

They seek to be absolved of an offence in which they took no part, and want God to be their witness.

At this point when everything is laid open, every soul will know the true nature of the deeds it did, realizing its inevitable outcome: "*There and then every soul will realize what it had done in the past.*" (Verse 30) What is abundantly clear to all at that moment is the fact that there is only one God to whom all shall return. Everything else is false: "*All will be brought back to God, their true Lord Supreme.*" (Verse 30)

There the idolaters will find nothing of what they used to claim and fabricate. All prove to have no real existence. "*All their invented falsehood will have forsaken them.*" (Verse 30) It is a vivid scene which is raised before our eyes so that we can examine all its details and the truth it reflects. It is painted in a few words which have an effect far superior to what a mere statement of facts supported by clear arguments would have produced.

Giving Life and Causing Death

The first round in this passage took us to the gathering of all on the Day of Resurrection when all false claims and fabrications are shown to have no validity whatsoever. God's is the only power on that day. Now the *sūrah* speaks of matters human beings see in their lives, and in their own souls, admitting that they are only done by God and subject to His control.

> Say: 'Who is it that provides for you from heaven and earth? Or, who is it that has power over hearing and sight? Who brings forth the living out of that which is dead, and brings forth the dead out of that which is alive? Who regulates all affairs?' They will say: 'God.' Say, then: 'Will you not, then, fear Him?' Such is God, your true Lord. Apart from the truth, what is left but error? How is it, then, that you turn away? (Verses 31–32)

The pagan Arabs, as has been explained, did not deny God's existence, nor did they deny that He is the One who creates, provides sustenance for His creation and controls the whole universe. They simply ascribed divinity to other beings whom they considered to be God's partners. They claimed that these were able to bring them nearer to God or that they had their own power, independent of God's. Here the *sūrah* addresses them taking their own beliefs as its starting point. It aims to alert their consciousness and make them reflect, so that they can discard their ill-conceived ideas. *"Say: 'Who is it that provides for you from heaven and earth?'"* (Verse 31) Who brings down the rain which quickens the land and brings up the plants? Who produces all the crops, birds, fish and animals? Who provides people with everything they get from the heavens and earth for their own and their animals' food? This is what they used to understand when reference was made to the provisions from heaven and earth. Reality however is much greater than this. Today, we can still discover new provisions that He gives us, and we can still uncover more and more about the laws of nature. People can use what God provides for them in beneficial or harmful ways, in line with their sound or false beliefs. They get their provisions from the surface or bottom of the earth; from water running in its courses on the surface of the earth or stored underground; from the sun with its heat and the moon and its light. Even the putridity of organic material contains something that is used in medicine to produce cures for diseases.

"Or, who is it that has power over hearing and sight?" (Verse 31) Who is it that gives these organs their power or deprives them of it; who makes them healthy or malfunctioning? Who is it that makes them see and hear what they like or dislike? Although that was then the limit of their understanding of the functioning of these senses, it was enough to enable them to understand the significance of such a question. However, we are still learning something new about the nature of hearing and sight, and the fine complexity of both these senses, to make the question wider in implication. The structure of the eye and the optic nerve, and how the whole system works to define what is seen, and also the structure of the ear, its different parts and how it captures sound frequencies are extraordinary wonders, particularly when they are compared to the most sophisticated machines of our modern scientific achievements. Yet although man-made machines are insignificant as compared with God's work, people still ignore the miracles of creation which are all around them in the universe and in their own souls.

"Who brings forth the living out of that which is dead, and brings forth the dead out of that which is alive?" (Verse 31) People considered everything that was motionless to be dead. On the other hand, motion and growth indicated life. Therefore the drift of the question was clear to them: it was no different from seeing a plant coming out of a seed and a seed contained in a plant; a chick coming out of an egg and an egg produced by a bird; and numerous other cycles of creation. To them this was especially remarkable, and it remains remarkable even though we have come to know that the seed and the egg should be classified among the living on account of the potential life they contain. Indeed life potential, with all its hidden qualities, hereditary characteristics and unique features, is one of the most remarkable and wonderful things made by God's will.

A pause to consider the phenomenon of a seed and a stone bringing forth a plant and a date tree, and also an egg and a cell bringing forth a chick and a human being, may lead to a whole lifetime of thinking and reflecting. Let us just consider where in the seed the roots, sticks, leaves and fruits lie hidden? Where in the date stone does the core, the bast, the tall trunk and fibres we see in the date tree hide? Where are the taste, flavour, colour and smell stored, and how do we account for what we see of the great variety of dates? Where in the egg do the bones, meat, feathers, colour, flapping of the wings and the singing of the bird hide? Even more remarkably, where in the female cell does the human being with all its complex characteristics hide? Where are a person's features stored until they are transmitted by genes that gather their qualities from past and distant generations? Where do the distinctive qualities of every human being come from: the way he talks, looks, turns his head, feels things around him, etc. and the features and qualities that he inherits from his parents, family and race, as well as those that give him his unique personality?

Is it sufficient to say that this endless world of creation lies hidden in a seed, a stone, an egg and a female cell? Is this sufficient to end our wonder? There is no escaping the recognition that it is all done by God's will and produced by His power.

Human beings continue to uncover some of the secrets of life and death, and how the living is brought forth out of the dead and the dead out of the living. At different stages, elements experience death or come back to life. All this adds to the great significance of the question asked here and its broader perspective. The food we eat dies as a result of cooking and exposure to heat, but it is then transformed inside the living body into blood, which in turn becomes dead waste as a result of body processes. The more we learn about this process the more remarkable it appears, and yet it continues during every moment of the night and day. Indeed life continues to be a great exciting mystery that poses for man a question he cannot answer unless he admits that it is God the Creator who gives life.

"*Who regulates all affairs?*" (Verse 31) This question applies to all that has just been mentioned and to everything else, whether it relates to the affairs of the universe or to human affairs. Who regulates the great universal system that conducts the movement of all worlds in such a fine and elaborate manner? Who regulates the cycle of life and sets it along its finely tuned system? Who regulates the social laws that govern human life, without the slightest deviation from its course? The list of such questions is endless.

"*They will say: 'God.'*" They, i.e. the Arabs who were the first to be addressed by the Qur'ān did not deny God's existence, or His control of these great issues. But as they deviated from the path of the truth, they began to associate partners with God, and to address worship rituals to such partners. Furthermore, they put into operation laws that God had not sanctioned.

"*Say: 'Will you not, then, fear Him?'*" (Verse 31) Since He is the One who provides sustenance, controls hearing and sight, brings the living out of the dead and the dead out of the living, and regulates all matters and affairs, should you not fear Him? The One who has all these attributes is indeed the true Lord who has no partners to be associated with Him.

Who Guides to the Truth

"*Such is God, your true Lord.*" (Verse 32) Since the truth is one and cannot be present in more than one form at the same time, then whoever goes beyond it is in fundamental error. "*Apart from the truth, what is left but error? How is it, then, that you turn away?*" (Verse 32)

When the truth is clearly evident, how can anyone look elsewhere for guidance?

The outcome of the unbelievers' deliberate denial of the truth, despite their acknowledgement of its basis, is that God has made it a law of human nature that those who deviate from the sound logic of nature and the overall laws of creation will not be believers: "*Thus is the word of your Lord proved true with regard to those who do evil: they will not believe.*" (Verse 33) He does not prevent them from believing. Indeed the pointers to the truth and true faith are everywhere in the universe, and its logical basis is acknowledged by them. It is simply because they themselves refuse to take the way leading to faith and deliberately turn their backs on the logical conclusion of the premise they accept. It is an outcome they choose by disregarding the logic of nature.

The *sūrah* then resumes its line of drawing attention to aspects of God's power and asks whether any of the partners the unbelievers associate with Him have any share in such power: "*Say: 'Does any of your partners [whom you associate with God] originate creation, and then bring it back [to life] again?' Say: 'It is God alone who originates creation and then brings it back [to life] again. How is it, then, that you are so misled?' Say: 'Does any of your partners [whom you associate with God] guide to the truth?' Say: 'God alone guides to the truth. Who is more worthy to be followed: He that guides to the truth, or he who cannot find the right way unless he is guided? What is then amiss with you? How do you judge?'*" (Verses 34–35)

The questions now addressed to them, concerning re-creation and guidance to the truth, are not taken for granted like the first group. These are posed on the basis of what they accept as true. They relate to conclusions they should arrive at with reflection. No answer is required of them. The answer is placed in front of them, outlining the conclusions to the premises they have accepted: "*Say: 'Does any of your partners [whom you associate with God] originate creation and then bring it back [to life] again?'*" (Verse 34)

They accept that God has initiated creation, but they do not acknowledge that He will bring it back to life. They refuse to believe in the resurrection, reckoning and reward. Yet God's purpose is not complete by simply originating creation, giving creatures their span of life, letting them die without receiving their reward for doing well and following divine guidance, or their punishment for deliberately following falsehood. That would be a journey cut short, and that would not be designed by a Creator whose attributes include deliberate planning and perfect wisdom. Indeed believing in the Day of Judgement is a logical requirement of believing in the wisdom, justice and mercy of the Creator. This fact needs to be stated clearly to them, since they believe that God is the Creator, and acknowledge that He is the One who brings the living out of the dead. In fact the second life is closely similar to the process of bringing what is alive out of what is dead: "*Say: 'It is God alone who originates creation and then brings it back [to life] again.'*" (Verse 34) It is singularly strange that they should turn away from this fact when they accept its premise: "*How is it, then, that you are so misled?*" (Verse 34) How is it that you choose error and accept false beliefs?

"*Say: 'Does any of your partners [whom you associate with God] guide to the truth?'*" (Verse 35) Does any such partner reveal scriptures, send messengers, lay down a law and a code of living, give warnings and direct people to the truth? Does any of them explain the signs and pointers that are available in the universe and within human nature, awakening minds that have been left in deep slumber and alerting disused faculties? They were aware of all this since God's Messenger presented it to them for their guidance. This was not something that they had already known and accepted, but rather something that actually took place before their very eyes. The Prophet was among them fulfilling the task God had assigned to him. Hence it is put to them as evidence of the truth they are called upon to acknowledge. "*Say: 'God alone guides to the truth.'*" (Verse 35)

This leads to another question with a ready answer: "*Who is more worthy to be followed: He that guides to the truth, or he who cannot find the right way unless he is guided?*" (Verse 35) There can only be a single answer to this question. Naturally, the one who guides mankind to the truth is the one to be followed, in preference to the one who is in need of guidance. This applies whether those who are worshipped are made of stone or trees, or whether they are stars or human beings. In fact it applies to Jesus Christ [peace be upon him]. Although God sent him to give guidance to people, being himself human, he too was in need of God's guidance. It therefore applies even more to those who are falsely claimed to be God's partners.

"What is then amiss with you? How do you judge?" (Verse 35) What has come over you that you clearly misjudge matters and deviate so badly from the truth?

When the questions put to them are completed, and the answers dictated by natural logic and accepted premises are clearly stated, the *sūrah* points out what they actually do in respect of reflection, arriving at conclusions, and formulating beliefs. They have no certainty in anything that relates to belief or worship. They do not base their arguments and beliefs on any fact that human nature and reason can accept as true. They indulge in conjecture, and that has nothing to do with the truth.

"Most of them follow nothing but mere conjecture. But conjecture can in no way be a substitute for truth. God has full knowledge of all that they do." (Verse 36) They think that God has partners, but they do not try to test such thoughts either by reasoning or in practical terms. They think that their forefathers would not have worshipped idols unless those idols had something to deserve worship. But they do not question this false premise, nor do they free their minds from the shackles of following such thoughts blindly. They assume that God would not reveal anything to a man from among them, but they do not question why God would not do so. They also assume that the Qur'ān is authored by Muḥammad, but they do not try to verify whether Muḥammad is capable of authoring the Qur'ān, when they themselves, human beings like him, are totally incapable of producing a *sūrah* similar to the Qur'ān. Thus they go about life nourishing a host of assumptions and thoughts that have no foundation. As the Qur'ān describes it, they thrive on conjecture but this does not give them anything of substance. It is God alone who knows fully what they do. *"God has full knowledge of all that they do."* (Verse 36)

A Book of God's Own Devising

The *sūrah* now begins a new round speaking of the Qur'ān itself. It starts with a categorical statement that there is no way that the Qur'ān could have been invented by anyone, followed by a challenge to the

79

unbelievers to produce a single *sūrah* like it. It then shows their judgement to be hasty, lacking solid ground. This is followed by stating the nature of their attitude to the Qur'ān, coupled with encouragement to the Prophet to remain steadfast regardless of the response he receives from them. The round concludes with a reference to the destiny awaiting those who are stubborn in their erroneous beliefs. It is a just and fitting destiny, determined by their deeds.

"*This Qur'ān could not have been devised by anyone other than God. It is a confirmation of [revelations] that went before it, and a full explanation of God's Book, about which there is no doubt. It certainly comes from the Lord of all the worlds. If they say: 'He has invented it,' say: 'Produce, then, one* sūrah *like it, and call for help on all you can other than God, if what you say is true.' Indeed they disbelieve what they cannot grasp, particularly since its inner meaning has not become clear to them. Likewise did those who lived before them disbelieve. But see what happened in the end to those wrongdoers. Some of them do believe in it, while others do not. But your Lord is fully aware of those who spread corruption. If they disbelieve you, then say: 'I shall bear the consequences of my deeds, and you your deeds. You are not accountable for what I do and I am not accountable for your doings.' Yet some of them [pretend to] listen to you; but can you make the deaf hear you, incapable as they are of using their reason? And some of them [pretend to] look towards you; but can you show the way to the blind, bereft of sight as they are? Indeed, God does not do the least wrong to mankind, but it is men who wrong themselves.*" (Verses 37–44)

"*This Qur'ān could not have been devised by anyone other than God.*" (Verse 37) Such unique characteristics of topic and expression; such perfection of order and harmony; such completeness of the faith it preaches and the code for human life it lays down; such a thorough concept of the nature of Godhead, as well as the nature of life, human beings and the universe could never have been designed by anyone other than God. Only He is able to combine all this, because He is the One who knows the beginnings of all things and their ends, the apparent and the hidden. No one else can devise a system that is perfect, free of shortcomings and based on perfect knowledge.

"*This Qur'ān could not have been devised by anyone other than God.*" (Verse 37) What is negated here is the very possibility that the Qur'ān could ever have been fabricated or authored by anyone other than God. This is much more comprehensive and emphatic.

"*It is a confirmation of [revelations] that went before it.*" (Verse 37) It confirms all the revelations and Scriptures given to earlier messengers. It confirms the original faith outlined by those messages and the good things they advocated. It is also "*a full explanation of God's Book.*" (Verse 37) It is the same Book, outlining the same message preached by all messengers. There may be differences of detail in these messages, but the basic principles are the same. The Qur'ān explains God's Book fully, making clear all the methods and means of goodness it outlines and how these are to be fulfilled and followed in human life. The faith is the same and the basic substance is the same, but the methods of goodness and the legislation outlined are given each time in a degree of detail that suits human progress and development. When mankind came of age, they were addressed by the Qur'ān as adults. They were no longer addressed by physical miracles that defy human intellect.

Moreover, it is a Book "*about which there is no doubt. It certainly comes from the Lord of all the worlds.*" (Verse 37) This is an assertion that the Qur'ān could never have been fabricated or attributed falsely to God. It is indeed a revelation by '*the Lord of all the worlds.*'

Having stated the truth about the Qur'ān, the *sūrah* speaks of a certain possibility: "*If they say: 'He has invented it.'*" (Verse 38) In other words, if Muhammad is alleged to have invented it let them then mobilize their resources and invent a single *sūrah* like it, if they can. "*Say: 'Produce, then, one* sūrah *like it, and call for help on all you can besides God, if what you say is true.*" (Verse 38)

The challenge is permanent, as is their inability to meet it. It continues for the rest of time and no one will ever be able to meet it. Anyone who appreciates the strength, beauty and artistic expression of the Arabic language will recognize that the Qur'ānic style is unique, and that no human being could produce anything similar to it. So will those who study human social systems and legal principles. If they study the system laid down in the Qur'ān, they will realize that its approach to the organization of the human community is absolutely unique. It enacts appropriate regulations for all aspects of human life, while at the same time allowing a sufficient degree of practicality and flexibility to meet any type of development. That is a task too great to be undertaken by a single human mind, or by the minds of any group of human beings in a single generation or throughout human history. The same applies to those who study human psychology and methods of influencing people on the one hand, and the Qur'ān and the way it addresses the human mind on the other.

It is not merely the incomparability of the Qur'ānic style and mode of expression; instead the absolutely miraculous nature of the Qur'ān is easily recognized by experts in diverse disciplines such as language, society, law and psychology.

Those who are adept at using artistic expression, and have an insight into fine literary styles are better able to appreciate the miracle of the Qur'ān in this particular aspect, while experts in the different disciplines of sociology, law, psychology are able to appreciate its superior treatment of their themes. Each will appreciate better than anyone else the miracle of the Qur'ān in their respective disciplines. I admit that it is practically impossible to describe this miracle and its true dimensions but I will nonetheless attempt to give a glimpse of its nature.

An Amazing Experience with the Qur'ān

The Qur'ān is readily distinguishable from any human expression. It has a powerful effect on people's hearts which no human style can achieve. Such an effect is sometimes felt by people who have no knowledge of Arabic. Some remarkable events, which may not be the rule, cannot have any other explanation. I am not giving any example witnessed by anyone else. I am only relating something that happened to me about 15 years ago, for which I have no less than six witnesses.[1]

We were seven Muslim passengers travelling on board an Egyptian ship across the Atlantic to New York. There were also 120 foreign passengers, none of whom was a Muslim. It occurred to us to hold Friday prayers on board, in the middle of the ocean. God knows that we were not that keen on the prayer itself, but we were driven to show our religious feelings when we saw a missionary exercising his mission with the passengers. He even approached us. The Captain, an

---

1. The author is referring here to his trip to the United States, in 1950, when he was sent on a scholarship to undertake research to determine the best means of developing education in Egyptian universities. – Editor's note.

Englishman, facilitated our task and allowed any of the crew and other workers, all of whom were Nubian Muslims, to join the prayer, provided that they were not on duty at the time. They were overjoyed by this, as it was, in their experience, the first time ever that Friday prayers had been held on board. I delivered the *khuṭbah*, or sermon, and led the prayers, while many of the foreign passengers were watching nearby.

When the prayer was over, many of them congratulated us on a 'successful service'. That was how they viewed our prayers. One particular lady, whom we were later informed was a Christian from Yugoslavia fleeing from the oppression of Tito's Communist regime, was particularly touched. In fact she could not control her feelings and her eyes were full of tears. She shook our hands warmly and said in broken English that she was profoundly touched by the discipline and spiritual calm of our prayers. She then asked which language the 'priest' was speaking. She simply could not imagine that prayers could be led by a layman, but we made sure to explain this point to her. She also said that although she could not understand a word of what was being said, the language had a remarkable musical rhythm. She then added something that was a great surprise to us all. She said that certain phrases or sentences which he used were different from the rest of his speech. They were more clearly musical with an even more profound rhythm. These phrases filled her with awe. It was as if the imām was deriving his speech from the Holy Spirit. We reflected on what she had said and concluded that she meant the Qur'ānic verses quoted in the *khuṭbah* and recited during the prayer. The whole thing was truly remarkable as the lady did not understand a word of Arabic.

As I have said, this is not the rule. Yet this incident, and similar ones reported by different people, confirm that the Qur'ān has some secret which enables certain hearts to react to it when they hear its recitation. It might have been that this lady had a keen religious sense which, coupled with the fact of her flight from Communist tyranny in her own country, refined her interaction with God's revelations. But why do we wonder at this when we see thousands of uneducated Muslims greatly influenced by the rhythm of the Qur'ān, despite their inability to understand it. In a sense, they are not much different from this Yugoslav lady.

I have felt it necessary to speak about this subtle power of the Qur'ān before turning to other aspects which are well known to those who are skilled in the art of expression and those who are endowed with a refined sense or who think and contemplate.

A distinctive feature of the Qur'ānic method of expression is that it tackles great issues in a space which, by human standards, is far too short. Nevertheless, it covers them in the fullest, finest, most vivid and accurate way, maintaining at the same time a perfect harmony between the words it uses, the style, rhythm, connotations and the overall feeling it generates. It combines artistic beauty with precision in a way that makes it impossible to replace one word with another, and does not allow the needs of fine style to overshadow those of precise meaning or vice versa. In this respect, it achieves a standard of excellence that surpasses anything that men of letters recognize as the zenith that can be attained by any human being.

This main feature brings about another distinctive characteristic of the Qur'ān, one which enables a single statement to provide different meanings that run side by side, with each given its fair share of clarity. There is no ambiguity or confusion between different meanings. Each aspect and each fact to which the text refers is given its full and appropriate space. Thus the same statement is quoted in different contexts but on each occasion it fits the context perfectly, as if it were only meant to express the particular issue in question. This feature is well known, and it only requires brief mention for people to appreciate it.

The Qur'ānic method of expression is also distinguished by its ability to paint pictures in a way no human expression can approximate. Anyone who tries to imitate it sounds confused and incoherent. How can people express the following ideas in the same way as the Qur'ān:

"*And We brought the Children of Israel across the sea; but Pharaoh and his legions pursued them with tyranny and aggression. But as he was about to drown, Pharaoh said: 'I have come to believe that there is no deity other than Him in whom the Children of Israel believe, and to Him I surrender myself.'*" (Verse 90) Up to this point, this is an account of certain events. But it is followed immediately with a direct remonstration brought up as though it were taking place right before us: "*Only now? But before this you were rebelling [against Us], and you*

84

spread corruption in the land. But today We shall save only your body, so that you may become a sign to those who will come after you." (Verses 91–92) This is then followed with a concluding comment on the scene itself: *"For a great many people do not heed Our signs."* (Verse 92)

"Say: 'What is weightiest in testimony?' Say: 'God is witness between me and you. This Qur'ān has been revealed to me that I may thereby warn you and all whom it may reach.'" (6: 19) So far this is an instruction received by God's Messenger. Then immediately we see the Messenger questioning his people: *"Will you in truth bear witness that there are other deities beside God?"* (6: 19) The next moment, we see him again receiving instructions concerning the very point he is questioning his people about and receiving their answer: *"Say: 'I bear no such witness.' Say: 'He is but one God. I disown all that you associate with Him.'"* (6: 19)

Note also the frequent switch of tense or address often employed in the Qur'ān, as in the following passage: *"On the day when He shall gather them all together, [He will say]: 'O you company of jinn! A great many human beings have you seduced.' Those who were their close friends among human beings will say: 'Our Lord, we have enjoyed each other's fellowship, and we have now reached the end of our term which You have appointed for us.' He will say: 'The fire shall be your abode, where you shall remain, unless God wills it otherwise.' Indeed, your Lord is Wise, All-knowing. In this manner do We cause the wrongdoers to be close allies of one another, because of that which they do. 'O you company of jinn and humans! Have there not come to you messengers from among yourselves who related to you My revelations and warned you of the coming of this your day?' They will reply: 'We bear witness against ourselves.' The life of this world has beguiled them. So they will bear witness against themselves that they were unbelievers. And so it is that your Lord would never destroy a community for its wrongdoing, while they remain unaware."* (6: 128–131)

There are numerous similar examples in the Qur'ān. Its style is thus totally different from any human style. Anyone who wishes to argue about this can try as hard as he wishes to produce something like it, but he will certainly fail. He will be totally unable to come up with any meaningful piece of writing, let alone having any degree of artistic beauty, inspiring rhythm and perfect coherence.

Characteristics of the Qur'ān

The Qur'ān addresses the human entity as a whole. It does not address different faculties such as logical reasoning, pulsating hearts or excited feelings, one at a time. It simply makes its appeal in the most direct manner, touching all human receptive faculties at once. Thus it generates feelings, impressions and concepts of the truth of existence that no other method known to mankind can ever generate. Moreover, all these are profound, comprehensive, precise, lucid and inimitably expressed.

I would like to quote here a few paragraphs from a book I am now working on[2] which may express this fact better. These speak of the Islamic approach in elucidating the constituent elements of the Islamic concept of life in a beautiful, comprehensive, coherent and balanced way. The most distinctive features of this approach are:

> Firstly, it portrays the facts as they are using a style that reveals all their aspects, dimensions, links and consequences. Comprehensive as it is, it does not complicate any fact or make it ambiguous. It then makes its address to all humanity, at all levels.[3] God has not wished to make the attainment of any standard of knowledge or education a necessary requirement for the proper perception of the Islamic concept of life. Faith is the first need in human life. When it is accepted by people, it formulates in their hearts and minds a concept which defines their method of dealing with the whole universe. It also gives them a method to follow in the pursuit of any branch of knowledge. This concept provides for them a complete explanation and understanding of the universe and what happens in it. Since it is founded on the truth of faith, God wants it to be the basis of all their knowledge and scientific study. This is the most solid basis since it is the ultimate truth.

---

2. This is the second volume of the author's work *Khaṣā'iṣ al-Taṣawwur al-Islāmī wa Muqawwimātuh*, or Distinctive Features of the Islamic Concept and its Constituent Elements. The first volume was published in 1963. The author wrote a few chapters of the second volume after his release from prison in 1964. These were posthumously published as the second volume. – Editor's note.

3. Human expression cannot achieve this, because every author addresses a particular level of understanding. Those who belong to a different level can hardly understand him.

All that man learns, and all the knowledge he attains, from any source other than faith remain within the field of probability. It is neither final nor absolute, not even when it relies on scientific experiment. Empirical science relies on analogy and induction to draw its conclusions. It is not based on thorough and exhaustive investigation and universal application. That is not possible for human beings to do in any experiment, even if we assume that all human observations and final conclusions are correct. The ultimate that scientific research can achieve is to conduct a number of experiments and make observations and conclusions that are applied generally. Scientists admit that their conclusions remain within the realm of probability; they are never final. Besides, every single experiment aims to determine the degree of probability of a certain aspect. Hence, the only certain knowledge that human beings can acquire is that which they receive from the One who knows all, and is fully aware of all secrets and minute details. He is the One who speaks the truth and explains the ultimate certainty.[4]

Secondly, it is free of any flaws of disjointedness or incoherence which are observed in scientific studies, philosophical treaties and refined artistic writings. It does not approach each aspect of a coherent, beautiful whole separately as all human styles of expression do. It portrays them all in an integrated approach which links perceptible features with the realm that lies beyond our reach. Thus it establishes a link between the truth of the universe, life and man and the truth of God; between this life and the life to come; and between our world here and the Supreme Society of angels. All this is done in a unique, inimitable style. When human beings try to imitate this characteristic, they fall far short and the outcome is incoherent, ambiguous, and ill-defined. This is the opposite of what we readily observe in Qur'ānic style.

Strong as the link is between different facts tackled in a particular Qur'ānic passage or *sūrah*, the emphasis on any one of them may

---

4. This is why on listening to the Qur'ān people feel it is clearly more authoritative than any other writing.

frequently change, yet the link remains clear. For example, when the emphasis is placed on explaining to people who their true Lord is, we find this great truth portrayed in describing His magnificent work in the universe and within human life, in our own world which we see and feel and in the world beyond. Elsewhere the emphasis may be on elucidating the truth about the universe and its existence. Here, then, we have the nature of the relationship between Godhead and the universe clearly outlined, with frequent references to the nature of life and living creatures and also to the natural laws God has set in operation in the universe at large.

Similarly, when the nature of man is emphasized, it is portrayed with its links with God, the universe and other living creatures; and also with the present world and the world beyond. If the emphasis happens to be on the life to come, this life is also discussed, and both are related to God and to other important facts. The same applies when the truth about the present life comes in for special emphasis.

Thirdly, the Qur'ān not only portrays the truth as an integrated whole with all its aspects in perfect harmony, but it also gives each aspect in this complete whole its due share of space and importance, commensurate with its weight on God's accurate scales. Hence the nature and qualities of God, and the question of godhead and servitude appear to be the dominant issues. Indeed explaining the facts relevant to these issues appears to be the basic theme of the Qur'ān.[5] Similarly, the theme of the world that lies beyond the reach of human perception, including God's will, predestination and the life to come, occupies substantial space. So does the nature of man, the universe and life, with each being given mutually complementary importance that fits with the harmony and complementarity of these questions in real life. Thus no important fact is overlooked, ignored or gloated over.

---

5. The reasons for attaching special importance to the theme of Godhead are fully discussed in the Prologue to this *sūrah*.

We have spoken elsewhere about the Islamic concept being well balanced. It admires the accuracy of the laws governing the material world and the perfect harmony between its various components. However, this admiration does not lead to making the material world a deity, as did some communities of old. In fact this is still done by some people in modern times when they ascribe divinity to material worlds or to stars and planets. Nor does the admiring look at the miracle of life and how it defines its functions and fulfils them, or its harmony with the universe around it, lead to giving it the position of a deity, as do some modern existentialists. Similarly the wonderful creation of man, his unique qualities and potential, manifesting themselves in his interaction with the universe, causes much admiration. However, this admiration does not lead to making man, or human intellect, a deity in one way or another, as the idealists generally do. On the other hand, the recognized majesty of the divine truth, or God Himself, does not lead to the discarding of the material world or to looking at it or at man with contempt, as Hindu, Buddhist and distorted Christian philosophies do. In fact, a well-balanced outlook is the main characteristic of the Islamic concept of life generally.

Similarly, the Qur'ānic method in presenting the constituent elements of this concept and the facts upon which it is based is also well balanced, giving prominence where it is due. Thus they are all clearly apparent every time the Qur'ān outlines this concept in its totality. This unique Qur'ānic quality is beyond the ability of human expression, refined as it may be.

Fourthly, the Qur'ān combines accuracy and precision with an inspirational vitality that imparts to these facts a rhythm, life and beauty unknown in any human presentation or expression. However, this accuracy does not encroach on a lively and beautiful style, nor does the demarcation spoil the rhythm and harmony.

Interaction with the Qur'ānic approach is the best way to appreciate it. Much as we try, we cannot fairly describe, in our human style, its main features so as to begin to appreciate it in the same way. Nor can our study of the main characteristics and constituent elements of the Islamic concept of life, man and the universe, be as complete as its picture given in the Qur'ān. Our attempt to present this study to people is made only because people have drawn far away from the Qur'ān. They have chosen to make their social environment vastly different from that which prevailed in the community which received the Qur'ānic revelations. They no longer experience the same circumstances and concerns of that community which established the Islamic society. Hence people are no longer able to appreciate the Qur'ānic approach and interact with it. Nor are they able to enjoy its beauty and finer characteristics.

Areas Unfathomed in Human Writings

The Qur'ān sometimes explains the basic truisms of faith in a way that the human mind would never attempt, because, by their nature, these are not things which preoccupy or attract human attention. A clear example is the verse which describes God's infinite knowledge: *"With Him are the keys to what lies beyond the reach of human perception: none knows them but He. He knows all that the land and sea contain; not a leaf falls but He knows it; and neither is there a grain in the earth's deep darkness, nor anything fresh or dry but is recorded in a clear book."* (6: 59) These broad places and situations, visible and hidden, are not normally frequented by human thought in this way, when it tries to express knowledge that embraces everything. Let us quote here a few paragraphs of what we stated in our commentary on this verse.

> Every time we look at this short verse, we cannot fail to recognize its miraculous style which tells of the author of the Qur'ān. One look at its subject matter is sufficient to make us absolutely certain that this is something no human being would say. Human intelligence does not stretch to limitless horizons when it describes perfect, unfailing knowledge. Instead, the human intellect has different characteristics and certain set limits, because its images reflect its own concerns. Why should human beings care about the number of leaves falling from trees all over the globe? Why should they bother about grains buried in the deep dark recesses

of the earth? What concern is it to them to know everything that is fresh or dry? People simply do not care about falling leaves, let alone about counting them. They care about the seeds they plant, hoping to have a good harvest. Otherwise, they would not care about the grains buried in the earth. They certainly like to use what they have of fresh and dry things, but none of these matters is thought of as evidence of perfect knowledge. It is only the Creator who knows and cares about every falling leaf, buried grain and the like, as He does about other things, fresh or dry.

No human being could ever contemplate that each falling leaf, buried grain, every fresh object and also every dry one should be recorded in a clear book. They cannot see any benefit to them from keeping such a record. But the Sovereign of the whole universe is the One who has all that recorded because everything in the whole universe, large or small, visible or hidden, distant or close, apparent or unknown, is part of His dominion and, as such, is accounted for.

This is an expansive scene, one which leaves a profound effect on the human mind. The human intellect does not even try to paint such a scene comprising the leaves falling from every tree throughout the world and every grain hidden in the soil and every fresh and dry thing on earth. Indeed, neither our eyes nor our imagination care to visualize it in the first place. Nevertheless, it is a powerful scene that tells us much about God's knowledge, reminding us that God oversees and records everything. His will takes care of what is large or small, highly important or infinitely insignificant, visible or hidden, distant or close, apparent or unknown.

Those of us who react to what we experience and have the talent of expression are keenly aware of our human limitations to visualize and express things. We know from personal experience that it does not occur to any human mind to paint such a scene and that no human being can use such a mode of expression. I invite anyone who disputes this to look into everything that human beings have ever written in an attempt to see if human literary talent has ever ventured in this direction. Indeed, this verse and similar ones in the Qur'ān are sufficient for us to know the Author of this glorious book.

If we look at the artistic excellence in this verse, we soon realize that it surpasses everything that human beings have ever attempted: "*With Him are the keys to what lies beyond the reach of human perception: none knows them but He.*" (Verse 59) The verse takes us first into the unfathomable reaches of the world beyond, stretching into time and place, as well as the past, present and future and into what takes place both in this life and in our imagination.

"*He knows all that the land and sea contain.*" (Verse 59). The picture here is of the seen world, stretching infinitely over the horizon so that the world we see is stretched into an infinite existence to provide harmony with the limitless nature of the world beyond.

"*Not a leaf falls, but He knows it.*" (Verse 59). This depicts the movement of death, the fall from above and disappearance after the end of life.

"*Neither is there a grain in the earth's deep darkness.*" (Verse 59). This depicts the movement of growth and life, starting in the deep and going up onto the surface. We see how the dead quickens and the idle moving forward with vigour.

"*Nor anything fresh or dry but is recorded in a clear book.*" (Verse 59) This is an overall generalization that comprises both life and death, the thriving and the withering away of everything that lives on earth. Who other than God would begin with such material in order to paint such an expansive scene? And who would give it such beauty and harmony to add to its excellence? Who other than God can do that?[6]

Let us now take another example expressing the same idea: "*He knows all that enters the earth, and all that comes out of it, as well as all that*

---

6. Sayyid Quṭb, *In the Shade of the Qur'ān*, Leicester, 2002, Vol. V. pp. 175–177.

descends from the skies, and all that ascends to them. And He alone is the Most-merciful, Truly-forgiving." (34: 2)

Reflect for a moment on this image drawn with the use of only a few words and you will see an endless number of things, movements, shapes, sizes, forms and abstractions that defy the imagination. Should all the people on earth dedicate their entire attention throughout their lives to monitoring and enumerating what takes place in a single moment, of all that to which this verse refers, they would not be able to compile a comprehensive list of which they would be certain.

How many things enter the earth in a single moment? How many grains are buried into all corners of the earth, and how many find their way into them? Think for a moment of the number of worms, insects, particles and crawlers that go underneath the surface of the earth throughout the globe. Think of the number of drops of water, gas molecules as well as rays and radiation that go into the earth at every point of its vast expanse. Think of all this and remember that it is all watched by God whose eyes never blink.

Then how many things come out of the earth? How many plants shoot up, springs issue forth, volcanoes erupt, and gases spread out? How many buried things reveal themselves, and how many insects come out of their hiding places? How many are those things, visible or invisible, known to humans or unknown, that come out of the earth in a single moment? The number is beyond human reckoning.

Reflect on the number of things that come down from the skies: the drops of rain, the meteors, the blazing rays and other rays that bring us light. Think also of every divine command brought down to accomplish God's will, and the mercy God bestows on the whole universe or on particular creatures; and think of all the provisions God grants to His servants in abundance or in restricted measure. All this comes down from the skies, as do numerous other things known only to God Himself.

Reflect also on what ascends to the skies: how many breaths of air come out of every plant, animal, human or other creature? How many supplications are addressed to God in public or in private, heard only by God? Think of the spirits of creatures that are gathered to God; the angels carrying God's orders, and other spirits that go about totally unknown to anyone other than God. Think also how many particles of vapour ascend from the seas, and how many gas molecules ascend from different types of creation.

How many of all these take place in a single moment? How much knowledge do human beings need to make a record of all that takes place in a single moment? Would they come close even if they devoted a lifetime to such counting and recording? But God's knowledge, which is complete and perfect, encompasses all that at every moment and every place. Indeed every heart and mind, every intention and thought, every movement and stoppage is under God's watchful eye. Yet His grace ensures that they remain private, and He also often forgives, for "*He alone is the Most-merciful, Truly-forgiving.*" (34: 2)

Indeed many similar verses of the Qur'ān indicate that it is not of human writing. Such cosmic thoughts do not occur to human beings, because there is nothing in human nature that gives rise to them. Moreover, the simple touches that serve to encompass a universal expanse indicate that they come from the Maker of the universe, whose style no one can emulate.

Certain things and happenings which appear to us to be of little significance are often used by the Qur'ān to prove great concepts. Here they are portrayed in a different light showing them to be very important indeed, and most fitting to prove the concepts in question. For example: "*It is We who have created you: why, then, do you not accept the truth? Have you ever considered that seed which you emit? Is it you who create it, or are We the source of its creation? We have indeed decreed that death shall be ever-present among you; but there is nothing to prevent Us from changing the nature of your existence and bringing you into being anew in a manner as yet unknown to you. And since you are indeed aware of the miracle of your coming into being in the first instance, why, then, do you not bethink yourselves of Us? Have you ever considered the seed which you cast upon the soil? Is it you who cause it to grow, or are We the cause of its growth? For, were it Our will, We could indeed turn it into chaff, and you would be left to wonder and to lament, 'Indeed we are ruined! Nay, but we have been deprived of our livelihood!' Have you ever considered the water which you drink? Is it you who cause it to come down from the clouds or are We the cause of its coming down? Were it Our will, We could make it burningly salty and bitter: why, then, do you not give thanks? Have you ever considered the fire which you kindle? Is it you who have brought into being the tree that serves as its fuel, or are We the cause of its coming into being? It is We who have made it a means to remind [you of Us], and a comfort for all who are lost and hungry in the wilderness [of their lives]. Extol, then, the limitless glory of your Lord's mighty name."* (56: 57–74)

The Qur'ān makes of such familiar phenomena universal issues of great importance, revealing the great laws in the universe, and formulating the basis of a profound faith and a complete way of existence. At the same time, it makes these familiar happenings the centre of thought and contemplation, a tool that refreshes hearts and souls and awakens feelings and sensitivities. It alerts people to phenomena which they tend to overlook although they are in front of them morning and evening. It makes them sensitive to the wonderful and miraculous events that take place in the universe. It does not leave them in need of special, preternatural and infrequent events. Nor does it require them to look for miracles and signs that are alien to them and to their lives, or to look far beyond the laws of nature that affect their own world. It does not lead them to dig into complex philosophies, entangled questions of logic, or scientific experiments that may not be comprehensible to all, in order to formulate in their minds a faith and a concept of life based on it.

They themselves are made by God, and the natural phenomena functioning all around them are set in operation by His will. Everything that He creates is miraculous. Moreover, the Qur'ān is His own book. Hence, it turns their minds to the miracles that are within them or present in their own world. It leads them by the hand to reflect on the miracles that are familiar to them, but because of this familiarity are overlooked and ignored. It opens their eyes to make them see the great secret that is embodied in their existence. It is the secret of the creative power and God's absolute oneness, and the secret of the eternal divine law that operates in their own selves and in the universe around them. This law embodies all the pointers to, and proofs of, the truth of faith. These are brought alive within their human nature.

This is the method followed in the Qur'ān as it portrays aspects of God's power seen in people's own creation, in the plants they grow, the water they drink and the fire they kindle. These are among the most basic things that they see all the time. It also portrays the moment when life on earth comes to its end, and the life of the other world begins. This is the moment which will be faced by everyone, when nothing within human power is of any avail. Thus the Qur'ān brings all human beings face to face with God's absolute power which controls the whole universe. There is no room for any argument. No excuse is valid. The truth stares people in the eye.

The Qur'ānic method of addressing human nature is itself a proof of its source. It is indeed the same source that has given the universe its existence. Its very structure follows the same method of building the universe. The most simple of material is used to produce the most sophisticated shapes and forms, as well as the largest and greatest of creatures. It is thought that the atom is the matter from which the universe is built, and the cell is the matter from which life is formed. Minute as it is, the atom is itself a miracle. Similarly, the tiny cell is a great wonder. In the Qur'ān, the most simple and familiar things are used to formulate the most profound religious beliefs and the broadest universal philosophy. The scenes portrayed are those known and experienced by everyone. They are concerned with offspring, plants, water, fire and death. Even the most primitive man, in his old cave has witnessed the inception of embryonic life, the shoot of a plant, the fall of water, the kindling of fire and the moment of death. On the basis of these scenes, familiar as they are to all human beings, the Qur'ān formulates its ideological beliefs. In this way, the Qur'ān is able to address its message to every human being in every community. But these simple and familiar scenes epitomize the great truth of the universe, and most profound secrets of God's ability. Simple as they are, they address human nature in general, and their greatness remains the central preoccupation of the most knowledgeable of scientists and scholars to the end of time.

Conjecture Preferred to Fact!

"*If they say: 'He has invented it,' say: 'Produce, then, one* sūrah *like it, and call for help on all you can other than God, if what you say is true.'*" (Verse 38) At this point, with the *sūrah* presenting this challenge, all argument is stopped and a clear statement is made to establish the fact that they rely only on conjecture, judging what they do not know.

Right judgement must be preceded by thorough knowledge, and not rely on personal preferences or unproved views. What they are judging is the revelation of the Qur'ān and the truth of its promises and warnings. They have denied all these without having any firm knowledge to justify their denial, and without waiting for its true interpretation: "*Indeed they disbelieve what they cannot grasp, particularly since its inner meaning has not become clear to them.*" (Verse 39) In this they have followed in the footsteps of former communities who rejected God's revelations and associated partners with their Lord. They should consider the fate of those earlier communities in order to know what awaits them if they continue to reject the faith. "*Likewise did those who lived before them disbelieve. But see what happened in the end to those wrongdoers.*" (Verse 39)

Although most of them deny something of which they do not have certain knowledge, and instead follow conjecture and caprice, there are those who do believe in the truth of this revealed book: "*Some of them do believe in it, while others do not. But your Lord is fully aware of those who spread corruption.*" (Verse 40) These spreaders of corruption are the unbelievers. Corruption on earth is certainly caused and mostly spread by turning away from belief in the true Lord. Indeed all corruption starts by submission to beings other than God, including the evil that follows such submission. This is the root cause of following one's desire in what affects oneself or others. It is this which leads to the rise of false gods which corrupt everything so that they can maintain their false lordship. They corrupt people's morals, spirits, thinking, concepts, as well as their interests and property, seeking only to preserve their own power. The history of mankind, old and new, is full of examples of such corruption spread by those who are devoid of faith.

Having explained their attitude to the Qur'ān the *sūrah* addresses the Prophet, telling him not to let himself be affected by their rejection of the truth. He is to disown them and their deeds, declaring that he has nothing to do with them, and by sticking to the truth, stating it clearly and decisively: "*If they disbelieve you, then say: 'I shall bear the consequences of my deeds, and you your deeds. You are not accountable for what I do and I am not accountable for your doings.'*" (Verse 41)

This directive to the Prophet is also meant to touch their consciences. They and their actions are disowned by the Prophet. Now they can face the fate they have been told about without his support. It is yet another way of awakening their hearts, just like a child stubbornly refusing to walk with his parents being left alone to face the consequences of having lost their support in an unexpected eventuality. Such warnings are often successful.

The *sūrah* goes on to portray how they behave with the Prophet. They listen to him and look at him, but they have already sealed their hearts and minds. Hence their faculty of perception cannot make any sense of what they hear and see: *"Yet some of them [pretend to] listen to you; but can you make the deaf hear you, incapable as they are of using their reason? And some of them [pretend to] look towards you; but can you show the way to the blind, bereft of sight as they are?"* (Verses 42–43)

Those who cannot use their reason to understand what they hear or appreciate what they see are always present in large numbers everywhere. The Prophet (peace be upon him) cannot do anything for them because they refuse to learn how to discern and reason. The Prophet cannot make the deaf hear or the blind see. Only God can do that. He, however, has set a law in operation and left His creatures to reap the results of their dealings according to this law. He has given them ears, eyes and minds to hear, see and reason with, so that they may follow the true guidance He sent them. If they decide to put these faculties out of order, they will reap the consequences according to His law. Such consequences are their fair reward, for God does not treat anyone with injustice: *"Indeed, God does not do the least wrong to mankind, but it is men who wrong themselves."* (Verse 44)

These last few verses are meant to reassure the Prophet and relieve his sorrow at their stubborn rejection of the truth. God reassures him that their rejection is not the result of any lack of effort on his part, or lack of conviction on the part of his message. It is simply that they behave as though they were deaf and blind. It is only God who gives ears and eyes their faculties. It has nothing to do with the message itself or the person who preaches it. These verses also provide a clear definition of the nature of servitude to God. The Prophet himself is a servant of God, and all his abilities remain within the limits of God's servants. The final say belongs to God alone.

When God Is the Witness

The next verses quickly touch the hearts of the unbelievers, portraying as they do a scene from the Day of Judgement. In this scene the whole of life which is so heavily present in their consciousness, and which encompasses all their concerns and preoccupations appears to be no more than a short trip which people undertake before returning to their permanent abode: *"On the Day when He will gather them together, [it will seem to them] as though they had not sojourned in this world more than an hour of a day, getting to know one another. Lost indeed will be those who [in their lifetime] disbelieved in meeting God and did not follow the right guidance."* (Verse 45)

In this very fast round, we see those who are gathered on the Day of Judgement to be totally bewildered. It all comes to them as if by total surprise. It is as if their journey through this life has been a very short one, lasting barely an hour in which they get to know one another before it is all over. Or we may take this as an analogy showing how we spend our whole lives just meeting and getting to know one another. Although it is given by way of example, it is a completely true statement. Do people ever complete the process of getting to know one another? We come and go, and each individual or group barely gets to know the rest.

Reflect, if you will, on individuals who are in conflict with one another all the time: have they got to know one another as they should do? And then those warring nations which constantly fight over material and petty gains, hardly able to finish one quarrel before starting another. Do they get to know each other? The comparison is drawn here in order to emphasize the fact that this present life is very short.

In this way the loss of those who give this momentary trip all their attention is highlighted. They deny the fact of their forthcoming meeting with God, and instead turn away from Him. They make no preparations for their meeting with God or for their much longer stay in the life to come: *"Lost indeed will be those who [in their lifetime] disbelieved in meeting God and did not follow the right guidance."* (Verse 45)

This is followed by an address to the Prophet concerning the warnings God gives to those who deny the truth of His revelations. It is a clear warning wrapped in a cover of mystery. They do not know whether it will come to pass within a day or so, or whether they will have to wait until the Day of Judgement. Thus it remains a constant threat to them, so that they may take heed and mend their ways. Gradually the passage which begins with a warning moves on to conclude with a description of the situation when nothing is of any use, and no one can buy his escape from God's punishment, not even if he had the whole world to offer. On the Day when God sits in judgement, no one shall suffer any injustice. Again we find here an example of the Qur'ānic method which links this life with the life to come, in just a few touching words. But it also describes the link between the two lives as it is in reality, and as they should always be viewed from an Islamic standpoint.

> *Whether We show you some of what We have promised them or We cause you to die, it is to Us that they shall return. God is witness of all that they do. To every community was sent a messenger. It is when their messenger had come to them that judgement was passed on them in all fairness; and never are they wronged. They say: 'When will this promise be fulfilled, if you are truthful?' Say: 'I have no control over any harm or benefit to myself, except as God may please. For every community a term has been appointed. When their time arrives, they can neither delay it by a single moment, nor indeed hasten it.' Say: 'Do but consider. Should His punishment befall you by night or by day, what could there be in it that the guilty ones should wish to hasten? Is it, then, when it has come to pass that you will believe in it? Is it now, while so far you have been asking for it to come speedily?' Then it will be said to the wrongdoers: 'Taste the long-lasting torment. Is this requital anything other than the just due for what you used to do?' They will ask you: 'Is all this true?' Say: 'Yes, by my Lord. It is most certainly true, and you will never be beyond God's reach.' Should every wrongdoer possess all that the earth contains, he will*

gladly offer it all as ransom. They will harbour feelings of remorse when they see the suffering. Judgement will be passed on them in all fairness; and they will not be wronged. (Verses 46–54)

This passage begins with a clear statement reaffirming the fact that such people will undoubtedly return to God, whether they experience some of what the Prophet has warned them against in his life or after his death. The return in both cases is to God who is a witness of all they do at all times, during the lifetime of the Prophet or afterwards. Nothing of what they do will ever be lost. The Prophet's death will not exempt them from facing the reckoning.

"*Whether We show you some of what We have promised them or We cause you to die, it is to Us that they shall return. God is witness of all that they do.*" (Verse 46) Everything takes place according to deliberate planning. Nothing is lost or changed on account of any emergencies or special circumstances. Every community is left to wait until its messenger comes to warn them and explain all the facts to them. Thus they are given their rights in accordance with the condition God has imposed upon Himself that He would not punish any community until He has sent them a messenger with a clear message. When this has taken place, they will have no excuse. They will be judged fairly, on the basis of their response to the messenger: "*To every community was sent a messenger. It is when their messenger had come to them that judgement was passed on them in all fairness; and never are they wronged.*" (Verse 47)

The last two verses should be taken as the basis of a proper understanding of the nature of Godhead and servitude to Him. The Qur'ān is keen to explain it at every occasion, in different ways and methods. Here the Prophet is told that what is to become of this faith and the people to whom it is addressed belongs entirely to God. The Prophet himself has no say in it. His role is that of conveying the message he has been given. Anything beyond that belongs to God alone. His lifetime may end and he may not see the end of those people who stubbornly opposed him or who tried to cause him harm. It is not imperative that God should let him see the fate of his opponents or how God will punish them. That is something determined by God alone. Every one of God's messengers should fulfil the task assigned to them of conveying God's message. When a messenger has done that, he then leaves everything to God to determine. Thus all creatures know their positions. The advocates of faith will not then be hasty trying to precipitate God's judgement, no matter how long they may take in advocating the message or how much hardship they are made to endure.

Why Precipitate God's Punishment?

"*They say: 'When will this promise be fulfilled, if you are truthful?'*" (Verse 48) The question was asked by way of a challenge. They were actually demanding that whatever the Prophet warned them against be fulfilled, and that God's judgement be made just as it had been on earlier communities which denied God's messengers. But the answer the Prophet is instructed to give makes all issues succinctly clear: "*Say: 'I have no control over any harm or benefit to myself, except as God may please. For every community a term has been appointed. When their time arrives, they can neither delay it by a single moment, nor indeed hasten it.'*" (Verse 49)

If God's Messenger does not have any power to bring harm or benefit to himself, he certainly cannot bring such harm or benefit to them either. It should be pointed out here that harm is mentioned before benefit because they were precipitating harm. In a different context, benefit is mentioned first because it is more fitting to the situation. This occurs in *Sūrah* 7, The Heights, or *Al-A'rāf*, when he says: "*Had I possessed knowledge of what lies beyond the reach of human perception, I would have availed myself of much that is good and no evil would have ever touched me.*" (7: 188)

"*Say: 'I have no power over any harm or benefit to myself, except as God may please.'*" (Verse 49) It is all, then, by God's will. He brings His word to pass and He puts His warnings into effect whenever He pleases. His law will never fail, and the term He has set will fall due as He has determined: "*For every community a term has been appointed. When their time arrives, they can neither delay it by a single moment, nor indeed hasten it.*" (Verse 49) The term may end with physical destruction, as happened to earlier communities, or it may take a metaphorical form, which leaves a community lost, vanquished. This may last for some time and the community may then rise again, or it may be permanent and the community continues its decline. Individuals may remain but its existence as a community is over. All this takes place in accordance with God's law which never changes. There is no element of coincidence, favouritism or prejudice. Only those communities which fulfil the requirements of vigorous existence will live, and those which abandon them will decline or die. It is clearly established that the Muslim community will lead an active and solid life if it follows God's Messenger who calls on it to take what ensures its continued life. Belief in the Prophet and his message is not sufficient on its own. Action is needed as clearly defined by Islam in all fields of life. The code of living laid down by God must be followed and the values He has set must be adhered to. Otherwise, the term set will come to pass as per God's law.

The *sūrah* then adds a surprising touch. The unbelievers are led from a position where they challenge and ridicule to one where they are threatened: "*Say: 'Do but consider. Should His punishment befall you by night or by day, what could there be in it that the guilty ones should wish to hasten?'*" (Verse 50) God's punishment will come at a time and place unknown to human beings. It may come during the night when people are asleep, or in the day when they are awake and alert. Yet their alertness will not prevent it. So why should they wish to hasten it when it brings them no good?

While they are still in shock at the idea that their punishment may be very close, the next verse delivers an even greater shock, showing that punishment as having actually occurred when it has not. This is done to alert people's consciences and heighten their feelings to its reality. "*Is it, then, when it has come to pass that you will believe in it? Is it now, while so far you have been asking for it to come speedily?*" (Verse 51) The image shows the punishment as having been inflicted, and they as having believed in it. It is as if they are being rebuked now for not believing when they had every reason to do so before they were punished. To complete this future scene, painted as if it is happening now, the next verse says: "*Then it will be said to the wrongdoers: 'Taste the long-lasting torment. Is this requital anything other than the just due for what you used to do?'*" (Verse 52) Thus the *sūrah* takes us to the moment of reckoning and punishment while a few moments and a couple of verses earlier we are still in this life, listening to God's address to His Messenger, telling him of the fate of those who persist in denying his message.

The scene concludes with the unbelievers asking the Prophet about whether the warning and punishment are really true. Deep inside, they are shaken. The answer is emphatic, asserted with an oath that it is most certain: "*They will ask you: 'Is all this true?' Say: 'Yes, by my Lord. It is most certainly true, and you will never be beyond God's reach.'*" (Verse 53) That is a remarkable reply indeed: *'Yes, by my Lord.'* I know my Lord and His power, and I do not make a false oath. I only swear to assert the truth in a most serious manner: "*It is most certainly true, and you will never be beyond God's reach.*" (Verse 53) He can always gather you and bring you to the reckoning and then administer His reward or punishment, as you deserve.

While we are still following this question and answer, the *sūrah* suddenly takes us deep into the time when people are made to account for their deeds and their fate is determined. First a supposition is made: "*Should every wrongdoer possess all that the earth contains, he will gladly offer it all as ransom.*" (Verse 54)

But such a ransom will not be accepted, even should it be offered. But before the verse is concluded, we see that what was supposed has come to pass and the whole matter is done and finished with: "*They will harbour feelings of remorse when they see the suffering.*" (Verse 54) It has all come as a great surprise which leaves them powerless. The image here is one of gloomy faces, full of sadness, their lips unable to utter a word: "*Judgement will be passed on them in all fairness; and they will not be wronged.*" (Verse 54) The whole scene which started only half a verse earlier as a supposed probability is concluded as a reality and a foregone conclusion. This is an example of how the Qur'ān paints impressive scenes that penetrate into our consciousness.

A Cure for What is in People's Hearts

To emphasize the concept of resurrection and reckoning the *sūrah* gives us yet another image of God's power as it appears in the heavens and the earth, life and death. It is a quick scene serving to reassert that what God promises will come to pass. This is followed by an appeal to all mankind to make the best use of, and receive the maximum benefit from the Qur'ān, which brings them an admonition, guidance and a cure for all that their hearts may harbour. "*Indeed, to God belongs all that is in the heavens and earth. God's promise always comes true, but most of them do not know it. He alone gives life and causes death, and to Him you shall all return. Mankind, there has come to you an admonition from your Lord, a cure for all that may be in your hearts, and guidance and grace for all believers. Say: 'In God's bounty and grace, in this let them rejoice; for this is better than all that they may amass.'*" (Verses 55–58)

We have first a clear and loud proclamation: "*Indeed, to God belongs all that is in the heavens and earth.*" (Verse 55) The One to whom everything in heaven and on earth belongs is certainly able to make His promise come true. No barrier or impediment can prevent Him from fulfilling it: "*God's promise always comes true, but most of them do not know it.*" (Verse 55) In their ignorance, they doubt this or deny it altogether. Then another of His great attributes is mentioned: "*He alone gives life and causes death.*" (Verse 56) The One who controls life and death is able to bring His creation back to life and hold them to account: "*To Him you shall all return.*" (Verse 56) This is a passing comment added to a scene of resurrection, reckoning, reward and punishment.

Then follows a comprehensive address to all people: "*Mankind, there has come to you an admonition from your Lord, a cure for all that may be in your hearts, and guidance and grace for all believers.*" (Verse 57) It is in this very book, about the origin of which you entertain doubts, that you have an admonition from your Lord. It is neither a fabricated book nor are its contents written by a human being. This admonition is meant to revive your hearts and cure you of all superstition, doubt and worry. It is given by way of reassurance, security and peace. Whoever has faith will find in it guidance along the road that leads to success, and a mercy from all error and punishment: "*Say: 'In God's bounty and grace, in this let them rejoice; for this is better than all that they may amass.'*" (Verse 58)

They should rejoice at the favours and grace which God has given them in abundance. Wealth and other worldly riches deserve no rejoicing because they all come to an end. Rejoicing should be subliminal, releasing people from the lure of worldly comforts and riches. Such items are here to serve people in life, not be served, to be controlled and not in control. Islam does not despise worldly comforts, nor does it encourage people to turn away from them. It only gives them their proper position, so that people enjoy them whilst retaining their free will, setting for themselves higher goals. For such people, having faith is God's grace, and the fulfilment of what faith prescribes is their goal. Beyond this, believers feel that they own the world, while it has no control over them.

An authentic report mentions that when the tax levied on the land and farms of Iraq arrived at the outskirts of Madinah, 'Umar went out to have a look at it, accompanied by a servant. 'Umar started counting the camels that the tax included, but they were too numerous. 'Umar repeated the words: 'Praise be to God; Thanks to God.' His servant said: 'This is indeed part of God's bounty and grace.' 'Umar said: 'You are wrong. It is not to such matters that the Qur'ānic verse refers when it commands: "*Say: 'In God's bounty and grace, in this let them rejoice; for this is better than all that they may amass.'*" (Verse 58)

Those early Muslims had a different sense of values. They realized that the greatest aspects of God's grace were admonition and guidance. Money, wealth and even victory over their enemies were all matters that came as a result. Hence, victory was assured to them, and wealth came to them with no effort on their part. The way the community of believers must follow is very clear. It is the one clearly marked out by the Qur'ān, and easily followed by the early Muslims who developed a thorough understanding of Islam. It is the only way to follow.

Neither wealth and property, nor material values determine people's status and position in this present life, let alone the life to come. Material provisions, facilities and values may be the cause of human misery, not only in the next world, but also in our present life. Hence, it is necessary to have different values to guide human life. These values assign to material provisions and facilities their proper position in people's lives. It is values that can make such material comforts the source of real happiness. Moreover, it is the system that regulates the life of a certain community that determines the value of material provisions in the life of that community, making them either a source of happiness or a cause of misery; a means of elevation or a cause of downfall. Hence the emphasis on the value of their faith to the believers: *"Mankind, there has come to you an admonition from your Lord, a cure for all that may be in your hearts, and guidance and grace for all believers. Say: 'In God's bounty and grace, in this let them rejoice; for this is better than all that they may amass.'"* (Verses 57–58)

Rejoice at God's Grace

Those who were first to receive the Qur'ān recognized this superior value. Hence 'Umar denied that the camels and cattle he, as the ruler of the Muslim state, received in land tax were aspects of the bounty and grace God bestowed on them, and for which they should rejoice. 'Umar had a keen insight into the Islamic faith. Hence, he realized that the most important aspects of God's grace and bounty were what God had revealed to them: an admonition from their Lord, a cure for what is in people's hearts, as well as guidance and mercy for believers. Material wealth had nothing to do with it. They appreciated the great change which Islam had brought about in their lives. They were able to remove themselves from the abyss of ignorance to something far superior.

Islam brings about people's freedom from enslavement to others, and ensures their submission to God alone. This determines that their concepts, values, morals and manners are placed on a much higher level. Their whole life is transformed from bondage to freedom. Material provisions, facilities and power all come as a result of such freedom, as happened in the history of the early Muslims. When they gained power and became the undisputed masters, they showed the rest of humanity how to believe in God, so that they too would enjoy what God bestows of His grace.

Those who lay too much emphasis on material values are the enemies of humanity. What they advocate is not promoted with good intent. Rather, what they want is to destroy the values inculcated by faith and the belief which makes people aspire to something higher than animal needs, without overlooking their own human needs. It gives them further necessities which they seek to fulfil together with their needs for food, shelter and sex.

Much fuss is being made of material values and production, making them people's central preoccupation. Thus human beings become no more than machines, whilst spiritual and moral values are lost and trampled on. Yet this does not come about by itself; it is all according to an elaborate plan which seeks to replace old idols with new ones, and treat these as the supreme power that controls all values.

When material production is thus transformed into an idol around which people turn in reverence, all values and considerations, including morality, family, honour, freedom and security, are sacrificed for its sake. Nothing is allowed to have a negative effect on material production. If anyone disputes that this is a worshipped idol, let him tell us what a worshipped idol is like. It is not necessary that idols be made of stone or wood. An idol may take the form of a certain value, a concept or principle.

The supreme value then must continue to be assigned to God's bounty and grace, epitomized in His guidance which cures people's hearts, gives them their freedom and attaches more importance to human values. Under this supreme value, people can continue to enjoy, and benefit from, the provisions God has given them and the material comforts generated by industrialization. They will feel their burden lightened by such comforts, but they will be free of the pressures characteristic of *jāhiliyyah* societies.

Without such a supreme value, material provisions, facilities and production become a curse that brings misery and distress to all humanity. In the absence of this supreme value, these are used to enhance animal values and needs at the expense of human ones. God certainly tells the truth as He says: "*Mankind, there has come to you an admonition from your Lord, a cure for all that may be in your hearts, and guidance and grace for all believers. Say: 'In God's bounty and grace, in this let them rejoice; for this is better than all that they may amass.'*" (Verses 57–58)

God's Grace and People's Ingratitude

Having highlighted God's bounty and grace, represented by His revelations and the guidance and cure they provide, the *sūrah* now speaks of people's practices that are at variance with God's guidance.

These are nothing less than an assault on God's authority whereby He makes things lawful or unlawful.

> *Say: 'Do but consider all the means of sustenance that God has bestowed on you! Some of it you then made unlawful, and some lawful.' Say: 'Has God given you leave to do so, or do you fabricate lies against God?' But what will they think, those who invent lies against God, on the Day of Resurrection? God is truly bountiful to mankind, but most of them are ungrateful.* (Verses 59–60)

The Prophet is instructed to ask them about the sustenance God has given them, especially in light of the fact that everything they have has been bestowed on them by Him. All this they should use in accordance with what He has legislated. Instead, though, they use it as they desire. Furthermore, without sanction from God, they make some of it lawful and some unlawful. In effect, an enactment of legislation, which is a manifestation of sovereignty. Yet sovereignty belongs to God alone. Hence they do what God has not given them permission to do. "*Say: 'Has God given you leave to do so, or do you fabricate lies against God?'*" (Verse 59)

This issue is frequently raised in the Qur'ān, because, next to believing in God's oneness, it is the most important issue. Indeed it is the main aspect of translating belief into reality. To acknowledge that God is the One who creates and sustains entails that He is the One to be worshipped and the One who determines all matters relating to human life. These include the means of sustenance God has provided. The unbelievers in Arabia acknowledged God as the Creator and the Provider of sustenance, as do some who call themselves Muslims today. Like these latter-day self-styled Muslims, those unbelievers also gave themselves the authority to prohibit part of what God gave them and to make others lawful. In this way then the Qur'ān paints them as both contrary and idolaters. The same description applies to all who are guilty of such contradiction, no matter what labels they give themselves. Islam is not a title that people attach to their names; it is a belief with practical implications.

Also like today's self-styled Muslims, the pagan Arabs used to claim that they had God's sanction for their actions, or what they even described as God's law. In *Sūrah* 6, Cattle, God mentions some of their claim: "*They say: 'Such cattle and crops are forbidden. None may eat of them save those whom we permit' – so they falsely claim. Other cattle they declare to be forbidden to burden their backs; and there are cattle over which they do not pronounce God's name, inventing [in all this] a lie against Him. He will surely requite them for their inventions.*" (6: 138) As is clear from this verse, they used to falsely claim that God wants this and not that, just as some Muslims today claim that what they legislate is God's own law.

God puts the whole issue clearly in front of them. He asks what they think His attitude will be like on the Day of Judgement when they make these false claims against Him: "*But what will they think, those who invent lies against God, on the Day of Resurrection?*" (Verse 60) This verse refers to all those who are guilty of fabrication against God. What do such people think their destiny will be on the Day of Judgement? It is a question to test even the most stubborn and hardened of unbelievers.

A Cure for Hearts

"*God is truly bountiful to mankind, but most of them are ungrateful.*" (Verse 60) God is always bountiful to mankind. He has placed on earth and in the universe the means of man's material sustenance. He has further given man the ability to know its sources as well as the natural laws that affect those sources, and to know how to enrich its variety of shapes and forms through analysis and synthesis. Indeed everything in the universe and every talent and potential people have is provided by God. Moreover, His bounty is epitomized in the code of living He has laid down, providing guidance for mankind and a cure for anything that may trouble their hearts and minds. When they implement this, they tap their highest potential and follow a way that brings about the best in the life of this world and in the life to come. They establish harmony between their human life and the life of the universe around them.

But most people do not show any gratitude for God's bounty. Instead they digress from His code, and ascribe partners to Him. This leads to their distress and misery, because they make no use of what God has revealed as a cure for what may trouble their hearts.

This is a profound truism. The Qur'ān is a cure for people's hearts in every connotation of the word 'cure'. It penetrates into people's hearts and minds just like a cure penetrates into a body weakened by illness. It makes its way through with its powerful rhythm and instructions which alert the natural human receptive mechanism, to open up and respond. It also penetrates into people's minds with its laws and regulations which guarantee the minimum conflict between groups and communities. It generates reassurance that justice will be done, that goodness will triumph and that the end will be good. Furthermore, it embraces numerous meanings and connotations that no human expression can imply. Yet they are all made clear in this remarkable verse.

Most people do not show any gratitude. They remain ungrateful although God is aware of everything, whether apparent or hidden. Nothing in the heavens or on earth escapes His knowledge. This is added here in order to awaken people's hearts and consciousness. It is followed by reassurance to the Prophet and his followers of God's care: the unbelievers who associate partners with God will not be able to cause them any harm.

Confusion Compounded

In whatever business you may be engaged, and whatever part you may recite of the Qur'ān, and whatever deed you [mankind] may do, We will be your witnesses from the moment you are engaged with it. Not even an atom's weight [of anything whatsoever] on earth or in heaven escapes your Lord, nor is there anything smaller or larger than that, but is recorded in a clear book. For certain, those who are close to God have nothing to fear, nor shall they grieve; for they do believe and remain God-fearing. Theirs are the glad tidings in the life of this world and in the life to come: there is no changing the word of God. This is the supreme triumph. Be not grieved by what they say. All might and glory belong to God alone. He alone hears all and knows all. Indeed, to God belong all those who are in the heavens and earth. Those who invoke other beings beside God do not follow any real partners with Him. They follow mere

111

conjecture, and they utter nothing but falsehood. It is He who has made the night for you, so that you may have rest, and the day, so that you may see. In this there are certainly signs for those who listen. (Verses 61–67)

The first verse in this passage reminds us that God is with us in all situations. *"In whatever business you may be engaged, and whatever part you may recite of the Qur'ān, and whatever deed you [mankind] may do, We will be your witnesses from the moment you are engaged with it."* (Verse 61) It is a feeling that brings reassurance and awe at the same time. For how is it that God is with us, witnessing whatever we do? God in His almightiness, the Creator who controls everything in the universe with total ease, is with each human being who, without God's care, is no more than a small particle floating aimlessly in the air. This is indeed awesome, yet at the same time, reassuring, inspiring us with confidence and security. We are not alone without good care and protection. God is with us at all times: *"In whatever business you may be engaged, and whatever part you may recite of the Qur'ān, and whatever deed you [mankind] may do, We will be your witnesses from the moment you are engaged with it."* (Verse 61) It is not merely God's knowledge that is complete, but His care and watch are also total: *"Not even an atom's weight [of anything whatsoever] on earth or in heaven escapes your Lord, nor is there anything smaller or larger than that, but is recorded in a clear book."* (Verse 61)

Let our imagination think of all the particles and atoms that are on earth or in heaven, and of what is smaller and larger, then remember that God's knowledge encompasses all. We are bound to experience awe and feel our own humility, but faith will reassure us and remind us of the peace that we should feel in God's presence. With such peace and reassurance, a proclamation is made: *"For certain, those who are close to God have nothing to fear, nor shall they grieve; for they do believe and remain God-fearing. Theirs are the glad tidings in the life of this world and in the life to come: there is no changing the word of God. This is the supreme triumph."* (Verses 62–64)

How could those who are close to God feel fear or experience grief when God is with them at every moment and in every action? These are the ones who watch God in all situations, trying always to do what pleases Him: "*They do believe and remain God-fearing.*" (Verse 63) What could cause them to feel fear or grieve when they have been given glad tidings that apply to both their present life and to their future life? This is a true promise that is never changed and never fails, for there is no changing of God's word. Indeed, "*this is the supreme triumph.*" (Verse 64)

Those whom the *sūrah* describes as being close to God are the true believers who are God-fearing. Faith is something that penetrates deep into the heart and to which credit is given by action, which, in turn means the implementation of God's commandments. This is how the concept of being close to God should be understood. By extension, those who command wealth and influence will achieve nothing: "*Be not grieved by what they say. All might and glory belong to God alone. He alone hears all and knows all.*" (Verse 65)

In this instance, might and glory are attributed to God alone. In a different context in the Qur'ān, they are also said to belong to the Prophet and the believers. Here the *sūrah* is speaking of God's protection of the believers, which makes it more fitting that might and glory should be shown as belonging to God alone, as indeed they are. The Prophet and the believers derive their power and glory from Him, while other people receive nothing of them at all. The mighty Quraysh were only a group of such other people. The Prophet (peace be upon him) enjoys God's protection, so he should not be saddened by what they say. God, who hears their plotting and knows their scheming, is with him, giving him and his followers all the protection they need.

Everyone in the heavens and the earth, whether human, *jinn* or angels, obedient or disobedient, are subject to His power: "*Indeed, to God belong all those who are in the heavens and earth.*" (Verse 66) The reference here is to animate creatures in order to emphasize that all of them, weak or strong, are under God's control. "*Those who invoke other beings beside God do not follow any real partners with Him.*" (Verse 66) Those presumed partners have no real partnership of any kind with God. Indeed those who claim them to be God's partners are uncertain of their claims: "*They follow mere conjecture, and they utter nothing but falsehood.*" (Verse 66)

This is followed by a statement portraying some aspects of God's power as reflected in the universe. These aspects are often overlooked because of familiarity: "*It is He who has made the night for you, so that you may have rest, and the day, so that you may see. In this there are certainly signs for those who listen.*" (Verse 67) The One who controls all stillness and movement, who makes the night a time for rest, and gives the day its light, enabling people to act and see, has absolute control over all people. Hence, He is able to protect those who are close to Him: "*In this there are certainly signs for those who listen.*" (Verse 67) They do not stop at the mere listening, but they also reflect and contemplate.

The Qur'ān often employs scenes from the universe when it discusses the subject of Godhead and servitude, because the universe, its existence and details, is a powerful witness which imposes its argument on human nature. The Qur'ān also addresses people drawing their attention to the harmony in their relationship with the universe. They actually feel this in their lives. The night in which they rest, and the day during which they are able to see, are two phenomena closely linked to their lives. The harmony between these phenomena and their lives is felt by all human beings, even those who are not conversant with scientific matters. Their innate nature understands the silent language of the universe.

Human beings were not deaf to the language of the universe until modern science revealed its secrets! Rather, people understand this language by their natural ability. Hence it is not surprising that God referred to this language so many centuries ago. Yet this language is self-renewing, taking into account every increase and progress in human knowledge. Indeed the richer people's knowledge, the greater their understanding of the language of the universe, provided that their hearts are enlightened with faith, and their minds alert to its address.

Fabricated Claims of Divinity

Among those who associate partners with God are those who allege that He has a son. Far be it from Him to need a son. The pagan Arabs in similar vein used to claim that the angels were God's daughters. The verses we are now looking at tackle this type of fabrication. They begin with providing irrefutable arguments that are relevant to this world and warn against punishment in the hereafter.

They say: 'God has taken unto Himself a son.' Limitless is He in His glory. Self-sufficient is He. To Him belongs all that is in the heavens and earth. No evidence whatever have you for this. Would you say about God something which you do not know? Say: 'Those who invent falsehood about God shall not be successful. They may have a brief enjoyment in this world, but then to Us they must return, and We will then make them suffer severe torment for their unbelief.'
(Verses 68–70)

The belief alleging that God has a son is naïve, based on a faulty concept of Godhead. One that does not appreciate the huge gulf between the nature of the eternal God, and the nature of mortal humans. Nor does it appreciate the great wisdom that allows mortals to procreate, so that they compensate for the short duration of their lives. This shortcoming does not apply to God.

Human beings die, and human life extends to an appointed time. It is God's wisdom that has allowed human life to continue until it reaches its ultimate point. Such continuity is made possible through procreation. Human beings get older and weaker. When they have children, their offspring compensate for their creeping weakness with the vitality of their youth, helping to continue the process of building human life on earth. Moreover, the young provide the necessary help to the elderly through their years of weakness. People also have to struggle within their environment, and against their enemies, whether human or animal. Hence they need support which is more likely to come from offspring. People also seek to have abundance of what they earn, and their children help them with their efforts which increase their earnings.

The same applies to all aspects that God has made necessary for the building of human life on earth, until the time appointed when God's will concerning its future is to be accomplished. None of this applies to God who does not need to have any continuity through offspring, or help in old age, or support in any endeavour. He has no need of anything. Hence there is no need for Him to have a son because His nature is such that He needs nothing to be accomplished by outside help. God has made human beings reproductive because, by nature, they have a definite need for such continuity.

Hence, the false claim that, *'God has taken unto Himself a son,'* is rebuffed by the assertion: *"Limitless is He in His glory. Self-sufficient is He. To Him belongs all that is in the heavens and earth."* (Verse 68)

"Limitless is He in His glory." This is said by way of emphasizing that His sublime nature is far above this level of thinking. *"Self-sufficient is He."* This is to stress that He is in no need of anything whatsoever, whether real or imaginary, which requires the presence of a son. It is well known that needs are the causes of what satisfies them. Nothing is given existence without a need or a purpose. *"To Him belongs all that is in the heavens and earth."* (Verse 68) Everything belongs to Him. He does not need a son in order to gain anything whatsoever. Hence, attributing a son to Him is idle play, and far be it from Him to admit idle play.

The Qur'ān does not enter into any theoretical debate about the nature of God or man of the type that prevails in many philosophies. Instead, it deals with the subject itself. Here it only briefly mentions man's need of offspring. This does not, however, apply to God who owns all that is in heavens and earth. This should be sufficient either to convince or silence them, without any need for theoretical argument.

They are then brought face to face with the reality which shows that they have no proof to support their claims. The Qur'ānic verse uses the term *'sultan'* which means authority, in place of 'evidence' because authority provides strength, and the one who has a proof to support his claim is in a position of strength: *"No evidence whatever have you for this."* (Verse 68) Indeed you have no argument, let alone solid proof: *"Would you say about God something which you do not know?"* (Verse 68)

To say something concerning a subject about which one knows nothing is unbecoming of intelligent human beings. When what is said is fabricated against God Himself, it becomes a terrible offence. For one thing, it contradicts all that is due to God of worship, respect and glorification, because it attributes to Him all that is associated with an event of imperfection and inability. Moreover, it is based on a faulty concept of the relationship between the Creator and His creation, leading to further errors in all relations between people, since the latter are essentially based on the former. All the authority claimed by the priests of pagan religions or by the Christian churches is based on the misconception of the relationship between God and His 'angel daughters' or between Him and Jesus Christ who is alleged to be His son. Moreover the concept of original sin, which has led to the practice of confession, and giving Christ's church an intermediary role between human beings and the One whom they describe as Christ's father, stems from a basic error in understanding the relationship between the Creator and His creation.

Hence the matter is not merely an erroneous belief, but rather, it is man's whole life that is affected. All the hostility that took place between the Church and scientists, and even between it and human intellect, is based on this fundamental error. This hostility was only brought to rest when society got shot of the Church's authority, and even of religion itself. Once the relationship between God and His creation is ill-conceived, much evil is bound to happen. Humanity has suffered this evil whenever materialistic doctrines have corrupted human life.

Hence the Islamic faith has taken extra care to make this relationship perfectly clear. God is the Creator, the Eternal, the Sustainer. The relationship between Him and all people, without exception, is that which exists between the Creator and His creation. The universe, life and the living exist according to certain laws that God has put into operation. These never fail and they apply to all people in equal measure, without favouritism or prejudice. Whoever observes these rules will be successful, and whoever puts them aside will end up the loser. All people will return to God, and He accepts no intercession. Everyone comes to Him on his or her own. They will have their individual reward for what they have done in this life. God will not treat anyone with injustice.

It is a simple faith that admits no erroneous interpretation. It does not take the human mind along any mysterious or confused way. Everyone stands in front of God in the same position. Everyone is addressed by God's message and is required to implement it. This ensures that relations between people are set on the right footing, as a result of forging the right and solid relationship between them and God.

"Say: 'Those who invent falsehood about God shall not be successful.'" (Verse 69) They will have no prosperity whatsoever, whether in this

life or in the life to come. True success is that which results from leading a life that is consistent with the laws God has set in operation. These lead to all goodness, elevating human beings to a higher level of humanity and setting their social structure on the right basis. Prosperity is not limited to material progress. Such progress is only superficial and temporary if it is combined with the destruction of human values, replacing them with animal values.

"*They may have a brief enjoyment in this world, but then to Us they must return, and We will then make them suffer severe torment for their unbelief.*" (Verse 70) Their enjoyment is brief and temporary. It has no permanent link with the enjoyment reserved for the hereafter. Indeed, it is followed by 'severe torment' for turning away from the laws of nature which God has devised.

3

Unheeded Warnings

Relate to them the story of Noah. He said to his people: 'My people! If my presence among you and my reminders to you of God's revelations are repugnant to you – well, in God have I placed my trust. Decide, then, what you are going to do, and [seek the help of] those whom you associate as partners with God. Be clear about your course of action, leaving no room for uncertainty, then carry out against me whatever you may have decided and give me no respite. (71)

وَٱتْلُ عَلَيْهِمْ نَبَأَ نُوحٍ إِذْ قَالَ لِقَوْمِهِۦ يَٰقَوْمِ إِن كَانَ كَبُرَ عَلَيْكُم مَّقَامِى وَتَذْكِيرِى بِـَٔايَٰتِ ٱللَّهِ فَعَلَى ٱللَّهِ تَوَكَّلْتُ فَأَجْمِعُوٓا۟ أَمْرَكُمْ وَشُرَكَآءَكُمْ ثُمَّ لَا يَكُنْ أَمْرُكُمْ عَلَيْكُمْ غُمَّةً ثُمَّ ٱقْضُوٓا۟ إِلَىَّ وَلَا تُنظِرُونِ ٧١

But if you turn away, [remember that] I have asked of you no reward whatsoever. My reward rests with none but God. I have been commanded to be one of those who surrender themselves to Him.' (72)

فَإِن تَوَلَّيْتُمْ فَمَا سَأَلْتُكُم مِّنْ أَجْرٍ إِنْ أَجْرِىَ إِلَّا عَلَى ٱللَّهِ وَأُمِرْتُ أَنْ أَكُونَ مِنَ ٱلْمُسْلِمِينَ ٧٢

But they disbelieved him. So We saved him and all those who joined him in the ark, and made them inherit the earth. And We drowned the others who denied Our revelations. Reflect on the fate of those who were fore-warned. (73)

فَكَذَّبُوهُ فَنَجَّيْنَهُ وَمَن مَّعَهُ فِي ٱلْفُلْكِ وَجَعَلْنَهُمْ خَلَٰئِفَ وَأَغْرَقْنَا ٱلَّذِينَ كَذَّبُواْ بِـَٔايَٰتِنَا فَٱنظُرْ كَيْفَ كَانَ عَٰقِبَةُ ٱلْمُنذَرِينَ ٧٣

Then after him We sent forth other messengers to their respective peoples, and they brought them clear evidence of the truth, but they would not believe in what they had once denied. Thus it is that We seal the hearts of those who transgress. (74)

ثُمَّ بَعَثْنَا مِنۢ بَعْدِهِ رُسُلًا إِلَىٰ قَوْمِهِمْ فَجَآءُوهُم بِٱلْبَيِّنَٰتِ فَمَا كَانُواْ لِيُؤْمِنُواْ بِمَا كَذَّبُواْ بِهِ مِن قَبْلُ كَذَٰلِكَ نَطْبَعُ عَلَىٰ قُلُوبِ ٱلْمُعْتَدِينَ ٧٤

Then after those [prophets] We sent Moses and Aaron with Our signs to Pharaoh and his nobles, but they persisted in their arrogance, for they were hardened offenders. (75)

ثُمَّ بَعَثْنَا مِنۢ بَعْدِهِم مُّوسَىٰ وَهَٰرُونَ إِلَىٰ فِرْعَوْنَ وَمَلَإِيْهِ بِـَٔايَٰتِنَا فَٱسْتَكْبَرُواْ وَكَانُواْ قَوْمًا مُّجْرِمِينَ ٧٥

When the truth came to them from Us, they said: 'This is clearly nothing but sorcery.' (76)

فَلَمَّا جَآءَهُمُ ٱلْحَقُّ مِنْ عِندِنَا قَالُواْ إِنَّ هَٰذَا لَسِحْرٌ مُّبِينٌ ٧٦

Moses replied: 'Do you say this to the truth when it has come to you? Can this be sorcery? But sorcerers will never be successful.' (77)

قَالَ مُوسَىٰٓ أَتَقُولُونَ لِلْحَقِّ لَمَّا جَآءَكُمْ أَسِحْرٌ هَٰذَا وَلَا يُفْلِحُ ٱلسَّٰحِرُونَ ٧٧

They said: 'Have you come to turn us away from what we found our forefathers believing in, so that the two of you might become supreme in the land? We will never believe in you.' (78)

قَالُوٓاْ أَجِئۡتَنَا لِتَلۡفِتَنَا عَمَّا وَجَدۡنَا عَلَيۡهِ ءَابَآءَنَا وَتَكُونَ لَكُمَا ٱلۡكِبۡرِيَآءُ فِي ٱلۡأَرۡضِ وَمَا نَحۡنُ لَكُمَا بِمُؤۡمِنِينَ ﴿٧٨﴾

Then Pharaoh commanded: 'Bring before me every learned sorcerer.' (79)

وَقَالَ فِرۡعَوۡنُ ٱئۡتُونِي بِكُلِّ سَٰحِرٍ عَلِيمٖ ﴿٧٩﴾

And when the sorcerers came, Moses said to them: 'Throw whatever you may wish to throw.' (80)

فَلَمَّا جَآءَ ٱلسَّحَرَةُ قَالَ لَهُم مُّوسَىٰٓ أَلۡقُواْ مَآ أَنتُم مُّلۡقُونَ ﴿٨٠﴾

And when they had thrown, Moses said to them: 'What you have contrived is mere sorcery which God will certainly bring to nothing. God does not further the work of those who spread corruption. (81)

فَلَمَّآ أَلۡقَوۡاْ قَالَ مُوسَىٰ مَا جِئۡتُم بِهِ ٱلسِّحۡرُۖ إِنَّ ٱللَّهَ سَيُبۡطِلُهُۥٓ إِنَّ ٱللَّهَ لَا يُصۡلِحُ عَمَلَ ٱلۡمُفۡسِدِينَ ﴿٨١﴾

By His words, God proves the truth to be true, much as the guilty may dislike it.' (82)

وَيُحِقُّ ٱللَّهُ ٱلۡحَقَّ بِكَلِمَٰتِهِۦ وَلَوۡ كَرِهَ ٱلۡمُجۡرِمُونَ ﴿٨٢﴾

None except a few of his people believed in Moses, for they feared Pharaoh and their nobles, lest they persecute them. Surely Pharaoh was mighty on earth and was indeed given to excesses. (83)

فَمَآ ءَامَنَ لِمُوسَىٰٓ إِلَّا ذُرِّيَّةٞ مِّن قَوۡمِهِۦ عَلَىٰ خَوۡفٖ مِّن فِرۡعَوۡنَ وَمَلَإِيْهِمۡ أَن يَفۡتِنَهُمۡۚ وَإِنَّ فِرۡعَوۡنَ لَعَالٖ فِي ٱلۡأَرۡضِ وَإِنَّهُۥ لَمِنَ ٱلۡمُسۡرِفِينَ ﴿٨٣﴾

Moses said: 'My people, if you believe in God, then place your trust in Him – if you have truly surrendered yourselves to Him.' (84)

وَقَالَ مُوسَىٰ يَٰقَوْمِ إِن كُنتُمْ ءَامَنتُم بِٱللَّهِ فَعَلَيْهِ تَوَكَّلُوٓاْ إِن كُنتُم مُّسْلِمِينَ ﴿٨٤﴾

They replied: 'In God have we placed our trust. Our Lord, do not let us suffer at the hands of evil-doing people. (85)

فَقَالُواْ عَلَى ٱللَّهِ تَوَكَّلْنَا رَبَّنَا لَا تَجْعَلْنَا فِتْنَةً لِّلْقَوْمِ ٱلظَّٰلِمِينَ ﴿٨٥﴾

Save us, by Your grace, from the people who disbelieve.' (86)

وَنَجِّنَا بِرَحْمَتِكَ مِنَ ٱلْقَوْمِ ٱلْكَٰفِرِينَ ﴿٨٦﴾

And thus did We inspire Moses and his brother: 'Take for your people some houses in Egypt, and make your houses places of worship, and be constant in prayer.' And give glad tidings to all believers. (87)

وَأَوْحَيْنَآ إِلَىٰ مُوسَىٰ وَأَخِيهِ أَن تَبَوَّءَا لِقَوْمِكُمَا بِمِصْرَ بُيُوتًا وَٱجْعَلُواْ بُيُوتَكُمْ قِبْلَةً وَأَقِيمُواْ ٱلصَّلَوٰةَ وَبَشِّرِ ٱلْمُؤْمِنِينَ ﴿٨٧﴾

Moses said, 'Our Lord! You have bestowed on Pharaoh and his nobles splendour and riches in this life, with the result that they have been leading people astray from Your path. Our Lord! Wipe out their riches and harden their hearts, so that they do not believe until they face the grievous suffering.' (88)

وَقَالَ مُوسَىٰ رَبَّنَآ إِنَّكَ ءَاتَيْتَ فِرْعَوْنَ وَمَلَأَهُۥ زِينَةً وَأَمْوَٰلًا فِى ٱلْحَيَوٰةِ ٱلدُّنْيَا رَبَّنَا لِيُضِلُّواْ عَن سَبِيلِكَ رَبَّنَا ٱطْمِسْ عَلَىٰٓ أَمْوَٰلِهِمْ وَٱشْدُدْ عَلَىٰ قُلُوبِهِمْ فَلَا يُؤْمِنُواْ حَتَّىٰ يَرَوُاْ ٱلْعَذَابَ ٱلْأَلِيمَ ﴿٨٨﴾

He replied: 'Your prayer is accepted. Continue, both of you, steadfastly on the right path, and do not follow the path of those who are devoid of knowledge.' (89)

قَالَ قَدْ أُجِيبَت دَّعْوَتُكُمَا فَٱسْتَقِيمَا وَلَا تَتَّبِعَآنِّ سَبِيلَ ٱلَّذِينَ لَا يَعْلَمُونَ ﴿٨٩﴾

And We brought the Children of Israel across the sea; but Pharaoh and his legions pursued them with tyranny and aggression. But as he was about to drown, Pharaoh said: 'I have come to believe that there is no deity other than Him in whom the Children of Israel believe, and to Him I surrender myself.' (90)

وَجَٰوَزْنَا بِبَنِيٓ إِسْرَٰٓءِيلَ ٱلْبَحْرَ فَأَتْبَعَهُمْ فِرْعَوْنُ وَجُنُودُهُۥ بَغْيًا وَعَدْوًا حَتَّىٰٓ إِذَآ أَدْرَكَهُ ٱلْغَرَقُ قَالَ ءَامَنتُ أَنَّهُۥ لَآ إِلَٰهَ إِلَّا ٱلَّذِىٓ ءَامَنَتْ بِهِۦ بَنُوٓا۟ إِسْرَٰٓءِيلَ وَأَنَا۠ مِنَ ٱلْمُسْلِمِينَ ﴿٩٠﴾

[But God said:] 'Only now? But before this you were rebelling [against Us], and you spread corruption in the land. (91)

ءَآلْـَٰٔنَ وَقَدْ عَصَيْتَ قَبْلُ وَكُنتَ مِنَ ٱلْمُفْسِدِينَ ﴿٩١﴾

But today We shall save only your body, so that you may become a sign to those who will come after you; for a great many people do not heed Our signs.' (92)

فَٱلْيَوْمَ نُنَجِّيكَ بِبَدَنِكَ لِتَكُونَ لِمَنْ خَلْفَكَ ءَايَةً وَإِنَّ كَثِيرًا مِّنَ ٱلنَّاسِ عَنْ ءَايَٰتِنَا لَغَٰفِلُونَ ﴿٩٢﴾

We settled the Children of Israel in a most goodly abode and We provided for them sustenance out of the good things of life. It was not until knowledge was given them that they began to disagree

وَلَقَدْ بَوَّأْنَا بَنِىٓ إِسْرَٰٓءِيلَ مُبَوَّأَ صِدْقٍ وَرَزَقْنَٰهُم مِّنَ ٱلطَّيِّبَٰتِ فَمَا ٱخْتَلَفُوا۟ حَتَّىٰ

among themselves. Your Lord will judge between them on the Day of Resurrection regarding that on which they differed. (93)

جَآءَهُمُ ٱلۡعِلۡمُ إِنَّ رَبَّكَ يَقۡضِى بَيۡنَهُمۡ يَوۡمَ ٱلۡقِيَٰمَةِ فِيمَا كَانُواْ فِيهِ يَخۡتَلِفُونَ ﴿٩٣﴾

If you are in doubt concerning what We have bestowed on you from on high, ask those who read the Scriptures [revealed] before you. It is surely the truth that has come to you from your Lord. Do not, then, be among the doubters. (94)

فَإِن كُنتَ فِى شَكٍّ مِّمَّآ أَنزَلۡنَآ إِلَيۡكَ فَسۡـَٔلِ ٱلَّذِينَ يَقۡرَءُونَ ٱلۡكِتَٰبَ مِن قَبۡلِكَ لَقَدۡ جَآءَكَ ٱلۡحَقُّ مِن رَّبِّكَ فَلَا تَكُونَنَّ مِنَ ٱلۡمُمۡتَرِينَ ﴿٩٤﴾

And do not be among those who deny God's revelations, for then you shall be among those who are lost. (95)

وَلَا تَكُونَنَّ مِنَ ٱلَّذِينَ كَذَّبُواْ بِـَٔايَٰتِ ٱللَّهِ فَتَكُونَ مِنَ ٱلۡخَٰسِرِينَ ﴿٩٥﴾

Surely, those against whom your Lord's word [of judgement] has come true will not believe, (96)

إِنَّ ٱلَّذِينَ حَقَّتۡ عَلَيۡهِمۡ كَلِمَتُ رَبِّكَ لَا يُؤۡمِنُونَ ﴿٩٦﴾

even though every sign should come to their knowledge, until they are faced with the grievous suffering. (97)

وَلَوۡ جَآءَتۡهُمۡ كُلُّ ءَايَةٍ حَتَّىٰ يَرَوُاْ ٱلۡعَذَابَ ٱلۡأَلِيمَ ﴿٩٧﴾

Had it believed, every community would have profited by its faith. It was so only with Jonah's people. When they believed, We lifted from them the suffering of disgrace in this life, and allowed them to enjoy things for a while. (98)

فَلَوۡلَا كَانَتۡ قَرۡيَةٌ ءَامَنَتۡ فَنَفَعَهَآ إِيمَٰنُهَآ إِلَّا قَوۡمَ يُونُسَ لَمَّآ ءَامَنُواْ كَشَفۡنَا عَنۡهُمۡ عَذَابَ ٱلۡخِزۡيِ فِى ٱلۡحَيَوٰةِ ٱلدُّنۡيَا وَمَتَّعۡنَٰهُمۡ إِلَىٰ حِينٍ ﴿٩٨﴾

Had your Lord so willed, all people on earth, in their entirety, would have believed. Do you, then, try to compel people to believe? (99)

وَلَوْ شَآءَ رَبُّكَ لَآمَنَ مَن فِى ٱلْأَرْضِ كُلُّهُمْ جَمِيعًا أَفَأَنتَ تُكْرِهُ ٱلنَّاسَ حَتَّىٰ يَكُونُوا۟ مُؤْمِنِينَ ٩٩

No human being can believe, except by God's leave. It is He who lays abomination on those who will not use their reason. (100)

وَمَا كَانَ لِنَفْسٍ أَن تُؤْمِنَ إِلَّا بِإِذْنِ ٱللَّهِ وَيَجْعَلُ ٱلرِّجْسَ عَلَى ٱلَّذِينَ لَا يَعْقِلُونَ ١٠٠

Say: 'Consider all that there is in the heavens and the earth.' But of what benefit could all signs and warnings be to people who will not believe? (101)

قُلِ ٱنظُرُوا۟ مَاذَا فِى ٱلسَّمَـٰوَٰتِ وَٱلْأَرْضِ وَمَا تُغْنِى ٱلْءَايَـٰتُ وَٱلنُّذُرُ عَن قَوْمٍ لَّا يُؤْمِنُونَ ١٠١

What are they waiting for except a repetition of the days [of calamity] experienced by those who have gone before them? Say: 'Wait, then, if you will. I am also waiting.' (102)

فَهَلْ يَنتَظِرُونَ إِلَّا مِثْلَ أَيَّامِ ٱلَّذِينَ خَلَوْا۟ مِن قَبْلِهِمْ قُلْ فَٱنتَظِرُوا۟ إِنِّى مَعَكُم مِّنَ ٱلْمُنتَظِرِينَ ١٠٢

Thereupon, We save Our messengers and those who believe. Thus have We willed it upon Ourselves: We save those who believe. (103)

ثُمَّ نُنَجِّى رُسُلَنَا وَٱلَّذِينَ ءَامَنُوا۟ كَذَٰلِكَ حَقًّا عَلَيْنَا نُنجِ ٱلْمُؤْمِنِينَ ١٠٣

Preview

Reference was made earlier in the *surah* to ancient communities and what happened to them when they denied the messages of their prophets. Another generation was made to succeed them: *"Indeed, We destroyed generations before your time when they persisted in their wrongdoing. The messengers sent to them brought them veritable evidence of the truth, but they would not believe. Thus do We reward the guilty. Then We made you their successors on earth, so that We might see how you behave."* (Verses 13–14)

Another reference was made to the fact that every community had a messenger sent to them to deliver God's message. *"To every community was sent a messenger. It is when their messenger had come to them that judgement was passed on them in all fairness; and never are they wronged."* (Verse 47)

Now the *surah* speaks in more detail about such earlier messages, highlighting certain aspects of the stories of Noah and Moses. The consequences of denying God's messages are emphasized in both accounts. A brief reference is also made to Jonah, whose community accepted the faith when they were about to be overtaken by God's punishment, and they were thus saved. This serves to encourage those who deny God to stop so that they spare themselves an end similar to that experienced by Noah's people and Pharaoh and his host.

The previous passage concluded with an order to the Prophet Muḥammad (peace be upon him) to declare that those who fabricate lies against God and associate partners with Him will come to an awful end: *"Say: "Those who invent falsehood about God shall not be successful. They may have a brief enjoyment in this world, but then to Us they must return, and We will then make them suffer severe torment for their unbelief.""* (Verses 69–70) This declaration follows a reassurance given to the Prophet that the believers *"who are close to God have nothing to fear, nor shall they grieve."* (Verse 62) The Prophet is also encouraged not to pay much attention to what the unbelievers say: *"Be not grieved by what they say. All might and glory belong to God alone. He alone hears all and knows all."* (Verse 65)

Now the Prophet is instructed to relate to them Noah's story and how he challenged his people. He was then saved with those believers

126

who followed him, while the unbelievers who were much stronger and larger in number were destroyed.

These stories serve to emphasize the meaning of the preceding passages. In fact, all stories mentioned in the Qur'ān serve a definite purpose. They are related in different styles, highlighting different episodes as may befit the context in which they occur. Here the stories of earlier prophets highlight the absurdity of the Makkans towards the Prophet Muḥammad (peace be upon him) and his small group of believers. They also stress the fact that those believers were firm in their faith despite facing an enemy mustering far superior forces.

Noah's Challenge

Relate to them the story of Noah. He said to his people: 'My people! If my presence among you and my reminders to you of God's revelations are repugnant to you – well, in God have I placed my trust. Decide, then, what you are going to do, and [seek the help of] those whom you associate as partners with God. Be clear about your course of action, leaving no room for uncertainty, then carry out against me whatever you may have decided and give me no respite. But if you turn away, [remember that] I have asked of you no reward whatsoever. My reward rests with none but God. I have been commanded to be one of those who surrender themselves to Him.' But they disbelieved him. So we saved him and all those who joined him in the ark, and made them inherit the earth. And we drowned the others who denied Our revelations. Reflect on the fate of those who were forewarned. (Verses 71–73)

Only the end part of Noah's story is mentioned here where we see him offering his people a final challenge. He had spent a very long time preaching and warning his people, but to no avail. There is no mention of the ark here, or of those who were taken on board and so saved from the great floods. The aim here is to highlight the challenge and the believers' reliance on God, as well as the saving of a small, powerless group of believers and the destruction of the great hordes of unbelievers. The *sūrah* reduces the whole story to a single episode so as to emphasize its final end. This is what is most fitting in the present context.

"*Relate to them the story of Noah. He said to his people: 'My people! If my presence among you and my reminders to you of God's revelations are repugnant to you – well, in God have I placed my trust. Decide, then, what you are going to do, and [seek the help of] those whom you associate as partners with God. Be clear about your course of action, leaving no room for uncertainty, then carry out against me whatever you may have decided and give me no respite.*" (Verse 71) Noah tells his people that if they are completely fed up with him, unable to tolerate his presence among them and his reminders of their duty to believe in God, then let that be as it may. He will continue along his way, unperturbed by their opposition, for "*in God have I placed my trust.*" He seeks no help from anyone else. "*Decide, then, what you are going to do, and [seek the help of] those whom you associate as partners with God.*" (Verse 71)

They may, for all he cares, mobilize all their forces and resources. "*Be clear about your course of action, leaving no room for uncertainty.*" (Verse 71) They are further told to make their position very clear, allowing no ambiguity or hesitation, and leaving no room for return. Then when they have done that, they are told: "*carry out against me [i.e. Noah] whatever you may have decided and give me no respite.*" (Verse 71)

It is a clear challenge thrown out by one who is absolutely certain of his ground and power. In fact he is inviting his opponents to attack him. What were the forces at his command facilitating such a challenge? He simply had faith, which gave him a power that is superior to everything else. Numbers, careful planning and firepower are of little use when compared to faith. He had God's support, and God does not abandon those who believe in Him. It is the challenge of one who relies on the source of real power, for faith establishes a bond between the believer and the One who has power over everything in the universe. It is neither an arrogant nor a foolhardy challenge. Rather, it is the challenge of true power.

Advocates of the divine faith have in God's messengers a fine example to follow. They should have unwavering confidence as they place their trust in God and face tyranny, whatever its source may be. Tyranny will not cause them any real or lasting damage, apart from perhaps some physical pain which God allows as a test of the believers. God does not abandon the believers to His and their enemies, but He lets them undergo this test so that true believers come through it unharmed. The end favours the believers when God's promise is fulfilled and they are victorious.

Having made his challenge clear, Noah says to his people: *"But if you turn away, [remember that] I have asked of you no reward whatsoever. My reward rests with none but God. I have been commanded to be one of those who surrender themselves to Him."* (Verse 72). If you turn a deaf ear to what I call on you to accept, then that is your choice. I have not asked for a reward for guiding you to the right path, so I do not fear that my compensation will be reduced as a result of your turning away. *"My reward rests with none but God."* (Verse 72) Your attitude will not tempt me to change my way in the least, for my orders are such that I must surrender myself completely to God: *"I have been commanded to be one of those who surrender themselves to Him."* (Verse 72)

What happened, then? *"They disbelieved him. So We saved him and all those who joined him in the ark, and made them inherit the earth. And We drowned the others who denied Our revelations. Reflect on the fate of those who were forewarned."* (Verse 73) All that happened is given in a very brief account: his rescue with the believers who followed him; their establishment as successors to the land and subsequent power; and the drowning of the multitude of unbelievers. *"Reflect on the fate of those who were forewarned."* (Verse 73) It is indeed something to be reflected upon by all people at all times, so that they may heed the lesson and follow in the footsteps of the believers who were saved.

The outcome was not merely the destruction of the unbelievers. Instead this was preceded by the saving of the believers from all danger, and their establishment in the land to rebuild human life on a sound basis.

Such is the law God has established and such is His promise to the believers. If they feel at any time that the road seems endless, they must realize that it is the only way, and that the outcome will certainly be in their favour. They must not precipitate the fulfilment of God's promise. God does not deceive believers, nor does He abandon them to their enemies. He only teaches and equips them with what is of help to them along their way.

Different Communities, Same Response

The *sūrah* then refers very briefly to a number of messengers who followed Noah, bringing clear evidence of the truth to their respective communities, and how the unbelievers received them: "*Then after him We sent forth other messengers to their respective peoples, and they brought them clear evidence of the truth, but they would not believe in what they had once denied. Thus it is that We seal the hearts of those who transgress.*" (Verse 74)

These messengers were given clear proof confirming the truth they preached. They presented these proofs to their peoples, but the *sūrah* says that those peoples were not to believe in what they had earlier denied. This statement may be taken to mean that they continued to deny God's message in the same way as they denied it prior to having such clear evidence. In other words, they stubbornly held to their attitude. It may also mean that the unbelievers who deny God's messages are classified in one group despite the passage of time, because they share the same nature. This means that present-day unbelievers would not believe in what their ancestors denied, or what they themselves denied through their ancestors. All carry the same attitude to faith and the revelations confirming it. They seal their hearts and minds against it. In this they transgress and exceed all limits, because they refuse to use their God-given ability to understand. "*Thus it is that We seal the hearts of those who transgress.*" (Verse 74)

This follows the divine rule that when a person turns a deaf ear and seals his mind to divine guidance, his heart and mind become totally unreceptive. It is not God who seals their hearts and minds to prevent them from accepting the faith, but the general rule applies to them as it applies in all situations.

Truth or Sorcery

Moses' story is given in rather more detail than Noah's. It starts at the point when Moses faces the rejection of his message coupled with a challenge, and concludes with the drowning of Pharaoh and his soldiers. The account includes situations which carry strong similarity with the attitude of the pagan Arabs in Makkah to the Prophet's message, as well as the attitude of his few followers.

The part of the story related here highlights five points before making a comment elucidating the purpose of relating it in this way. The five points are given in quick succession as follows: "*Then after those [prophets] We sent Moses and Aaron with Our signs to Pharaoh and his nobles, but they persisted in their arrogance, for they were hardened offenders. When the truth came to them from Us, they said: 'This is clearly nothing but sorcery.' Moses replied: 'Do you say this to the truth when it has come to you? Can this be sorcery? But sorcerers will never be successful.' They said: 'Have you come to turn us away from what we found our forefathers believing in, so that the two of you might become supreme in the land? We will never believe in you.'*" (Verses 75–78)

The signs which Moses brought to Pharaoh and his nobles are the nine mentioned in *Sūrah* 7, The Heights. They are not mentioned here in detail because the context does not require such detail. What is important in the present context is the attitude of Pharaoh and his group when they received these signs: "*They persisted in their arrogance, for they were hardened offenders.*" (Verse 75)

"*When the truth came to them from Us...*" (Verse 76) The source of these signs is emphasized here, '*from Us*', to show clearly their terrible offence when they describe as '*clear sorcery*' the truth sent to them by God.

It is with limitless arrogance that they thus describe the truth without any evidence to support their claim. The statement sounds as if it is a standard one reiterated by all those who deny God's messages. As reported at the beginning of the *sūrah*, the pagan Arabs in Makkah said the same thing, despite the wide difference in time and place between the two communities and the great difference between the signs delivered by Moses and the Qur'ān.

"*Moses replied: 'Do you say this to the truth when it has come to you? Can this be sorcery? But sorcerers will never be successful.'*" (Verse 77) A part of Moses' first objection is deleted because it is indicated by his second one. It is as if he said to them: "Do you say to the truth when it has come to you that it is sorcery? Can this be sorcery?" The first question expresses horror that the truth is described as sorcery, and the second wonders that anyone should actually say it is so. Sorcery does not aim to provide guidance to people, and it does not include a faith or a clear idea about Godhead and His relationship with His servants. It cannot outline a code of living. Indeed sorcery cannot be confused with God's message. No sorcerer ever intended to work for such objectives or move in such a direction. Sorcerers' work is all false, playing tricks on people's imagination. Hence they cannot be successful.

At this point, the nobles supporting Pharaoh reveal their true motives for rejecting the truth: "*They said: 'Have you come to turn us away from what we found our forefathers believing in, so that the two of you might become supreme in the land? We will never believe in you.'*" (Verse 78) They feared that the new call would destroy their inherited beliefs which formed the foundation of their political and economic systems. They feared that they would lose their power which was conferred on them by the superstitious beliefs they promoted.

This is indeed the old and new reason which motivates tyrants to oppose every call to believe in God and follow His message. Hence, they fabricate all sorts of excuses, make false accusations against the advocates of the true faith, and brutally suppress them. It is their desire to remain 'supreme in the land' that forms their strongest motive. Their supremacy is based on false beliefs which the tyrants are keen to preserve in people's minds, despite their fallacy and what they may involve of superstition or deception. They know that when people's minds are open to receive the true faith, and their hearts are illumined with the new light, then that represents a danger to their long established values and positions. Indeed it shakes their very foundation and authority as perceived by the masses.

The divine faith preached by all prophets aims to establish the truth that God is the only deity and the Lord of the universe. All false deities that usurp God's authority and claim Lordship must be removed.

Tyranny never allows the truth to be presented to the masses, because it represents a general declaration liberating mankind from servitude to any authority other than God's. Tyranny realizes that its very existence is threatened by this declaration. Hence, it suppresses it with all the power at its disposal.

This is the true reason for the suppression of the Islamic call throughout history. The intelligent people of the Quraysh could not have been blind to the truth of the Prophet's message and its sublime aspects. They could not have been unaware of the falsehood of their idolatrous beliefs. But they feared for their power and position. They realized that they could only maintain these through their false beliefs, just like the nobles in Pharaoh's court. Hence they all said: "*We will never believe in you.*" (Verse 78)

Fear Barring Belief

Apparently accusing Moses of sorcery sounded good to Pharaoh and his nobles. They most probably felt they could make their accusation stick in people's minds. Hence, they wanted to challenge Moses, for the signs he exhibited seemed to them to be similar to the sorcery they knew and practised. They hoped that the challenge would show Moses to be no more than a highly skilled sorcerer. This would remove all danger to their hereditary authority, or to their monopoly of power, which was their main objective. These were, in all likelihood, the true reasons for holding this sorcery to be fair.

> *Then Pharaoh commanded: 'Bring before me every learned sorcerer.' And when the sorcerers came, Moses said to them: 'Throw whatever you may wish to throw.' And when they had thrown, Moses said to them: 'What you have contrived is mere sorcery which God will certainly bring to nothing. God does not further the work of those who spread corruption. By His words, God proves the truth to be true, much as the guilty may dislike it.* (Verses 79–82)

We note here how the build-up to the challenge is given very briefly, because it is the outcome that is most relevant. When Moses said: '*What you have contrived is mere sorcery,*' he was actually replying to the accusation levelled at him. There is no real substance to sorcery. It is all tricks and deception that dazzles and bewitches people. It has no higher call, and is far from constructive. It builds nothing within the community. What Moses brought was indeed a revealed book bestowed on him from on high. His statement that 'God will certainly bring [sorcery] to nothing,' demonstrates his great trust in his Lord, who will never allow sorcery, which is wicked, to score any real success: 'God does not further the work of those who spread corruption.' These were the ones who used their sorcery to lead people astray from the right path and prevent them from following divine guidance.

'By His words, God proves the truth to be true.' (Verse 82) The phrase, 'His words', refers here either to His expression of His will to create or do something, as when He says to something 'Be' and it comes into being as a result, or to His revelations. 'Much as the guilty may dislike it.' (Verse 82) Their dislike does not disrupt or impede the realization of God's will. This is indeed what actually took place: sorcery was shown to come to nothing, and the truth was triumphant. However, the triumph of the truth is not mentioned at this time because the purpose intended here is served in a different way.

Here the curtains are drawn, and when they are lifted again we see Moses with those who accepted his message and believed with him. They are a small group of people. This is one of the lessons to be drawn here: "None except a few of his people believed in Moses, for they feared Pharaoh and their nobles, lest they persecute them. Surely Pharaoh was mighty on earth and was indeed given to excesses. Moses said: 'My people, if you believe in God, then place your trust in Him – if you have truly surrendered yourselves to Him.' They replied: 'In God have we placed our trust. Our Lord, do not let us suffer at the hands of evil-doing people. Save us, by Your grace, from the people who disbelieve.' And thus did We inspire Moses and his brother: 'Take for your people some houses in Egypt, and make your houses places of worship, and be constant in prayer.' And give glad tidings to all believers." (Verses 83–87)

The Arabic text uses the term dhurriyyah when it refers to those who believed with Moses. This term connotes a small number among the younger generation. What we understand here is that, among the Israelites, those who declared their belief and joined Moses were young people, not the bulk of the Children of Israel. There were fears that these young people might be put under severe pressure to revert back to their old ways. They might fear the persecution of Pharaoh and his authority, or the pressure that might be brought to bear on them by the leaders of their own community who have their own interests with those in authority. Pressure was also expected to be brought on them by the weaklings within their community, because these normally side with everyone who has any authority. This applies particularly to the Israelites. Needless to say, Pharaoh enjoyed great authority, and he was a tyrant who indulged in all sorts of excess. He did not hesitate to take any brutal action when he felt the need for it.

In such a situation the only course is to rely on faith in order to dispel worries and reassure people, helping them to stick to the truth they have recognized: *"Moses said: 'My people, if you believe in God, then place your trust in Him – if you have truly surrendered yourselves to Him.'"* (Verse 84) Placing one's trust in God is evidence of firm belief. Furthermore, it is the element of strength which is added to what the weaker and smaller group may have to enable it to win its confrontation with mighty tyranny. Moses mentions both faith and self-surrender, making the reliance on God and placing one's trust in Him the natural outcome of both. Those believers made the right response to their prophet's call: *"They replied: 'In God have we placed our trust.'"* (Verse 85)

They then addressed a fitting supplication to God: *"Our Lord, do not let us suffer at the hands of evil-doing people."* (Verse 85) This means that they prayed to God not to give the tyrants physical power over them, so that those tyrants and their followers do not feel that their faith is superior since they are able to win their confrontation against the believers. Such a temporary victory may take place in any situation where God wants to let people be tempted by it, so that they go deeper into error. Hence the believers pray to God not to let the tyrants have power over them even if the purpose was to lead the tyrants further astray.

The next verse adds a prayer which is even clearer with regard to the desired outcome: *"Save us, by Your grace, from the people who disbelieve."* (Verse 86) These prayers do not conflict with placing their trust in

135

God and seeking His support. Indeed they make such reliance on Him clearer. A believer does not wish for hardship and does not aspire to be the victim of tyranny, but when he is tested by what tyrants do to him, he remains steadfast.

No Hope of a Positive Response

Thus, the two lines were drawn and the two communities were clearly identified. Some people responded positively to Moses. God then advised him and his brother, the Prophet Aaron, to choose special houses for the Children of Israel, so that they would be ready to leave Egypt at the appointed time. He also instructed them to purify their homes and their bodies, and to trust to God: "*And thus did We inspire Moses and his brother: 'Take for your people some houses in Egypt, and make your houses places of worship, and be constant in prayer.' And give glad tidings to all believers.*" (Verse 87)

This may be considered an exercise of 'spiritual mobilization', running alongside ordinary mobilization. Both are necessary for individuals and communities alike, particularly before battles and during times of hardship. Some people may dismiss spiritual mobilization as being of little consequence, but experience shows that faith continues to be the most important weapon in battle. Held by a soldier who is devoid of faith, military hardware is of little benefit when the going gets tough. This mustering is not something only the Children of Israel should do. Instead it pertains to all hard core believers in God. It is an experience based on pure faith. Believers may find themselves persecuted in a society which is devoid of faith, where tyranny is hardened by brute force, and generally people have lost their integrity and values, and where the whole environment is rotten, as was true of Pharaoh's realm. In such a situation, God tells them to abandon the *jāhiliyyah* society, with all its evil and corruption, as much as that is practical, so that they can establish their own community and purge, train and organize themselves in waiting for the fulfilment of His promise. They should also boycott the places of worship of the unbelieving society, while making use of their own homes as places of worship. In this way they can worship God in the proper manner, and make that worship an exercise of self organization.

Having despaired of any positive response from Pharaoh and his nobles, Moses turned to his Lord with a supplication that He destroy the Egyptians' property and riches because these had lured them away from the truth, so compromising their faith. Thus they had sunk deep into error. He further prayed that the rich remain hardened in their disbelief, so that they would face a grievous punishment. God answered his supplication: "*Moses said, 'Our Lord! You have bestowed on Pharaoh and his nobles splendour and riches in this life, with the result that they have been leading people astray from Your path. Our Lord! Wipe out their riches and harden their hearts, so that they do not believe until they face the grievous suffering.' He replied: 'Your prayer is accepted. Continue, both of you, steadfastly on the right path, and do not follow the path of those who are devoid of knowledge.'*" (Verses 88–89)

Moses begins his prayer with a statement: "*Our Lord! You have bestowed on Pharaoh and his nobles splendour and riches in this life.*" (Verse 88) These riches and splendour become a means to turn people away from Your path, either by the lure that they constitute or by the power they give to those who have them enabling them to humiliate or lead others astray. There is no doubt that if the corrupt people are the ones who have all the splendour and riches, a situation is created where many people are shaken because they do not realize that these riches are no more than a test. In comparison to God's bounty, whether it is bestowed in this life or in the hereafter, they are of no value. Moses appeals to God to destroy these riches, so that the nobles no longer have the means to tempt and pressurize people away from the right path. The rest of his supplication, that Pharaoh and his nobles not believe until they witness the suffering, is the prayer of one who has despaired that any of them will ever recognize the truth. Hence, he wants them to be hardened even further until they face their due punishment. Repentance then is not acceptable, because it does not signify any real regret, or any positive change based on free choice.

"*He replied: 'Your prayer is accepted.'*" (Verse 89) That then brings the matter to its due end. "*Continue, both of you, steadfastly on the right path.*" (Verse 89) Follow that path until the end, paying no regard to anything different. "*Do not follow the path of those who are devoid of knowledge.*" (Verse 89) Such people move along without guidance.

Their plans are flawed, and they lack certainty. Hence they are worried about their destiny, unsure of the path they follow.

When Accepting the Faith Means Nothing

The next scene depicts the event as it actually happened: "*And We brought the Children of Israel across the sea; but Pharaoh and his legions pursued them with tyranny and aggression. But as he was about to drown, Pharaoh said: 'I have come to believe that there is no deity other than Him in whom the Children of Israel believe, and to Him I surrender myself.' [But God said:] 'Only now? But before this you were rebelling [against Us], and you spread corruption in the land. But today We shall save only your body, so that you may become a sign to those who will come after you; for a great many people do not heed Our signs.*" (Verses 90–92)

This is a highly decisive point in the story of defiance and rejection of truth. It is shown here only very briefly, because the purpose of mentioning it in this *sūrah* is to demonstrate the result of the dispute. What is shown is the fact that God protects the believers and punishes those who choose to be His enemies, paying little attention to the signs and messages that call on them to believe in Him. They persist in disbelief until they are overwhelmed by God's punishment, when believing is of no avail. This was also explained earlier in the *sūrah*: "*To every community was sent a messenger. It is when their messenger had come to them that judgement was passed on them in all fairness; and never are they wronged. They say: 'When will this promise be fulfilled, if you are truthful?' Say: 'I have no control over any harm or benefit to myself, except as God may please. For every community a term has been appointed. When their time arrives, they can neither delay it by a single moment, nor indeed hasten it.' Say: 'Do but consider. Should His punishment befall you by night or by day, what could there be in it that the guilty ones should wish to hasten? Is it, then, when it has come to pass that you will believe in it? Is it now, while so far you have been asking for it to come speedily?'*" (Verses 47–51)

> *And We brought the Children of Israel across the sea; but Pharaoh and his legions pursued them with tyranny and aggression. But as*

he was about to drown, Pharaoh said: 'I have come to believe that there is no deity other than Him in whom the Children of Israel believe, and to Him I surrender myself.' [But God said:] 'Only now? But before this you were rebelling [against Us], and you spread corruption in the land. But today We shall save only your body, so that you may become a sign to those who will come after you; for a great many people do not heed Our signs. (Verses 90–92)

The story is meant, then, to confirm and assert the warnings: "*And We brought the Children of Israel across the sea.*" (Verse 90) They managed to cross it under Our guidance and protection. This statement, coming at this point, and attributing the guidance to God alone, is highly significant. "*But Pharaoh and his legions pursued them with tyranny and aggression.*" (Verse 90) They were not chasing them to follow their suit and accept divine guidance, nor was the chasing in defence of any rightful claim they might have had, but was rather an act of aggression and tyranny. Then, in no time at all, the story moves from a scene of brute tyrannical force to one of drowning: "*But as he was about to drown,*" staring death in the eye, "*Pharaoh said: 'I have come to believe that there is no deity other than Him in whom the Children of Israel believe, and to Him I surrender myself.'*" His masks had now fallen away. He was no longer the mighty ruler whose wishes were instantly obeyed. He had shrunk and looked humiliated. Not only did he declare that he believed in God, in whom the Children of Israel believed; he went further to submit himself in total surrender. "*[But God said:] 'Only now? But before this you were rebelling [against Us], and you spread corruption in the land. But today We shall save only your body, so that you may become a sign to those who will come after you; for a great many people do not heed Our signs.'*" (Verses 91–92)

But the response he received came as a total shock, as God said to him: "*Only now? But before this you were rebelling [against Us], and you spread corruption in the land.*" (Verse 91) You believe now, when you no longer have any choice or means of escape? You have been arrogant in your disbelief, rejecting all messages and warnings. "*But today We shall save only your body.*" (Verse 92) His body would remain intact, uneaten by sharks or other sea creatures. It would not be allowed to drift with the waves, but would be saved so that his end would be known to all and sundry: "*So that you may become a sign to those who will come after you.*" (Verse 92) It may be that when others see your body they will take heed and realize that defying God and His warnings brings certain doom. The fact is that "*a great many people do not heed Our signs.*" (Verse 92) They do not turn to them with open hearts and minds, nor do they consider their significance, be they evident in the great universe or within their own selves.

The final scene in this tragedy of corruption, defiance, disobedience and tyranny is clearly shown and the curtains are drawn. The *sūrah* then continues with a brief statement of what happened to the Children of Israel over several generations: "*We settled the Children of Israel in a most goodly abode and We provided for them sustenance out of the good things of life. It was not until knowledge was given them that they began to disagree among themselves. Your Lord will judge between them on the Day of Resurrection regarding that on which they differed.*" (Verse 93)

For 'abode' the Arabic statement uses a term which signifies security, but adds to it a description of sincerity. This gives the added connotation of a secure settlement which is not easily threatened. Sincerity and truth do not experience the sort of unease that are associated with lying and invention. The Children of Israel were settled in their secure abode after several experiences that are not mentioned here because they do not relate to the purpose of the *sūrah*. They further enjoyed goodly provisions until they started to disobey God, at which time these provisions were forbidden them. The *sūrah* only states that they started to argue about matters of religion as well as worldly matters. These disputes were not the result of ignorance. They only began after knowledge of the truth had been given to them. But they used that knowledge to arrive at false interpretations of religious matters.

Since the context here is one of giving support to those who accept the faith and ensuring the defeat of tyranny, the *sūrah* does not dwell on what the Children of Israel perpetrated after that, nor does it give any account of their disputes. It turns the page, leaving judgement on all this to God alone: "*Your Lord will judge between them on the Day of Resurrection regarding that on which they differed.*" (Verse 93) The story thus maintains its seriousness and the effect is in no way diminished.

No Doubts Entertained

Now the *sūrah* begins its comments on the accounts it gives of the stories of Moses and Noah with their peoples. At the outset, it reassures the Prophet by telling him what happened to other messengers God sent before his time. It also explains to him the real reason for his people's denial of the truth. He is told that what these people lack is not more signs and clear proofs of this truth. It is simply the fulfilment of human nature with all that God has placed in it of aptitude to follow guidance or error and to be good or evil. A brief account of the Prophet Jonah's history is then added, mentioning how his people believed in the nick of time when God's punishment was about to overwhelm them. Their acceptance of the faith ensured the lifting of that punishment. This is given by way of encouraging the Arabs who denied the truth to accept it before their time too was up. The passage concludes with outlining the basic issues which the stories of past nations given in the Qur'ān are meant to emphasize. They confirm that the laws God has set in operation will apply to later communities in as much as they applied to earlier ones. This spells doom and suffering to the unbelievers who deny God and His message, while the messengers and those who follow them shall be saved. This is a commitment God has made and a law He has set. It will always come true.

> *If you are in doubt concerning what We have bestowed on you from on high, ask those who read the Scriptures [revealed] before you. It is surely the truth that has come to you from your Lord. Do not, then, be among the doubters. And do not be among those who deny God's revelations, for then you shall be among those who are lost. Surely, those against whom your Lord's word [of judgement] has come true will not believe, even though every sign should come to their knowledge, until they are faced with the grievous suffering. Had it believed, every community would have profited by its faith. It was so only with Jonah's people. When they believed, We lifted from them the suffering of disgrace in this life, and allowed them to*

141

enjoy things for a while. Had your Lord so willed, all people on earth, in their entirety, would have believed. Do you, then, try to compel people to believe? No human being can believe, except by God's leave. It is He who lays abomination on those who will not use their reason. Say: 'Consider all that there is in the heavens and the earth.' But of what benefit could all signs and warnings be to people who will not believe? What are they waiting for except a repetition of the days [of calamity] experienced by those who have gone before them? Say: 'Wait, then, if you will. I am also waiting.' Thereupon, We save Our messengers and those who believe. Thus have We willed it upon Ourselves: We save those who believe. (Verses 94–103)

The previous passage was concerned with the attitude of the Children of Israel who had received revelations from God. They were aware of Noah and his community's story, and they were also fully aware of Moses and his experience with Pharaoh, which was given in detail in their Scriptures. The *sūrah* now addresses the Prophet telling him that if he is in doubt concerning God's revelations, including the history of past communities, then he should ask those who received revelations before his time. They have full knowledge of what they read in those Scriptures: "*If you are in doubt concerning what We have bestowed on you from on high, ask those who read the Scriptures [revealed] before you. It is surely the truth that has come to you from your Lord. Do not, then, be among the doubters.*" (Verse 94)

But the Prophet (peace be upon him) was not in doubt concerning his revelations. It is reported that when this verse was revealed, the Prophet said, "I do not doubt, and I am not going to ask." Why is it, then, that he is told to ask if he is in doubt? And why is this followed by the statement that "*it is surely the truth that has come to you from your Lord*"? It is certainly more than enough for him to know that this statement is made by God.

This directive gives us an idea of the difficult situation that prevailed in Makkah after the Prophet was taken on his night journey to Jerusalem and ascended from there to heaven. Some people who had previously declared their acceptance of Islam now denied it, as they could not believe this. What aggravated the matter even more was the fact that shortly before this, the Prophet lost his wife, Khadījah, and his uncle, Abū Ṭālib, who had both provided him with much-needed support. They died within a short period of each other. Moreover, the unbelievers in Makkah increased their physical persecution of the Prophet and those who believed in his message. The new faith was practically confined to Makkah, as the Quraysh, the predominant tribe in Arabia, fought hard to stop it from spreading to other tribes. All these circumstances weighed heavily on the Prophet's heart. Hence, he needed the reassurance that God gives him with this assertion, making it clear that his message is the message of truth.

Moreover, the doubters and those who deny God's message are assigned their place: *"And do not be among those who deny God's revelations, for then you shall be among those who are lost."* (Verse 95) This exposure of the doubters serves to give them another chance to return to the truth. If the Prophet neither doubts nor asks questions when he is permitted to do so, then he must be absolutely certain that what has been given to him is the truth which admits no doubt. This serves as encouragement to others not to doubt or waver.

Moreover, this gives us an insight into the method God has laid down for the Muslim community. It must make sure of whatever remains uncertain. It can do so by asking those who have been endowed with great knowledge. It should ask even if the matter concerns something of the basic essentials of faith, because a Muslim is required to make sure of his faith and the law he implements. He must not follow anyone else unless he knows for certain that that person follows the truth.

One may well ask here whether there is any conflict or contradiction between the permission to ask others when one is in doubt and the subsequent directive not to be 'one of the doubters'? There is certainly neither conflict nor contradiction. What is to be avoided is remaining in doubt so that it becomes a permanent condition, without any attempt by the doubter to remove his doubts and reach a stage of certitude. For prolonged doubt is a very bad situation which leads to neither benefit nor knowledge.

Since what has been given to the Prophet is the truth that admits no doubt, how is it then that some people continue to deny it and adopt an unreasonably stubborn attitude? The answer is that God's law is such that when one does not seek guidance, one will not find it, and one who does not open his eyes and heart to the light will not see it. A person who wastes his perceptions will not benefit by what he perceives, and will end up in error. Whatever proofs and signs are available will remain of no use to him. Hence, the law God has set in operation will work against him, and God's word of punishment will overtake him: "*Surely, those against whom your Lord's word [of punishment] has come true will not believe, even though every sign should come to their knowledge, until they are faced with the grievous suffering.*" (Verses 96–97)

At this point, acknowledgement of the truth and accepting the faith will not benefit them because it does not flow from their own choice. There is no longer any chance to test that faith in everyday life. The *sūrah* confirmed all this earlier when it depicted Pharaoh crying out at the point of drowning: "*I have come to believe that there is no deity other than Him in whom the Children of Israel believe, and to Him I surrender myself.*" (Verse 90) But he was told: "*'Only now? But before this you were rebelling [against Us], and you spread corruption in the land.'*" (Verse 91)

As we are assured of the inevitability of the operation of God's laws and that their outcome will never fail to apply in accordance with what people choose for themselves in this life, a window of hope is opened. Salvation is possible when the wrongdoers stop denying the truth and declare their belief before they are overtaken by God's punishment.

Even When Punishment is Due

"*Had it believed, every community would have profited by its faith. It was so only with Jonah's people. When they believed, We lifted from them the suffering of disgrace in this life, and allowed them to enjoy things for a while.*" (Verse 98) The way this verse is phrased expresses a dear wish concerning past events. This means that what was hoped for did not take place. *'Had it believed, every community'* of those that have been mentioned would have profited by accepting the faith. But these communities did not believe as whole communities. Only a minority of each community accepted the divine faith. Hence, disbelief was the predominant feature of these communities. Jonah's people were the one exception. This verse uses the term 'town' to refer to communities thereby indicating that God's messages were centred in urban areas, and not among nomadic peoples.

The *sūrah* does not provide a detailed account of the history of the Prophet Jonah and his people. It only refers to their end, because this is what is relevant here. It is sufficient that we learn that Jonah's people were about to suffer a humiliating punishment. Then, when, at the last minute, they declared their acceptance of the divine faith and believed in God and His message, the punishment was lifted and they were allowed to enjoy life for a while. Had they persisted in their disbelief, God's punishment would have overtaken them, in accordance with the law that determines consequences on the basis of people's actions.

This makes two points very clear. The first is an urgent address to those who deny the truth to save themselves if only at the last minute, as Jonah's people did. This is the immediate purpose behind the reference to their history.

The second point is that God's law was not suspended or disrupted when the punishment was lifted and Jonah's people were left to enjoy life for a further period. In fact God's law took its full course. The law meant that they would be punished if they persisted in disbelief up to the point of punishment. But Jonah's people changed their attitude just before, and so God's law to lift the punishment was implemented. This shows that people are free to choose their line of action, but any action they do choose will have its natural consequences determined by God.

This is followed by a general rule concerning faith and its acceptance or rejection: *"Had your Lord so willed, all people on earth, in their entirety, would have believed. Do you, then, try to compel people to believe? No human being can believe, except by God's leave. It is He who lays abomination on those who will not use their reason."* (Verses 99–100)

Had God so willed, He would have created the human race in a different mould, allowing it to know only the path of faith, as He has done with the angels. Or He would have given human beings a single susceptibility leading them all to acceptance of the faith. In His wisdom, which we may or may not understand, God has created man with a dual susceptibility towards good and evil, to follow guidance or sink into error. He has given man free-will to choose his path. Furthermore, God has so willed that when any human being uses his feelings and faculties to understand the signs pointing to the way to faith, and when he reflects on the revelations and proofs given by God's messengers, he will accept the divine faith. His belief will lead him along the way to salvation. On the other hand, when man shuts his mind and faculties to faith, his heart will be hardened and his mind closed. This leads him to deny the truth and, in consequence, to suffer the punishment God has determined for all unbelievers.

This means that accepting the faith is a matter of choice. The Prophet does not compel anyone to believe, because there can be no compulsion in matters determined by reason and conscience: "*Do you, then, try to compel people to believe?*" (Verse 99) This is a rhetorical question which serves to emphasize that compulsion is not possible.

"*No human being can believe, except by God's leave.*" (Verse 100) This is again in accordance with the law God has set in operation and which we have already explained. No person will attain to faith if they follow the route which does not lead to faith. This statement does not mean that anyone will ever be prevented from attaining to faith if he wants to believe and follows the road of faith. What it means is that no one reaches belief and faith without following the proper steps along the route leading to faith. When a person makes this choice, God provides His guidance to that person who will then believe, by God's leave. In other words, nothing happens except by God's will. People follow their freely chosen ways, and God determines the consequences of every type of action. The result is the sum of these consequences. They receive their reward on the basis of how conscientiously they seek to be properly guided.

This is confirmed by the ending of the same verse: "*It is He who lays abomination on those who will not use their reason.*" (Verse 100) Those who choose to shut their minds and decide not to reflect on the signs and proofs pointing to the right faith will suffer abomination, i.e. the worst type of spiritual impurity. This is what they deserve for not using their reason, which has resulted in their disbelief and denial of the truth.

This is further explained by stating that signs and warnings will be of no benefit to people who will not believe. They do not reflect on them when they see them everywhere in the world around them: "*Say: 'Consider all that there is in the heavens and the earth.' But of what benefit could all signs and warnings be to people who will not believe?*" (Verse 101) Whether we take the final part of this verse as a rhetorical question or a straightforward statement, it signifies the same thing. There are numerous signs and pointers to the truth all around us in the heavens and the earth, but none of these will benefit the unbelievers, because they have chosen to close their eyes and minds to them.

Minds Shut to All Evidence

Before we move further we need to reflect briefly on the verse that says: "*Say: 'Consider all that there is in the heavens and the earth.' But of what benefit could all signs and warnings be to people who will not believe?*" (Verse 101)

The community which was the first to be addressed by the Qur'ān had very little scientific knowledge of what exists in the heavens and earth. But the fact is that human nature communicates with the universe in which we live in a language that is both rich and subtle at the same time. When human nature is alert and receptive, the universe has much to tell it and it listens carefully.

The Qur'ānic approach to the formulation of an Islamic concept in human consciousness makes use of what exists in the heavens and earth. It derives inspiration from the universe, and directs the human faculties of vision, hearing, perception and understanding to its discourse, without trying to disturb the balance and harmony that exist in the universe. It does not make of the universe a deity directing human life, as narrow-minded materialists claim with their 'scientific socialism'. True science and knowledge have nothing to do with all their nonsense.

Reflection on what exists in the heavens and earth gives the human heart and mind a wealth of feelings, responses and influences, as well as meaningful interaction with the universe. All this helps man to be receptive to everything in the universe that points to God's existence, majesty, power, planning, wisdom and perfect knowledge.

With the passage of time, human knowledge of the universe increases. A human being who sees God's light and follows His guidance benefits greatly from increased knowledge. He is better able to know the universe and interact with it. He joins the universe in glorifying God, for: *"There is nothing that exists but celebrates His praises, although you may not understand their praises."* (17: 44) Only a person whose heart nurtures its bond with God understands such praises. When human knowledge is devoid of the light of faith, it increases human misery as it leads people further away from God and deprives them of the happiness that comes with faith.

"But of what benefit could all signs and warnings be to people who will not believe?" (Verse 101) What is the benefit of signs and warnings when hearts are hardened, minds are shut, receptive faculties are left idle and the whole human being is isolated from the universe, unable to listen to its glorification of God?

The Qur'ānic method of explaining the nature of God shows the universe and life generally as a great exhibition in which the truth of God's existence is seen most vividly through its extensive action. Its presence overwhelms all human faculties. This method does not make of God's existence a topic for debate. Indeed the way the Qur'ān looks at the universe and what we see in it fills our hearts with the fact of God's existence so as to leave no room for arguing about it. The Qur'ān speaks directly of the results of this existence in the whole universe, and its influence on human conscience and human life in general.

In its method, the Qur'ān relies on a basic element in the make up of human beings. After all, it is God who has created man and He knows best what He has created: *"It is We who have created man, and We know the promptings of his soul."* (50: 16) There is a basic need in human nature to have faith and to believe in a deity. In fact, when human nature is uncorrupted, it experiences a strong inner feeling directing it towards belief in a single God. The purpose of true faith is not to initiate this need to believe in God. That feeling is basic to human nature. True faith seeks to put man's concept of God on a proper footing, and to make the true God, who is the only deity in the universe, known to man, with all His attributes. It is to know God properly, not to establish His existence, that the true faith works. For it also aims to make man aware of the effects on human life of God's existence, i.e. His Lordship and Sovereignty. Indeed the mere doubt of God's existence, let alone denying it altogether, is indicative of an imbalance in human nature, and a malfunctioning of its faculties of perception. Such malfunctioning is not rectified by argument and logic.

This universe knows God, believes in Him and submits itself to Him. Every living thing in it celebrates God's praises, except for a few humans. Mankind lives in this universe where the echoes of faith in God and submission to Him are heard everywhere, as are God's praises and glorification. Therefore, someone whose nature does not perceive all this is one whose natural qualities of perception are not functioning properly. Argument is not the proper way to address such a heart and mind. The correct way is to try to alert man's faculties of perception, and awaken his nature so that it may resume its proper function. Drawing man's attention, as well as his heart and mind, to what exists in the heavens and the earth is one of the methods the Qur'ān uses to awaken human hearts.

Those unbelievers among the pagan Arabs, and others who adopt a similar attitude, neither responded nor reflected. What were they waiting for, then? God's law will always remain in operation. The destiny of those who deny the truth is well known, and they cannot expect that God's law will not apply to them. God may give them a chance, and may withhold their punishment for a while, but those who persist in denying Him will suffer in the end: "*What are they waiting for except a repetition of the days [of calamity] experienced by those who have gone before them? Say: 'Wait, then, if you will. I am also waiting.'*" (Verse 102) This is a threat that puts an end to all argument while it fills hearts with fear.

This passage is then concluded with the final outcome of every message and every opposition to it, making plain the lessons of the histories reported in the *sūrah*: "*We save Our messengers and those who believe. Thus have We willed it upon Ourselves: We save those who believe.*" (Verse 103) This is the promise God has made: the seed of faith will retain its healthy function. It will be safe after every type of persecution to which its advocates are subjected. It will survive every denial and every torture inflicted on its advocates. The stories related in this *sūrah*, and elsewhere in the Qur'ān confirm this. Hence, the believers should be reassured.

4

Clarification of Issues

Say: 'Mankind, if you are still in doubt as to what my faith is, then [know that] I do not worship those whom you worship beside God, but I worship God alone who will cause all of you to die. I have been commanded to be one of those who believe. (104)

قُل يَٰٓأَيُّهَا ٱلنَّاسُ إِن كُنتُمْ فِى شَكٍّ مِّن دِينِى فَلَآ أَعْبُدُ ٱلَّذِينَ تَعْبُدُونَ مِن دُونِ ٱللَّهِ وَلَٰكِنْ أَعْبُدُ ٱللَّهَ ٱلَّذِى يَتَوَفَّىٰكُمْ وَأُمِرْتُ أَنْ أَكُونَ مِنَ ٱلْمُؤْمِنِينَ ﴿١٠٤﴾

And adhere exclusively and sincerely to the true faith, and do not be one of those who associate partners with God. (105)

وَأَنْ أَقِمْ وَجْهَكَ لِلدِّينِ حَنِيفًا وَلَا تَكُونَنَّ مِنَ ٱلْمُشْرِكِينَ ﴿١٠٥﴾

Do not invoke, instead of God, anything that can neither benefit nor harm you. For if you do, you will surely be among the wrongdoers.' (106)

وَلَا تَدْعُ مِن دُونِ ٱللَّهِ مَا لَا يَنفَعُكَ وَلَا يَضُرُّكَ فَإِن فَعَلْتَ فَإِنَّكَ إِذًا مِّنَ ٱلظَّٰلِمِينَ ﴿١٠٦﴾

Should God afflict you with any hardship, none other than He can remove it; and if He wills any good for you, none can withhold His bounty. He bestows it on whomsoever He wills. He is truly Forgiving, truly Merciful. (107)

وَإِن يَمْسَسْكَ ٱللَّهُ بِضُرٍّ فَلَا كَاشِفَ لَهُۥٓ إِلَّا هُوَ وَإِن يُرِدْكَ بِخَيْرٍ فَلَا رَآدَّ لِفَضْلِهِۦ يُصِيبُ بِهِۦ مَن يَشَآءُ مِنْ عِبَادِهِۦ وَهُوَ ٱلْغَفُورُ ٱلرَّحِيمُ ﴿١٠٧﴾

Say: 'Mankind, the truth has come to you from your Lord. Whoever chooses to follow the true guidance, does so for his own good; and whoever chooses to go astray, does so at his own peril. I am not responsible for your conduct.' (108)

قُلْ يَـٰٓأَيُّهَا ٱلنَّاسُ قَدْ جَآءَكُمُ ٱلْحَقُّ مِن رَّبِّكُمْ فَمَنِ ٱهْتَدَىٰ فَإِنَّمَا يَهْتَدِى لِنَفْسِهِۦ وَمَن ضَلَّ فَإِنَّمَا يَضِلُّ عَلَيْهَا وَمَآ أَنَا۟ عَلَيْكُم بِوَكِيلٍ ۝

Follow whatever is revealed to you, and be patient in adversity, until God shall give His judgement. He is the best of all judges. (109)

وَٱتَّبِعْ مَا يُوحَىٰٓ إِلَيْكَ وَٱصْبِرْ حَتَّىٰ يَحْكُمَ ٱللَّهُ وَهُوَ خَيْرُ ٱلْحَـٰكِمِينَ ۝

Preview

In this its final passage, the *sūrah* brings to an end our sojourn of the universe, and reflection on aspects of human constitution, and the realms of feeling and thought. It is as if we are returning home with a wealth of riches, as also looking for relaxation after a long journey. The *sūrah* has dwelt on the central theme of faith with its main issues: the oneness of God, who has no partners and who admits no mediation or mediators; His absolute sovereignty and overpowering will; the laws He has set in operation which no one can amend or change; the truth of revelation which makes the true faith clear to all; the resurrection and the reckoning and reward on the Day of Judgement. All these issues have been clarified with historical accounts and illustrated with fine examples and analogies. Now they are summed up in a short passage. The Prophet is instructed to declare these principles to mankind, making clear that he will continue along the line he has followed until God has judged between him and those who oppose him. He is indeed the best of all judges.

Perseverance until Final Judgement

"Say: 'Mankind, if you are still in doubt as to what my faith is, then [know that] I do not worship those whom you worship beside God, but I worship God alone who will cause all of you to die. I have been commanded to be one of those who believe.'" (Verse 104) Here the Prophet is told to address all mankind, although the address is meant in the first instance to the Arabs in Makkah who believed in a multiplicity of deities. He tells them that if they are in doubt about the truth of the faith to which he is calling, then their doubts will never turn him away from the truth which he is preaching. He is not going to change his way so as to worship their false gods. Instead, *"I worship God alone who will cause all of you to die."* (Verse 104) He is the One who determines everyone's span of life and the time when everyone dies. Emphasizing this aspect here is significant because it reminds them of God's power over them. He is the One to be worshipped, not those false deities which cannot give life or cause death. He is also told to make his own instructions plain to them: *"I have been commanded to be one of those who believe."* (Verse 104) He fulfils his orders as they are given to him, without going beyond his limits.

"And adhere exclusively and sincerely to the true faith, and do not be one of those who associate partners with God." (Verse 105) Here the style changes into a direct order, which is given in such a way that it sounds as if it is being given now in front of them all. This is far more effective. *"Adhere exclusively and sincerely to the true faith,"* turning to God alone and accepting what He has revealed to you as the complete truth. *"And do not be one of those who associate partners with God."* (Verse 105) This re-emphasizes the meaning of sincere and exclusive adherence to the true faith and being one of the believers. The emphasis takes the form of a direct prohibition of associating partners with God which follows a direct order to believe. *"Do not invoke, instead of God, anything that can neither benefit nor harm you. For if you do, you will surely be among the wrongdoers."* (Verse 106) Do not appeal to any of those beings whom the unbelievers associate with God, for they cannot bring you any benefit or cause you any harm. If you do appeal to them, you will put yourself among

the wrongdoers, because God is fair to all, and He does not show any favouritism to anyone.

"*Should God afflict you with any hardship, none other than He can remove it; and if He wills any good for you, none can withhold His bounty. He bestows it on whomsoever He wills. He is truly Forgiving, truly Merciful.*" (Verse 107) God has set certain laws in operation whereby harm and benefit inevitably affect human beings when they expose themselves to their causes. So if harm afflicts you through the operation of God's laws, then no one can remove that harm unless you follow the right course of action. This means that you should cease to expose yourself to the causes of harm if you are aware of them or appeal to God to make them known to you if you do not know them. Similarly, if you follow His laws which generate benefit for you, no one will be able to stop that benefit. It will always be granted by God to those of His servants who decide to follow the means to achieve it. This is His general will and *modus operandi*. Furthermore, "*He is truly Forgiving, truly Merciful.*" (Verse 107) He forgives past sins when one sincerely repents. Furthermore, He is merciful to His servants, forgiving them their errors and increasing their reward for their good deeds when they adhere to the true path.

This is the sum of faith, as illustrated in this *sūrah*. The Prophet is ordered to declare it to mankind, and the order is given to him as though he is standing in front of them. The order is directed at each individual in person. It is a remarkably inspiring and effective method. The Prophet makes his declaration, facing up to material power, numerical strength, ignorant beliefs and a long history of associating partners with God. He makes his declaration, as commanded by God, with force and maximum clarity, when he has only a small number of followers in Makkah where the power is decidedly with the unbelievers. Thus he fulfils his duty towards the truth he is advocating, showing his unshakeable certainty in faith.

This brings us to the final declaration to all people: "*Say: 'Mankind, the truth has come to you from your Lord. Whoever chooses to follow the true guidance, does so for his own good; and whoever chooses to go astray, does so at his own peril. I am not responsible for your conduct.'*" (Verse 108) It is the final, decisive word which makes it clear that everyone chooses his or her way as they please after the truth has been given to all by their Lord. Hence, "*whoever chooses to follow the true guidance, does so for his own good; and whoever chooses to go astray, does so at his own peril.*" (Verse 108) The Prophet is not required to force people to follow divine guidance. He only conveys to them his message and leaves them to choose freely, making it clear that everyone will bear the results of his or her choice.

The final address to the Prophet tells him to follow what he has been instructed and to persevere until God has made His judgement: "*Follow whatever is revealed to you, and be patient in adversity, until God shall give His judgement. He is the best of all judges.*" (Verse 109) The conclusion is in perfect harmony with the opening of the *sūrah* and its contents, following the unique method of the Qur'ān.

SŪRAH 11

Hūd

Prologue

This *surah* is a Makkan revelation, despite that in some copies of the Qur'ān it is said that verses 12, 17 and 114 were revealed in Madinah. A glance at these verses within the context of the *surah* shows that they occur in their perfect settings. It is difficult to imagine that the *surah* was without these verses from the outset, or that they were added later on. Besides, these verses speak about subjects that are essentially part of what Makkan revelations address, namely faith and the Quraysh's attitude to it, how their attitude affected the Prophet and his small band of followers, and how the Qur'ān dispelled these effects.

The *surah* as a whole followed the revelation of *Surah* 10, Jonah, which succeeded *Surah* 17, The Night Journey. This gives us a clear idea of the timing of its revelation, in the middle of a very difficult period in the early history of Islam. It was preceded by the deaths of Abū Ṭālib, the Prophet's uncle who protected him against all harm from the unbelievers, and Khadījah, his wife whose comforting influence was of great help to the Prophet. Their deaths enabled the unbelievers to become bolder and harsher in their opposition, particularly after the Prophet's night journey to Jerusalem, from where he ascended to heaven before returning to Makkah in the same night.

The unbelievers ridiculed the event to such an extent that some people even renounced Islam. Furthermore, the Prophet missed Khadījah whom he loved dearly. The hostility towards him and his message was at its fiercest. Indeed, his efforts to win more support yielded few results; almost no one from Makkah and its surrounding area being prepared to embrace Islam. This continued until the first group of the *Anṣār* accepted Islam, delivering their pledges to the Prophet at 'Aqabah.

Ibn Isḥāq reports:

> Both Khadījah bint Khuwaylid and Abū Ṭālib died in the same year. This meant a succession of tragedies for the Prophet, because Khadījah provided him with honest and true support, and listened to his complaints, while his uncle was a mainstay of support, providing protection and ensuring his safety. Both events took place three years before his migration to Madinah. After Abū Ṭālib's death, the Quraysh were able to cause him more trouble than they could ever perpetrate during his uncle's life."

> Things were so bad for the Prophet that a wretched person stopped him on the street and threw dust over his head. The Prophet then went home and one of his daughters was crying as she washed the dirt off his head. The Prophet said to her: "Do not cry, child. God will certainly protect your father." He remarked more than once: "The Quraysh could not cause me much harm before Abū Ṭālib's death."[1]

Al-Maqrīzī says: "The Prophet found things too hard after their deaths, and he called that year, the year of sorrow. He used to say: 'The Quraysh could not do me much harm until Abū Ṭālib had died.' In fact, Abū Ṭālib was his only protector in his own clan.

It is during this period that the two *sūrahs*, Jonah and Hūd, were revealed, following *Sūrah* 17, The Night Journey, and *Sūrah* 25, The Criterion. All these *sūrahs* give a clear impression of the time and the extent of the Quraysh's hostility. In this present *sūrah* we also have the reassurances given to the Prophet and his followers. These comfort him in his loneliness in the midst of a hostile environment.

---

1. Ibn Hishām, *Al-Sīrah al-Nabawiyyah*, Dār al-Qalam, Beirut, n.d., Vol. 2, pp. 57–58.

Several Messengers, One Message

The nature and general atmosphere of the period is reflected in the *sūrah* in different ways. One of these is a general review of the progress of divine faith in human history, starting with Noah and leading up to the last Messenger, the Prophet Muḥammad. It makes clear that all messages were based on the same fundamental principles: submission to God alone, worshipping Him without the association of any partners, and following only the guidance provided by God's messengers in both submission and worship. These are coupled with the belief that this present life is only a test, with the reward given only in the life to come. Freedom of choice between truth and falsehood, which God has given to man, is the basis of this test.

The Prophet was sent as a messenger and given *"a book, with verses which have been perfected and distinctly spelled out, bestowed on you by One who is Wise, All-aware."* (Verse 1) The basic contents of this book are:

> *Worship none but God. I come to you from Him as a warner and a bearer of glad tidings. Seek forgiveness of your Lord, and then turn towards Him in repentance, and He will grant you a goodly enjoyment of life for an appointed term. He will grant everyone with merit a full reward for his merit. But if you turn away, I dread for you the suffering of a great day. To God you shall all return, and He has power over all things. (Verses 2–4)*

This was by no means an unprecedented message. It was the same as advocated by Noah, Hūd, Ṣāliḥ, Shu'ayb, Moses and many others.

> *We sent forth Noah to his people: 'I have come to you with a plain warning. Worship none but God. I certainly fear that suffering should befall you on a grievous day.' (Verses 25–26)*

> *To 'Ād, We sent their brother Hūd. He said: 'My people! Worship God alone; you have no deity other than Him. You are indeed inventors of falsehood. No reward do I ask of you, my people, for this [message]. My reward rests with Him who brought me into being. Will you not, then, use your reason? My people! Seek your Lord's forgiveness, and then turn to Him in repentance. He will cause the*

sky to rain abundance on you, and will add strength to your strength. Do not turn away as guilty criminals.' (Verses 50–52)

To Thamūd, We sent their brother Ṣāliḥ. He said: 'My people! Worship God alone. You have no deity other than Him. He it is who brought you into being out of the earth and settled you therein. Seek His forgiveness and then turn to Him in repentance. My Lord is ever near. He answers all.' (Verse 61)

And to Madyan We sent their brother Shu'ayb. He said: 'My people! Worship God alone. You have no deity other than Him. Do not give short measure and weight. I see you now in a happy state, yet I dread lest suffering befall you on a fateful day which will encompass all. My people, always give full measure and weight, in all fairness, and do not deprive people of what is rightfully theirs, and do not spread corruption on earth by wicked actions. That which rests with God is better for you, if you truly believe. I am not your keeper.' (Verses 84–86)

We see clearly that all these messengers delivered the same message, advocating the same principles.

A Community Apart

Again the *sūrah* reflects the nature of the period as it describes God's messengers' attitudes to the hostility, ridicule, threats and physical harm they met. They all persevered, confident that what they preached was the truth, and that God's support would inevitably be granted. The result in this life, and indeed in the life to come, confirmed their belief when the believers were saved while the unbelievers were destroyed.

In its account of Noah, the *sūrah* portrays this scene:

The notables of his people who disbelieved said: 'We see you but a mortal man like ourselves. Nor can we see anyone following you except the most abject among us; those who are rash and undiscerning. We do not consider that you are in any way superior to us: indeed we think you are liars.' Noah said: 'Think, my people! If I take my stand on a clear evidence from my Lord, and He has favoured me with grace from Himself, to which you have remained blind, can we force it upon you when you are averse to it? And, my people, I ask of you no money in return; my reward rests with none but God. Nor will I drive away those who believe; they will surely meet their Lord, whereas in you I see people with no awareness [of right and wrong]. And, my people, who would protect me from God were I to drive them away? Will you not reflect? I do not say to you that God's treasures are with me, or that I know what lies beyond the reach of human perception. Nor do I say: I am an angel. Nor do I say of those whom you eye with contempt that God will never grant them any good. God knows best what is in their hearts – for then I would indeed be a wrongdoer.' 'Noah,' they replied, 'you have argued with us, and argued to excess. Bring upon us that with which you have been threatening us, if you are a man of truth.' He said: 'Only God can bring it upon you, if He so wills. You cannot be immune.' (Verses 27–33)

Then a little later, the *surah* paints a picture of the floods and how those who opposed Noah were drowned while those who believed with him were all saved.

In the history of Hūd, we are presented with the following scene:

They replied: 'Hūd, you have brought us no clear evidence. We are not forsaking our gods on your mere word, nor will we believe in you. All we can say is that one of our gods may have smitten you with something evil.' He said: 'I call God to witness, and you, too, bear witness, that I disassociate myself from all those you claim to be partners with God. Scheme against me, all of you, if you will, and give me no respite. Indeed I have placed my trust in God, my Lord and your Lord. There is no living creature which He does not hold by its forelock. Straight indeed is my Lord's way. But if you turn away, I have delivered to you the message with which I was sent to you. My Lord may replace you with another people. You can do Him no harm. My Lord watches over all things.' (Verses 53–57)

Then we see the outcome of their rejection:

And so, when Our judgement came to pass, by Our grace We saved Hūd and those who shared his faith. We have indeed saved them from severe suffering. Such were the 'Ād. They denied their Lord's revelations, disobeyed His messengers, and followed the bidding of every arrogant, unrestrained tyrant. They were pursued by a curse in this world and on the Day of Judgement. Indeed, the ʿĀd denied their Lord. Oh, away with the ʿĀd, the people of Hūd. (Verses 58–60)

And in its account of Ṣāliḥ and his people the *sūrah* portrays this scene:

They answered: 'Ṣāliḥ! Great hopes did we place in you before this. Would you now forbid us to worship what our forefathers worshipped? We are indeed in grave doubt about that to which you call us.' He said: 'Think, my people! If I take my stand on a clear evidence from my Lord who has bestowed on me His grace, who will save me from God were I to disobey Him? You are, in such a case, only aggravating my ruin.' (Verses 62–63)

They persist in their rejection and slaughter the she-camel God sent them as a sign confirming Ṣāliḥ's message. Thus, their fate is sealed:

When Our judgement came to pass, by Our grace We saved Ṣāliḥ and those who shared his faith from the ignominy of that day. Indeed, your Lord is Powerful, Almighty. The blast overtook the wrongdoers, and when morning came, they lay lifeless on the ground, in their very homes, as though they had never prospered there. Thamūd denied their Lord! Oh, away with Thamūd. (Verses 66–68)

Of Shuʿayb and his people we have the following account:

They said: 'Shuʿayb, do your prayers compel you to demand of us that we should renounce all that our forefathers worshipped, or that we refrain from doing what we please with our property? You are indeed the one who is clement and right-minded!' He said: 'Think, my people! If I take my stand on a clear evidence from my Lord and He has provided me with goodly sustenance which He alone can give? I have no desire to do, in opposition to you, what I ask you not to do. All that I desire is to set things to rights in so far as it lies within my power. My success depends on God alone. In Him have I placed my trust, and to Him I always turn. My people, let not your disagreement with me bring upon you a fate similar to those that befell the peoples of Noah, Hūd or Ṣāliḥ; nor were Lot's people far away from you. Hence, pray to your Lord to forgive you your sins, and then turn towards Him in repentance. My Lord is indeed Merciful and All-loving.' They said: 'Shuʿayb, we cannot understand much of what you say. But we do see clearly how weak you are in our midst. Were it not for your family, we would have stoned you. You do not command a position of great respect among us.' Said he: 'My people, do you hold my family in greater esteem than God? You have turned your backs on Him. My Lord encompasses [with His might] all that you do. Do what you will, my people, and so will I. You shall come to know who shall be visited by suffering that will cover him with ignominy, and who is a liar. Watch, then [for what is coming], and I shall watch with you.' (Verses 87–93)

The outcome is also portrayed:

When Our judgement came to pass, by Our grace We saved Shuʿayb and those who shared his faith. The blast overtook the wrongdoers, and when morning came, they lay lifeless on the ground, in their very homes, as though they had never prospered there. Oh, away with the people of Madyan, even as the Thamūd have been done away with! (Verses 94–95)

Comforting the Prophet

These historical accounts demonstrate to the Prophet that opposition to his message is echoed by the opposition earlier messengers received. But they all received God's support and enjoyed His care. He is directed to separate himself from those who reject his message, in the same way as earlier messengers disassociated themselves from their own people, pursuing the truth that was given to them. Moreover, the histories given are, in themselves, proof of the Prophet's claim to receive God's message and revelations.

At the end of its account of Noah's history, the *sūrah* provides this comment:

These accounts of things that have passed We now reveal to you. Neither you nor your people knew them before this. Be, then, patient in adversity; for the future belongs to those who are God-fearing. (Verse 49)

As the *sūrah* draws to a close, fairly lengthy comments ensue:

These are some of the accounts of past communities which We relate to you. Some still remain while others are extinct, like a field mown-down. No wrong did We do to them, but it was they who wronged themselves. Those deities of theirs which they were keen to invoke instead of God availed them nothing when your Lord's judgement came to pass; they only added to their ruin. Such is your Lord's punishment whenever He takes to task any community which is bent on evil-doing; His punishment is indeed grievous, severe. (Verses 100–102)

Indeed, We gave the Scriptures to Moses, and there was strife over them. Had it not been for a decree that had already gone forth from your Lord, judgement would have been passed on them. Yet, they are in grave doubt concerning that. To each and all your Lord will surely give their full due for whatever they may have done. He is indeed aware of all that they do. Follow, then, the right course as you are bidden, together with those who, with you, have turned to Him; and let none of you transgress. Surely, He sees all that you do. Put no trust in those who do wrong, lest the fire touch you. You would, then, have none to protect you from God, nor would you find any help. Attend to your prayers at both ends of the day and in the early watches of the night. Surely, good deeds erase evil ones. This is a reminder for those who are thoughtful. And be patient in adversity; God does not fail to reward those who do good. (Verses 110–115)

All that We relate to you of the histories of earlier messengers is a means by which We strengthen your heart. Through these [accounts] there has come to you the truth, as well as an admonition and a reminder for all believers. Say to those who will not believe: 'Do whatever lies within your power, and so shall we. Wait if you will;

we too are waiting.' God alone knows whatever is hidden in the heavens and the earth. All authority over all matters belongs to Him alone. Worship Him, then, and place your trust in Him alone. Your Lord is not unaware of what you do. (Verses 120–123)

All this serves to outline the practical aspect of Qur'ānic directives. Essentially, the historical accounts are given in the Qur'ān in order to serve as guidelines in the battle against *jāhiliyyah*. These guidelines are meant to enable the advocates of Islam to face up to all eventualities with suitable action.

Different Uses of Historical Events

In the Prologue to the preceding *sūrah*, Jonah, we wrote:

The last Makkan revelations discussed in this work were *Sūrahs* 6 and 7, Cattle and The Heights. Although these two *sūrahs* are placed together in their Qur'ānic order, they did not have the same sequence in the chronological order of revelation. They are followed in the Qur'ān by *Sūrahs* 8 and 9, The Spoils of War and The Repentance, which feature the special characteristics and themes of the later part of the Qur'ān revealed in Madinah. Now, however, we have two Makkan *sūrahs*, Jonah and Hūd, which have the same sequence in both chronological order and Qur'ānic arrangement. We note a remarkable similarity between the two earlier Makkan *sūrahs* and the two present ones, both in subject matter and presentation. *Sūrah* 6, Cattle, concentrates on the essence of faith, confronting the unbelievers with it and refuting all erring beliefs and practices. *Sūrah* 7, The Heights, on the other hand, speaks about the practical implementation of faith in human life and its confrontation with *jāhiliyyah* during different periods of history. The same is true of the two *sūrahs* in this volume, Jonah and Hūd. However, *Sūrah* 6 is distinguished from *Sūrah* 10 by its very powerful rhythm, quick pulse and sophistication of scene and movement. *Sūrah* 10, on the other hand, has a more relaxed rhythm and easy flow of scene and movement. *Sūrahs* 7 and 11, The Heights and Hūd display great similarity in theme, presentation and rhythm. Nevertheless, every *sūrah* in the Qur'ān has its own character, special features and distinctive properties.

We need to elaborate a little here. *Sūrah* Jonah includes brief historical references, with a very short account of Noah, and a general reference to subsequent messengers, before giving a reasonably detailed account of Moses, and concluding with a brief reference to Jonah. But these historical accounts are given only as examples, confirming the basic beliefs the *sūrah* concentrates upon.

In the present *sūrah*, historical accounts constitute a major component. Although they confirm the basic beliefs outlined in the *sūrah*, it is clear that this review of the progress of divine faith in human history is the primary objective. Hence, the *sūrah* has three clearly marked sections: the opening passage covers all basic beliefs; then we have the histories of earlier prophets which take a very sizeable portion; and finally the *sūrah* comments on the historical progress of faith. Neither the opening remarks nor the concluding comments are long.

It is also clear that these three sections effectively and coherently contribute to the establishment of the ideological basis of faith, which is the primary objective of the whole *sūrah*. In each section basic beliefs are stated in the best way suited to that section and its purpose.

The essential facts the *sūrah* wants to establish are:

1. That which the Prophet Muḥammad preached and what was preached by earlier messengers is the same basic truth revealed to them from on high. Its basis is complete submission to God alone, as directed by God's messengers only, and to separate people into two communities based on their acceptance or rejection of such submission.

   • The opening passage includes the following verses speaking of the nature of the Prophet's message:

   Alif. Lām. Rā. *This is a book, with verses which have been perfected and distinctly spelled out, bestowed on you by One who is Wise, All-aware. Worship none but God. I come to you from Him as a warner and a bearer of glad tidings.* (Verses 1–2)

If they say: 'He has invented it', say: 'Produce, then, ten invented sūrahs like it, and call for help on all you can other than God, if what you say is true.' If they do not respond to you, know that it [the Qur'ān] has been bestowed from on high with God's knowledge, and that there is no deity other than Him. Will you then submit yourselves to Him? (Verses 13–14)

- In the historical accounts of earlier prophets, there are numerous verses that state the nature of their message and the way they separated themselves from the rest of their people on the basis of faith. Here are some examples:

  We sent forth Noah to his people: 'I have come to you with a plain warning. Worship none but God. I certainly fear that suffering should befall you on a grievous day.' (Verses 25–26)

  Noah said: 'Think, my people! If I take my stand on a clear evidence from my Lord, and He has favoured me with grace from Himself, to which you have remained blind, can we force it upon you when you are averse to it?' (Verse 28)

  Noah called out to his Lord, saying: 'Lord, my son is of my family. Surely Your promise always comes true, and You are the most just of judges.' 'Noah,' He answered, 'he was not of your family; his was an unrighteous conduct. Do not question Me about matters of which you have no knowledge. I admonish you lest you become one of the ignorant.' (Verses 45–46)

  To 'Ād, We sent their brother Hūd. He said: 'My people! Worship God alone; you have no deity other than Him. You are indeed inventors of falsehood.' (Verse 50)

  To Thamūd, We sent their brother Ṣāliḥ. He said: 'My people! Worship God alone. You have no deity other than Him. He it is who brought you into being out of the earth and settled you therein. Seek His forgiveness and then turn to Him in repentance. My Lord is ever near. He answers all.' (Verse 61)

He said: 'Think, my people! If I take my stand on a clear evidence from my Lord who has bestowed on me His grace, who will save me from God were I to disobey Him? You are, in such a case, only aggravating my ruin.' (Verse 63)

And to Madyan We sent their brother Shuʿayb. He said: 'My people! Worship God alone. You have no deity other than Him.' (Verse 84)

'Think, my people! If I take my stand on a clear evidence from my Lord and He has provided me with goodly sustenance which He alone can give?' (Verse 88)

• The following verses address the same points in the final passage:

Put no trust in those who do wrong, lest the fire touch you. You would, then, have none to protect you from God, nor would you find any help. (Verse 113)

God alone knows whatever is hidden in the heavens and the earth. All authority over all matters belongs to Him alone. Worship Him, then, and place your trust in Him alone. Your Lord is not unaware of what you do. (Verse 123)

Thus all three sections converge to establish this truth.

2. In order that people should acknowledge that all Lordship belongs to God alone, the *sūrah* provides them with a clear concept of God, making it clear to them that they remain in His grasp in this life, and that to Him they will return on the Day of Resurrection when they receive their reward. Again all three sections work hand in hand to establish this truth.

• To give but a few examples, in the opening passage we read:

They cover up their breasts in order to hide from Him. Surely, when they cover themselves with their garments, He knows all that they keep secret as well as all that they bring into the open. He has full knowledge of what is in people's hearts.

There is no living creature on earth but depends for its sustenance on God; and He knows its habitation and its resting-place. All this is in a clear record. He it is who has created the heavens and the earth in six days, whereas His throne has rested upon water, so that He may test you [to make manifest] which of you is best in conduct. Yet if you say to them: 'You shall be raised again after death,' those who disbelieve are sure to say: 'This is nothing but plain sorcery.' If We defer their suffering for a definite term, they are sure to say: 'What is holding it back?' On the day when it befalls them there will be nothing to avert it from them; and they shall be overwhelmed by that which they used to deride. (Verses 5–8)

As for those who desire only the life of this world and its bounties, We shall fully repay them in this life for all they do, and they shall suffer no diminution of their just dues. It is they who, in the life to come, shall have nothing but the fire. In vain shall be all that they have done in this world, and worthless shall be all their actions. (Verses 15–16)

• In the historical accounts we have some definitive statements, such as:

Indeed I have placed my trust in God, my Lord and your Lord. There is no living creature which He does not hold by its forelock. Straight indeed is my Lord's way. But if you turn away, I have delivered to you the message with which I was sent to you. My Lord may replace you with another people. You can do Him no harm. My Lord watches over all things. (Verses 56–57)

To Thamūd, We sent their brother Ṣāliḥ. He said: 'My people! Worship God alone. You have no deity other than Him. He it is who brought you into being out of the earth and settled you therein. Seek His forgiveness and then turn to Him in repentance. My Lord is ever near. He answers all.' (Verse 61)

- And in the concluding passage we have verses like:

  Such is your Lord's punishment whenever He takes to task any community which is bent on evil-doing; His punishment is indeed grievous, severe. (Verse 102)

  To each and all your Lord will surely give their full due for whatever they may have done. He is indeed aware of all that they do. (Verse 111)

  Had your Lord so willed, He would have made all mankind one single community. As it is, they continue to differ, except those upon whom your Lord has bestowed His grace. And to this end He created them. The word of your Lord shall be fulfilled: 'I shall certainly fill hell with jinn *and humans all.'* (Verses 118–119)

Thus, all three sections of the *sūrah* complement each other in driving home the nature of Godhead and the nature of the hereafter.

It is not the existence of God that the *sūrah* wants to prove. Rather, it is God's sole Lordship in human life, as indeed in the rest of the universe. There was little or no dispute over God's existence. Divine messages were primarily concerned with God's Lordship. The same applies to the final message of Islam. This is a question of submission to God alone, ascribing no partners to Him, and of obedience to Him in all respects. All people's affairs must be referred to Him, and settled in accordance with His law. The verses we have quoted make this amply clear.

Varied Effects

The *sūrah* provides strong incentives and gives stern warnings. There is the incentive of enjoying the best in this life and in the life to come for those who respond positively to the call to submit to God alone. It promises much of what is good and beneficial for humanity. It also warns against forfeiting all that is good in this life or in the hereafter, and threatens immediate or deferred punishment for those who turn their backs on the divine message. It explains that the tyrannical leaders of those who reject the message reward their followers by leading them to hell. (See verses 15–24, 52, 57, 96–99, etc.)

The long historical accounts confirm that both the incentives and warnings are fulfilled throughout the course of divine faith. It highlights the destruction of the unbelievers and the salvation of the believers. The flood scene that destroyed Noah's people is particularly effective, and it is here that the *sūrah's* powerful rhythm reaches its zenith. (See verses 36–44)

The *sūrah* also portrays how the human soul responds to events that bring blessings or hardship. Those who reject the faith and who hasten their own punishment in reckless defiance are shown their inevitable judgement, their grief when they are deprived of their comforts and luxuries, and their arrogance when their hardship is lifted and blessings again come their way:

> *If We defer their suffering for a definite term, they are sure to say: 'What is holding it back?' On the day when it befalls them there will be nothing to avert it from them; and they shall be overwhelmed by that which they used to deride. And thus it is: if We let man taste some of Our grace, and then take it away from him, he becomes utterly in despair, totally ungrateful. And if We let him taste ease and plenty after hardship has visited him, he is sure to say: 'Gone is all affliction from me,' and he grows jubilant and boastful. Not so are the ones who are patient in adversity and do righteous deeds. They shall have forgiveness and a great reward.* (Verses 8–11)

We also have a number of scenes of the Day of Judgement and the position of the unbelievers there and how they speak to their Lord whose revelations they denied, and whose messengers they opposed. We see the great humiliation they suffer on that day, when they receive no support from any quarter. (See verses 18–22, 103–108)

Another particularly powerful effect is that produced by the statement that God Almighty is always present with us, fully aware of what we conceal in our hearts, while we remain totally unaware of His presence or His knowledge that disregards nothing.

> *To God you shall all return, and He has power over all things. They cover up their breasts in order to hide from Him. Surely,*

when they cover themselves with their garments, He knows all that they keep secret as well as all that they bring into the open. He has full knowledge of what is in people's hearts. There is no living creature on earth but depends for its sustenance on God; and He knows its habitation and its resting-place. All this is in a clear record. (Verses 4–6)

Indeed I have placed my trust in God, my Lord and your Lord. There is no living creature which He does not hold by its forelock. Straight indeed is my Lord's way. (Verse 56)

Another highly effective element is the *sūrah's* review of the historical progress of the divine faith under the leadership of God's noble messengers. Each of them faced up to the erring *jāhiliyyah*, saying the same words, clearly, powerfully and decisively. Each demonstrated his unshakeable faith and unparalleled reassurance. This is shown in some of the verses we have already quoted. Other examples will be discussed as they occur in the *sūrah*. This unity of the messengers and their attitudes in confronting *jāhiliyyah*, employing exactly the same words, heightens the effect of the *sūrah*.

I

The Message Spelled Out

Sūrah Hūd

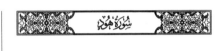

In the Name of God, the Merciful, the Beneficent

Alif. Lām. Rā. This is a book, with verses which have been perfected and distinctly spelled out, bestowed on you by One who is Wise, All-aware. (1)

Worship none but God. I come to you from Him as a warner and a bearer of glad tidings. (2)

Seek forgiveness of your Lord, and then turn towards Him in repentance, and He will grant you a goodly enjoyment of life for an appointed term. He will grant everyone with merit a full reward for his merit. But if you turn away, I dread for you the suffering of a great Day. (3)

173

To God you shall all return, and He has power over all things. (4)

إِلَى ٱللَّهِ مَرْجِعُكُمْ وَهُوَ عَلَىٰ كُلِّ شَىْءٍ قَدِيرٌ ٤

They cover up their breasts in order to hide from Him. Surely, when they cover themselves with their garments, He knows all that they keep secret as well as all that they bring into the open. He has full knowledge of what is in people's hearts. (5)

أَلَا إِنَّهُمْ يَثْنُونَ صُدُورَهُمْ لِيَسْتَخْفُوا۟ مِنْهُ أَلَا حِينَ يَسْتَغْشُونَ ثِيَابَهُمْ يَعْلَمُ مَا يُسِرُّونَ وَمَا يُعْلِنُونَ إِنَّهُۥ عَلِيمٌۢ بِذَاتِ ٱلصُّدُورِ ٥

There is no living creature on earth but depends for its sustenance on God; and He knows its habitation and its resting-place. All this is in a clear record. (6)

وَمَا مِن دَآبَّةٍ فِى ٱلْأَرْضِ إِلَّا عَلَى ٱللَّهِ رِزْقُهَا وَيَعْلَمُ مُسْتَقَرَّهَا وَمُسْتَوْدَعَهَا كُلٌّ فِى كِتَٰبٍ مُّبِينٍ ٦

He it is who has created the heavens and the earth in six days, whereas His throne has rested upon water, so that He may test you [to make manifest] which of you is best in conduct. Yet if you say to them: 'You shall be raised again after death,' those who disbelieve are sure to say: 'This is nothing but plain sorcery.' (7)

وَهُوَ ٱلَّذِى خَلَقَ ٱلسَّمَٰوَٰتِ وَٱلْأَرْضَ فِى سِتَّةِ أَيَّامٍ وَكَانَ عَرْشُهُۥ عَلَى ٱلْمَآءِ لِيَبْلُوَكُمْ أَيُّكُمْ أَحْسَنُ عَمَلًا وَلَئِن قُلْتَ إِنَّكُم مَّبْعُوثُونَ مِنۢ بَعْدِ ٱلْمَوْتِ لَيَقُولَنَّ ٱلَّذِينَ كَفَرُوٓا۟ إِنْ هَٰذَآ إِلَّا سِحْرٌ مُّبِينٌ ٧

If We defer their suffering for a definite term, they are sure to say: 'What is holding it back?' On the day when it befalls them there will be nothing to avert it from them; and they shall be overwhelmed by that which they used to deride. (8)

وَلَئِنْ أَخَّرْنَا عَنْهُمُ ٱلْعَذَابَ إِلَىٰٓ أُمَّةٍ مَّعْدُودَةٍ لَّيَقُولُنَّ مَا يَحْبِسُهُۥٓ أَلَا يَوْمَ يَأْتِيهِمْ لَيْسَ مَصْرُوفًا عَنْهُمْ وَحَاقَ بِهِم مَّا كَانُوا۟ بِهِۦ يَسْتَهْزِءُونَ ٨

And thus it is: if We let man taste some of Our grace, and then take it away from him, he becomes utterly in despair, totally ungrateful. (9)

وَلَئِنْ أَذَقْنَا ٱلْإِنسَـٰنَ مِنَّا رَحْمَةً ثُمَّ نَزَعْنَـٰهَا مِنْهُ إِنَّهُۥ لَيَـُٔوسٌ كَفُورٌ ۝

And if We let him taste ease and plenty after hardship has visited him, he is sure to say: 'Gone is all affliction from me,' and he grows jubilant and boastful. (10)

وَلَئِنْ أَذَقْنَـٰهُ نَعْمَآءَ بَعْدَ ضَرَّآءَ مَسَّتْهُ لَيَقُولَنَّ ذَهَبَ ٱلسَّيِّـَٔاتُ عَنِّىٓ إِنَّهُۥ لَفَرِحٌ فَخُورٌ ۝

Not so are the ones who are patient in adversity and do righteous deeds. They shall have forgiveness and a great reward. (11)

إِلَّا ٱلَّذِينَ صَبَرُوا۟ وَعَمِلُوا۟ ٱلصَّـٰلِحَـٰتِ أُو۟لَـٰٓئِكَ لَهُم مَّغْفِرَةٌ وَأَجْرٌ كَبِيرٌ ۝

Is it, then, conceivable that you may omit any part of what is being revealed to you and feel distressed in your heart at their saying: 'Why has not a treasure been bestowed on him from on high?' – or, 'Why has not an angel come with him?' You are only a warner, whereas God has everything in His care. (12)

فَلَعَلَّكَ تَارِكٌۢ بَعْضَ مَا يُوحَىٰٓ إِلَيْكَ وَضَآئِقٌۢ بِهِۦ صَدْرُكَ أَن يَقُولُوا۟ لَوْلَآ أُنزِلَ عَلَيْهِ كَنزٌ أَوْ جَآءَ مَعَهُۥ مَلَكٌ إِنَّمَآ أَنتَ نَذِيرٌ وَٱللَّهُ عَلَىٰ كُلِّ شَىْءٍ وَكِيلٌ ۝

If they say: 'He has invented it,' say: 'Produce, then, ten invented *surahs* like it, and call for help on all you can other than God, if what you say is true.' (13)

أَمْ يَقُولُونَ ٱفْتَرَىٰهُ قُلْ فَأْتُوا۟ بِعَشْرِ سُوَرٍ مِّثْلِهِۦ مُفْتَرَيَـٰتٍ وَٱدْعُوا۟ مَنِ ٱسْتَطَعْتُم مِّن دُونِ ٱللَّهِ إِن كُنتُمْ صَـٰدِقِينَ ۝

If they do not respond to you, know that it [the Qur'ān] has been bestowed from on high with God's knowledge, and that there is no deity other than Him. Will you then submit yourselves to Him? (14)

فَإِلَّمۡ يَسۡتَجِيبُواْ لَكُمۡ فَٱعۡلَمُوٓاْ أَنَّمَآ أُنزِلَ بِعِلۡمِ ٱللَّهِ وَأَن لَّآ إِلَٰهَ إِلَّا هُوَ فَهَلۡ أَنتُم مُّسۡلِمُونَ ١٤

As for those who desire only the life of this world and its bounties, We shall fully repay them in this life for all they do, and they shall suffer no diminution of their just dues. (15)

مَن كَانَ يُرِيدُ ٱلۡحَيَوٰةَ ٱلدُّنۡيَا وَزِينَتَهَا نُوَفِّ إِلَيۡهِمۡ أَعۡمَٰلَهُمۡ فِيهَا وَهُمۡ فِيهَا لَا يُبۡخَسُونَ ١٥

It is they who, in the life to come, shall have nothing but the fire. In vain shall be all that they have done in this world, and worthless shall be all their actions. (16)

أُوْلَٰٓئِكَ ٱلَّذِينَ لَيۡسَ لَهُمۡ فِي ٱلۡأَخِرَةِ إِلَّا ٱلنَّارُ وَحَبِطَ مَا صَنَعُواْ فِيهَا وَبَٰطِلٌ مَّا كَانُواْ يَعۡمَلُونَ ١٦

Have you considered him who takes his stand on a clear evidence from his Lord, followed by a testimony from Him, which is preceded by the Book of Moses [revealed as] a guide and a mercy [to people]? These believe in it. As for those, of any group, who deny its truth, the fire is their appointed place. So, be not in doubt concerning it; it is the truth from your Lord, even though most people do not believe. (17)

أَفَمَن كَانَ عَلَىٰ بَيِّنَةٖ مِّن رَّبِّهِۦ وَيَتۡلُوهُ شَاهِدٌ مِّنۡهُ وَمِن قَبۡلِهِۦ كِتَٰبُ مُوسَىٰٓ إِمَامًا وَرَحۡمَةً أُوْلَٰٓئِكَ يُؤۡمِنُونَ بِهِۦ وَمَن يَكۡفُرۡ بِهِۦ مِنَ ٱلۡأَحۡزَابِ فَٱلنَّارُ مَوۡعِدُهُۥ فَلَا تَكُ فِي مِرۡيَةٖ مِّنۡهُ إِنَّهُ ٱلۡحَقُّ مِن رَّبِّكَ وَلَٰكِنَّ أَكۡثَرَ ٱلنَّاسِ لَا يُؤۡمِنُونَ ١٧

Who could be more wicked than one who invents lies against God? These shall be brought before their Lord, and witnesses shall say: 'These are they who lied against their Lord.' God's curse is on the wrongdoers, (18)

وَمَنْ أَظْلَمُ مِمَّنِ ٱفْتَرَىٰ عَلَى ٱللَّهِ كَذِبًا أُوْلَٰٓئِكَ يُعْرَضُونَ عَلَىٰ رَبِّهِمْ وَيَقُولُ ٱلْأَشْهَٰدُ هَٰٓؤُلَآءِ ٱلَّذِينَ كَذَبُواْ عَلَىٰ رَبِّهِمْ أَلَا لَعْنَةُ ٱللَّهِ عَلَى ٱلظَّٰلِمِينَ ۝

who debar others from the path of God and seek to make it crooked, and who deny the life to come. (19)

ٱلَّذِينَ يَصُدُّونَ عَن سَبِيلِ ٱللَّهِ وَيَبْغُونَهَا عِوَجًا وَهُم بِٱلْأَخِرَةِ هُمْ كَٰفِرُونَ ۝

Never can they be immune [from punishment] on earth, nor have they any friends to protect them from God. Their suffering shall be doubled. They could not bear to hear, and they used not to see. (20)

أُوْلَٰٓئِكَ لَمْ يَكُونُواْ مُعْجِزِينَ فِي ٱلْأَرْضِ وَمَا كَانَ لَهُم مِّن دُونِ ٱللَّهِ مِنْ أَوْلِيَآءَ يُضَٰعَفُ لَهُمُ ٱلْعَذَابُ مَا كَانُواْ يَسْتَطِيعُونَ ٱلسَّمْعَ وَمَا كَانُواْ يُبْصِرُونَ ۝

These are the ones who have lost their own souls, and that which they used to invent shall fail them. (21)

أُوْلَٰٓئِكَ ٱلَّذِينَ خَسِرُوٓاْ أَنفُسَهُمْ وَضَلَّ عَنْهُم مَّا كَانُواْ يَفْتَرُونَ ۝

Most certainly, it is they who in the life to come shall be the greatest losers. (22)

لَا جَرَمَ أَنَّهُمْ فِي ٱلْأَخِرَةِ هُمُ ٱلْأَخْسَرُونَ ۝

Those who believe and do righteous deeds and humble themselves before their Lord are destined for paradise, and there shall they abide. (23)

إِنَّ ٱلَّذِينَ ءَامَنُواْ وَعَمِلُواْ ٱلصَّٰلِحَٰتِ وَأَخْبَتُوٓاْ إِلَىٰ رَبِّهِمْ أُوْلَٰٓئِكَ أَصْحَٰبُ ٱلْجَنَّةِ هُمْ فِيهَا خَٰلِدُونَ ۝

The case of the two parties is like that of the one who is blind and deaf and the one who sees and hears. Can the two be deemed equal? Will you not take heed? (24)

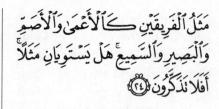

Preview

This first passage of the *sūrah* is like an introduction, followed by several accounts of past communities to whom God sent His messengers. These are then followed by a similar passage that reinforces the message the *sūrah* is meant to put across. In this introductory passage, all the fundamental issues of the Islamic faith are presented. These include self-surrender to God alone; addressing all worship to Him, associating no partners with Him; believing in the resurrection when people's actions in this life are reckoned and their rewards determined; making clear for mankind who their true Lord is, outlining His attributes that have a strong effect on their life and on the universe around them; describing the nature of the Godhead and what being a servant of God means in practice; and, finally, the fact that all will submit to God in the life to come as they do in this present life.

This introductory passage also includes an explanation of the nature of the divine message and the messenger delivering it. It adds some comfort for God's Messenger who was facing determined opposition and resistance during a particularly difficult period in Makkah. The *sūrah* throws out a challenge to all unbelievers who reject the Qur'ān to produce ten *sūrahs* like the Qur'ān. If their claim is true that the Qur'ān is a human fabrication, then they should be able to produce ten similarly fabricated *sūrahs*. This challenge serves to reassure the Prophet and his followers because it is a challenge proffered by God which the unbelievers cannot meet.

This challenge is coupled with a very stern warning to those who deny the divine message. It tells them of the suffering that awaits them in the life to come. The irony is that they hasten this punishment when they cannot tolerate that God's mercy be withdrawn from them in this present life, or that they should go through a testing period during it. Either situation is much easier to bear than the suffering in the hereafter.

This warning is then depicted in a scene of the Day of Judgement, portraying the attitude of the different groups of unbelievers who reject the Qur'ān. We see their total inability, even when they seek help from their friends and patrons, to save themselves from the suffering that is coupled with ignominy, reproach and condemnation. In contrast, the believers who do righteous deeds are shown awaiting their fine reward in a life of complete bliss. Following the Qur'ānic method of drawing analogies to express its meaning more succinctly, we have finally a quick scene showing both parties: *"The case of the two parties is like that of the one who is blind and deaf and the one who sees and hears. Can the two be deemed equal? Will you not take heed?"* (Verse 24)

The Main Issues

Alif. Lām. Rā. This is a book, with verses which have been perfected and distinctly spelled out, bestowed on you by One who is Wise, All-aware. Worship none but God. I come to you from Him as a warner and a bearer of glad tidings. Seek forgiveness of your Lord, and then turn towards Him in repentance, and He will grant you a goodly enjoyment of life for an appointed term. He will grant everyone with merit a full reward for his merit. But if you turn away, I dread for you the suffering of a great Day. To God you shall all return, and He has power over all things. (Verses 1–4)

These four opening verses set out the main fundamental principles of the Islamic faith:

- Confirmation of the facts of revelation and the divine message;
- Submission to God alone who has no partners;
- God's reward in this life and in the hereafter to those who follow His guidance and implement His code of living;
- His punishment in the hereafter of those who disbelieve, and the fact that all creatures, believers and unbelievers alike, will ultimately return to God;
- His absolute power and limitless authority.

'*Alif. Lām. Rā.*' These words stand for the letters, A, L, R. Like other single letters which occur at the beginning of other *sūrahs*, they set a challenge to the unbelievers. The challenge is that God's book is composed of such letters as people use in their speech and writing, but no matter how they try, they will not be able to produce anything similar to it. These three letters constitute the subject of the first sentence, while the rest of the first verse is its predicate.

"*This is a book, with verses which have been perfected and distinctly spelled out, bestowed on you by One who is Wise, All-aware.*" (Verse 1) The Arabic term which is rendered in translation as *have been perfected* also denotes firmness of structure and precision of meaning. Every word, every phrase is used carefully to deliver exactly the required meaning. There is no conflict or contradiction between its verses which are all *distinctly spelled out.* Each is used at its right place, under a proper heading, in order to impart a precise meaning.

Obviously the one who has so firmly perfected them, and distinctly spelled them out, is not the Messenger; he is God: "*bestowed on you by One who is Wise, All-aware.*" (Verse 1) His wisdom helps to mould their firm structure, and His comprehensive knowledge helps to give clarity to their detail. Furthermore, they come from Him directly, as delivered to His Messenger, without any distortion or alteration.

But what do they tell us? First, an outline of the basics of faith: "*Worship none but God,*" signifies that man should submit himself only to God, and obey none but Him. "*I come to you from Him as a warner and a bearer of glad tidings.*" (Verse 2) This refers to the message and its dual purpose.

"*Seek forgiveness of your Lord and then turn towards Him in repentance.*" (Verse 3) Whenever a sin is committed, it must be followed by a return to God and submission to Him. "*He will grant you a goodly enjoyment of life for an appointed term. He will grant everyone with merit a full reward for his merit.*" (Verse 3) Good reward then awaits those who repent and seek forgiveness. "*But if you turn away, I dread for you the suffering of a great Day.*" (Verse 3) This is a self-evident threat to those who turn away. Finally, the return to God who has absolute power: "*To God you shall all return, and He has power over all things.*" (Verse 4)

These then are the principles on which the whole structure of the Islamic faith is raised. Indeed, no religion can establish itself and delineate a complete way of life for mankind without first establishing these principles.

That all people should submit themselves to God alone is the central point in matters of faith. It is the point where people are either liberated from the shackles of myth, superstition and false authority or they continue to be enslaved by diverse deities, people who claim to be intermediaries between God and ordinary people, rulers and dictators who usurp God's sovereignty and authority to rule and legislate, thereby subjugating others.

No social or moral system, whether national or international, can be established on clear and well-defined principles, which are not subject to personal desire and distorted interpretations, unless the doctrine of God's oneness is clearly and precisely established. People cannot release themselves from the pressures of fear, humility and anxiety, and enjoy the true noble status with which God has favoured them unless the concept of God's absolute power and sovereignty is accepted without question, entertaining no rival claim, in any form, by anyone.

Throughout history the conflict between Islam and other systems, and the battle between truth and falsehood, have not been over the fact that God is the Lord of the universe who conducts its affairs and establishes its laws of nature. The conflict has always been over who is the Lord of mankind, who enacts their laws, conducts their affairs and to whom they must submit. Tyrants of all colours and creeds have been usurping this right for themselves. By practising it in life they subjugate people to their own power and enslave them. The divine messages and the Prophets, as well as the advocates of Islam, have always struggled to regain this usurped right in order to establish a society which acknowledges that only God has this right.

God has no need for anyone. His kingdom is neither increased by the obedience and worship of believers, nor is it decreased by the disobedience of anyone or by the tyranny of dictators. It is human beings who live in abject humility when they submit themselves to anyone other than God. On the other hand, they gain in dignity, nobility and honour when they submit to God alone and free themselves from subjugation to anyone else. Since God wants people to live in dignity and honour, He has sent His messengers with the task of returning mankind to the worship of Him alone and to liberate them from subjugation by their fellow men. This is for people's own good, not for the benefit of God who has no need for anyone.

Submission to God alone means the acknowledgement of His Lordship which, in turn, means that He is the master who can conduct their affairs by His legislation and commandment. This is the subject matter of God's book, as stated at the opening of this *sūrah*: "*This is a book, with verses which have been perfected and distinctly spelled out, bestowed on you by One who is Wise, All-aware. Worship none but God.*" (Verses 1–2) Indeed this is the meaning of worship as recognized by the Arabs in whose language the Qur'ān was revealed.

The acknowledgement of the message is essential to the acceptance of the concepts the message aims to establish. Any doubt that all this comes from God destroys its due respect in peoples' minds and consciences. Those who think that it comes from Muḥammad, no matter what degree of greatness they assign to Muḥammad, cannot look on it with the same degree of respect which makes people hesitate before violating any of its major principles or minor details. Indeed the feeling that the message and the faith it establishes come from God is the one which causes those who contravene it to feel uneasy until they eventually return to God. It also makes the believers stand firm and resist any pressure to which they may be subjected.

Acceptance of the message also provides a controlling factor which defines what God wants of His servants. Thus in matters of faith and submission to God people acknowledge only one source. No one will then be able to claim that what he says or legislates comes from God. He will be confronted with the fact that his claim is false.

In all doctrines and social set-ups based on *jāhiliyyah* people and institutions claim sovereignty and the authority to establish values and traditions, but then say: 'This comes from God.' Such confusion cannot be resolved unless God's word is derived from one source, namely, God's Messenger.

To seek forgiveness for one's sins is evidence that one's heart is alive, recognizes the offence committed and is keen to repent. Repentance means to actually refrain from committing sins and starting to do what God has bidden us to do. This is the practical meaning of repentance. Without it, it has no real existence, and cannot be accepted; and no forgiveness can be granted. If someone claims that he has decided to mend his ways and be a true Muslim, without submitting himself to God alone, and accepting only His legislation, conveyed to us through the Prophet, his claim remains false. It is belied by his submission to some authority other than God's.

Giving glad tidings to those who repent and warning those who turn away are fundamental to the message and its propagation. They utilize the two elements of hope and fear, which are well established in human nature, and which together give very strong and genuine motivation.

To believe in the hereafter is necessary for us to feel that beyond this life there is divine wisdom, and that the goodness to which the divine messages have called is the purpose of life. Therefore, it must be rewarded either in this life or in the hereafter, when human life reaches its perfection. Those who deviate from the way of life God has established are those who sink down and suffer. This should work as a safeguard for human nature against deviation. Thus, when someone is overcome by a fleeting desire or yields to temptation, he soon turns towards his Lord in repentance. Thus life continues in its good way on this planet. To believe in the Day of Judgement is, therefore, not only a method for gaining reward in the hereafter, as some people may think; it also provides motivation to be good in this life and to work for its proper development. Such development is not an end in itself; it is simply a means to establish the sort of life which suits man in whom God has blown of His own spirit, and elevated him above many of His creatures in order to make the goal of his life much more sublime than the goal of animal life.

This explains why the verses of the Qur'ān, perfected and clearly spelled out as they are, call upon us to seek God's forgiveness and turn to Him in repentance. Such is the beginning of good action which God rewards both in this life and in the life to come. Good action is not merely having good intentions and offering worship rituals. It is the type of action that seeks to make human life better in every sense of the word.

The promised reward is certain to come: "*He will grant you a goodly enjoyment of life for an appointed term. He will grant everyone with merit a full reward for his merit.*" (Verse 3) In as far as this life is concerned, goodly enjoyment may refer to the quality of life, or to having abundance and plenty. Where the life to come is concerned, it includes both quality and quantity, as well as comforts and pleasures that no human being can begin to imagine.

Let us consider what goodly enjoyment in this life represents. We often see many good people who always seek God's forgiveness and turn to Him in repentance and who work hard advocating His message enduring a life of poverty. Where is this goodly enjoyment, then?

To understand the wider significance of the Qur'ānic text, we need to look at life from a broad angle, so as to see it comprehensively and not a mere fleeting glimpse. When any community puts in place a good system based on belief in God, submission to Him alone, acknowledgement of His Lordship as the only God, and promoting good and productive work, it will inevitably enjoy progress, a comfortable standard of living and a generally good life. Furthermore, it benefits by an equity between effort and reward, and experiences a feeling of contentedness and reassurance in the life of its individual members. Therefore, when we notice that those who are good in themselves and work hard in a particular community have to endure a life of stinted means, we conclude that that community does not implement a system based on belief in God and so does not ensure equity between effort and reward.

Nevertheless, those good and hard-working individuals in such a community will still have goodly enjoyment, even though they may be poor and subjected to harm and persecution. This was indeed the case when the idolaters in Makkah persecuted the small number of believers that responded to the call of Islam. It remains the case in many communities today, where the advocates of the divine message are subjected to much persecution. This is by no means a fanciful claim. The fact that a believer has a direct relation with God, and is reassured of the eventual outcome, more than compensates for whatever hardship he endures in this present life. Indeed, it provides goodly enjoyment for anyone who moves even a single step above the material sense.

We do not say this in order to encourage those who suffer injustice and who receive only a miserable reward for their efforts to accept such injustice. Islam does not approve of this, nor does it sit idle when faced with injustice. The Muslim community, and Muslim individuals as well, are required to remove such injustice so as to ensure goodly enjoyment for all those who work hard. We say this because it is true and it is often experienced by believers who endure poverty and limited means.

"*He will grant everyone with merit a full reward for his merit.*" (Verse 3) Some commentators are of the view that this applies to the hereafter. I feel that it is of general import, making it applicable to both this life and the life to come. But we need to look at it in the same way as we explained what 'goodly enjoyment' in this present life means, because, in this sense, it is achievable in all situations. A person who has merit will receive his reward at the moment he uses his merit in a good way. He will enjoy contentedness and reassurance, and strengthen his relations with God as he uses his merit to seek God's pleasure. His reward in the life to come will be an added blessing.

"*But if you turn away, I dread for you the suffering of a great Day.*" (Verse 3) This refers to the punishment meted out on the Day of Judgement. Some commentators say that this statement refers to the unbelievers' suffering at the Battle of Badr. When the Qur'ān speaks of a 'great day' in a general sense, this is a reference to the Day of Judgement.

This sense is reinforced by the next verse: "*To God you shall all return, and He has power over all things.*" (Verse 4) Returning to God occurs in this world and the next, at every moment and in all situations. However, Qur'ānic usage confirms that when such an expression is used, it means the return that comes after this life is over.

"*He has power over all things.*" (Verse 4) This again reinforces the meaning we have outlined, because stating that God has power over all things fits in with the concept of resurrection which the unbelievers found too difficult to accept.

Hiding Away from God

Having thus given a brief outline of what the Qur'ān, the book with perfected and clearly spelled-out verses, contains, the *sūrah* goes on to describe how some of them receive these verses when they are read to them by God's Messenger. It describes the physical movements they make, hanging their heads down and covering their breasts to hide from God. It tells them of the absurdity of such action when God sees them even in their most private situations, and is fully aware of every move made by every creature on earth.

> *They cover up their breasts in order to hide from Him. Surely, when they cover themselves with their garments, He knows all that they keep secret as well as all that they bring into the open. He has full knowledge of what is in people's hearts. There is no living creature on earth but depends for its sustenance on God; and He knows its habitation and its resting-place. All this is in a clear record.* (Verses 5–6)

These two verses portray an awe-inspiring scene worthy of careful study. It is enough to contemplate the fact that God has knowledge of, and power over, everything, while people of His own creation try to hide away from Him when His Messenger conveys His message.

The first verse portrays what the unbelievers did when the Prophet tried to recite to them God's revelations. They covered their breasts and hung their heads down in order to hide from God, even though they felt, in the depth of their hearts, that He was the originator of this revelation. This they intimated on more than one occasion. The same verse shows how futile such action is. God, who sent down this revelation, is watching them as they hide and as they come out of hiding. In the inimitable style of the Qur'ān this meaning is presented in an awesome personal and private situation. When they go to bed, alone, in the darkness of the night, with all their clothes and covers on, God remains with them. He sees what takes place in such a private situation, and He has power over them in this condition, as well as in any other condition: "*Surely, when they cover themselves with their garments, He knows all that they keep secret as well as all that they bring into the open.*" (Verse 5)

God certainly knows what is much more deeply hidden and what is kept much more secret. Their shrouds and coverings cannot hide anything from His knowledge. In such a private situation, however, man feels that he is alone, unseen by anyone. Hence, the Qur'ān touches his conscience and alerts him to what he may overlook: "*He has full knowledge of what is in people's hearts.*" (Verse 5)

He is, indeed, aware of the secrets people keep closely guarded. They are well hidden in people's breasts and kept there permanently. For this reason they are described in the Arabic original as belonging to the bosom, as if they were inseparable. They are, nevertheless, known to God, who is well aware of every action, whisper and movement.

"*There is no living creature on earth but depends for its sustenance on God; and He knows its habitation and its resting-place. All this is in a clear record.*" (Verse 6) This is another example of God's knowledge which encompasses everything. All the creatures which live on earth; every human being and every animal, whether it walks, flies, crawls or creeps; and every creature which lives underneath the soil or in the depths of the sea is known to God. He it is who provides them with sustenance and He knows where each one of them abides and where it lies down, where it comes and where it goes. Each single one of them is part of His very detailed knowledge.

Here the Qur'ān gives us an elaborate picture of God's knowledge of His creation. Contemplating this image fills us with awe. The matter, however, does not end with mere knowledge. God also provides sustenance for every single one of this infinite number of creatures. Our minds are even less capable of imagining how all this happens, unless God favours us with some inspiration.

Out of His free-will, God has chosen to provide sustenance to every living creature on earth. He, therefore, has given the earth the ability to meet the needs of all these creatures, and has given these creatures the ability to get their sustenance which is available on earth in some form or another. Creatures want their provisions in different forms: raw, cultivated, manufactured, resulting from chemical processes or in any other form which generates food. Some creatures for example, like fleas and mosquitoes, feed on blood which is fully digested food.

This comprehensive picture of providing sustenance is the one befitting God's wisdom, grace and compassion as manifested in the way He has created the universe, and the way He has created all creatures with the abilities He has given them. This applies most particularly to man who is put in charge of this planet, and who is given the ability to analyse and synthesise, to grow and produce, to change the face of the earth and develop all life situations as he goes about seeking production by the abilities and powers that God has planted in this universe. In this he also depends on natural laws which make the universe conducive to producing all that it does for the sustenance of all living creatures.

This verse does not mean that every creature has its own pre-determined provisions which will not fail to come about even if he chooses not to work for them. Had this been the case, why would God require us to work and utilize the laws of nature? What would be the wisdom of giving all these creatures the abilities He has given them? How would life develop? How would man play his important role in this development?

Every creature has its sustenance; this is a fact. This sustenance is available in the universe, provided by God and He has established laws of nature which make production commensurate with effort. No one, therefore, can remain idle, thinking that the heavens will shower gold or silver on them. The heavens and earth, however, are full of sustenance which is sufficient for all creatures. They need to work in order to obtain their sustenance according to God's laws which neither favour any creature over another nor do ever fail.

However, what people earn can be divided into good and bad. Both come as a result of work and effort. They certainly differ in quality, as well as in the use and results to which they are put.

We should not overlook the contrast provided here by mentioning 'living creatures' and their sustenance, and the goodly enjoyment mentioned in Verse 3 which we have already discussed. The perfect style of the Qur'ān does not overlook the use of such finer elements that enhance the beauty of construction and effect.

Matching Science with the Qur'ān

The *sūrah* moves ahead by giving people a clearer idea of their true Lord, drawing their attention to the fact that He has created the heavens and the earth according to a certain system, with well-defined stages, to serve a definite purpose. It points out certain manifestations of God's power and wisdom which fit well with the theme of resurrection and reckoning, action and reward: *"He it is who has created the heavens and the earth in six days, whereas His throne has rested upon water, so that He may test you [to make manifest] which of you is best in conduct. Yet if you say to them: 'You shall be raised again after death,' those who disbelieve are sure to say: 'This is nothing but plain sorcery.'"* (Verse 7)

The verse speaks of the creation of the heavens and the earth in six days, which we discussed when commenting on Verse 3 of *Sūrah* 10, Jonah, page 40 in this volume. This creation is mentioned here in order to establish that there is a definite link between the system which holds the universe together and the system that regulates human life: *"So that He may test you [to make manifest] which of you is best in conduct."* (Verse 7)

What is new in this reference to God's creation is the addition of a parenthetical clause: *"His throne has rested upon water."* This signifies that when God created the heavens and the earth, that is, when He brought them into existence in their final shape and form, water was there and God's throne rested on water.

Where, how and in what condition was this water? How did God's throne rest on it? These are questions which are not answered in the Qur'ānic text. It is not for any commentator who knows his limits to add anything to what the Qur'ānic statement signifies. In such matters, what God has chosen not to reveal to us we cannot know from any other source.

Nor is it for us to try to find some endorsement of any Qur'ānic statement by what we call 'scientific' theories, even if the Qur'ānic statement, at its face value, fits well with any particular theory. 'Scientific' theories are always liable to be turned upside down whenever scientists, having tested a new assumption, discover that it provides a more credible explanation of natural and universal phenomena than the earlier theory. Every Qur'ānic statement is true regardless of whether or not science discovers the fact it states. There is a difference between what we consider to be a scientific fact and what is a scientific theory. A scientific fact is subject to experiment, but it remains always within the realm of probability. It is never taken as absolute. On the other hand, a scientific theory is based on an assumption which aims to explain a certain natural phenomenon or phenomena. It admits changes and amendments. It may even be proved wrong. Hence, it cannot be used to explain any Qur'ānic statement, nor can it be supported by the Qur'ān. Its scope is different from that of the divine book.

To seek compatibility between Qur'ānic statements and scientific theories betrays a lack of seriousness in one's faith in the Qur'ān and one's acceptance of it as true and as revealed by God who is well aware of all things. It betrays an overall fascination with science, giving it a far greater role than its natural one. Those who think that by attempting to establish compatibility between the Qur'ān and science do the Qur'ān and faith a service should be careful. Defeat has crept into their hearts. A faith which depends on the findings of ever-changing human knowledge and human science in order to be more firmly established is one which needs to be reviewed. The Qur'ān comes first. What it states is always true. It is immaterial whether scientific theories are in agreement or disagreement with the Qur'ān. Experimental scientific facts operate within a different area to that of the Qur'ān. The Qur'ān has left such facts to us to work with them freely, and make whatever conclusions our experiments establish. On the other hand, the Qur'ān takes upon itself the task of establishing in the human mind the values of righteousness and sound reasoning and liberating it from delusion, superstition and myth. It also seeks to establish a way of life which ensures that the human mind remains sound, free and active. It gives it the freedom to operate within its scope and establish by its own experiments whatever practical facts it concludes. The Qur'ān only rarely mentions scientific facts, such as that water is the source of life and the element common to all living creatures, and that all living creatures have been created in pairs, even self-fertilizing plants which contain both male and female cells.[1]

Let us now reflect on this verse from the proper point of view, that is, faith and life: *"He it is who has created the heavens and the earth in six days, whereas His throne has rested upon water, so that He may test you [to make manifest] which of you is best in conduct."* (Verse 7)

He has created the heavens and the earth in six days. There are several points not expressly stated here, but referred to later in the *sūrah*. He has created them in this span of time to make them suitable for the emergence of human life. He has also created man and made the earth and part of the heavens subject to His will. He Himself exercises His

---

1. For a more detailed discussion of the subject of the Qur'ān and science, see Vol. I, pp. 259–264 (Revised edition 2003), and Vol. V, pp. 177–178.

power over the whole universe: *"so that He may test you [to determine] which of you is best in conduct."* Here, the text seems to make the creation of the heavens and the earth in six days, coupled with the fact that God has power over the whole universe, a test for man. This adds to the seriousness of the test and makes people feel their own importance.

As God, the Creator, has endowed the earth and the heavens with what makes the emergence of the human race possible, He has equipped man with certain abilities and made his nature responsive to the law which governs the universe. He has also left him an area of free choice. Man is, therefore, capable of choosing the path of right guidance, whereupon he is helped by God. Or he can choose the path which leads him astray, and which God lets him follow. He leaves people to do whatever they want, so that He can test them and see who is the best in conduct. He does not, however, test them to find anything out. Indeed He knows, and there is no limit to His knowledge. Instead He tests them to make their secret actions appear on the surface. They then receive their reward or punishment according to God's will and justice.

Denial of the resurrection and the reckoning and the handing out of rewards sounds very strange in this context. When it is stated that testing people is linked with the creation of the heavens and the earth and is essential to this universal system and the laws of existence, those who deny it sound both absurd and totally unaware of the major facts of the creation of this universe. For this reason they are surprised and stunned by these facts: *"Yet if you say to them: 'You shall be raised again after death,' those who disbelieve are sure to say: 'This is nothing but plain sorcery.'"* (Verse 7)

What a strange claim. How false it sounds in the light of the preceding Qur'ānic statement!

Man in Different Moods

In their denial of the Day of Judgement, the unbelievers are seen to be totally unaware of its close relation to the law that governs the whole universe. They demonstrate the same ignorance concerning punishment in this life. They question the fact that they have not already been overtaken by suffering and punishment. They wonder at the delay: *"If We defer their suffering for a definite term, they are sure to say: 'What is holding it back?' On the day when it befalls them there will be nothing to avert it from them; and they shall be overwhelmed by that which they used to deride."* (Verse 8)

Where earlier prophets had produced miracles, it was to no avail for their communities which continued to reject their messages. Immediate punishment was thus their lot. This was due to the fact that the messages delivered by those prophets were addressed to a specific community, or generation. And the miracles they produced were witnessed only by that generation.

The Prophet Muḥammad, however, was given the task of delivering the final message, addressed to all generations and all communities. The miracle supporting his message was not a material one. It could, therefore, be preserved so that it could be contemplated and accepted by generation after generation. It is divine wisdom, then, that has ruled out the infliction on his community of an exterminating punishment. However, such punishment may be visited on groups or individuals of this community at particular times. The same applies to the Jews and Christians, who received earlier Scriptures, and who also have never been subjected to the sort of catastrophe that had eliminated earlier communities.

In their ignorance the unbelievers here question why their punishment, if any, is delayed. They do not realize that it is delayed only to an appointed time. Nor do they recognize that behind this delay lies God's wisdom and compassion. When the suffering overwhelms them, as it will surely do, they will have no means of averting it. It will encompass them all for their derision, evidenced by their questioning: *"On the day when it befalls them there will be nothing to avert it from them; and they shall be overwhelmed by that which they used to deride."* (Verse 8)

A believer, indeed anyone who takes a serious view of things, does not ask for God's punishment to be hastened. Such people know that if punishment is deferred, such deferment is as a result of God's compassion and wisdom, so that those who are more responsive to faith may eventually accept it. Indeed in the period during which God chose not to inflict overwhelming punishment on the Quraysh unbelievers many of them adopted Islam and served it well afterwards. Of their offspring many were good servants of Islam. These are only partial manifestations of God's purpose and wisdom. He alone knows it in full. Man, with his finite reason and hasty view, cannot know it all.

The rest of the passage describes aspects of the psychology of man, a remarkable creature who, without faith, remains short-sighted, inconsistent and vacillating: *"And thus it is: if We let man taste some of Our grace, and then take it away from him, he becomes utterly in despair, totally ungrateful. And if We let him taste ease and plenty after hardship has visited him, he is sure to say: 'Gone is all affliction from me,' and he grows jubilant and boastful. Not so are the ones who are patient in adversity and do righteous deeds. They shall have forgiveness and a great reward."* (Verses 9–11)

This is a perfectly accurate picture of man as he is: hasty, short-sighted, living only for the present, influenced only by present circumstances, forgetful of what has passed and heedless of what may follow. He is either in despair once God's grace is removed from him, ungrateful for what he has enjoyed, or overly jubilant, boastful and arrogant when ease and plenty are his lot. He does not persevere when he tastes hardship, hoping and praying that God will have mercy on him and lighten his hardship. Nor does he moderate his jubilation when he enjoys God's abundant bounty, or consider that it may be withdrawn.

"Not so are the ones who are patient in adversity." (Verse 11) Such people remain steadfast when they enjoy ease and plenty and when they endure adversity. Many people may be too proud to show weakness when they suffer any hardship. But few indeed are those who do not give themselves airs when they enjoy bliss and affluence. *"And do righteous deeds,"* in both situations. *"They shall have forgiveness and a great reward,"* for their commendable attitude in both situations. A serious view of faith, manifested in righteous deeds, is the only thing that protects man from despair during hardship and from arrogance during times of ease and plenty. It is the only factor which helps man adopt a consistent attitude in both situations. With faith man feels his link with God. He is thus not overwhelmed by adversity. Nor is he proud and insolent when he enjoys abundance. To a believer both situations are beneficial. As the Prophet says, only a believer derives benefit from both situations.

Short-Sighted Requests

Those who betray a total ignorance of God's purpose and wisdom in creating the universe and man demand that the messengers be angels or, at least, accompanied by angels. They underestimate the value of the message and demand that a messenger be given vast treasure. Here the *sūrah* addresses the Prophet and asks what he is going to do about such people.

> *Is it, then, conceivable that you may omit any part of what is being revealed to you and feel distressed in your heart at their saying: 'Why has not a treasure been bestowed on him from on high?' – or, 'Why has not an angel come with him?' You are only a warner, whereas God has everything in His care.* (Verse 12)

This verse does not present a direct question. Instead it imparts the impression that any human being would be distressed at such ignorance, stupidity and intransigence. Basically, the Prophet is being asked whether his distress and irritation at such people would make him leave out some parts of the revelations he receives from God, so as to avoid the sort of answers other prophets received from their communities.

The ending of the verse, however, clearly states that the Prophet's duty is to warn them: '*You are only a warner.*' Such people need to be warned. Hence this aspect of the Prophet's role is emphasized here.

As you do your duty you know that "*God has everything in His care.*" He will do with them what He wills, according to the laws He has established, and He will hold them accountable for what they do. The Prophet is not responsible for either their acceptance or denial of faith. He is only a warner.

This last verse lets us know the difficulties the Prophet faced at this time, and how he felt his burden to be very heavy indeed. It reminds us of the unbelievers' intransigence, hostility and conceit. Few were they at this time who responded favourably to the Prophet's call, and they endured great hardship. Yet, revelations continued to be bestowed on him from on high providing encouragement and reassurance.

A Challenge Never to be Met

The unbelievers often claimed that the Qur'ān was a forgery, invented by the Prophet. Here, he is instructed to challenge them to produce ten *sūrahs* similar to the Qur'ān, and to that end, they are able to seek the help of whomever they like: "*If they say: 'He has invented it,' say: 'Produce, then, ten invented* sūrahs *like it, and call for help on all you can other than God, if what you say is true.'*" (Verse 13) The same sort of challenge occurs in the preceding *sūrah*, Jonah, but there they are only challenged to produce one *sūrah* like the Qur'ān. So why are they now challenged to produce ten *sūrahs*?

Earlier commentators on the Qur'ān say that the challenge was narrowed down chronologically. They were first challenged to produce a book like the Qur'ān, then ten *sūrahs* and later the challenge was reduced to one *sūrah*. There is, however, no evidence to support this claim. It appears that *Sūrah* 10, Jonah, was revealed earlier than the present one, Hūd. The challenge there was to produce one *sūrah* while here it is ten. It is true that the chronological order of the revelation of verses does not necessarily follow the order of the revelation of the *sūrahs* in which they occur. Furthermore, more than one *sūrah* could have been revealed at the same time. A later verse could have been attached to an earlier *sūrah*. We have, nevertheless, no evidence to prove that the verse which contains the challenge in *Sūrah* 10 was revealed at a later date than the challenge in the present *sūrah*. We simply cannot make such an arbitrary claim.

In his commentary on the Qur'ān, *Al-Manār*, the eminent scholar, Rashīd Riḍā', tries hard to explain the challenge made here to the unbelievers to produce ten *sūrahs*. He claims this challenge is concerned with the historical accounts given in the Qur'ān. He says that up to the time this *sūrah* was revealed God's revelations included only ten *sūrahs* with such detailed accounts. In this connection, the production of a single *sūrah* would be much more difficult for them because of the different styles in which the historical accounts are told in the Qur'ān. If they were to imitate the Qur'ān they would have needed ten *sūrahs* to produce similar stories.[2]

---

2. Muḥammad Rashīd Riḍā', *Al-Manār*, Vol. 12, pp. 32–41.

The matter is, in my view, much easier than this. The challenge took into consideration the particular circumstances of those making the accusation that the Qur'ān was invented. As the process of its revelation continued, the Qur'ān dealt with particular conditions and cases. Each time, its response was the one most fitting to the case in hand. Hence, the challenge was once to produce a Qur'ān like the one revealed. In other situations it required them to produce a single *sūrah*, or ten *sūrahs*. No chronological order needs to be taken into consideration. The purpose was to challenge them to produce anything like the Qur'ān, in full or in part. The challenge indeed related to the quality of the Qur'ān, not to any quantity of it. Needless to say, in quality, a single *sūrah* is the same as the Qur'ān in full.

"*And call for help on all you can other than God, if what you say is true.*" (Verse 13) The challenge included anyone they cared to call to their aid: their deities whom they claimed to be God's partners, their finest poets as well as those among them who were endowed with the best literary talents. All they had to do to prove their allegation that the Qur'ān was invented, was produce ten *sūrahs* like those of the Qur'ān.

But all the help you seek will produce nothing. So, "*if they do not respond to you,*" then it should be enough for you to come to know the truth of revelation: "*know that it [the Qur'ān] has been bestowed from on high with God's knowledge.*" (Verse 14) He alone has the ability to bestow the Qur'ān. Only His knowledge could have produced it the way it is.

They must also realize "*that there is no deity other than Him.*" (Verse 14) This is the net result of the inability of their gods to help compose ten *sūrahs* similar to those God revealed. The self-evident conclusion then is that there is only one God who alone is able to reveal such a Scripture.

Having stated this fact, which does not admit any contradiction, the verse concludes with a question which allows for only one answer, unless it be by those who stubbornly refuse to admit the obvious. The question is "*Will you then submit yourselves to Him?*" (Verse 14)

Despite their failure to meet the challenge, their stubborn rejection of the self-evident truth continued. Their rejection was motivated by their unwillingness to relinquish their privileges in this life. They had the wealth and power to subjugate and deprive others of a chance to respond to the call of freedom, dignity and justice, the call to believe that there is no deity but God. Therefore, the following verse describes their true situation and their inevitable destiny: "*As for those who desire only the life of this world and its bounties, We shall fully repay them in this life for all they do, and they shall suffer no diminution of their just dues. It is they who, in the life to come, shall have nothing but the fire. In vain shall be all that they have done in this world, and worthless shall be all their actions.*" (Verses 15–16)

Efforts made in this life will produce their results. This is so whether the person who exercises such efforts limits his aspirations to his immediate benefit or has higher aspirations. Hence, the person whose cares are limited to this life and its luxuries and who pins his ambitions to only what this life can offer will have his results in this world to enjoy them as he wishes until the arrival of his appointed time. He will, however, have nothing in the hereafter but the fire of hell, because he has not taken the hereafter into account and has not worked for it. He receives the rewards of his worldly actions in this world. It is natural that such work will be worthless in the hereafter. The Arabic expression provides a very apt image of an action which seems to bring fat results in this world but leads to destruction in the next.

We see all around us people, individuals and communities, whose aspirations do not go beyond this world, and who actually have abundant enjoyment. We need not wonder about and question this. For this is the rule God has established for this life: "*As for those who desire only the life of this world and its bounties, We shall fully repay them in this life for all they do, and they shall suffer no diminution of their just dues.*" (Verse 15)

Having accepted this rule, we must not forget that these very people could have gone about their lives doing the same things but pinning their aspirations to the hereafter and observing God's laws in their lives. Had they done so, they would have had, as a result, the same bounties in this world and received, in addition, the bounties of the life to come.

To work for the hereafter is no impediment to working for this world. Indeed it is the same action provided that it is done with an eye to earning God's pleasure. To observe God's laws does not limit our scope of action or reduce its effects. Indeed, it increases and blesses both the effort and the result: it makes both our earnings and our enjoyment of what we earn good and blessed, and then it enhances our enjoyment of the limitless pleasures in the hereafter. The only restriction is that we should not seek the enjoyment of what is forbidden. For what is forbidden leads to ruin, not only in the hereafter, but here as well, though the latter may be delayed. This law of nature applies to both individuals and communities alike. History is a witness to the destiny of every community which over-indulged itself in forbidden desires.

Having explained these issues with such clarity, the *sūrah* points out the pagan Arabs' attitude towards the Prophet, the truth God revealed to him, the Qur'ān which testifies that what he stands for is evidenced by clear proof given by God, and that he is a messenger sent by God. Not only so, but the revelations given to Moses also testify to these facts. The aim here being to support the Prophet and the small group of believers who accepted his message. The Qur'ān also warns the unbelievers who reject his message that they will suffer the fire of hell. It paints a picture of the Day of Judgement, whereby their suffering is compounded by humiliation. This is a just retribution for their arrogance. They are unable to escape God's punishment, and cannot find anyone to support them against God. Hence they are the losers as compared with the believers. A tangible image is drawn portraying the wide gulf between the two groups, their natures and attitudes, as well as their respective positions in this life and in the hereafter.

Testimony in Support of Clear Evidence

Have you considered him who takes his stand on a clear evidence from his Lord, followed by a testimony from Him, which is preceded by the Book of Moses [revealed as] a guide and a mercy [to people]? These believe in it. As for those, of any group, who deny its truth, the fire is their appointed place. So, be not in doubt concerning it; it is the truth from your Lord, even though most people do not believe. Who could be more wicked than one who invents lies against God? These shall be brought before their Lord, and witnesses shall say: 'These are they who lied against their Lord.' God's curse is on the wrongdoers, who debar others from the path of God and seek to make it crooked, and who deny the life to come. Never can they be immune [from punishment] on earth, nor have they any friends to protect them from God. Their suffering shall be doubled. They could not bear to hear, and they used not to see. These are the ones who have lost their own souls, and that which they used to invent shall fail them. Most certainly, it is they who in the life to come shall be the greatest losers. Those who believe and do righteous deeds and humble themselves before their Lord are destined for Paradise, and there shall they abide. The case of the two parties is like that of the one who is blind and deaf and the one who sees and hears. Can the two be deemed equal? Will you not take heed? (Verses 17–24)

These verses, with varying rhythm and a multitude of pointers and references, give us an impression of what the small group of early believers faced during that critical period of the history of Islam. It tells us that the situation needed to be clearly defined and faced with positive action.

The Qur'ān cannot be truly appreciated except by those who fight the same battle as the early believers and look to the Qur'ān for guidance and instruction. Those who try to understand the meaning of the Qur'ān in a cold and detached academic manner cannot appreciate its true nature as long as they remain away from its battle. The Qur'ān never reveals its secrets to those who opt for safety and comfort even if their choice requires them to submit to some authority other than God's.

"Have you considered him who takes his stand on a clear evidence from his Lord, followed by a testimony from Him, which is preceded by the Book of Moses [revealed as] a guide and a mercy [to people]? These believe in it. As for those, of any group, who deny its truth, the fire is their appointed place. So, be not in doubt concerning it; it is the truth from your Lord, even though most people do not believe." (Verse 17) Qur'ānic commentators express different views about the meaning of this verse, depending upon their understanding of the referent of each of the third person pronouns used: *'him who takes his stand on a clear evidence from his Lord,' 'a testimony from him,'* and *'[it is] followed by'.*[3] To my mind, the weightier view is to say that the one

---

3. Translators of the Qur'ān also give different renderings of this verse, since they rely on commentators to give them a clear interpretation of the meaning of each verse. The task of both commentators and translators is made even harder because Arabic uses the same form of third person pronoun for 'he' and 'it'. In our translation of this verse we follow its meaning as given by the author. – Editor's note.

'*who takes his stand on a clear evidence from his Lord*' is the Prophet Muḥammad (peace be upon him), and, by extension, everyone who believes in his message. The next phrase, '*followed by a testimony from Him*,' means that the Prophet is followed by a witness giving a testimony to the truth of his message and prophethood. This witness is the Qur'ān which is, by itself, proof of its being revealed from God, as no one can produce anything similar to it. '*Which is preceded by*,' again refers to the Qur'ān as a witness, while '*the Book of Moses*' also testifies to the truthfulness of the Prophet as it contains clear references to him as the final prophet, and also by the fact that in its original form, the Torah, which is the Book of Moses, is in full agreement with the Qur'ān.

What confirms this understanding, in my view, is the fact that there is a single and coherent mode of expression running throughout the *sūrah* as it describes the relationship between God and His messengers. They find within themselves clear evidence giving them unshakeable certainty that it is God who sends down revelations to them. Hence, their belief in God is solid, never shaken by doubt. The Prophet Noah says to his community: "*Think, my people! If I take my stand on a clear evidence from my Lord, and He has favoured me with grace from Himself, to which you have remained blind, can we force it upon you when you are averse to it?*" (Verse 28) Ṣāliḥ (peace be upon him) also says the same words to his community: "*Think, my people! If I take my stand on a clear evidence from my Lord who has bestowed on me His grace, who will save me from God were I to disobey Him? You are, in such a case, only aggravating my ruin.*" (Verse 63) And the Prophet Shu'ayb also says the same: "*Think, my people! If I take my stand on a clear evidence from my Lord and He has provided me with goodly sustenance which He alone can give…*" (Verse 88) There is here evidently a line of expression describing the same relationship between all noble messengers and their Lord. It describes what they feel deep in their hearts about the truth of Godhead, and the truth of their contact with Him through revelations. This single mode of expression is deliberately used throughout the *sūrah* in order to emphasize that the Prophet Muḥammad's relationship with God is the same as that of earlier messengers. This is sufficient to prove the falsehood of all the unbelievers' claims. It also serves to reassure him and his followers that his message is the truth preached by all previous messengers and accepted by all their followers who submitted themselves to God alone.

Thus, the overall meaning of this verse is as follows: consider this Prophet to whose honesty and truthfulness all evidence points. He takes his stand on clear evidence which he finds in his innermost soul, granted to him by his Lord. This clear evidence is followed by a testimony from God, which is the Qur'ān, a book with clear characteristics confirming its divine source. He is further supported by another testimony which was given long before him, that is, the Torah, the book revealed to Moses to be a constitution for the Children of Israel and a mercy bestowed on them from on high. The Torah gives evidence to the truthfulness of the Prophet, God's Messenger, in two ways: it tells plainly of his message and prophethood, and it includes the same ideological principles of the universal religion acceptable to God. Is it right, then, that such a prophet should face hostility, stubborn rejection, a denial of his message and accusations of forgery? This is singularly odd, considering all the evidence confirming and endorsing his message.

It then portrays the attitude of believers in the Qur'ān and those, of all races, colours and communities, who deny it, and shows the punishment awaiting them in the hereafter. It reassures the Prophet and the believers that what they have is the truth. They should not, therefore, be disturbed by the unbelievers' attitude despite the fact that they formed the majority at that time.

"*These believe in it. As for those, of any group, who deny its truth, the fire is their appointed place. So, be not in doubt concerning it; it is the truth from your Lord, even though most people do not believe.*" (Verse 17) Some commentators find the first sentence in this section of the verse problematic. If the one who '*takes his stand on a clear evidence from his Lord,*' is the Prophet in person, as we have explained, then the pronoun '*these*' is problematic because it is plural referring to a group who believe in God's revelations and the proof it contains. But there is no problem really. The pronoun '*it*' in this sentence, '*These believe in it,*' refers to the 'testimony' which is the Qur'ān. Thus, there is nothing unusual in saying, '*These believe in it,*' meaning that they believe in the Qur'ān. Indeed the Prophet was the first to believe in what was revealed to him, followed by those who accepted his message:

"*The Messenger believes in what has been revealed to him by his Lord, and so do all the believers. Each one of them believes in God, His angels, His books and His messengers.*" (2: 285) The present verse refers to him and includes with him those who have accepted his message and believed in the faith which he conveyed to them. This is a method of expression often used in the Qur'ān.

"*As for those, of any group, who deny its truth, the fire is their appointed place.*" (Verse 17) The appointment will not fail, for God [limitless is He in His glory] is the One who has appointed it.

Unshakeable Belief in the Truth

"*So, be not in doubt concerning it; it is the truth from your Lord, even though most people do not believe.*" (Verse 17) The Prophet never entertained any doubt about the truthfulness of the revelations he was receiving. How could he have doubted when he had taken his stand on clear evidence from his Lord? However, this divine instruction, coming immediately after all the pointers and evidence made in this verse, suggests that the Prophet was concerned that his call had not made any real headway in Makkah and that it faced determined opposition from many quarters. He therefore needed some reassurance, as did the small group of his followers. Such reassurance is granted here by God, the Merciful.

The advocates of Islamic revival face a similar situation wherever they happen to be. They have to confront all sorts of rejection, hostility, ridicule, persecution as well as physical and moral repression. All forces of *jāhiliyyah*, local and international, are marshalled against them. They are subjected to the most ghastly and wicked forms of repression. Conversely, those who conduct such persecution are treated as heroes. In their present difficulty, the advocates of Islam will be well advised to understand this verse fully, with all that it states and implies. They are in urgent need of the reassurance provided by God's appropriate affirmation: "*Be not in doubt concerning it; it is the truth from your Lord, even though most people do not believe.*" (Verse 17)

Advocates of Islam need to find within themselves a share of the clear, divine evidence God's messengers had in their hearts. They need to feel His mercy which God's messengers never doubted for a moment and through which they confirmed their commitment regardless of the great difficulties they faced: "*Think, my people! If I take my stand on a clear evidence from my Lord who has bestowed on me His grace, who will save me from God were I to disobey Him? You are, in such a case, only aggravating my ruin.*" (Verse 63)

Advocates of Islam nowadays face a situation that is not dissimilar to the situations faced by God's messengers (peace be upon them). In fact, our situation today is similar to that which prevailed when the Prophet conveyed his message to all of humanity. He faced the *jāhiliyyah* into which humanity had sunk after it was put on the path of Islam [i.e. submission to God] by Abraham, Ishmael, Isaac, Jacob, Joseph, Moses, Aaron, David, Solomon, John, Jesus and the rest of the prophets.

Jāhiliyyah may or may not recognize the existence of God. In either form it appoints for people deities who rule over them in a way that is different from that revealed by God. It establishes for mankind values, traditions and legislations which make them submit to these deities, and not to God. The Islamic message to all of humanity is to renounce these false deities in order to return to God. We should believe in Him as our only Lord, submit ourselves to Him, follow only His legislation and obey only His commandments. This is indeed what starts the grinding battle between monotheism and polytheism, Islam and *jāhiliyyah*, the advocates of Islamic revival and the tyrants who rule the world in the name of their false deities.

Hence, it is necessary for advocates of Islam to refer to the Qur'ān where they may find a picture of their own situation and the battle they are fighting. This is what we mean when we say that this Qur'ān can only be appreciated by those who fight its battle, and who face situations similar to those that existed at the time of its revelation and for which it provided guidance and instruction.

The *sūrah* moves on to confront those who deny the validity of the Qur'ān and who blatantly lie against God and the Prophet alleging that the Qur'ān is fabricated. The confrontation starts with a scene from the Day of Judgement when the liars are brought to account before their Lord. Here, everything that can be described as lies against God is included: their allegation that God did not reveal the Qur'ān, their association of partners with Him and their claims that Lordship of this earth, which is an attribute of God's, belongs to them. When they are brought before their Lord on the Day of Judgement all their allegations are publicized so that everyone witnesses their fabrications and falsehood. On the other side stand the believers, happy, reassured, awaiting their fine reward. The two groups are compared to someone who is blind and deaf, and another who is in full possession of his seeing and hearing faculties.

> *Who could be more wicked than one who invents lies against God? These shall be brought before their Lord, and witnesses shall say: 'These are they who lied against their Lord.' God's curse is on the wrongdoers, who debar others from the path of God and seek to make it crooked, and who deny the life to come. Never can they be immune [from punishment] on earth, nor have they any friends to protect them from God. Their suffering shall be doubled. They could not bear to hear, and they used not to see. These are the ones who have lost their own souls, and that which they used to invent shall fail them. Most certainly, it is they who in the life to come shall be the greatest losers. Those who believe and do righteous deeds and humble themselves before their Lord are destined for Paradise, and there shall they abide. The case of the two parties is like that of the one who is blind and deaf and the one who sees and hears. Can the two be deemed equal? Will you not take heed? (Verses 18–24)*

The Greatest Losers

To invent any lie is to commit a terrible crime against truth and against the person concerned. How much more terrible the crime becomes then when the lies are fabricated against God? The culprits then "*shall be brought before their Lord, and witnesses shall say: 'These are they who lied against their Lord.'*" (Verse 18) It is a scene where their crime is publicized and they are disgraced. They are singularly pointed out and everyone is made aware that their lies were '*against their Lord*'. The scene carries an air of defamation, and is followed by a suitably appropriate curse: "*God's curse is on the wrongdoers.*" (Verse 18)

This curse is invoked by the witnesses, who are the angels, the messengers and the believers, or probably, all mankind. Thus, humiliation awaits them on that vast stage where they are brought to account. Or, perhaps, it is God's final decision in their case along with the humiliation and the disgrace which they are made to endure in front of all people. In this case it should be read not as an invocation, but as a statement of fact: "*God's curse is on the wrongdoers.*" The wrongdoers are those who associate partners with God and who fabricate lies against Him in order to debar others from His path.

"*And seek to make it crooked.*" (Verse 19) They do not wish to act with honesty and sincerity. They do not like to behave in a straightforward manner. They prefer crookedness and deviousness. The pronoun '*it*' used here refers to either the path of God or to life generally. The truth about them is emphasized, for they are those '*who deny the life to come.*' The Arabic expression here is much more emphatic, so that the enormity of their crime is portrayed in sharp relief.

Those who ascribe partners to God (limitless is He in His glory) are the wrongdoers who, indeed, wish all life to be crooked. For they deliberately take themselves away from the straightforward and honest path of Islam. Submission to any deity other than God can only bring about crookedness in every aspect of human existence. When people submit themselves to deities other than God Almighty, they bring humiliation into their own lives, whereas God wants them to enjoy dignity. They perpetrate injustice and oppression while God wants life to be based on justice and fair play. They also waste their own efforts as they try to make their own deities look big and blow up their images so that they can fill the place which belongs to God alone.

These people, cursed and turned away as they are, can never "*be immune from punishment on earth.*" (Verse 20) God is always able to punish them in this life, if He so wishes. "*Nor have they any friends to protect them*" or to support them against God. It is, however, His will to defer their punishment to the future life, so that they will endure torment in this world and in the world to come. "*Their suffering shall be doubled.*" (Verse 20) They have wasted their senses, and lived as if they were dispossessed of their faculties of hearing and seeing: "*They could not bear to hear, and they used not to see.*" (Verse 20)

"*These are the ones who have lost their own souls.*" (Verse 21) This is indeed the most terrible loss. For he who has lost his own soul cannot benefit from anything he gains in its place. These people have wasted their lives. They could not appreciate their dignity which is best fulfilled by lifting themselves above submission to anyone other than God. They incurred their loss when they denied the hereafter and fabricated lies against their Lord with the expectation that they would never meet Him. In the life to come they will find that they have lost their souls.

"That which they used to invent shall fail them." (Verse 21) Their fabrications will go amiss. They cannot find the lies they invented against God. They will all disappear. *"Most certainly, it is they who in the life to come shall be the greatest losers."* (Verse 22) What loss can be greater than theirs when they have lost their own souls both in this life and in the life to come?

Contrasted with their situation is that of those who believe and maintain good and proper action. These are reassured, have total trust in their Lord, undisturbed by any doubt or worry: *"Those who believe and do righteous deeds and humble themselves before their Lord are destined for Paradise, and there shall they abide."* (Verse 23) The Arabic expression used for 'humbling themselves' also denotes submission, trust and reassurance. It depicts a believer's relationship with his Lord which is one of complete satisfaction, security and freedom from all worry.

We have finally a very vivid image of each of the two groups. The first is like a person who cannot see because he is blind, and cannot hear because he is deaf. He does not put his senses and faculties to their ultimate use, serving his mind, so that he can think, reason and contemplate. He is indeed deprived of all his senses and faculties. The other group are like a person who sees and hears and is, therefore, rightly guided by his senses. *"The case of the two parties is like that of the one who is blind and deaf and the one who sees and hears."* (Verse 24) This image is then followed by a rhetorical question: *"Can the two be deemed equal? Will you not take heed?"* (Verse 24) The whole issue does not require more than taking heed. It is a simple, straightforward issue.

2

A Historical Perspective

We sent forth Noah to his people: 'I have come to you with a plain warning. (25)

وَلَقَدۡ أَرۡسَلۡنَا نُوحًا إِلَىٰ قَوۡمِهِۦ إِنِّي لَكُمۡ نَذِيرٌ مُّبِينٌ ﴿٢٥﴾

Worship none but God. I certainly fear that suffering should befall you on a grievous day.' (26)

أَن لَّا تَعۡبُدُوٓاْ إِلَّا ٱللَّهَ إِنِّيٓ أَخَافُ عَلَيۡكُمۡ عَذَابَ يَوۡمٍ أَلِيمٍ ﴿٢٦﴾

The notables of his people who disbelieved said: 'We see you but a mortal man like ourselves. Nor can we see anyone following you except the most abject among us; those who are rash and un-discerning. We do not consider that you are in any way superior to us: indeed we think you are liars.' (27)

فَقَالَ ٱلۡمَلَأُ ٱلَّذِينَ كَفَرُواْ مِن قَوۡمِهِۦ مَا نَرَىٰكَ إِلَّا بَشَرًا مِّثۡلَنَا وَمَا نَرَىٰكَ ٱتَّبَعَكَ إِلَّا ٱلَّذِينَ هُمۡ أَرَاذِلُنَا بَادِيَ ٱلرَّأۡيِ وَمَا نَرَىٰ لَكُمۡ عَلَيۡنَا مِن فَضۡلٍ بَلۡ نَظُنُّكُمۡ كَٰذِبِينَ ﴿٢٧﴾

Noah said: 'Think, my people! If I take my stand on a clear evidence from my Lord, and He has favoured me with grace from Himself, to which you have remained blind, can we force it upon you when you are averse to it? (28)

قَالَ يَٰقَوۡمِ أَرَءَيۡتُمۡ إِن كُنتُ عَلَىٰ بَيِّنَةٍ مِّن رَّبِّي وَءَاتَىٰنِي رَحۡمَةً مِّنۡ عِندِهِۦ فَعُمِّيَتۡ عَلَيۡكُمۡ أَنُلۡزِمُكُمُوهَا وَأَنتُمۡ لَهَا كَٰرِهُونَ ﴿٢٨﴾

And, my people, I ask of you no money in return; my reward rests with none but God. Nor will I drive away those who believe; they will surely meet their Lord, whereas in you I see people with no awareness [of right and wrong]. (29)

وَيَٰقَوْمِ لَآ أَسْـَٔلُكُمْ عَلَيْهِ مَالًا إِنْ أَجْرِىَ إِلَّا عَلَى ٱللَّهِ وَمَآ أَنَا۠ بِطَارِدِ ٱلَّذِينَ ءَامَنُوٓا۟ إِنَّهُم مُّلَٰقُوا۟ رَبِّهِمْ وَلَٰكِنِّىٓ أَرَىٰكُمْ قَوْمًا تَجْهَلُونَ ﴿٢٩﴾

And, my people, who would protect me from God were I to drive them away? Will you not reflect? (30)

وَيَٰقَوْمِ مَن يَنصُرُنِى مِنَ ٱللَّهِ إِن طَرَدتُّهُمْ أَفَلَا تَذَكَّرُونَ ﴿٣٠﴾

I do not say to you that God's treasures are with me, or that I know what lies beyond the reach of human perception. Nor do I say: I am an angel. Nor do I say of those whom you eye with contempt that God will never grant them any good. God knows best what is in their hearts – for then I would indeed be a wrongdoer.' (31)

وَلَآ أَقُولُ لَكُمْ عِندِى خَزَآئِنُ ٱللَّهِ وَلَآ أَعْلَمُ ٱلْغَيْبَ وَلَآ أَقُولُ إِنِّى مَلَكٌ وَلَآ أَقُولُ لِلَّذِينَ تَزْدَرِىٓ أَعْيُنُكُمْ لَن يُؤْتِيَهُمُ ٱللَّهُ خَيْرًا ٱللَّهُ أَعْلَمُ بِمَا فِىٓ أَنفُسِهِمْ إِنِّىٓ إِذًا لَّمِنَ ٱلظَّٰلِمِينَ ﴿٣١﴾

'Noah,' they replied, 'you have argued with us, and argued to excess. Bring upon us that with which you have been threatening us, if you are a man of truth.' (32)

قَالُوا۟ يَٰنُوحُ قَدْ جَٰدَلْتَنَا فَأَكْثَرْتَ جِدَٰلَنَا فَأْتِنَا بِمَا تَعِدُنَآ إِن كُنتَ مِنَ ٱلصَّٰدِقِينَ ﴿٣٢﴾

He said: 'Only God can bring it upon you, if He so wills. You cannot be immune. (33)

قَالَ إِنَّمَا يَأْتِيكُم بِهِ ٱللَّهُ إِن شَآءَ وَمَآ أَنتُم بِمُعْجِزِينَ ﴿٣٣﴾

Nor will my counsel benefit you, much as I desire to give you good counsel, if it is God's will to let you remain in error. He is your Lord and to Him you shall return.' (34)

وَلَا يَنفَعُكُمْ نُصْحِى إِنْ أَرَدتُّ أَنْ أَنصَحَ لَكُمْ إِن كَانَ ٱللَّهُ يُرِيدُ أَن يُغْوِيَكُمْ هُوَرَبُّكُمْ وَإِلَيْهِ تُرْجَعُونَ ٣٤

Do they claim that he [i.e. Muḥammad] has invented it? Say: 'If I have invented it, upon me be this crime of mine, but I am innocent of the crimes you perpetrate.' (35)

أَمْ يَقُولُونَ ٱفْتَرَىٰهُ قُلْ إِنِ ٱفْتَرَيْتُهُ فَعَلَىَّ إِجْرَامِى وَأَنَا۟ بَرِىٓءٌ مِّمَّا تُجْرِمُونَ ٣٥

Noah received this revelation: 'None of your people will believe now apart from those who have already accepted the faith. Do not be in distress over anything they may do. (36)

وَأُوحِىَ إِلَىٰ نُوحٍ أَنَّهُۥ لَن يُؤْمِنَ مِن قَوْمِكَ إِلَّا مَن قَدْ ءَامَنَ فَلَا تَبْتَئِسْ بِمَا كَانُوا۟ يَفْعَلُونَ ٣٦

Build the ark under Our eyes, and according to Our inspiration. Do not appeal to Me on behalf of the wrongdoers. They shall be drowned.' (37)

وَٱصْنَعِ ٱلْفُلْكَ بِأَعْيُنِنَا وَوَحْيِنَا وَلَا تُخَٰطِبْنِى فِى ٱلَّذِينَ ظَلَمُوٓا۟ إِنَّهُم مُّغْرَقُونَ ٣٧

So he set himself on building the ark. And whenever a group of his people passed by him they scoffed at him. He said: 'If you are scoffing at us, we are indeed scoffing at you, just as you are scoffing at us. (38)

وَيَصْنَعُ ٱلْفُلْكَ وَكُلَّمَا مَرَّ عَلَيْهِ مَلَأٌ مِّن قَوْمِهِۦ سَخِرُوا۟ مِنْهُ قَالَ إِن تَسْخَرُوا۟ مِنَّا فَإِنَّا نَسْخَرُ مِنكُمْ كَمَا تَسْخَرُونَ ٣٨

You will surely come to know who it is that will be visited by suffering that will cover him with ignominy, and who will be afflicted by long-lasting suffering.' (39)

فَسَوْفَ تَعْلَمُونَ مَن يَأْتِيهِ عَذَابٌ يُخْزِيهِ وَيَحِلُّ عَلَيْهِ عَذَابٌ مُّقِيمٌ ۝

Until, when Our will came to pass and the fountains of the earth gushed forth, We said [to Noah]: 'Take into it a pair of every species, as well as your family, except those against whom Our word has passed, and all those who have accepted the faith.' None believed with him except a few. (40)

حَتَّىٰٓ إِذَا جَآءَ أَمْرُنَا وَفَارَ ٱلتَّنُّورُ قُلْنَا ٱحْمِلْ فِيهَا مِن كُلٍّ زَوْجَيْنِ ٱثْنَيْنِ وَأَهْلَكَ إِلَّا مَن سَبَقَ عَلَيْهِ ٱلْقَوْلُ وَمَنْ ءَامَنَ وَمَآ ءَامَنَ مَعَهُۥٓ إِلَّا قَلِيلٌ ۝

He said to them: 'Embark in it. In the name of God be its course and its riding at anchor. My Lord indeed is Much-Forgiving, Merciful.' (41)

وَقَالَ ٱرْكَبُواْ فِيهَا بِسْمِ ٱللَّهِ مَجْر۪ىٰهَا وَمُرْسَىٰهَآ إِنَّ رَبِّى لَغَفُورٌ رَّحِيمٌ ۝

And it sailed with them amid waves towering like mountains. Noah cried out to a son of his who stood apart [from the rest]: 'Embark with us, my child, and do not stay with the unbelievers.' (42)

وَهِىَ تَجْرِى بِهِمْ فِى مَوْجٍ كَٱلْجِبَالِ وَنَادَىٰ نُوحٌ ٱبْنَهُۥ وَكَانَ فِى مَعْزِلٍ يَٰبُنَىَّ ٱرْكَب مَّعَنَا وَلَا تَكُن مَّعَ ٱلْكَٰفِرِينَ ۝

He answered: 'I shall seek refuge in a mountain, which will afford me protection from the water.' Said (Noah): 'Today there is no protection for anyone from God's judgement, except those who shall enjoy His mercy.' Thereupon waves rose up between them and he was among those who were drowned. (43)

قَالَ سَـَٔاوِىٓ إِلَىٰ جَبَلٍ يَعْصِمُنِى مِنَ ٱلْمَآءِ قَالَ لَا عَاصِمَ ٱلْيَوْمَ مِنْ أَمْرِ ٱللَّهِ إِلَّا مَن رَّحِمَ وَحَالَ بَيْنَهُمَا ٱلْمَوْجُ فَكَانَ مِنَ ٱلْمُغْرَقِينَ ٤٣

And the word was spoken: 'Earth, swallow up your waters. Heaven, cease (your rain).' Thus the waters sank into the earth, and God's will was done, and the ark came to rest on Mount Jūdī. The word was spoken: 'Away with these evil-doing folk.' (44)

وَقِيلَ يَـٰٓأَرْضُ ٱبْلَعِى مَآءَكِ وَيَـٰسَمَآءُ أَقْلِعِى وَغِيضَ ٱلْمَآءُ وَقُضِىَ ٱلْأَمْرُ وَٱسْتَوَتْ عَلَى ٱلْجُودِىِّ وَقِيلَ بُعْدًا لِّلْقَوْمِ ٱلظَّـٰلِمِينَ ٤٤

Noah called out to his Lord, saying: 'Lord, my son is of my family. Surely Your promise always comes true, and You are the most just of judges.' (45)

وَنَادَىٰ نُوحٌ رَّبَّهُ فَقَالَ رَبِّ إِنَّ ٱبْنِى مِنْ أَهْلِى وَإِنَّ وَعْدَكَ ٱلْحَقُّ وَأَنتَ أَحْكَمُ ٱلْحَـٰكِمِينَ ٤٥

'Noah,' He answered, 'he was not of your family; his was an unrighteous conduct. Do not question Me about matters of which you have no knowledge. I admonish you lest you become one of the ignorant.' (46)

قَالَ يَـٰنُوحُ إِنَّهُ لَيْسَ مِنْ أَهْلِكَ إِنَّهُ عَمَلٌ غَيْرُ صَـٰلِحٍ فَلَا تَسْـَٔلْنِ مَا لَيْسَ لَكَ بِهِۦ عِلْمٌ إِنِّىٓ أَعِظُكَ أَن تَكُونَ مِنَ ٱلْجَـٰهِلِينَ ٤٦

Said (Noah): 'My Lord, I do indeed seek refuge with You from ever questioning You about anything of which I have no knowledge. Unless You grant me forgiveness and have mercy on me I shall be among the losers.' (47)

قَالَ رَبِّ إِنِّيٓ أَعُوذُ بِكَ أَنْ أَسْـَٔلَكَ مَا لَيْسَ لِي بِهِۦ عِلْمٌ وَإِلَّا تَغْفِرْ لِي وَتَرْحَمْنِيٓ أَكُن مِّنَ ٱلْخَٰسِرِينَ ٤٧

The word was spoken: 'Noah, disembark in peace from Us, and with Our blessings upon you as well as upon generations from those who are with you. As for other folk, We shall let them have enjoyment, and then there will befall them grievous suffering from Us.' (48)

قِيلَ يَٰنُوحُ ٱهْبِطْ بِسَلَٰمٍ مِّنَّا وَبَرَكَٰتٍ عَلَيْكَ وَعَلَىٰٓ أُمَمٍ مِّمَّن مَّعَكَ وَأُمَمٌ سَنُمَتِّعُهُمْ ثُمَّ يَمَسُّهُم مِّنَّا عَذَابٌ أَلِيمٌ ٤٨

These accounts of things that have passed We now reveal to you. Neither you nor your people knew them before this. Be, then, patient in adversity; for the future belongs to those who are God-fearing. (49)

تِلْكَ مِنْ أَنۢبَآءِ ٱلْغَيْبِ نُوحِيهَآ إِلَيْكَ مَا كُنتَ تَعْلَمُهَآ أَنتَ وَلَا قَوْمُكَ مِن قَبْلِ هَٰذَا فَٱصْبِرْ إِنَّ ٱلْعَٰقِبَةَ لِلْمُتَّقِينَ ٤٩

Preview

Historical accounts form the main part of this *sūrah*, but they are not independent of its theme. They are related to confirm the great truths it aims to establish. This is apparent from the *sūrah's* very opening verses: "*This is a book, with verses which have been perfected and distinctly spelled out, bestowed on you by One who is Wise, All-aware. Worship none but God. I come to you from Him as a warner and a bearer of glad tidings. Seek forgiveness of your Lord, and then turn towards Him in repentance, and He will grant you a goodly enjoyment of life for an appointed term. He will grant everyone with merit a full reward for his merit. But if you turn away, I dread for you the suffering of a great Day. To God you shall all return, and He has power over all things."* (Verses 1–4)

The opening passage of the *sūrah* emphasizes these truths: it reflects on God's creation of the heavens and earth, explains the wonders of human creation, and speaks about the Day of Judgement. Now the *sūrah* takes us back in history to tell us of earlier communities and how they received the message of truth. Thus it recounts the call to faith over many centuries, providing rather detailed accounts of earlier prophets. This is particularly true in the case of Noah and the great flood. These accounts include the arguments over the basic issues of faith as outlined at the *sūrah*'s opening, and asserted by every messenger. Those who deny the faith are the same throughout history: they share the same mentality and nature.

The historical accounts in this *sūrah* are given in chronological order, starting with Noah, then Hūd and Ṣāliḥ. We then move on to Abraham, Lot, Shu'ayb and Moses. Thus they serve as a reminder to later generations of the fate of their predecessors.

When a Prophet is Described as a Liar

"We sent forth Noah to his people: 'I have come to you with a plain warning. Worship none but God. I certainly fear that suffering should befall you on a grievous day.'" (Verses 25–26) These are practically the same words as used by Prophet Muḥammad (peace be upon him) and as outlined in the Qur'ān. This use of almost exactly the same wording to express the main theme is deliberate, as it emphasizes the unity of the message and the unity of the faith. We assume that what is given here is the meaning of what Noah said to his people, not the exact words, because we do not know what language was used by Noah and his community.

"We sent forth Noah to his people: 'I have come to you with a plain warning.'" (Verse 25) The text does not include any intervening clause such as 'and he said to them', because the Qur'ān paints the scene and we see it as if it is happening now, not as a part of ancient history.

213

Moreover, it gives a brief statement summing up the purpose of the message in one fundamental truth: "*I have come to you with a plain warning.*" This is much more emphatic.

This is followed by another brief statement summing up the central theme of the message: "*Worship none but God.*" (Verse 26) This is the main issue of faith and the subject matter of the warning. But what is the warning all about: "*I certainly fear that suffering should befall you on a grievous day.*" (Verse 26) Thus the message is conveyed and the warning given in a few brief statements. It should be noted here that the Arabic wording should give the meaning that the day itself is in grief, awe or pain, but it is naturally not so. It is simply described as such to indicate that it senses the pain suffered by people. How about the people themselves, then?

"*The notables of his people who disbelieved said: 'We see you but a mortal man like ourselves. Nor can we see anyone following you except the most abject among us; those who are rash and undiscerning. We do not consider that you are in any way superior to us: indeed we think you are liars.'*" (Verse 27) This is the response of the elders who assume leadership of the community. It is practically the same response Prophet Muḥammad received from the Quraysh elders, his own tribesmen. They express the same doubts, utter the same accusations, show the same arrogance and give overall the same answer that betrays their ignorance and stupidity.

We find here the same doubt entertained by the ignorant who think that the human race is too low to be entrusted with God's message. If God wants to send a message, then let it be delivered by an angel or some other creature. This ignorant misgiving stems from a lack of trust in the human race. It stands to reason that God would have given man adequate abilities and talents to fulfil his function as vicegerent. He has also enabled certain individuals to carry and deliver God's message. These are chosen by God who knows best the special qualities with which He has equipped them.

Another mark of ignorance is what such people say about the choice of messenger. They maintain that he should have been chosen from among the elders who exercise power and influence in the community. This betrays a total ignorance of the real values attached to human beings, the race assigned the task of building life on earth. These values have nothing to do with wealth, position, or influence in society. Instead, they have much to do with the soul and its purity, openness, the ability to receive revelations, a willingness to be true to one's trust, perseverance in the face of difficulties and other such noble qualities. But the notables among Noah's people, like the notables among every prophet's community, are blinded by their worldly positions and unable to perceive these more subtle qualities. They cannot visualize what is noble.

"*We see you but a mortal man like ourselves.*" (Verse 27) This is their first argument, but the second is much worse: "*Nor can we see anyone following you except the most abject among us; those who are rash and undiscerning.*" (Verse 27) They describe the poor among them as '*the most abject*'. This is the way notables always look at the poor who have not been endowed with riches or power. Yet it is mainly such lowly folk who followed the earlier prophets. Such people are, by their nature, more likely to respond to a call which liberates the subjugated and establishes a bond between them and God Almighty. Their nature has not been corrupted by the power of wealth and luxury. Nor are they held back by their interests and social appearances. They have nothing to lose as a result of accepting the true faith. The faith based on God's oneness is indeed the real message of liberating mankind at every stage in history. Hence, it was opposed by tyrants everywhere who try to turn people away from it, levelling at it all sorts of false accusations.

"*Nor can we see anyone following you except the most abject among us, those who are rash and undiscerning.*" This is an accusation which those in power level at the believers, accusing them of being rash, unthinking. The implication being that they would not follow suit. It does not become them to go along the same way as the unthinking, unreflecting masses or to sit idle without trying to turn the believers away from their faith.

"*We do not consider that you are in any way superior to us: indeed we think you are liars.*" (Verse 27) Here they group together the messenger and those who follow him. They see nothing in the believers that makes them more likely to be right or following proper guidance. Had the message being advocated been right and good, they would have seen it for what it is and accepted it, without allowing those who are '*abject*' to beat them to it. They apply here the same erroneous standards that make honour commensurate with wealth, understanding with influence and position, and knowledge with power. Such standards and values gain the upper hand when the faith based on God's oneness gives way to *jāhiliyyah*, and into some form of paganism, even though it may appear in bright attire.[1] This is definitely a setback for humanity. It reduces the importance of the values that equip man to fulfil the task God has assigned to him on earth, and make him worthy of receiving God's message.

"Indeed we think you are liars." (Verse 27) This is the last accusation levelled at the Prophet Noah and his followers. The accusation is expressed in a gentle way that befits their social standing in society. They say, *'we think you,'* because an accusation made in absolute and clear terms is more suited to the unthinking masses. Such a form of expression and blatant accusation is beneath the ruling classes in their higher status.

The same type of argument and accusation has been repeated time and again, ever since the Prophet Noah. This is the attitude of people who have full pockets but empty hearts and minds. Their arrogance is limitless.

A Prophet's Passionate Plea

Kind and dignified, the Prophet Noah is full of confidence that his message is the message of truth. He trusts that it comes from God, and is fully aware that his path has been set clearly for him and that his method of operation is sound and honest. He remains unaffected by the false accusations, insolence and blind rejection with which his message has been received. He applies his own values and maintains his own standards. He does not make false claims or accusations as they have done. Nor does he try to give himself any false image or impart anything alien to his message.

"Noah said: 'Think, my people! If I take my stand on a clear evidence from my Lord, and He has favoured me with grace from Himself, to

---

1. In the US, a person's position is commensurate with his income or bank balance. The new pagan *jāhiliyyah* spreads from the US to the rest of the world, including the Orient which claims to be Islamic!

which you have remained blind, can we force it upon you when you are averse to it? And, my people, I ask of you no money in return; my reward rests with none but God. Nor will I drive away those who believe; they will surely meet their Lord, whereas in you I see people with no awareness [of right and wrong]. And, my people, who would protect me from God were I to drive them away? Will you not reflect? I do not say to you that God's treasures are with me, or that I know what lies beyond the reach of human perception. Nor do I say: I am an angel. Nor do I say of those whom you eye with contempt that God will never grant them any good. God knows best what is in their hearts – for then I would indeed be a wrongdoer.'" (Verses 28–31)

He addresses people with kindness and friendliness stressing his relationship to them: 'My people,' you object to my message saying: *'We see you but a mortal man like ourselves.'* Yet I have a relationship with my Lord which is absolutely clear to me and firmly established in my conscience. This is something that you have not been granted. What if God has bestowed on me His grace, selecting me to carry His message? This is indeed a great mercy He has shown me. Yet what if both conditions are true, but you remain blind to them, because you are not open minded enough? *"Can we force it upon you?"* (Verse 28) It is not for me to try to force you to accept it *"when you are averse to it."* (Verse 28)

Here we see Noah trying gently to awaken their consciences, making them feel the importance of the values to which they have been blind and making them aware of the characteristics they tend to overlook when it comes to the message and the person selected to carry it. He explains to them that these matters are not decided on the basis of their superficial criteria. At the same time he establishes the right principle that faith must be based on conviction, and that conviction is the result of study and reflection. Compulsion, arbitrary authority and conceit have no bearing on faith and conviction.

"And, my people, I ask of you no money in return; my reward rests with none but God. Nor will I drive away those who believe; they will surely meet their Lord, whereas in you I see people with no awareness [of right and wrong]." (Verse 29) Those whom you describe as the most

abject among you, Noah explains, have responded positively to my call and accepted the faith. I seek no financial gain for my call, and as such, I cannot favour the rich over the poor. All my people are equal as far as I am concerned. He who does not seek pecuniary reward from people cannot make any distinction on the basis of wealth. *"My reward rests with none but God."* He is the only One from whom reward may be forthcoming.

"Nor will I drive away those who believe." (Verse 29) This statement implies that Noah's people either demanded or hinted that if he drove them away, they might consider accepting his faith. They claim that they cannot degrade themselves by meeting with such abject people or take the same route as they. Noah's statement though is very emphatic: I am not going to drive them away. I cannot bring myself to do so when they have believed. Their fate is decided by their Lord, not by me: *"They will surely meet their Lord, whereas in you I see people with no awareness."* (Verse 29) You are unaware of the true values by which people achieve their status with God. You are also unaware that all people shall return to Him.

"My people, who would protect me from God, were I to drive them away?" (Verse 30) Who will shield me from God if I contravene His rules and treat the believers among His servants unjustly, when they enjoy His pleasure? Who will protect me from Him if I confirm the false, worldly values which He sent me to change: *"Will you not reflect?"* (Verse 30) Your methods and conditions have certainly caused you to neglect the standards of a true and upright nature.

He then introduces himself and his message. His presentation is simple, devoid of any ornament and decoration, free of all false standards and values. He reminds them of the true values, looking with contempt on all superficial ones. He disowns all superficiality and states his message as it is, pure and simple, with no false claims. He who wants it, let him take it as it is: as pure as God made it.

"I do not say to you that God's treasures are with me." I do not claim that I am rich or that I can make any of you rich. *"Or that I know what lies beyond the reach of human perception."* (Verse 31) I do not make any claim of any super-human status or allege that my relationship with God exceeds the fact that I have been entrusted with this message. *"Nor do I say: I am an angel."* (Verse 31) I do not claim to have a

position which you think to be higher than that of man, so that I may gain favour or high position from you. *"Nor do I say of those whom you eye with contempt that God will never grant them any good,"* so that I satisfy your pride or accommodate your standards and values. *"God knows best what is in their hearts."* (Verse 31) I have to go by what I see. To me, they appear deserving of honour and hope that God will grant them of His bounty. *"For then I would indeed be a wrongdoer."* (Verse 31) If I made such false claims I would be unjust to the very truth I have come to convey. I would also be unjust to myself, exposed to God's wrath, and I would be unjust to other people to whom I gave a status other than that given them by God.

Thus Noah (peace be upon him) disowns all false values and assumed pretences. He presents his message clearly: real, great, free of all falsehood. He faces them with the clarity and strength of the truth. At the same time he makes a gentle and friendly exposition of the simple truth so that they may look it in the face and decide upon their line of action. No pretence, no flattery, no attempt to win any favour with anyone at the expense of the message and its simple nature. In this Noah sets an example for all advocates of the Islamic message in all generations and provides them with a lesson in how to confront the people of authority with the simple truth, without any attempt to compromise, or flatter, but with the sort of friendliness which is not associated with submission.

At this point, it was clear to the notables that they had no chance of winning the argument. They stiffened their attitude, became determined not to accept any proof of Noah's case, logical and natural as it certainly was. Then they finally rallied themselves in order to deliver a challenge to Noah.

"'Noah,' they replied, 'you have argued with us, and argued to excess. Bring upon us that with which you have been threatening us, if you are a man of truth.'" (Verse 32) This is nothing short of deceit, an attempt to cover up their weakness by putting on a display of strength. It is a challenge made in order to mask their dread of the truth's strength.

Noah, however, remains unaffected by their outright rejection and challenge. He maintains the noble attitude befitting a noble prophet. He continues to explain to them the truth and the facts which they have ignored when they invite him to bring on the suffering he has warned against. He restates the fact that he is only a messenger whose task is to deliver a message. Their punishment is left to God who has absolute control over their destiny. He alone decides, at His own discretion, whether it is appropriate to punish them here and now or to delay their punishment until a later date. God's will must come to pass, and Noah has no power over it. As a messenger, he has to continue to explain the truth to his people until the last moment. Their rejection and challenge must not deter him from fulfilling his task. Hence, he says to them: "*Only God can bring it upon you, if He so wills. You cannot be immune. Nor will my counsel benefit you, much as I desire to give you good counsel, if it is God's will to let you remain in error. He is your Lord and to Him you shall return.*" (Verses 33–34)

If God's law determines that you will perish because of your rejection of the truth, His law will be fulfilled, regardless of my advice. It is not that God will deprive you of benefiting by my advice. It is what you do with yourselves that will, according to God's law, take you away from the right path. You cannot defy God or make yourselves immune from Him. You are always within His reach. He has absolute power over you and over your lives. You cannot escape meeting Him when He brings you to account and decides your reward: "*He is your Lord and to Him you shall return.*" (Verse 34)

Prophets Act on Their Instructions

At this juncture in Noah's story we have a remarkable pause. The *sūrah* makes brief reference to the reception of a similar message by the Quraysh unbelievers. There is a remarkable similarity of attitudes, as the Quraysh claim that Muḥammad too invented these stories. The *sūrah* quickly refutes their claims before returning to Noah: "*Do they claim that he [i.e. Muḥammad] has invented it? Say: 'If I have invented it, upon me be this crime of mine, but I am innocent of the crimes you perpetrate.'*" (Verse 35) To fabricate a falsehood is to commit a crime. Hence, the Prophet is instructed to tell the Quraysh: if I have made any such fabrication, I will bear the responsibility for it. Since I am aware that it is a crime to make such fabrications, it is highly unlikely that I would do so. I am, however, innocent of all your crimes, including your false allegations, your rejection of God's message and your associating partners with God. This interjection however does not interrupt the Qur'ānic story, rather it serves the purpose of the *sūrah*.

In the next scene we see Noah receiving God's revelations and commandments. "*Noah received this revelation: 'None of your people will believe now apart from those who have already accepted the faith. Do not be in distress over anything they may do. Build the ark under Our eyes, and according to Our inspiration. Do not appeal to Me on behalf of the wrongdoers. They shall be drowned.'*" (Verses 36–37)

Everything has come to an end: the advocacy of God's message, the warning, and the argument. "*None of your people will believe now apart from those who have already accepted the faith.*" (Verse 36) Those who are susceptible to faith have already accepted it. The others are hopeless. God, who knows best what is feasible and what is not, and knows His servants well, has informed Noah of this. Hence, it is pointless to continue with the argument. He is told not to grieve at their rejection or their mockery. "*Do not be in distress over anything they may do.*" (Verse 36) God's will has come to pass.

"*Build the ark under Our eyes, and according to Our inspiration.*" (Verse 37) We will look after you and give you instructions as you do so. "*Do not appeal to Me on behalf of the wrongdoers. They shall be drowned.*" (Verse 37) Their destiny has been decided and you are not to plead their case. You can neither pray for them to be guided to the truth, nor can you pray for their punishment. Prayers are to no avail when God's will comes to pass. It is mentioned elsewhere in the Qur'ān[2] that he prayed for their destruction. It is understood that his despair came only after he received this revelation.

The next scene shows Noah building the ark, having given up arguing with his people and calling on them to accept the faith: "*So he set himself on building the ark. And whenever a group of his people passed by him they scoffed at him. He said: 'If you are scoffing at us, we are indeed scoffing at you, just as you are scoffing at us.'*" (Verse 38)

The present tense is used here to portray the scene. This brings the scene to life. We see everything happening in front of us now. Noah builds the ark and group after group of his insolent people pass by and scoff at him. They scoff at the man who said he was a messenger from

---

2. *Sūrah* 71, Verses 26–27. – Editor's note.

God and argued long with them, but who now busies himself making a boat. They mock him because they can only see what appears to them. Noah, on the other hand, is full of confidence as he tells them that their mockery will rebound: "*If you are scoffing at us, we are indeed scoffing at you, just as you are scoffing at us.*" (Verse 38) We will scoff at you because you cannot visualize that God has a definite purpose beyond all this, and you cannot imagine what awaits you: "*You will surely come to know who it is that will be visited by suffering that will cover him with ignominy, and who will be afflicted by long-lasting suffering.*" (Verse 39) Will this apply to us or to you when everything will be revealed?

A scene of mobilization follows as the awaited moment draws near: "*Until, when Our will came to pass and the fountains of the earth gushed forth, We said [to Noah]: 'Take into it a pair of every species, as well as your family, except those against whom Our word has passed, and all those who have accepted the faith.' None believed with him except a few.*" (Verse 40)

The Arabic phrase translated here as '*the fountains of the earth gushed forth*' could also be literally translated as 'the oven boiled'. There are varying reports about the meaning of this phrase. To pursue each one in an attempt to determine the precise meaning is to go into a maze without guidance. Hence, we confine ourselves to the limits of the text adding nothing to it. The most that we can say is that this phrase may be a reference to a certain signal from God to Noah. It might, on the other hand, have accompanied the execution of God's will as water started to gush forth from the earth and rain poured down in torrents.

When this took place, God said to Noah: "*Take into it a pair of every species, as well as your family, except those against whom Our word has passed, and all those who have accepted the faith.*" (Verse 40) It appears that the whole process was revealed to Noah step by step at the right moment. He first received orders to build the ark and he did. The *sūrah* does not tell us at the beginning why the ark was built, nor does it tell us that Noah was informed of the purpose, until "*when Our will came to pass and the fountains of the earth gushed forth,*" then, he received his instructions for the following stage: "*Take into it a pair of every species, as well as your family, except those against whom Our word has passed, and all those who have accepted the faith.*" (Verse 40)

Again the reports we have vary as to the meaning of the expression, *'a pair of every species.'* They smack of much exaggeration. We, however, will not let imagination carry us away in order to give this statement a precise interpretation. We will only say that Noah was ordered to take into the ark a pair of all such living species as he could take.

"As well as your family, except those against whom Our word has passed," that is, those who deserved to be punished by God in accordance with the law He has laid down. *"And all those who have accepted the faith,"* meaning those who did not belong to his family. These, however, were very few as the Qur'ānic statement makes very clear.

Noah carried out his instructions as they were given to him. *"He said to them: 'Embark in it. In the name of God be its course and its riding at anchor. My Lord indeed is Much-Forgiving, Merciful.'"* (Verse 41) This statement indicates that he put himself and the ark in God's hands and trusted in Him. The ark would float and anchor under God's watchful eyes. For, what could Noah and his people do to steer the ark to safety in such a deluge?

A Rebellious Son

We then have the very awesome scene of the flood. *"And it sailed with them amid waves towering like mountains. Noah cried out to a son of his who stood apart [from the rest]: 'Embark with us, my child, and do not stay with the unbelievers.' He answered: 'I shall seek refuge in a mountain, which will afford me protection from the water.' Said (Noah): 'Today there is no protection for anyone from God's judgement, except those who shall enjoy His mercy.' Thereupon waves rose up between them and he was among those who were drowned."* (Verses 42–43)

Two elements of fear are at work here: one emanates from nature, stormy but silent as it is; and the other is felt in one's innermost soul. Both converge as the ark moves on amidst waves as high as mountains. At this terrible, decisive moment, Noah looks in a certain direction and sees one of his sons who has not joined them in the ark. Paternal emotion is roused in Noah and he calls out to his stray child: *"Embark with us, my child, and do not stay with the unbelievers."* (Verse 42)

Disobedient as he is, the son does not respond to his loving father. A conceited youth, he does not realize the extent of the terrible event which is taking place. He says: "*I shall seek refuge in a mountain, which will afford me protection from the water.*" (Verse 43) Aware of the terrible reality, the father pleads with him for the last time: "*Today there is no protection for anyone from God's judgement, except those who shall enjoy His mercy.*" (Verse 43) In an instant, the scene changes and the towering waves swallow everything up: "*Thereupon waves rose up between them and he was among those who were drowned.*" (Verse 43)

Today as we read this account it is as if we see these events happening now before our very own eyes. The ark is sailing amid huge waves, Noah, the worried father makes one plea after another; his conceited young son insolently turns his back, and then suddenly a towering wave settles the issue. Everything is over as if the dialogue did not take place.

The element of fear and worry in this scene is measured by its depth in the human soul, in the exchange between father and son. It is also measured by its extent in nature, as the waves rise high to submerge the tops of the mountains. Both elements are equal. This is a distinctive feature of artistic imagery in the Qur'ān.

The storm subsides, an air of calmness spreads, the matter is settled and God's will is done. The words used here give the impression of something coming to a complete standstill. "*And the word was spoken: 'Earth, swallow up your waters. Heaven, cease (your rain).' Thus the waters sank into the earth, and God's will was done, and the ark came to rest on Mount Jūdī. The word was spoken: 'Away with these evil-doing folk.'*" (Verse 44) The earth and the heavens are addressed as if they were human beings. Both comply with the commandment. The earth swallows up its water and the heaven stops raining. Furthermore, the earth's surface was soon dry, as excess waters penetrated deep underground.

"*God's will was done and the ark came to rest on Mount Jūdī.*" (Verse 44) That was its final stop. "*The word was spoken: 'Away with these evil-doing folk.'*" (Verse 44) We are not told who said this, but it generates the impression that the whole affair need not be considered again. Let the evil-doers disappear beyond God's mercy for they deserve to be expelled; let them be banished from memory, for they do not deserve to be remembered.

A Father's Plea

Now that the storm has subsided and the ark has come to rest, the paternal love of a distressed father is once again felt by Noah. He makes this appeal to God: "*Noah called out to his Lord, saying: 'Lord, my son is of my family. Surely Your promise always comes true, and You are the most just of judges.'*" (Verse 45) Noah makes clear that he has absolutely no doubt that God is just and wise. Nothing He does is without reason. Yet he has been promised that his family will be safe and now he requests that God fulfil the promise He made to spare his family. God's answer states the fact which Noah has overlooked. By God's standards and according to His principles, one's family are not necessarily one's blood relations. The true relationship is that of faith. This son was not a believer, and as such he was not a member of the family of Noah, the Prophet.

The answer is firm and emphatic. Indeed there is an element of reproach and warning in the answer: "*'Noah,' He answered, 'he was not of your family; his was an unrighteous conduct. Do not question Me about matters of which you have no knowledge. I admonish you lest you become one of the ignorant.'*" (Verse 46) A great principle of this religion states that the paramount relationship that exists between individuals is not one based on family affinity: "*He was not of your family; his was an unrighteous conduct.*" Your relationship with him is thus severed despite the fact that he was your own son. Since the basic tie between the two of you does not exist, no other tie has any significance.

Since Noah's prayer requested the fulfilment of a promise which he felt had not happened, the answer includes an implicit reproach and warning: "*Do not question Me about matters of which you have no knowledge. I admonish you lest you become one of the ignorant.*" (Verse 46) The admonition is needed lest Noah become one of those who are ignorant of the real ties and relationships, or unaware of God's promise and its interpretation. For God's promise has been done and Noah's true family has been saved. Noah, a true believer and God's humble servant, trembles with fear that he may have erred in what he said to his Lord. He, therefore, appeals to Him, praying for His forgiveness: "*My Lord, I do indeed seek refuge with You from ever questioning You about anything of which I have no knowledge.*"

Unless You grant me forgiveness and have mercy on me I shall be among the losers." (Verse 47)

God has mercy on Noah and he is reassured. He is given blessings which are also extended to the good people of his offspring. The others, however, will receive severe punishment: "*The word was spoken: 'Noah, disembark in peace from Us, and with Our blessings upon you as well as upon generations from those who are with you. As for other folk, We shall let them have enjoyment, and then there will befall them grievous suffering from Us.'*" (Verse 48) The end is clear: he and those who believe of his offspring will be saved and will enjoy a magnificent reward. Those who prefer the enjoyment of this worldly life, however, will have it for a while but will then be overtaken by severe punishment. The same glad tidings and the same warnings which were made at the opening of the *sūrah* are confirmed by the story in order to make them much more real to those whom the Qur'ān addresses.

The commentary on this history is summarized in one verse: "*These accounts of things that have passed We now reveal to you. Neither you nor your people knew them before this. Be, then, patient in adversity; for the future belongs to those who are God-fearing.*" (Verse 49) This sums up the objectives of relating such stories in the Qur'ān:

- It establishes the fact of revelation denied by the unbelievers. These stories were unknown to the Prophet and to his people. It was part of God's knowledge and the Prophet could not have known about it except through revelation from the One who knows all.
- It also establishes the fact that the true faith has always been the same, ever since Noah, the second father of mankind. The message of the Prophet uses almost the same expressions as Noah.
- The objections and the accusations made by those who denied the message of the Prophet are always the same. Furthermore, the glad tidings and the warnings made by the Prophet will surely come to pass. This story is then a testimony from history.
- Another fact which is established by this comment is that God's laws will not fail. They do not favour anyone: "*The future belongs to those who are God-fearing.*" They are the ones who will prosper and who will be given power.

- It also establishes the true tie that exists between individuals and generations. It is the tie of faith, the same faith which holds together all believers in God, the only Lord of the universe. All generations of believers have in common the fact that they submit themselves to Him alone and ascribe divinity to no one else.

The Origin of Monotheistic Religions

People often wonder whether the great flood engulfed the whole earth or just the area where Noah and his people lived. What were the boundaries of that area in the ancient world or in the new one? We simply have no definite answer for any of these questions. But then the significance of the story is in no way affected by our lack of knowledge on this point. Taken at face value, the Qur'ānic text suggests that the people of Noah constituted all mankind at that particular time. Their land was the only inhabited area of the earth. Secondly, the floods must have swept through this whole area, drowning all living creatures, except those saved in the ark.

This is sufficient for us to understand that great event which undoubtedly happened, since no lesser source than the Qur'ān tells us about it. Our history books, on the other hand, record nothing about that ancient period. The writing of history is a relatively modern art that has recorded only a fraction of the events witnessed by mankind. Besides, whatever is recorded by history is subject to error, falsification and distortion. Hence, we need not seek history's confirmation for anything which we are certain has happened, since we are told about it by God who revealed the Qur'ān.

The legends of different communities often speak of a flood far back in their history, one caused by the erring ways of their ancestors. The stories related in the Old Testament also mention the flood that overwhelmed Noah's people. None of this, however, should be discussed in conjunction with the Qur'ānic account of the flood, because that would mix the true and accurate account of the Qur'ān with myths of unknown origin and poor authenticity. However, the fact that such myths exist and are told in different communities suggests that the floods covered the lands of these communities, or that its memory travelled with the offspring of those who were saved.

We should also remember that neither the Old Testament, which includes Jewish Scriptures, nor the New Testament with its Christian Scriptures is the text revealed by God. All copies of the Torah that God revealed to Moses were burnt by the Babylonians when they enslaved the Jews. It was rewritten several centuries later by Ezra – who is probably the one mentioned in *Sūrah* 9 as Uzayr – about five centuries before the birth of Jesus Christ. He recorded what remained of the original Torah, but the rest is of human authorship. The Gospels, on the other hand, include only what Christ's disciples and their students could remember one century after Christ's life on earth had ended. Numerous stories and legends were subsequently added to them. Hence, we cannot rely on these Scriptures to establish certainty on any matter.

This is anyway a side issue. What we need to do is try to understand the moral of this great event. Indeed, the story drives home several lessons which we will now briefly discuss.

As we have seen, Noah's people were immersed in *jāhiliyyah*. Hardened in their evil ways, they stubbornly rejected his message based on God's oneness and the need for all people to submit themselves to Him only. Noah's people were Adam's progeny, and we know from Adam's history related in *Sūrahs* 7 and 2, The Heights and The Cow, that his fall was the prelude for him and his offspring to be charged with the task of building the earth. This was the purpose behind his creation. God gave him the qualities and abilities necessary to perform this task after He had told him how to repent and seek forgiveness for his error. Adam received certain commandments from his Lord and God forgave him his sin. He then pledged to God, along with his wife and offspring, that they would always follow God's guidance and never listen to Satan, their eternal enemy.

Adam, then, descended to earth with the right faith: submitting himself to God, following His guidance. He did, no doubt, teach his children the meaning of Islam, i.e. submission to God. Hence, this submission, or Islam in the general sense of the word, was the first faith ever known to man on earth. There was no other faith alongside it. Hence, if Noah's people, a later generation, were so immersed in the type of ignorance, or *jāhiliyyah*, described in this *sūrah* we can state, in all certainty, that such *jāhiliyyah*, with all that it entailed of paganism, legends, idols, false concepts and traditions, is something more recent than the pure faith of Islam with which human life on earth started. Man's deviation from the monotheistic faith based on submission to God, i.e. Islam, in its broader sense, took place as a result of Satan's machinations. As the enemy of both God and man, Satan always exploits people's weaknesses whenever they become lax in their observance of God's commandments and deviate from His guidance. God has created man and granted him a measure of free choice, by which he is tested. With this measure he can choose to hold fast to God's guidance, fortifying himself against his enemy. Or he can deviate from God's guidance and follow any other way. When he deviates, even slightly, Satan overpowers him, eventually, pushing him to that state of ignorance experienced by Adam's offspring. Yet Adam was a prophet who taught the faith based on submission to God.

The fact that the first faith ever known on earth was Islam, or submission to God alone, makes it imperative for us to reject as conjecture the theses advanced by the masters of Comparative Religion and other evolutionists. These claim that monotheism is a recent development in human religion, preceded by several stages and forms of polytheism and dualism, worship of natural forces, spirits, planets, etc. Whatever research is made in this connection follows a particular methodology predetermined by historical, psychological and political factors. This methodology destroys the basis of divine religions, and the very concept of revelation and divine messages, in order to establish that all religions are a human product. Once this is established it can easily be claimed that religions developed as human thought advanced.

Some of those who write in defence of Islam err, unwittingly endorsing the theories of specialists in the history of religion who conduct their research along such predetermined lines. While defending Islam so enthusiastically they unwittingly destroy the basis of the Islamic faith as stated in the Qur'ān with absolute clarity. The Qur'ān states that Adam (peace be upon him) descended on earth with the faith of Islam. It also states that Noah (peace be upon him) faced a later generation that had installed ignorance in place of Islam. He advocated basically the same faith based on the absolute oneness of God; i.e. the Islamic faith in its broader sense. The same cycle repeated itself after Noah with mankind abandoning Islam to adopt different *jāhiliyyah* doctrines. All prophets were sent with the same message of God's oneness, calling on mankind to submit themselves to God alone. At no point was there any development in the divine faith in as much as it relates to the basics of faith. Evolution, expansion and advancement addressed only the laws that accompanied the same faith. An enlightened study of the development of *jāhiliyyah* doctrines does not lead to the conclusion that people progressed to monotheism. It rather shows that the monotheistic faith, preached by successive prophets and messengers, left more traces in succeeding generations, even after they had deviated from true faith, to make their doctrines nearer to the monotheistic origins. Belief in God's oneness dates back much further than all pagan religions. This faith was complete right from the start, because it was not the result of human thinking or increased human knowledge. It was given to man by God, and as such it was true and complete from the outset.

This is clearly established in the Qur'ān. It is not for any Muslim scholar either to depart from what is stated so clearly in the Qur'ān or to follow professors of Comparative Religion as they grope for a coherent theory.

Devoting a chapter to the origins of faith in his book, *Allah*, or God, Abbas Mahmood al-Aqqad, writes:

Human beliefs developed in parallel to human development in scientific knowledge and other skills. Thus, early beliefs fit with the standards of early human life, as did human scientific knowledge and skills. This means that such early knowledge in the scientific field was no more advanced than early beliefs and worship. Neither field reflects a clearer grasp of the truth.

Moreover, human efforts to formulate a true concept of religion must have been harder and longer lasting than those related to science and industry. The greatest truth in the universe must be harder to achieve than the truth of different areas addressed at times by science and at others by industry.

People remained ignorant of how the sun functions, although it is the clearest thing our eyes see and our bodies feel. For a long time, the common belief was that it was the sun that orbited the earth. They explained its movement and other aspects in much the same way as they sought to explain mysteries and interpret dreams. People's ignorance of the nature of the sun, which may be true even today, never prompted anyone to deny its existence.

This means that our reference to the origins of religion in the early periods of *jāhiliyyah* does not indicate that religiosity was false, or that it meant a search for the impossible. All that it shows is that the greatest truth is too momentous to be comprehended in full in one generation. People must gather it in stages, one generation after another, in the same way as they do with smaller truths of which their senses are more cognizant. However, the greatest truth requires them to put more toil and effort into the process.

Studies in Comparative Religion have unravelled a multitude of myths and superstitions in which early humanity believed. Traces of these continue to be found among primitive communities or nations of ancient civilization. It was never presumed that such studies could make any different discoveries, or that early beliefs could be anything other than such myths. Indeed, this is the logical conclusion which scholars expected. They did not expect to unearth anything that could be the basis of a completely new outlook on the essence of belief. A scholar who imagines that his research in primitive faiths could lead him to conclude that the early humans recognized the fundamental universal truth, complete and pure, is only pursuing a mirage.[3]

In another chapter, on the 'Stages of Belief in God', al-Aqqad writes:

Scholars of Comparative Religion identify three main stages of belief in primitive communities: polytheism, henotheism and monotheism.

In the polytheistic era, early tribes worshipped scores or even hundreds of deities. In this era, it was often the case that a large family would have its own deity which members of the family worshipped. Alternatively, they may have a charm or a symbol which deputized for the deity in accepting prayers and offerings.

In the second stage, deities continued to be worshipped in their hundreds. However, one of them begins to acquire greater

---

3. A.M. al-'Aqqad, *Allah*, Cairo, 1960, pp. 13–14

prominence, either because it is the deity of the largest tribe commanding the allegiance of other tribes, or because it commanded higher authority, such as the god of rain in a land that depends on rain for irrigation, or the deity commanding wind in an area often hit by hurricanes.

The third stage witnesses the rise of nations. Each nation congregates around the same worship although different deities dominate different provinces. It could happen in this stage that one nation imposes its own religious worship on another, in the same way as it imposes its political authority. It may also accept that the deity of the defeated nation should submit to the higher authority of the deity of the victor nation, yet the former continued to be worshipped by its defeated adherents.

A nation attains this stage of deficient monotheism only after going through different stages of expanding human knowledge that makes old legends and superstitions no longer acceptable. Thus, God is described in terms that are closer to perfection and holiness than were given to old deities worshipped during the polytheistic stage. Worship becomes associated with contemplation and reflection, and with God's will and superior wisdom. The main deity is often thought of as the only true Lord, while other deities are reduced to a rank similar to that of angels or gods that incurred the displeasure of the superior deity.[4]

It is clear from al-Aqqad's views and what he attributes to other authorities in Comparative Religion that the origin of religious belief lies with human beings. Thus, it reflects their rational, scientific, political and civilizational development. Progress followed its consistent line, starting with polytheism, then moving to dualism and finishing with monotheism. Indeed this is clear in the first sentence the author writes in his Introduction: "This book discusses the rise of the belief in God, from the time man worshipped a deity until he recognized the One God and purified his belief in God's oneness."

Without a doubt, God states in His glorious book, the Qur'ān, most clearly and decisively, something that is at variance with what al-Aqqad has written, influenced as he is by scholars of Comparative

4. Ibid., pp. 28–29

Religion. What God clearly states is that Adam, the first man on earth, was fully aware of the truth of God's oneness. He knew it to be pure, unmixed with any trace of polytheism or dualism, and he knew the meaning of submission to God alone and its practical manifestation in following only God's legislation. He also communicated this faith to his children, leading to the existence of several generations in the earliest period of human history who knew no belief other than God's oneness and no faith other than submission to God, or Islam. As time went by, and generations of Adam's progeny succeeded one another, deviation crept in, perhaps towards dualism and perhaps towards polytheism. Nonetheless people began to submit to a multitude of false deities. Then the Prophet Noah brought back the divine faith of monotheism. The flood drowned all those who persisted with their erroneous beliefs. Only those who believed in God's oneness were saved. They were the ones who rejected all forms of polytheism and the association of partners with God. We may say without fear of contradiction that several generations after Noah continued to live under the divine faith, Islam, based on pure monotheism. But then again, with the passage of time, deviation crept in and people started to move away from the true faith. This was the case with every one of God's messengers: "*Before your time We never sent a messenger without having revealed to him that there is no deity other than Me. Therefore, you shall worship Me alone.*" (21: 25)

This is certainly at variance with what specialists in Comparative Religion and al-Aqqad conclude. The two approaches are diametrically opposed in methodology and conclusion. We should remember that the views of academics and writers are theories that may contradict one another, which means that none provides a final and confirmed judgement, even by human standards.

Needless to say, when God unequivocally states something that is contradicted by others, the statement to follow is God's. This applies particularly to those who write in defence of Islam, aiming to clarify misconceptions about Islam and the origin of faith. For there is no service to Islam by undermining the fact that it came to us in the form of revelations bestowed by God. No human being has invented it. It preached the basic truth of God's oneness from the very first day, and never entertained any idea or concept that is at variance with the truth of God's oneness. Nor did it preach any concept other than that of God's oneness in any of the divine messages.

These brief remarks demonstrate the grave danger we expose ourselves to if we borrow our basic concepts from un-Islamic sources. They also show how deeply Western thought influences people who follow its methodologies, even when they try to defend Islam and refute accusations levelled at it by those who are hostile. "*Surely this Qur'ān shows the way to that which is most upright.*" (17: 9)

Ties and Families

Another point to reflect on in Noah's history as told in this *sūrah* concerns his son, whom he was told did not belong to his family. This outlines an important aspect of the nature of the Islamic faith and how it works in human life. We need first to remind ourselves of some verses in this respect:

> *Noah received this revelation: 'None of your people will believe now apart from those who have already accepted the faith. Do not be in distress over anything they may do.'* (Verse 36)

> *When Our will came to pass and the fountains of the earth gushed forth, We said [to Noah]: 'Take into it a pair of every species, as well as your family, except those against whom Our word has passed, and all those who have accepted the faith.' None believed with him except a few.* (Verse 40)

> *And it sailed with them amid waves towering like mountains. Noah cried out to a son of his who stood apart [from the rest]: 'Embark with us, my child, and do not stay with the unbelievers.' He answered: 'I shall seek refuge in a mountain, which will afford me protection from the water.' Said (Noah): 'Today there is no protection for anyone from God's judgement, except those who shall enjoy His mercy.' Thereupon waves rose up between them and he was among those who were drowned.* (Verses 42–43)

> *Noah called out to his Lord, saying: 'Lord, my son is of my family. Surely Your promise always comes true, and You are the most just of judges.' 'Noah,' He answered, 'he was not of your family; his was an*

unrighteous conduct. Do not question Me about matters of which you have no knowledge. I admonish you lest you become one of the ignorant.' Said (Noah): 'My Lord, I do indeed seek refuge with You from ever questioning You about anything of which I have no knowledge. Unless You grant me forgiveness and have mercy on me I shall be among the losers.' (Verses 45–47)

The tie which binds people together in the Islamic faith is unique. It relates to certain objectives and aspirations which are peculiar to this divine constitution.

This tie of Islamic society has nothing to do with family or blood relations, land or country, tribe or nation, colour or language, race or sex, profession or class. All such ties may exist between two individuals, yet their relations may, nevertheless, still be severed. When Noah pleaded with his Lord: *'Lord, my son is of my family,'* he was told by God: *'Noah, he was not of your family.'* The reason why his own son was not considered to belong to his family was then explained to him: *'His was an unrighteous conduct.'* The tie of faith which would have linked them together did not exist: *'Do not question Me about matters of which you have no knowledge.'* Thus, Noah was mistaken when he considered that his son belonged to his family. He simply did not, despite the fact that he was Noah's own son.

This is a clear, distinctive landmark which distinguishes the Islamic view of all ties and relationships. Different modes of *jāhiliyyah* make different ties paramount, such as those of blood, family, land, country, tribe, nation, colour, language, race, profession or class. They sometimes give prominence to common interests, common history or common destiny. All these are *jāhiliyyah* considerations that are fundamentally in conflict with the Islamic viewpoint.

The Islamic code of living, represented by the Qur'ān and the *Sunnah*, endeavours to educate the Muslim community so that it observes this distinctive landmark in its general outlook.

In this *sūrah*, Noah and his son provide the example of what happens between father and son. The Qur'ān gives numerous other examples in order to establish the true nature of the only tie which Islam recognizes. The story of Abraham and his father, related in *Sūrah* 19, Maryam, is an example of a son's relationship with his father: "*Mention*

*in the Book Abraham. He certainly was a man of truth and a prophet.
He said to his father: 'My father! Why do you worship something that
neither hears nor sees and can be of no avail whatever to you? My father!
There has come to me knowledge which you do not have. Follow me,
and I shall guide you along a straight path. My father! Do not worship
Satan, for Satan has indeed rebelled against [God] the Most Gracious.
My father! I dread lest a scourge will fall upon you from the Most Gracious,
and then you will become one of Satan's friends.' He answered: 'Are you
renouncing my gods, Abraham? If you do not desist, I shall most certainly
have you stoned. Now begone from me for good!' Abraham replied: 'Peace
be on you. I shall pray to my Lord to forgive you; for He has always been
very kind to me. But I shall withdraw from you all and from whatever
you invoke instead of God, and I shall pray to my Lord alone. Perhaps, by
my prayer to my Lord I shall not be unblest.' When he had withdrawn
from them and from all that they were worshipping instead of God, We
bestowed on him Isaac and Jacob, each of whom We made a prophet. We
bestowed on them of Our mercy and We granted them the high honour
of [conveying] the truth."* (19: 41–50)

Another example, as stated in *Sūrah* 2, The Cow, concerns Abraham
and his seed, and what God taught him concerning them. When
Abraham made his pledge to God, he was given the happy news that
the message would continue in his seed, but the wrongdoers were
entitled to nothing of it.

> *When his Lord tested Abraham with certain commandments and
> he fulfilled them, He said, 'I have appointed you a leader of
> mankind.' Abraham asked, 'And what of my descendants?' God said,
> 'My covenant does not apply to the wrongdoers.'* (2: 124)

> *Abraham said, 'Lord, make this a land of security and make
> provisions of fruits for those of its people who believe in God and the
> Last Day.' God said, 'And as for he who disbelieves, I shall let him
> enjoy life for a while and then I shall drive him to suffering through
> the fire; and what a terrible end!'* (2: 126)

The Qur'ān also gives us two examples of matrimonial relationships.
On the one hand we have the prophets Noah and Lot and their wives,
while on the other we have Pharaoh and his wife. "*God has set an example*

of unbelievers: the wife of Noah and the wife of Lot. They were married to two of Our righteous servants, but they betrayed them. Their husbands could not avail them anything against God. The word has been spoken, 'Enter the fire, together with those who shall enter it.' And God has also set an example of believers: the wife of Pharaoh, who said: 'Lord, build for me a house in heaven with You, and deliver me from Pharaoh and his doings. Deliver me from all evil-doing folk.'" (66: 10–11)

Other examples are also given in the Qur'ān where strong ties, which might have otherwise existed between believers and unbelievers, were of no significance when the tie of faith did not exist. There is the case of Abraham and his followers and the example of the people of the cave who deserted their community. With respect to the first God says: *"You have had a good example in Abraham and those who followed him, when they said to their people: 'We are quit of you and of all that you worship instead of God. We reject whatever you believe. Between us and you there has arisen enmity and hatred lasting until such a time as you come to believe in God alone.'"* (60: 4)

And regarding the young men of the cave, God tells us: *"Do you think that the People of the Cave and the Inscription were a wonder among Our signs? When those youths betook themselves to the Cave, they said: 'Our Lord! Bestow on us Your grace, and provide for us right guidance in our affair.' So We drew [a veil] over their ears in the Cave, for a number of years, and then We awakened them so that We may know which of the two parties managed to calculate the time they had tarried. We shall relate to you their story in all truth. They were young men who had believed in their Lord, so We increased them in guidance. We put courage in their hearts, so that they stood up and said: 'Our Lord is the Lord of the heavens and the earth. Never shall we call upon any deity other than Him: if we did, we should indeed utter an enormity! These people of ours have taken for worship deities other than Him, without being able to show any convincing proof of their beliefs. Who does more wrong than he who invents a lie about God? Hence, now that you have withdrawn from them and all that they worship instead of God, betake yourselves to the Cave. God may well spread His grace over you and make fitting arrangements for you in your affairs.'"* (18: 9–16)

All these examples make the issue absolutely clear for the Muslim community. The only tie which brings people together in Islamic society is the one of faith. Numerous verses in the Qur'ān remind Muslims to hold fast to this view and establish it clearly in society. Here are some examples:

> You cannot find people who believe in God and the Last Day and love anyone who contends against God and His Messenger, even though they be their fathers, sons, brothers or kindred. It is such [believers] in whose hearts He has inscribed faith, and whom He has strengthened with inspiration from Himself, and whom [in time] He will admit into gardens through which running waters flow, therein to abide. Well-pleased is God with them, and well-pleased are they with Him. They are God's partisans. Most certainly the partisans of God shall be successful. (58: 22)

> Believers! Do not take My enemies, who are your enemies as well, for your allies, showing them affection even though they reject the truth that has come to you, and they have driven the Messengers and yourselves away, because you believe in God, your Lord. If you have gone forth to strive for My cause, and out of a longing for My goodly acceptance, [do not] incline towards them in secret affection, for I am fully aware of all that you may conceal and all that you may do openly. Any of you who does this has already strayed from the right path. (60: 1)

> Neither your kinsfolk nor your own children will be of any benefit to you on the Day of Resurrection, when He will decide between you. God sees all that you do. You have had a good example in Abraham and those who followed him, when they said to their people: 'We are quit of you and of all that you worship instead of God. We reject whatever you believe. Between us and you there has arisen enmity and hatred lasting until such a time as you come to believe in God alone.' (60: 3–4)

> Believers, do not take your fathers and brothers for allies if they choose unbelief in preference to faith. Those of you who take them for allies are indeed wrongdoers. (9: 23)

> Believers, do not take the Jews and the Christians for your allies. They are allies of one another. Whoever of you allies himself with

them is indeed one of them. God does not bestow His guidance on the wrongdoers. (5: 51)

Islamic society is basically and organically distinguished from all other social orders, old and new, by this very basic principle which governs its relations with others. There can be no way which combines Islam with the adoption of any tie other than that of faith as the basis of society. Those who claim to be Muslims and then establish their social orders on the basis of ties which Islam has demolished are either ignorant of Islam or reject Islam. In either case Islam does not accept their claim as it has no practical application in their lives.

The Nature of Islamic Society

We will now consider some aspects of the divine wisdom behind making faith the supreme tie of Islamic society.

Faith is indeed the noblest characteristic of man which distinguishes him from animals. It relates to the spiritual side of human existence which no class of animal shares. Indeed, even the most hardened atheists have come to acknowledge that faith is an essential quality that categorically distinguishes man from animals.

Hence, in a society which achieves the highest standard of human civilization, faith must be the constituent tie, because it is man's most distinctive quality. Indeed, no human grouping can be based on anything which man shares with animals, such as land, meadows, interests and borders; for these are akin to an animal enclosure with its fencing. Nor can a human society be based on ties of blood, ancestry, clan, nation, race, language or colour. Again, all these are common to both man and animals. Man is indeed distinguished from animals by his reason and what relates to his heart and mind.

Similarly, faith is closely linked to another factor that distinguishes man from animals, namely, his free-will and ability to choose. Every human being is able to choose his or her own faith when they attain a reasonable standard of maturity. Thus human beings are able to determine the type of society in which they choose to live, and the type of ideological, social, political, economic and moral system they advocate.

By contrast, no human being is able to choose his ancestry, colour, community or race. Nor can he determine in which geographical area to be born, which mother tongue to speak, or indeed any of the ties on which *jāhiliyyah* communities are based. All these are determined before a human being is born. If his destiny, both in this life and the life to come, or indeed in only this life, is based on considerations in which he has no say, then his free choice is negated. Thus, one of the most essential and distinctive characteristics of his humanity, which God has established, is lost.

When a community is based on the tie of faith, and not on any consideration in which man has no say, it can establish a society that is open to all. People of diverse races, colours, languages, lands and ethnic origins will freely choose to join this society, knowing that nothing can stop them from doing so and no artificial barriers are erected to prevent them from joining. What determines their ability to join are man's most distinctive qualities. All human potential and talents thus contribute to the establishment of a civilization that benefits by the qualities of all races. It never closes the door to any talent because of colour, race, family or land.

When Islamic society was built on this basis, it gave prominence to the distinctive qualities of man, in preference to those that man shares with other creatures. It soon achieved spectacular results for its being open to all, erecting none of the artificial obstacles that are more suited to animals. The special characteristics of different human races and communities were able to work together, without barriers, and they soon produced a superior human structure. In that superior Islamic community, Arabs, Persians, Syrians, Egyptians, North Africans, Turks, Chinese, Indians, Byzantines, Greeks, Indonesians and Africans, as well as many others, brought in their diverse talents to contribute to the building of Islamic civilization. It was never an Arab or national civilization, but an Islamic one based on faith.

All were equal in that society, strengthened by a strong tie of love, and sharing a common objective. Their unifying tie was always their belief in the One God, their only Lord. No other grouping in human history has ever been able to achieve such unity and equality.

In history, the best known grouping of different communities in the past was that of the Roman Empire, which included a large variety

240

of races, languages and peoples. But that group did not come about through any distinctively human characteristic, nor was it based on an ideal like faith. It was, on the one hand, based on class, dividing people into masters and slaves throughout the Empire. On the other, it was racist, giving the Romans superiority over all others. Hence, it never aspired to the level attained by Islamic society.

In recent history similar groupings flourished, such as the British Empire. Yet it was largely an heir to the Roman Empire in as much as it was nationalistic and exploitative, promoting the superiority of the British people and exploiting the resources of Britain's colonies. The same applies to all European empires: the Spanish and Portuguese at one stage, and later the French. They were all in the same low category.

Communism tried to establish a different type of grouping that overcame barriers of race, nation, land, language and colour. But it was established on a class rather than human basis. Whilst the Romans gave superiority to the aristocrats, Communism gave it to the Proletariat. Its main emotion was its unabating grudge against other classes. Such a small, hateful group could not promote anything other than man's worst qualities. Its ideal was to enhance and promote the animal aspects in human life, which it considered to be man's basic needs. These were food, shelter and sex. Needless to say, these are the basic needs of animals. It also considered human history as nothing more than a search for food.[5]

Islam, which follows a method laid down by God, is unique in promoting and enhancing the most distinctive human qualities to building human society. This certainly remains exclusive to Islam. Those who abandon the Islamic way in preference for any other method based on racial, national, patriotic or class values are indeed the enemies of man. They do not want man to benefit by his God-given superior qualities, nor do they want human society to benefit from the best talents and potential of its constituent races, bringing all their experiences into a harmonious whole.[6]

---

5. It should be noted that the author wrote this in the early 1960s, when Egypt was moving strongly towards the Communist Bloc. – Editor's note.

6. The last six paragraphs are quoted in full in the author's book, *Milestones*. Although the book has been translated into English, we preferred to produce our own translation, so as to deliver the same style as employed in the current work. – Editor's note.

It should be mentioned that some of those to whom God refers when He says: "*Those to whom We granted revelation know it as well as they know their own children,*" are hostile to Islam, yet they know its points of strength and its method of action. They have not overlooked the fact that making faith the basis on which a community is founded is one of Islam's major strengths. Since they want to destroy Islamic society, or at least weaken it to a degree that enables them to control it, avenge themselves on Islam, exploit its followers and their land and resources, they are keen to disrupt the basis on which it is founded. They try hard to divert Muslims from the worship of God alone so that they turn to the worship of new idols whether it be fatherland, nation, or race. Such neo-idolatry came to prominence under different names during different epochs of history, such as *Shu'ūbiyyah* and Turanian nationalism, and more recently Arab nationalism. At times, these idols are given different names, each supported by a different group. Such groups engage in in-fighting within a single Islamic society founded on faith and regulated by Islamic law. Their aim is to weaken the foundation of Islamic society and make anyone who rejects their idols an outlaw in his community or a traitor to his country.

The most hostile camp that continues to undermine the solid foundation of Islamic society are the Jews. They successfully employed nationalism as a weapon to destroy Christendom, dividing it into several political entities, each with its own national church. In this way they were able to break through the Christian grouping within which they were encircled. Now they are trying the same tactic to divide the Muslim community.

The same was done by Christian imperialists in the Muslim world. They tried for centuries to stir ethnic, racial and national hatred within the Muslim community that embraces all ethnic entities on an equal footing. In this way, they were able to satisfy their ancient grudges against Islam, inherited from the days of the Crusades. They managed to tame the Muslims into accepting European imperialism. They will continue to do so until God enables the Muslims to destroy this evil neo-idolatry. This will open the way for the new rise of Islamic society on its solid and unique foundation.

A Unique Community

People cannot extricate themselves from the state of pagan *jāhiliyyah* as a community unless the basis which brings them together is that of faith. Submission to God alone is not complete unless this rule is established in their minds and in their community.

There must be only one sacred thing which is revered. There can never be a multiple of 'sacred' things. The community must have a single slogan. There must be only one *qiblah* [i.e. direction faced in prayer] which remains the focus of everyone's wholehearted attention.

Idol worship is not confined to worshipping idols made of stone or gold, or even to worshipping legendary gods; it can take numerous forms and shapes. Islam, however, cannot tolerate that people fight under the banners of such false gods when it calls on them to believe in God alone and to submit themselves to Him only. For this reason Islam divides all mankind into two nations: the nation of Muslims who follow the prophets, each in his own time until the last Messenger was sent to mankind as a whole, and the nation of non-Muslims who worship all forms of tyrannical idols.

When God identified the Muslim nation, He defined it as the nation of the followers of His messengers, each in his own time, and then said: "*Your community is but one community, and I am your only Lord, therefore worship Me alone.*" (21: 92) He did not tell the Arabs that they belonged to the Arab nation, either when they were ignorant, or when they were Muslim. Nor did He tell the Jews that their nation was that of the Children of Israel, or the Hebrew nation, both when they lived in ignorance and in those periods when they submitted themselves to God alone. The Prophet's companions, Salmān, the Persian, and Ṣuhayb, the Byzantine, and Bilāl, the Abyssinian, were not considered to belong to Persia, Byzantium or Abyssinia. Indeed, the Prophet said to all Muslims, Arabs, Persians, Romans and Abyssinians alike: your community is that of the believers who have earned the title of Muslims by submitting themselves truly to God throughout the ages, during the times of Moses, Aaron, Abraham, Lot, Noah, David, Solomon, Job, Ishmael, Idrīs, Dhulkifl, Zachariah, John and Mary as mentioned in *Sūrah* 21, verses 48–91.

This is the Muslim nation according to God's definition. He who wishes to take a line other than God's, let him do so, but he must not claim to belong to Islam. We, who have submitted ourselves to God alone, acknowledge no nation as ours except the one God has defined for us. He indeed tells the truth and He is the best of judges.

For Whom Miracles Happen

Finally, let us reflect on the value assigned by God to a small community of Muslims. Only a handful of people, numbering no more than twelve according to some reports, were the net result of Noah's efforts in calling people to God. This is a period which extended over 950 years, according to the Qur'ān, the only reliable and certain source in this connection.

Yet this handful of people, the fruit of such a difficult campaign, was so important that God changed the established universal phenomena for its sake. He let the floods drown everything and every living soul on inhabited land. He then made this handful of people the only heirs of the earth and mankind's second seed. They were the people entrusted with the rebuilding of the earth.

This is indeed something which must not be taken lightly. The small groups of people who work for an Islamic revival today face a state of *jāhiliyyah* which has tightened its grip around the whole earth. These advocates feel weak and lonely as they face the forces of *jāhiliyyah*, and suffer all sorts of persecution, hardship and torture. They must, however, contemplate the example of Noah's people very seriously and learn its special significance.

The fact that the Muslim seed is planted on earth is something which weighs very heavily in God's measure. It is something which He considers so deserving that He destroys all the forces of *jāhiliyyah* on earth for its sake: their land, civilization, installations, physical power and achievements. It also deserves that He protects this seed and looks after it until it is safely entrenched and able to build the earth anew.

Noah (peace be upon him) built the ark according to God's instructions and under His protection: "*Build the ark under Our eyes, and according to Our inspiration. Do not appeal to Me on behalf of the wrongdoers. They shall be drowned.*" (Verse 37) When Noah's people chased and repulsed him and spread all sorts of fabrications about him, as God tells us, he appealed to God, his Lord, and declared to Him that he was overcome: *"Noah's people called it a lie; and they accused Our servant of lying, saying, 'Mad is he!' And he was repulsed. So he called out to his Lord: 'I am defeated; come to my help.'"* (54: 9–10) He called on Him to take revenge as he saw fit. At that moment God let certain natural forces of great magnitude to be at the service of His defeated servant: *"We caused the gates of heaven to open with water pouring down in torrents, and caused the earth to burst forth with springs, so that the waters met for a predestined purpose."* (54: 11–12) While these awesome forces were doing their work at such a fearful level, God Himself, limitless is He in His glory, looked after His defeated servant: *"We carried him on that vessel made of planks and nails, which floated under Our eyes: a recompense for him who had been rejected with ingratitude."* (54: 13–14)

The vanguard of Islamic revival in every age and place must pause and contemplate this majestic scene as they are chased and overcome by the forces of *jāhiliyyah*. Such people deserve that God put in their employ awesome natural forces; these need not be the floods, for they are only one form: *"The forces of your Lord are known fully only to Him."* (48: 4) Their task is only to remain steadfast and to continue on their way. They must be aware of the source of their strength and appeal to Him, remaining steadfast until He brings about the accomplishment of His will. They must be certain within themselves that He has power over everything in the heavens and on earth and that He will never let His servants be overcome by His enemies. They will certainly have to undergo a period of education and test; but once they pass this test God will assign a certain role to them to accomplish on earth under His protection.

This is indeed the lesson we learn from that great universal event. No one who faces *jāhiliyyah* with the message of Islam should think for one moment that God will abandon him to such forces when he calls on people to worship God alone. He must not at any moment measure his own strength against the forces of *jāhiliyyah*, believing that he stands alone against these or think that God will desert him when he cries out to Him that he is defeated and helpless.

The forces of the two camps cannot be evenly matched. *Jāhiliyyah* has its own forces, but those who call on people to submit to God rely on God's power. God can put at their service, whenever He chooses, some natural elements, the weakest of which can destroy all *jāhiliyyah*, attacking it from whence it does not expect.

The test period may be prolonged as God wishes. Noah continued to preach his message to his people for 950 years, having no more than twelve believers to show for his efforts. Yet this handful of people was so valuable, in God's measure, that He destroyed all erring mankind, so that the handful of believers would inherit the earth and establish the good seed in it.

The age of miracles is not over. Miracles occur indeed every moment, according to God's will. God, however, may substitute certain forms of miracles for others, as befits every period and age. Certain miracles may be so minute that some people may not even observe them. Those who believe in God, however, detect His will in everything they see and appreciate its unique results.

Those who follow the path leading to God's pleasure need only fulfil their duties as best as they can and leave matters to God with trust and confidence. When they are defeated they should cry out to Him who can help them, in the same way as God's noble servant, Noah, did: "*So he called out to his Lord: 'I am defeated; come to my help.'*" (54: 10) All they need to do afterwards is await God's help. Such waiting is a form of worship, so they are rewarded for it.

Once again we observe that the Qur'ān reveals its treasures only to those who fight its battle, for the cause of God, having the Qur'ān as their guide. They alone live a similar experience to that which took place at the time the Qur'ān was revealed. Hence they can appreciate its meaning fully, because they feel that it addresses them directly in the same way as the first Muslims were addressed.

Praise be to God at the beginning and at the end.

3

The Promise That Never Fails

To 'Ād, We sent their brother Hūd. He said: 'My people! Worship God alone; you have no deity other than Him. You are indeed inventors of falsehood. (50)

وَإِلَىٰ عَادٍ أَخَاهُمْ هُودًا قَالَ يَٰقَوْمِ ٱعْبُدُوا ٱللَّهَ مَا لَكُم مِّنْ إِلَٰهٍ غَيْرُهُۥ إِنْ أَنتُمْ إِلَّا مُفْتَرُونَ ﴿٥٠﴾

No reward do I ask of you, my people, for this [message]. My reward rests with Him who brought me into being. Will you not, then, use your reason? (51)

يَٰقَوْمِ لَآ أَسْـَٔلُكُمْ عَلَيْهِ أَجْرًا إِنْ أَجْرِيَ إِلَّا عَلَى ٱلَّذِى فَطَرَنِىٓ أَفَلَا تَعْقِلُونَ ﴿٥١﴾

My people! Seek your Lord's forgiveness, and then turn to Him in repentance. He will cause the sky to rain abundance on you, and will add strength to your strength. Do not turn away as guilty criminals.' (52)

وَيَٰقَوْمِ ٱسْتَغْفِرُوا رَبَّكُمْ ثُمَّ تُوبُوٓا إِلَيْهِ يُرْسِلِ ٱلسَّمَآءَ عَلَيْكُم مِّدْرَارًا وَيَزِدْكُمْ قُوَّةً إِلَىٰ قُوَّتِكُمْ وَلَا تَتَوَلَّوْا مُجْرِمِينَ ﴿٥٢﴾

They replied: 'Hūd, you have brought us no clear evidence. We are not forsaking our gods on your mere word, nor will we believe in you. (53)

قَالُوا يَٰهُودُ مَا جِئْتَنَا بِبَيِّنَةٍ وَمَا نَحْنُ بِتَارِكِىٓ ءَالِهَتِنَا عَن قَوْلِكَ وَمَا نَحْنُ لَكَ بِمُؤْمِنِينَ ﴿٥٣﴾

All we can say is that one of our gods may have smitten you with something evil.' He said: 'I call God to witness, and you, too, bear witness, that I disassociate myself from all those you claim to be partners with God. (54)

إِن نَّقُولُ إِلَّا ٱعْتَرَىٰكَ بَعْضُ ءَالِهَتِنَا بِسُوٓءٍ قَالَ إِنِّي أُشْهِدُ ٱللَّهَ وَٱشْهَدُوٓاْ أَنِّي بَرِيٓءٌ مِّمَّا تُشْرِكُونَ ۝

Scheme against me, all of you, if you will, and give me no respite. (55)

مِن دُونِهِۦ فَكِيدُونِي جَمِيعًا ثُمَّ لَا تُنظِرُونِ ۝

Indeed I have placed my trust in God, my Lord and your Lord. There is no living creature which He does not hold by its forelock. Straight indeed is my Lord's way. (56)

إِنِّي تَوَكَّلْتُ عَلَى ٱللَّهِ رَبِّي وَرَبِّكُم مَّا مِن دَآبَّةٍ إِلَّا هُوَ ءَاخِذٌۢ بِنَاصِيَتِهَآ إِنَّ رَبِّي عَلَىٰ صِرَٰطٍ مُّسْتَقِيمٍ ۝

But if you turn away, I have delivered to you the message with which I was sent to you. My Lord may replace you with another people. You can do Him no harm. My Lord watches over all things.' (57)

فَإِن تَوَلَّوْاْ فَقَدْ أَبْلَغْتُكُم مَّآ أُرْسِلْتُ بِهِۦٓ إِلَيْكُمْ وَيَسْتَخْلِفُ رَبِّي قَوْمًا غَيْرَكُمْ وَلَا تَضُرُّونَهُۥ شَيْـًٔا إِنَّ رَبِّي عَلَىٰ كُلِّ شَيْءٍ حَفِيظٌ ۝

And so, when Our judgement came to pass, by Our grace We saved Hūd and those who shared his faith. We have indeed saved them from severe suffering. (58)

وَلَمَّا جَآءَ أَمْرُنَا نَجَّيْنَا هُودًا وَٱلَّذِينَ ءَامَنُواْ مَعَهُۥ بِرَحْمَةٍ مِّنَّا وَنَجَّيْنَٰهُم مِّنْ عَذَابٍ غَلِيظٍ ۝

Such were the 'Ād. They denied their Lord's revelations, disobeyed His messengers, and followed the bidding of every arrogant, unrestrained tyrant. (59)

وَتِلْكَ عَادٌ جَحَدُوا بِـَٔايَـٰتِ رَبِّهِمْ وَعَصَوْا رُسُلَهُۥ وَٱتَّبَعُوٓا أَمْرَ كُلِّ جَبَّارٍ عَنِيدٍ ٥٩

They were pursued by a curse in this world and on the Day of Judgement. Indeed, the 'Ād denied their Lord. Oh, away with the 'Ād, the people of Hūd. (60)

وَأُتْبِعُوا فِى هَـٰذِهِ ٱلدُّنْيَا لَعْنَةً وَيَوْمَ ٱلْقِيَـٰمَةِ أَلَآ إِنَّ عَادًا كَفَرُوا رَبَّهُمْ أَلَا بُعْدًا لِّعَادٍ قَوْمِ هُودٍ ٦٠

To Thamūd, We sent their brother Ṣāliḥ. He said: 'My people! Worship God alone. You have no deity other than Him. He it is who brought you into being out of the earth and settled you therein. Seek His forgiveness and then turn to Him in repentance. My Lord is ever near. He answers all.' (61)

وَإِلَىٰ ثَمُودَ أَخَاهُمْ صَـٰلِحًا قَالَ يَـٰقَوْمِ ٱعْبُدُوا ٱللَّهَ مَا لَكُم مِّنْ إِلَـٰهٍ غَيْرُهُۥ هُوَ أَنشَأَكُم مِّنَ ٱلْأَرْضِ وَٱسْتَعْمَرَكُمْ فِيهَا فَٱسْتَغْفِرُوهُ ثُمَّ تُوبُوٓا إِلَيْهِ إِنَّ رَبِّى قَرِيبٌ مُّجِيبٌ ٦١

They answered: 'Ṣāliḥ! Great hopes did we place in you before this. Would you now forbid us to worship what our forefathers worshipped? We are indeed in grave doubt about that to which you call us.' (62)

قَالُوا يَـٰصَـٰلِحُ قَدْ كُنتَ فِينَا مَرْجُوًّا قَبْلَ هَـٰذَآ أَتَنْهَىٰنَآ أَن نَّعْبُدَ مَا يَعْبُدُ ءَابَآؤُنَا وَإِنَّنَا لَفِى شَكٍّ مِّمَّا تَدْعُونَآ إِلَيْهِ مُرِيبٍ ٦٢

He said: 'Think, my people! If I take my stand on a clear evidence from my Lord who has bestowed on me His grace, who will save me from God were I to disobey Him? You are, in such a case, only aggravating my ruin. (63)

قَالَ يَٰقَوْمِ أَرَءَيْتُمْ إِن كُنتُ عَلَىٰ بَيِّنَةٍ مِّن رَّبِّى وَءَاتَنِى مِنْهُ رَحْمَةً فَمَن يَنصُرُنِى مِنَ ٱللَّهِ إِنْ عَصَيْتُهُۥ فَمَا تَزِيدُونَنِى غَيْرَ تَخْسِيرٍ ۝

And, my people, here is God's she-camel, a clear sign for you. Leave her to graze at will in God's land, and do her no harm, lest speedy punishment befall you.' (64)

وَيَٰقَوْمِ هَٰذِهِۦ نَاقَةُ ٱللَّهِ لَكُمْ ءَايَةً فَذَرُوهَا تَأْكُلْ فِىٓ أَرْضِ ٱللَّهِ وَلَا تَمَسُّوهَا بِسُوٓءٍ فَيَأْخُذَكُمْ عَذَابٌ قَرِيبٌ ۝

Yet they cruelly slaughtered her. He said: 'You have just three more days to enjoy life in your homes. This is a promise which will not be belied.' (65)

فَعَقَرُوهَا فَقَالَ تَمَتَّعُوا۟ فِى دَارِكُمْ ثَلَٰثَةَ أَيَّامٍ ذَٰلِكَ وَعْدٌ غَيْرُ مَكْذُوبٍ ۝

When Our judgement came to pass, by Our grace We saved Ṣāliḥ and those who shared his faith from the ignominy of that day. Indeed, your Lord is Powerful, Almighty. (66)

فَلَمَّا جَآءَ أَمْرُنَا نَجَّيْنَا صَٰلِحًا وَٱلَّذِينَ ءَامَنُوا۟ مَعَهُۥ بِرَحْمَةٍ مِّنَّا وَمِنْ خِزْىِ يَوْمِئِذٍ إِنَّ رَبَّكَ هُوَ ٱلْقَوِىُّ ٱلْعَزِيزُ ۝

The blast overtook the wrong-doers, and when morning came, they lay lifeless on the ground, in their very homes, (67)

وَأَخَذَ ٱلَّذِينَ ظَلَمُوا۟ ٱلصَّيْحَةُ فَأَصْبَحُوا۟ فِى دِيَٰرِهِمْ جَٰثِمِينَ ۝

As though they had never prospered there. Thamūd denied their Lord! Oh, away with the Thamūd. (68)

كَأَن لَّمْ يَغْنَوْا۟ فِيهَآ أَلَآ إِنَّ ثَمُودَا۟ كَفَرُوا۟ رَبَّهُمْ أَلَا بُعْدًا لِّثَمُودَ ۝

Preview

So Noah's people became past history: the great majority who denied his message were drowned and forgotten. They were banished from life on earth as also from God's grace. The survivors were established on earth in fulfilment of God's promise: *"The future belongs to those who are God-fearing."* (Verse 49). God's promise to Noah is summed up in the following verse: *"The word was spoken: 'Noah, disembark in peace from Us, and with Our blessings upon you as well as upon generations from those who are with you. As for other folk, We shall let them have enjoyment, and then there will befall them grievous suffering from Us.'"* (Verse 48) As time passed and history took its course, God's promise was fulfilled. The 'Ād were part of Noah's offspring who dispersed on earth, as were the Thamūd. Both of these communities deserved to be punished: *"As for other folk, We shall let them have enjoyment, and then there will befall them grievous suffering from Us."*

A full cycle had turned and the forces of *jāhiliyyah* were back in full sway. Successive generations of mankind, whose number is known only to God, must have lived and passed away, having been guided by true submission to God. This means that they lived according to Islam, which was the faith of their parents, Adam and Eve. They remained so until Satan cajoled them from the straight path, which, in turn, gave rise to the kind of *jāhiliyyah* Noah faced. Noah (peace be upon him), however, was saved with his followers by God. The rest of mankind were destroyed in the floods, in response to Noah's prayers. Again, numerous generations, known only to God, adopted as the basis of their social order the principle of submission to God. They continued to do so until Satan was able once again to cause them to stray. The peoples of 'Ād and Thamūd belonged to *jāhiliyyah*.

The 'Ād were a tribe living at al-Aḥqāf, or the sand dunes, in the south of the Arabian peninsula. The Thamūd lived in the townships of al-Ḥijr, an area between Madinah and Tabūk in North Arabia. Both tribes were extremely powerful and affluent. Both also deviated from the right path and chose idol worship in preference to the worship of God alone. They accused God's messengers of fabricating lies. Hence, their histories are full of lessons for the believers, confirming the facts outlined in the opening passage of the *sūrah*.

Health, Rain and the God-Fearing

> *To ʿĀd, We sent their brother Hūd. He said: 'My people! Worship God alone; you have no deity other than Him. You are indeed inventors of falsehood. No reward do I ask of you, my people, for this [message]. My reward rests with Him who brought me into being. Will you not, then, use your reason? My people! Seek your Lord's forgiveness, and then turn to Him in repentance. He will cause the sky to rain abundance on you, and will add strength to your strength. Do not turn away as guilty criminals.'* (Verses 50–52)

Hūd belonged to the tribe of ʿĀd. He was, then, their brother, tied to them by the blood relations that bind all tribesmen. This tie is emphasized here because it should generate confidence, compassion and honest counsel between brethren. Hence, their attitude towards their brother and prophet seems very odd and exceedingly repugnant. The parting of the ways between the ʿĀd and their brother comes about because of an ideological conflict. Thus the concept of the invalidity of all ties when the bond of faith is non-existent is strongly emphasized. This bond is thus given prominence in Islamic society, making absolutely clear the nature of Islamic faith and its line of action.

Hūd commences his call recognizing that he and his people belong to the same community. They are united together by ties of family, clan, tribe and land. They end up, however, as two different nations: one submissive to God and another worshipping deities beside Him. The two are in conflict. God's promise to give victory to the believers and to destroy the unbelievers comes to pass only when the parting of the ways takes place and the two sides are clearly distinguished and separated. The Prophet and those who believe in God with him disassociate themselves from their people and consider all their former ties with them as invalid. They no longer have any loyalty to their former people and former leadership. They are loyal only to God, their Lord, and to their own 'islamic' leadership which called on them to submit themselves to God alone. Only at this moment when issues are clearly outlined and directions totally marked out, with no meeting point in the middle, are they given victory.

"*To 'Ād, We sent their brother Hūd.*" (Verse 50) In the same way as Noah was previously sent to his people. He said: "*My people!*" His appeal is friendly, reminding them of the ties that unite them together so that they may have confidence in what he says. He would not have cheated his own people.

"*Worship God alone; you have no deity other than Him.*" (Verse 50) These are the very same words with which every messenger addressed his people. Deviation certainly took place after the believers with Noah disembarked from the ark. Perhaps the first deviant step was an attempt to glorify their small group who were saved in the ark with Noah. This glorification might have increased gradually with successive generations until their spirits were represented in trees and stones supposedly providing some sort of beneficial qualities. With the passage of time these stones and trees became idols which were worshipped and served by priests who made people submit to the will of others in the name of such claimed idols. This is only one of the numerous forms of *jāhiliyyah* which can overtake society. We have to remember that any deviation, even by one step, from the line of the absolute oneness of God and total submission to Him will inevitably be followed by further steps which take mankind far away from the right path.

In any case Hūd's people were idolaters who did not submit themselves to God alone. His messenger, therefore, made the same address to them as every messenger addressed his people: "*My people! Worship God alone; you have no deity other than Him. You are indeed inventors of falsehood.*" (Verse 50) False inventions are the idols you worship alongside God.

Hūd then hastens to make it clear to his people that he is giving them honest and sincere counsel, for no ulterior motive, and that he seeks no reward from them. He expects his reward from God who has brought him into existence. Hūd's statement, '*No reward do I ask of you*', suggests that he was implicitly or explicitly accused of trying to serve some personal interest when he made his call. Hence his comment: "*Will you not, then, use your reason?*" (Verse 51) It is indeed singular that people should imagine that a messenger from God would seek personal gain from human beings, when God, who has sent him, is the One who provides all people with their sustenance.

Hūd then directs them to seek God's forgiveness and to turn to Him in repentance. The *sūrah* here repeats the same words stated at its opening as quoted from Muḥammad, the last Messenger. Hūd indeed gave his people the same promise and the same warning as Muḥammad did thousands of years later. *"My people! Seek your Lord's forgiveness, and then turn to Him in repentance. He will cause the sky to rain abundance on you, and will add strength to your strength. Do not turn away as guilty criminals."* (Verse 52)

To seek God's forgiveness and to repent of one's sins opens a new page and sets for people a new way to follow, where good intentions are translated into good actions. Their reward, then, will be abundant. *"He will cause the sky to rain abundance on you."* They will have the rain they need for their farms and animals. They will prosper and have great harvests as a result of the abundant rain. *"And will add strength to your strength."* Their strength, for which they were renowned, would certainly increase. *"Do not turn away as guilty criminals."* The only thing which may withhold all this is their own attitude if they choose to turn away from God and accuse His messenger of fabrication.

Reflecting on Hūd's promise we note that it relates to rain and strength. How can these depend on seeking God's forgiveness and repenting of one's sins, when they are directly influenced by the natural laws which operate in the universe?

As far as the increase in strength is concerned, the explanation is easy. When people purify their hearts and commit themselves to good action, they inevitably add to their strength. They enjoy better health because they eat in moderation and their diet is free from harmful things. Their consciences are relaxed, free of tension; they have confidence in God and His mercy. Their social life is also healthier because they implement God's law which ensures man's freedom and dignity. They maintain their equality in front of God. Besides, faith taps the resources of all those who contribute to man's task of building the earth, without the deviation of false gods.

False deities need from their promoters and worshippers, at times, an acknowledgement that they have or exercise some of God's attributes, such as ability, knowledge, might or mercy. Only then do people submit to them. The lordship claimed by false deities needs to be coupled with godhead so that it can control people. All this requires sustained effort. It also requires that believers who submit themselves to God alone exert great effort to establish the truth and counter the effects of the promotion of such false deities.

People who do not implement God's laws in their lives may be powerful, but their power is only temporary. It will eventually collapse, according to God's laws, because it is not based on solid foundations. Such power is derived from only one side of natural law, such as hard work, discipline and a high standard of production. But these do not last. The fact that the social order and the spiritual side of life are not well founded will bring about their collapse.

Rain, on the other hand, seems to occur according to natural phenomena. This does not however preclude that rain may be beneficial in a certain time and place while it is harmful and destructive in others. God may decide to give life through rain to a certain people, or make rain the undoing of others. He may, if He chooses, fulfil His promises as well as His warnings through the manipulation of natural phenomena. After all, He is the Creator of these phenomena, and the Creator of both cause and effect. His will remains free and absolute. He accomplishes His purpose in whatever way He chooses.

A Lesson in Futile Argument

Such was the sum of the message presented by Hūd to his people. It appears that it was not supported by a miracle to convince those who persisted with unbelief. Perhaps this was so because the floods were still alive in people's memories. In another *sūrah* that gives an account of Hūd and his people we learn that he reminded them of what happened to Noah's people when they rejected God's message. However, his people still entertained bad thoughts about him: "*They replied: 'Hūd, you have brought us no clear evidence. We are not forsaking our gods on your mere word, nor will we believe in you. All we can say is that one of our gods may have smitten you with something evil.'*" (Verses 53–54)

Hūd's people had gone so far astray that they thought him deranged, that one of their deities had smitten him with something evil. They claimed that Hūd did not bring them any clear evidence of his message. Little did they consider that no evidence is needed to prove God's oneness. All that people need to accept this truism is to be properly reminded of it and guided on the line of thought they should follow. They only needed to consult their consciences. They were, however, not prepared to do that. They told God's Messenger point blank that they were not prepared to abandon their false gods just because he, Hūd, encouraged them to do so, without clear proof of the truthfulness of his message. They simply did not believe him: "*We are not forsaking our gods on your mere word, nor will we believe in you.*" (Verse 53)

There was little Hūd could do at this point apart from throwing down a challenge to them and putting his trust entirely in God. In this way, he delivered a final warning to those who denied him and his message, disassociating himself completely from their erring practices.

> *He said: 'I call God to witness, and you, too, bear witness, that I disassociate myself from all those you claim to be partners with God. Scheme against me, all of you, if you will, and give me no respite. Indeed I have placed my trust in God, my Lord and your Lord. There is no living creature which He does not hold by its forelock. Straight indeed is my Lord's way. But if you turn away, I have delivered to you the message with which I was sent to you. My Lord may replace you with another people. You can do Him no harm. My Lord watches over all things.'* (Verses 54–57)

Hūd's statement shows how he cut himself off completely from them, despite the fact that they were his brethren. He was not happy to stay among them when they had chosen a way different from God's. With the tie of faith severed the two sides had nothing to hold them together. Hūd asked God to be his witness as he disassociated himself from them altogether. He also asked them to be his witnesses so that there could be no doubt as to his final position. Throughout, Hūd had the dignity, confidence and reassurance which faith imparts.

Indeed, Hud's attitude is very impressive as he single-handedly confronted his people who were gigantic in stature, rough, impertinent and so ignorant as to believe that their false idols could possess anyone with evil or cause him to be deranged. He goes further and challenges them to cause him any harm they could, allowing him no respite. A man full of faith, Hūd was confident that God's promises would be fulfilled; he was assured of His support. It is a faith so strong that God's promise of support is a tangible reality in which there can be no doubt. He can see it and feel it. It is not a promise for the future which is unknown; it is a reality which is there to see and feel.

Destruction of the 'Ād

"He said: 'I call God to witness, and you, too, bear witness, that I disassociate myself from all those you claim to be partners with God.'" (Verse 54) I call God to be my witness that I am innocent of all those you associate with Him as His partners. You also should testify for me that I have disclaimed all your false gods. Assemble together, all of you and all your invented gods whom you claim to have smitten me with evil and scheme together against me, giving me not a moment's notice, for I do not fear anything from you. *"Indeed I have placed my trust in God, my Lord and your Lord."* (Verse 56) Your denials and rejection notwithstanding, the truth remains that God is the Lord of us all. He is indeed the only Lord of the universe. He has no partners.

"There is no living creature which He does not hold by its forelock." (Verse 56) This is a very real image of God's power. It portrays Him as holding every creature[1] that walks on the earth by its forelock, whether man or animal. He has indeed power over them all. His power is depicted so vividly that it fits well with the strength, roughness and insensibility of the people Hūd was addressing. This is followed by a statement that divine laws never fail: *"Straight indeed is my Lord's way."* (Verse 56) All this reflects the combination of Hūd's strength and determination. Why should he fear anything the 'Ād may cause when they cannot have power over him unless God wills?

When an advocate of God's cause feels this truth within himself, he is left with no doubt as to his own destiny. He feels no hesitation to go along his way. The truth we mean here is that of Godhead which is clearly felt by those who truly believe in God.

---

1. It should be mentioned here that the word used in the Qur'ān for 'living creature' generally refers to animals. In its broader use, as in this instance, it refers to all living creatures. Shades of its narrower meaning, i.e. animals, however, are always present. – Editor's note.

When Hūd has made his challenge, relying on God's might which he portrays in its most majestic form, he warns his people that he has done his duty, conveyed his message and has left them to face God's power: *"If you turn away, still, I have delivered to you the message with which I was sent to you. My Lord may replace you with another people."* (Verse 57) Such people would be more worthy of God's message because they would follow His guidance after Hūd's people had been destroyed. They have no power to cause God any harm. Their departure leaves no vacuum whatsoever. And God will surely protect His good servants and enforce His laws. The wicked have no escape: *"You can do Him no harm. My Lord watches over all things."* (Verse 57)

This was the decisive word. All argument is over and the warnings are fulfilled: *"When Our judgement came to pass, by Our grace We saved Hūd and those who shared his faith. We have indeed saved them from severe suffering."* (Verse 58) Hūd and his followers were saved by a direct act of God's mercy which singled them out and kept them safe from the general punishment which engulfed their people. The punishment is described as 'severe suffering' because this fits with the general atmosphere and with the fact that the 'Ād were rough tyrants. Now, even though they have been removed, their crimes are recorded against them and they are pursued with a curse: *"Such were the 'Ād. They denied their Lord's revelations, disobeyed His messengers, and followed the bidding of every arrogant, unrestrained tyrant. They were pursued by a curse in this world and on the Day of Judgement. Indeed, the 'Ād denied their Lord. Oh, away with the 'Ād, the people of Hūd."* (Verses 59–60)

"Such were the 'Ād." They are far away, although just a moment ago they were shown engulfed by their punishment. Yet now they are gone, lost and forgotten.

"They denied their Lord's revelations, disobeyed His messengers." (Verse 59) They disobeyed only one messenger, but since all God's messengers preach the same message, whoever disobeys one messenger, disobeys them all. The use of the plural in reference to revelations and messengers also has a stylistic purpose. Their crime is made to look much more horrid and ghastly when we realize that they have denied revelations and disobeyed messengers. *"And followed the bidding of every arrogant, unrestrained tyrant."* (Verse 59) They are required to liberate themselves from the tyranny of anyone who wants

to impose authority over them. They must think for themselves and exercise their freedom of choice. They cannot just waste their humanity by accepting the role of blind followers.

Thus we realize that the issue between Hūd and the 'Ād was that of God's Lordship over all people, and their submission to Him alone. It is the issue of sovereignty and to whom it belongs. Who is the Lord to whom all must submit? This is apparent in God's words: "*Such were the 'Ād. They denied their Lord's revelations, disobeyed His messengers, and followed the bidding of every arrogant, unrestrained tyrant.*" They were punished for their disobedience of God's messenger and their following of the bidding of tyrants. Islam, on the other hand, requires its followers to obey God's messengers, because their bidding comes from Him. At the same time Muslims must also disobey all tyrants. This is indeed the parting of the ways between Islam and *jāhiliyyah*, submission to God and denial of His message.

It is abundantly clear, then, that the message of God's unity emphasizes first of all the need to liberate man from submission to anyone other than God, and the need to revolt against the authority of all tyrants who impose themselves as gods. It considers the forfeiture of freedom by the blind following of tyrants, a capital crime of disbelief in and denial of God. Such perpetrators deserve to be destroyed in this life and punished in the hereafter. God has created man to be free, to worship no fellow creature and to maintain his freedom in the face of any chief or leader. This is the essence of man's nobility. If man does not protect it, he deserves no kindness from God. No community of people can claim to have any degree of dignity and humanity when they submit themselves to anyone other than God. Those who do submit to their fellow creatures, and obey their legislation, cannot be excused. After all, they are the majority while the tyrants are a small minority. If the majority want to liberate themselves they need only to sacrifice a small portion of what they actually sacrifice at the altars of tyrants. They willingly pay them the tax of being humiliated in every respect.

The Real Issue of Contention

Let us pause here a little to reflect briefly on the history of Hūd with his people, within the context of the *sūrah*. The Qur'ān gives this account of the history of the age-old call to Islam in order to provide landmarks for the advocates of Islam throughout all generations. These landmarks are not only relevant to the first Muslim community, the first to be addressed by the Qur'ān, and the first to make it its operational guide as opposed to *jāhiliyyah*, but also to every Muslim community which stands up to *jāhiliyyah* anywhere in the world, at any time. This is what makes the Qur'ān the permanent constitution of the Islamic message and the manual of every Islamic movement.

Every time the Qur'ān mentions the approach of any messenger sent by God to any people, it quotes the messenger as saying: *"My people, worship God alone. You have no deity other than Him."* I have repeatedly stated that *"worship God alone"* means total submission to Him alone in all matters which relate to this life or to the hereafter. This is indeed the original meaning of the word. The dictionary shows the word *'abada* [which we now use primarily to denote worship] as meaning: to yield, submit and to lower one's rank to another. A *mu'abbad* road is one which has been levelled to facilitate travelling. *'Abbada* is to enslave; that is, to cause someone to submit to another. The Arabs who were first addressed by the Qur'ān did not confine the import of the term *'abada* to mere worship rituals. Indeed, when the Arabs were first addressed by this term in Makkah, no worship rituals had then been assigned to them. They understood it to mean that they were required to submit themselves to God alone in all their life affairs and to renounce submission to anyone else. The Prophet defined 'worship' in one of his pronouncements as meaning 'compliance', not as offering worship rituals. He was answering 'Adī ibn Ḥātim's question about the Jews and the Christians and their treatment of their rabbis and monks as gods. He said: "Yes, indeed. They (meaning the rabbis and monks) made lawful to them what God has forbidden, and forbade them what God has made lawful, and they complied. This is how they worshipped them."

The term 'worship' has come to signify worship rituals since these are one form of showing submission to God. This form does not by any means, however, encompass the full meaning of 'worship'. When the clear meanings of 'religion' and 'worship' faded from peoples' minds, they started to think that people abandon Islam only if they offer worship rituals to anyone other than God, such as idols and statues. They believe that if they avoid this particular form of *jāhiliyyah* they are protected against atheism, polytheism or any other form of *jāhiliyyah* generally and remain Muslims who could not be deprived of this status. They would thus continue to enjoy all the privileges of a Muslim with regard to the protection of life, honour and property.

This is a blatant fallacy based on distortions of the word 'worship' which decides whether a person is Muslim or not. This term signifies total submission to God in all matters and all affairs. As we have already said, this is the linguistic meaning of the word and the specific definition of it by the Prophet. When the Prophet has so clearly defined a certain term, no one can provide any other definition.

I have stated this very important concept in this commentary, *In the Shade of the Qur'ān*, and in all the works God has enabled me to write about the nature of Islam and its method of operation. In the story of the Prophet Hūd, as given in this *sūrah*, we have a statement which defines the real issue of contention between Hūd and his people, the faith he preached, based on submission to God alone, and the *jāhiliyyah* they practised. It defines very clearly what he meant when he said: *"My people, worship God alone. You have no deity other than Him."* He certainly did not mean to tell his people not to offer worship rituals to anyone other than God, as imagined by those who give the term 'worship' the very narrow meaning of rituals. He meant total submission to God alone and the rejection of any false god or tyrant. The crime for which the 'Ād, Hūd's people deserved to be punished, and to be pursued by a curse in this life and in the life to come, was not merely the offering of worship rituals to someone other than God. It was rather that *"they denied their Lord's revelations, disobeyed His messengers, and followed the bidding of every arrogant, unrestrained tyrant."* (Verse 59)

Their denial of God's revelations is manifest in their disobedience of His messengers and their following of arrogant tyrants. All these actions refer to the same thing. When any people disobey God's commands, they do indeed deny God's revelations and disobey His messengers. They thus go beyond the pale of Islam into polytheism. We have already shown that Islam, in its broad sense, is the original status with which human life on earth started. It is indeed the faith brought by Adam when he fell from heaven and was put in charge of this earth. It is the faith Noah re-established on earth as he disembarked after the floods. People, however, will continue to deviate from Islam and sink back into *jāhiliyyah* until the call of Islam is successful in bringing them back to Islam. The cycle has continued until the present time.

Indeed, had the true essence of worship been the mere offering of worship rituals, it would not have warranted the sending of all God's messengers. It would not have warranted the great efforts exerted by those Prophets (peace be upon them all) and the hard suffering to which the advocates of Islam have been subjected throughout the ages. Saving mankind, however, from submission to creatures of all sorts and returning them to submission to God in all matters is indeed worth that heavy price.

The establishment of the oneness of God, the only God, Lord and Sustainer in the universe, and the only source of legislation in all matters, and the establishment of the only way of life acceptable to God are all aims which merit the sending of God's messengers. They also merit the exertion of great efforts by the messengers as well as the endurance of all the suffering the advocates of Islam have experienced throughout history. This is not because God needs to achieve these aims: He is in need of nothing and no one. They are worthy aims simply because human life cannot be put right, reformed, elevated and become worthy of man without the establishment of the faith based on God's oneness.

Faith, the Truth and Human Welfare

Let us now pause a little to listen to the Prophet Hūd speaking to his people: "*My people! Seek your Lord's forgiveness, and then turn to Him in repentance. He will cause the sky to rain abundance on you, and will add strength to your strength. Do not turn away as guilty criminals.*" (Verse 52) It is the same idea mentioned at the beginning of the *sūrah*, when the Prophet Muḥammad called on his people to believe in Islam: "*Seek forgiveness of your Lord, and then turn towards Him in repentance, and He will grant you a goodly enjoyment of life for an appointed term. He will grant everyone with merit a full reward for his merit. But if you turn away, I dread for you the suffering of a great Day.*" (Verse 3)

These statements establish the relation between the values of faith and the values of human life. They make it abundantly clear that the universe and its governing laws and phenomena have a close relationship with the truth contained in this religion. The whole idea needs to be clarified and properly stated, especially for those who have not yet felt the existence of this relationship.

The truth which this religion seeks to establish is not separate from the truth represented by the fact that God is the Lord of the universe, or the truth of the creation of the heavens and the earth. This whole truth is reflected in the nature of the universe and its overall laws and phenomena. We find that the Qur'ān often links the truth represented in God's Lordship, and Godhead generally, with the truth manifested in the perfection of the heavens and the earth. It links the truth represented in submission to God alone in this life with the truth manifest in the submission of all mankind to Him on the Day of Judgement and in reward or punishment for people's good or evil actions. For example:

We have not created the heavens and the earth and all that is between them in mere idle play. Had We willed to indulge in a pastime, We would indeed have found one near at hand; if such had been Our will at all! Nay, but We hurl the truth against falsehood, and it crushes the latter, and behold, it withers away. But woe to you for all the falsehoods you ascribe [to Us]. To Him belong all those who are in the heavens and on earth. Those that are with Him are never too proud to worship Him and never grow weary of that. They extol His limitless glory by night and day, tirelessly. Or have they taken for worship some earthly deities who can restore the dead to life? Had there been in heaven or on earth any deities other than God, both would surely have fallen into ruin! But limitless in His glory is God, Lord of the Throne, and exalted is He above all that they attribute to Him! He cannot be questioned about whatever He does, whereas they shall be questioned. Or have they taken for worship some deities besides Him? Say: 'Produce your convincing proof. This is the message of those who are with me and the message of those before me.' But nay, most of them do not know the truth, and so they stubbornly turn away. Before your time We never sent a messenger without having revealed to him that there is no deity other than Me. Therefore, you shall worship Me alone. (21: 16–25)

Mankind! If you are in doubt as to the resurrection, remember that We have created you out of dust, then out of a drop of sperm, then out of a germ-cell, then out of an embryonic lump complete and yet incomplete, so that We might make things clear to you. We cause to rest in the [mothers'] wombs whatever We please for an appointed term, and then We bring you forth as infants, that you may grow up and attain your prime. Some of you die young, and some live on to abject old age when all that they once knew they know no more. You can see the earth dry and barren; and [suddenly,] when We send down water upon it, it stirs and swells and puts forth every kind of radiant bloom. That is because God alone is the Ultimate Truth; and He alone brings the dead to life; and He has the power to will anything. And that the Last Hour is certain to come, beyond any doubt; and that God will certainly resurrect all who are in their graves. (22: 5–7)

Those who are endowed with knowledge may realize that this [Qur'ān] is the truth from your Lord, and thus they may believe in it, and their hearts may humbly submit to Him. God will surely guide those who believe to a straight path. Yet the unbelievers will not cease to be in doubt about Him until the Last Hour comes suddenly upon them, or suffering befalls them on a day with no more [days] to follow. On that day, all dominion shall belong to God. He shall judge between them. Thus, all who believe and do righteous deeds shall find themselves in gardens of bliss, whereas for the unbelievers who have denied Our revelations there shall be shameful suffering in store. As for those who leave their homes to serve God's cause, and are then slain or die, God will most certainly grant them a goodly provision. God is indeed the most munificent provider. He will most certainly admit them to a place with which they shall be well pleased. God is surely All-knowing, Most-forbearing. Thus shall it be. If one retaliates only to the extent of the injury he has received, and then is wronged again, God will certainly succour him. God is certainly the One who absolves sin, Much-forgiving. Thus it is, because God causes the night to pass into the day, and the day to pass into the night; and because God hears all and sees all. Thus it is, because God alone is the Ultimate Truth, and all that people invoke beside Him is sheer falsehood, and because God alone is Most High, Great. Are you not aware that God sends down water from the skies, whereupon the earth becomes green. God is unfathomable in His wisdom, All-aware. To Him belongs all that is in the heavens and on earth. God alone is indeed free of all want, worthy of all praise. Do you not see that God has made subservient to you all that is on earth, and the ships that sail the sea at His bidding? He it is who holds the celestial bodies, so that they may not fall upon the earth except by His leave. Most compassionate is God, and merciful to mankind. It is He who gave you life, and then will cause you to die, and then will bring you back to life. Bereft of all gratitude is man. To every community We have appointed ways of worship, which they should observe. Let them not draw you into disputes on this score, but call [them all] to your Lord. You are indeed on the right way. (22: 54–67)

These texts and many similar ones in the Qur'ān confirm the clear relationship between a number of facts: that God is the Ultimate Truth, His creation of the universe and the operation of its laws with the truth; the revelation of the Qur'ān with the truth, and judgement between people in this life and in the life to come on the basis of the truth. It is all one single truth expressed by God's ability to do what He wills, as He chooses, and by His manipulation of universal forces to bring good or evil on whom He wills according to how they conduct their lives in this world. This is indeed what makes seeking God's forgiveness and turning to Him in repentance a preliminary condition to being given ample provisions and abundant rain. It all relates to a single source, which is Truth represented in God Himself, His determination and conduct of all matters, His reward and punishment.

Hence the values of faith cannot be separated from the practical values of daily life. Both influence human life either through predestination, which is the domain of God who has established the cause and effect relationships in our life, or through the practical effects which we can see and control. These effects are produced by our acceptance or rejection of faith.

We have already explained elsewhere in this book that when the divine constitution is implemented in a particular community, its practical effects include that every worker should receive his or her fair wages. Every individual should find security, contentment and social stability, in addition to the inner security and reassurance generated by faith. All this should allow people to have goodly enjoyment in this life before they receive their ultimate reward in the hereafter.

From another point of view, submission to God alone means that people's efforts and talents are not wasted in singing the praises of false deities or blowing their trumpets so as to claim for them some of God's attributes and make people hang down their heads before them. Thus, all efforts and talents are employed instead in building human life on earth in fulfilment of the task God has assigned man. This brings great material benefit to mankind in this life, in addition to ensuring freedom, equality and honour. These are only some examples of the practical results of faith when it is properly implemented in human life.

Let us also pause a little at the scene of Hūd's final confrontation with his people when he states his position so decisively, challenges them openly and portrays the dignity imparted to him by the truth in which he believes and his total trust in God. *"He said: 'I call God to witness, and you, too, bear witness, that I disassociate myself from all those you claim to be partners with God. Scheme against me, all of you, if you will, and give me no respite. Indeed I have placed my trust in God, my Lord and your Lord. There is no living creature which He does not hold by its forelock. Straight indeed is my Lord's way. But if you turn away, I have delivered to you the message with which I was sent to you. My Lord may replace you with another people. You can do Him no harm. My Lord watches over all things.'"* (Verses 54–57)

Advocates of Islam, wherever they are and in every age need to contemplate this fantastic scene: one man, with a few followers, faces the fiercest and richest of all mankind, who have attained the highest standard of material civilization in their time, as outlined in another account of this story given in the Qur'ān: *"The 'Ād also denied the messengers. Their brother Hūd said to them: 'Will you not be conscious of God? I am an honest messenger sent to you. Be then conscious of God and follow me. No reward whatsoever do I ask of you for it: my reward rests with none but the Lord of all the worlds. Will you build a monument on every high place for vain delight? You raise strong fortresses, hoping that you may last forever. When you exercise your power, you do so like cruel tyrants. Have fear of God, and follow me. Fear Him who has given you all the things you know. He has given you flocks and children, gardens and fountains. Indeed, I fear lest suffering befall you on an awesome day.' They replied: 'It is all one to us whether you preach to us or you are not one of those who preach. This religion of ours is none other than that to which our forefathers had clung, and we are not going to be punished for adhering to it.'"* (26: 123–138)

Like Hūd, advocates of Islam must feel the truth of their Lord very clearly within themselves in order to be able to stand up with dignity to the tyrannical forces of *jāhiliyyah* all around them. They must confront physical power as well as the power of industry, wealth, human knowledge, governmental regimes, sophisticated machinery, equipment and the like, knowing that God holds every creature by its forelock. We are all the same before God.

They must at one point confront their people with an uncompromising attitude. The same people are then divided into two different nations: one which submits to God alone and one which does not. When this confrontation takes place, God fulfils His promise to grant victory to His servants. Throughout the history of the divine message, God only resolves the issue between His servants and His enemies in a direct way when the believers have confronted the unbelievers on the basis of faith and made their choice of submission to God alone known to them. In this way they state clearly that they belong to God's party and rely on Him alone, and have no support except that which He grants.

High Hopes, Arrogance and a Woeful Doom

Let us now move on with the *sūrah* and look at the account it gives of the Prophet Ṣāliḥ and his people, Thamūd: *"To Thamūd, We sent their brother Ṣāliḥ. He said: 'My people! Worship God alone. You have no deity other than Him. He it is who brought you into being out of the earth and settled you therein. Seek His forgiveness and then turn to Him in repentance. My Lord is ever near. He answers all.'"* (Verse 61)

We again encounter the same words outlining the same basic issue, and the same course of action. Ṣāliḥ calls on people to believe in God's oneness, to seek His forgiveness and to feel His presence with them wherever they are and whatever they are doing. Ṣāliḥ also reminds them that they originate from the earth. This refers to the origin of the human race as well as to the fact that every human being depends on the nourishment that he receives from the earth, or from the elements which are available in it, for his growth. Despite this origin they are put in charge of the earth and given the task of building it. This applies to the human race generally and to the Thamūd in particular, in their period of history.

All this, however, does not deter them from associating partners with God. Ṣāliḥ, therefore, calls on them to *"Seek His forgiveness and then turn to Him in repentance."* (Verse 61) If they do so, He will respond favourably and answer their prayers: *"My Lord is ever near. He answers all."* (Verse 61) Note here the use of the possessive pronoun *"My Lord"* and the attributes which are chosen here, *"ever near, He answers all."* Coming so close together, they give the impression of the reality of Godhead as felt by one of the chosen elite of believers. They impart an air of friendliness, compassion and very real contact between the benevolent prophet's heart and the hearts of his audience.

Their hearts, however, have been blinded by their corruption. They are no longer responsive. Hence, they do not feel the beauty or the majesty of the reality of Godhead, nor do they appreciate the friendliness and the care with which Ṣāliḥ addresses them. On the contrary, they are surprised and start to doubt their trusted brother. *"They answered: 'Ṣāliḥ! Great hopes did we place in you before this. Would you now forbid us to worship what our forefathers worshipped? We are indeed in grave doubt about that to which you call us.'"* (Verse 62)

They tell him that they had placed great hopes in him. Where once they had appreciated his wide knowledge, honesty, sensibility and wisdom, they are now totally disappointed. Why? *"Would you now forbid us to worship what our forefathers worshipped?"* (Verse 62) To them, that was the calamity. They expected anything but this. And this raised grave doubts in their minds about everything Ṣāliḥ had said. *"We are indeed in grave doubt about that to which you call us."* (Verse 62)

Thus, the Thamūd are puzzled by what is straightforward. They consider as strange and singular what is right and clear. They are amazed that their brother, Ṣāliḥ, should call them to worship God alone. Their astonishment, however, is not based on any evidence, argument, or intellectual thought. They are astonished only because their forefathers worshipped such false gods. People can indeed reach this level of blindness. They base their beliefs on nothing more than the fact that their forefathers believed in the same thing. Once again we find that the faith based on God's oneness is, in essence, a call for the complete and total liberation of the human mind from its bonds of blind imitation of the past, and from the shackles of legendary illusions.

The Thamūd's attitude towards Ṣāliḥ and their statement, *"Great hopes did we place in you before this,"* remind us of the great trust the Quraysh had shown in Muḥammad (peace be upon him) and his honesty. When he, however, called on them to believe in God alone, they denounced him in the same way as Ṣāliḥ was denounced by his people. They accused him of being a sorcerer and a fabricator. They preferred to forget their own testimony to his honesty. The same attitude is always repeated.

Like Noah, his great-grandfather, Ṣāliḥ puts this simple question to his people: *"Think, my people! If I take my stand on a clear evidence from my Lord who has bestowed on me His grace, who will save me from God were I to disobey Him? You are, in such a case, only aggravating my ruin."* (Verse 63) If I have clear proof, and I feel it within me to be absolutely certain that my path is the right path, and if God has bestowed His grace on me by choosing me to deliver His message, and has given me the qualities which make me qualified for this task, who will protect me from God if, in order to preserve your hopes and trust in me, I disobey Him by not conveying to you His message? Would your hopes which you have placed in me be of any use to me against God? *"Who will save me from God were I to disobey Him?"* You raise before me nothing more than the prospect of double ruin. I will incur God's anger in addition to being deprived of the honour of being His messenger and will suffer the ignominy of this world in addition to the punishment of the hereafter. What a compound loss!

"And, my people, here is God's she-camel, a clear sign for you. Leave her to graze at will in God's land, and do her no harm, lest speedy

punishment befall you." (Verse 64) The *sūrah* does not give here any description of the she-camel to which Ṣāliḥ refers as a sign given to them. However, she is *'God's she-camel,'* sent to them in particular so as to be *'a clear sign for you.'* This suggests that the she-camel had certain distinctive qualities by which they knew that it was a sign from God. They were told to allow the she-camel to graze at will in God's land and to do her no harm, or else, they would suffer a speedy punishment. The structure of the sentence in the original Arabic suggests that the punishment would fall immediately and overwhelm them totally.

"Yet they cruelly slaughtered her. He said: 'You have just three more days to enjoy life in your homes. This is a promise which will not be belied." (Verse 65) Despite Ṣāliḥ's warnings, they hamstrung the she-camel and killed her. The Arabic text uses for 'slaughter' a term that indicates that they struck her hamstrings with swords before killing her. Their action was evidence of their corruption and apathy. We note that the text here does not allow for any time passing between the appearance of the she-camel and their killing of her. It is evident that this sign from their Lord did not affect their attitude to Ṣāliḥ's message. Hence, they had to be punished.

They were given a respite of three days, and were told that that was the time left for them to enjoy themselves. The punishment would then surely follow: *"When Our judgement came to pass, by Our grace We saved Ṣāliḥ and those who shared his faith from the ignominy of that day. Indeed, your Lord is Powerful, Almighty."* (Verse 66) At the appointed time Ṣāliḥ and those who followed him were saved by God's grace. A special act of kindness was done to them and they were saved the humiliating destiny of the rest of the Thamūd, who died, having heard the dreadful cry, with everyone in the same position they were in before the cry.

"Indeed your Lord is Powerful, Almighty." Nothing can stand in His way and no people, powerful as they may be, can escape His judgement. Those who are on His side will always have their dignity intact.

The *sūrah* then portrays a scene which makes us wonder at the Thamūd and the speed with which they were destroyed: *"The blast overtook the wrongdoers, and when morning came, they lay lifeless on the ground, in their very homes, as though they had never prospered there."* (Verses 67–68) It is as if they never dwelled or prospered in their magnificent dwellings. It is a scene which fills us with wonder. Nothing more than a glance separates life from death. The whole life of a human being is no more than a momentary affair.

The final comment is the usual one in the *sūrah*. It records the guilt of the people punished, the curse which pursued them and the fact that they were removed from existence and memory: *"The Thamūd denied their Lord! Oh, away with the Thamūd."* (Verse 68)

Historical Similarities

This is another episode of the history of the divine message to mankind. It is the same message, speaking about the essence of Islam, in the broad sense of the word: to worship God and submit to Him alone, associating no partners with Him. Again we are faced with a state of *jāhiliyyah* that follows deviation from the divine faith based on God's oneness. Like the 'Ād before them, the Thamūd descended from the believers saved in Noah's ark, but they deviated from the right faith and ended up in a dreadful state of *jāhiliyyah*. Ṣāliḥ was sent to return them to the true faith.

They are given a miraculous sign, as they asked for, but this does not lead them to believe; rather, it makes them more hostile and they cruelly slaughter the she-camel.

The Arab idolaters also demanded that the Prophet bring them some miraculous sign to help them accept his message. But the sign given to Ṣāliḥ's people benefitted them nothing. To believe in God does not require miracles: the message is both simple and straightforward when approached with clear thinking. *Jāhiliyyah*, however, seals both hearts and minds leaving people in a state of ignorance.

Again we find here the truth of Godhead as manifested in the heart of one of the noble messengers chosen to deliver His message. It is stated by Ṣāliḥ, as he is quoted in the Qur'ān: *"Think, my people! If I take my stand on a clear evidence from my Lord who has bestowed on me His grace, who will save me from God were I to disobey Him? You are, in such a case, only aggravating my ruin."* (Verse 63) He says this after having given them a clear description of his Lord as he feels His presence in his own heart: *"My Lord is ever near. He answers all."* (Verse 61)

Nowhere are the beauty, majesty and perfection of the reality of Godhead better reflected than in the hearts of this noble group of God's chosen people. These hearts stand out as a clear, unstained exhibition of this great reality.

We also find here how *jāhiliyyah* considers as erroneous what is clearly right, and looks at the truth as extremely singular! Ṣāliḥ was much appreciated by his people because of his fine character, clear thinking and wisdom. His people placed great hope in him. But once he had delivered his message to them, they looked upon him with much disappointment. Why this sudden change? It was only because he called on them to submit themselves to God alone. This was at variance with what they had learnt from their forefathers. When the human heart deviates even slightly from the true faith, its error takes it so far away as to make it unable to appreciate the truth, simple and logical as it is. By contrast, such deviant hearts are able to accept deviation that flies in the face of natural and rational logic.

Ṣāliḥ called on his people: "*My people! Worship God alone. You have no deity other than Him. He it is who brought you into being out of the earth and settled you therein.*" (Verse 61) He thus appealed to them by what they could easily recognize as natural and irrefutable evidence based on how they were brought into being. Never had they claimed that they were the ones who brought themselves into being, ensured their survival and provided themselves with the sustenance available on earth. They did not deny that it was God who brought them into being. But they did not follow this through to its logical outcome, namely, submission to God alone and following His guidance. This indeed was the essence of what Ṣāliḥ called on them to do: "*Worship God alone. You have no deity other than Him.*"

It is, then, not the issue of Godhead that is subject to contention. As always, it is the issue of God's Lordship and sovereignty and man's submission and obedience. This is the same issue throughout the battle between Islam and *jāhiliyyah*.

4

Abraham's Special Guests

Our messengers came to Abraham with good news. They bade him peace, and he answered: 'Peace [be to you].' He then hastened to bring them a roasted calf. (69)

وَلَقَدْ جَاءَتْ رُسُلُنَا إِبْرَٰهِيمَ بِالْبُشْرَىٰ قَالُوا۟ سَلَٰمًا قَالَ سَلَٰمٌ فَمَا لَبِثَ أَن جَاءَ بِعِجْلٍ حَنِيذٍ ۝

But when he saw that their hands did not reach out to it, he felt their conduct strange and became apprehensive of them. They said: 'Do not be alarmed. We are sent to the people of Lot.' (70)

فَلَمَّا رَءَا أَيْدِيَهُمْ لَا تَصِلُ إِلَيْهِ نَكِرَهُمْ وَأَوْجَسَ مِنْهُمْ خِيفَةً قَالُوا۟ لَا تَخَفْ إِنَّا أُرْسِلْنَا إِلَىٰ قَوْمِ لُوطٍ ۝

His wife, standing nearby, laughed; whereupon We gave her the happy news of [her giving birth to] Isaac and, after Isaac, Jacob. (71)

وَٱمْرَأَتُهُۥ قَآئِمَةٌ فَضَحِكَتْ فَبَشَّرْنَٰهَا بِإِسْحَٰقَ وَمِن وَرَآءِ إِسْحَٰقَ يَعْقُوبَ ۝

Said she: 'Woe is me! Shall I bear a child, now that I am an old woman and this my husband is well-advanced in years? This is a strange thing indeed.' (72)

قَالَتْ يَٰوَيْلَتَىٰٓ ءَأَلِدُ وَأَنَا۠ عَجُوزٌ وَهَٰذَا بَعْلِى شَيْخًا إِنَّ هَٰذَا لَشَىْءٌ عَجِيبٌ ۝

They said: 'Do you marvel at God's decree? May God's mercy and blessings be upon you, people of this house. He is indeed ever to be praised, Glorious.' (73)

قَالُوٓاْ أَتَعْجَبِينَ مِنْ أَمْرِ ٱللَّهِ رَحْمَتُ ٱللَّهِ وَبَرَكَٰتُهُۥ عَلَيْكُمْ أَهْلَ ٱلْبَيْتِ إِنَّهُۥ حَمِيدٌ مَّجِيدٌ ۝

When his fear had left Abraham, and he received the happy news, he began to plead with Us for Lot's people. (74)

فَلَمَّا ذَهَبَ عَنْ إِبْرَٰهِيمَ ٱلرَّوْعُ وَجَآءَتْهُ ٱلْبُشْرَىٰ يُجَٰدِلُنَا فِى قَوْمِ لُوطٍ ۝

Abraham was indeed most clement, tender-hearted, and devout. (75)

إِنَّ إِبْرَٰهِيمَ لَحَلِيمٌ أَوَّٰهٌ مُّنِيبٌ ۝

Abraham! Leave off all this [pleading]. Your Lord's judgement must come to pass. They shall be afflicted by an irrevocable torment. (76)

يَٰٓإِبْرَٰهِيمُ أَعْرِضْ عَنْ هَٰذَآ إِنَّهُۥ قَدْ جَآءَ أَمْرُ رَبِّكَ وَإِنَّهُمْ ءَاتِيهِمْ عَذَابٌ غَيْرُ مَرْدُودٍ ۝

When Our messengers came to Lot he was troubled on their account, for he was powerless to offer them protection. He said: 'This is a woeful day.' (77)

وَلَمَّا جَآءَتْ رُسُلُنَا لُوطًا سِىٓءَ بِهِمْ وَضَاقَ بِهِمْ ذَرْعًا وَقَالَ هَٰذَا يَوْمٌ عَصِيبٌ ۝

His people came running towards him, for they had been long keen on abominable practices. He said: 'My people! Here are my daughters: they are purer for you. Have fear of God and do not disgrace me by wronging my guests. Is there not one right-minded man among you?' (78)

وَجَآءَهُۥ قَوْمُهُۥ يُهْرَعُونَ إِلَيْهِ وَمِن قَبْلُ كَانُواْ يَعْمَلُونَ ٱلسَّيِّـَٔاتِ قَالَ يَٰقَوْمِ هَٰٓؤُلَآءِ بَنَاتِى هُنَّ أَطْهَرُ لَكُمْ فَٱتَّقُواْ ٱللَّهَ وَلَا تُخْزُونِ فِى ضَيْفِىٓ أَلَيْسَ مِنكُمْ رَجُلٌ رَّشِيدٌ ۝

They answered: 'You know we have no need of your daughters; and indeed you well know what we want.' (79)

قَالُواْ لَقَدْ عَلِمْتَ مَا لَنَا فِى بَنَاتِكَ مِنْ حَقٍّ وَإِنَّكَ لَتَعْلَمُ مَا نُرِيدُ ۝

He said: 'Would that with you I had real strength, or that I could lean on some mighty support.' (80)

قَالَ لَوْ أَنَّ لِى بِكُمْ قُوَّةً أَوْ ءَاوِىٓ إِلَىٰ رُكْنٍ شَدِيدٍ ۝

[The angels] said: 'Lot, we are messengers from your Lord. They shall not touch you. Depart with your household, during the night, and let none of you look back, except for your wife. She shall suffer the same fate which is to befall them. Their appointed time is the morning. Is not the morning near?' (81)

قَالُواْ يَٰلُوطُ إِنَّا رُسُلُ رَبِّكَ لَن يَصِلُوٓاْ إِلَيْكَ فَأَسْرِ بِأَهْلِكَ بِقِطْعٍ مِّنَ ٱلَّيْلِ وَلَا يَلْتَفِتْ مِنكُمْ أَحَدٌ إِلَّا ٱمْرَأَتَكَ إِنَّهُ مُصِيبُهَا مَآ أَصَابَهُمْ إِنَّ مَوْعِدَهُمُ ٱلصُّبْحُ أَلَيْسَ ٱلصُّبْحُ بِقَرِيبٍ ۝

When Our Judgement came to pass We turned those [towns] upside down, and rained on them stones of clay, ranged one upon another, (82)

فَلَمَّا جَآءَ أَمْرُنَا جَعَلْنَا عَٰلِيَهَا سَافِلَهَا وَأَمْطَرْنَا عَلَيْهَا حِجَارَةً مِّن سِجِّيلٍ مَّنضُودٍ ۝

marked out as from your Lord. Nor is such [punishment] far from the wrongdoers. (83)

مُّسَوَّمَةً عِندَ رَبِّكَ وَمَا هِىَ مِنَ ٱلظَّٰلِمِينَ بِبَعِيدٍ ۝

Preview

· This *surah* gives a brief history of the people who were left in charge of the earth after Noah's time. It refers to certain communities which received God's blessings and to others which incurred His displeasure and deserved His punishment. We now have a reference to a part of Abraham's story in which we witness God's blessings. This leads to the story of Lot's people who suffered a painful end. In both stories the dual promise God made to Noah is fulfilled. God's promise ran as follows: *"The word was spoken: 'Noah, disembark in peace from Us, and with Our blessings upon you as well as upon generations from those who are with you. As for other folk, We shall let them have enjoyment, and then there will befall them grievous suffering from Us.'"* (Verse 48) Thus, some of the offspring of those saved in the ark were to receive God's blessings, while other communities were left to enjoy themselves for a while before terrible punishment overwhelmed them for their misdeeds. The blessings are given to Abraham and his seed through both his sons: Isaac and his children who were the Israelite prophets, and Ishmael whose offspring included Muḥammad, the last of God's messengers.

Good News for Abraham

The account of Abraham opens here with the fact that he was to receive good news: *"Our messengers came to Abraham with good news."* (Verse 69) We are not told immediately what the good news was. This would come at the right moment, when his wife was present. The messengers were angels whose identity is left a mystery. Although some commentators on the Qur'ān mention names and numbers, we prefer not to speculate, since we have no evidence to support such contentions.

"They bade him peace, and he answered: 'Peace [be to you].'" (Verse 69) Abraham had emigrated from his birthplace in Iraq, crossed the Jordan and settled in the land of the Canaanites which was largely a desert. Following the Bedouin tradition of hospitality, Abraham immediately went about preparing food for his guests. *"He then hastened to bring them a roasted calf."* (Verse 69) He gets a fat calf, roasts and prepares it. He presents it to his guests who, as we have already said, were angels. Angels, however, do not eat what human beings eat. Hence, they could not partake of the calf, and this worried Abraham: *"When he saw that their hands did not reach out to it, he felt*

their conduct strange and became apprehensive of them." (Verse 70) A guest who does not eat of the food given him causes worry. He makes his host nervous that he intends some kind of treachery. To this day, country people and Bedouins consider it a grave crime to act treacherously towards someone with whom they have shared food. Hence, if they refuse to eat someone's food, their action suggests that they either intend to do harm or that they do not trust the host's intentions. Hence, the messengers reveal their identity to Abraham and tell him about their mission: *"They said: 'Do not be alarmed. We are sent to the people of Lot.'"* (Verse 70)

Abraham realized what sending angels to Lot's people meant, but then something else happens and the subject is changed: *"His wife, standing nearby, laughed."* (Verse 71) She might have been pleased by the imminent destruction of the evil-doers! Then she is given her own news: *"whereupon We gave her the happy news of [her giving birth to] Isaac and, after Isaac, Jacob."* (Verse 71) She was an old woman who had never given birth to a child. Hence, the news of giving birth to Isaac was extremely surprising. Yet, it was happy news of double significance because Isaac would have offspring of his own. Jacob would be born to him. Any woman, especially a sterile one, would be overjoyed at such news. But she is also confused and her confusion is evident: *"Said she: 'Woe is me! Shall I bear a child now that I am an old woman, and this my husband is well-advanced in years? This is a strange thing indeed.'"* (Verse 72)

It is strange indeed. All women cease to menstruate after a certain age. When this happens, they can no longer conceive. But nothing is strange when God wills it: *"They said: 'Do you marvel at God's decree? May God's mercy and blessings be upon you, people of this house. He is indeed ever to be praised, Glorious.'"* (Verse 73)

Familiar or Miraculous?

Nothing that God does should be considered strange. When it is the norm for something to happen in a particular fashion, this does not mean that that fashion is unchangeable. The norm can be broken when God so chooses, for a particular purpose of His own. The purpose here is to bestow His mercy and promised blessings to the believers in that household. Yet, when the norm is broken, whatever takes place as a result occurs in accordance with the overall divine laws of nature which we do not know in full. We cannot judge God's laws according to what happens during a short, limited period of time.

Those who try to restrict God's will to the laws of nature familiar to them are ignorant of the reality of Godhead as stated by God in His book. Whatever God states is true. Our human minds have no say in all this. Even those who restrict God's will to what He Himself has stated to be His law are again unaware of the true nature of Godhead. God's will is free and not restricted by His laws.

It is true that God conducts the affairs of this universe according to the laws He has set for it. This is, however, different from restricting God's will to these natural laws after they have been set in operation. The laws of nature work by God's will all the time. They are not automatic. At any time, God may choose to cause His natural laws to operate in a different way. Whenever this happens natural laws will change to the new fashion God has determined. The overall law of nature which governs the operation of all other laws is that which states that God's will is free and absolute. Every time any particular law operates, it does so according to God's free and absolute will.

At this point, Abraham was reassured. He was delighted by the good news given him by God's messengers. This, however, did not make him overlook Lot and his people. Lot was his nephew who had emigrated with him from their birthplace and who lived in the neighbouring area. He realized that the messengers, or the angels were sent to destroy Lot's people. Compassionate and tender-hearted as Abraham was, he could not bear that the whole community should be so destroyed. He began to plead for them. "*When his fear had left Abraham, and he received the happy news, he began to plead with Us for Lot's people. Abraham was indeed most clement, tender-hearted, and devout.*" (Verses 74–75)

Abraham is described in the text as clement, tender-hearted and devout. He did not lose his temper easily, he prayed to God with sincerity, and he always turned to his Lord in repentance. All these qualities prompted Abraham to plead for Lot's people. We do not know how this pleading was conducted, because the Qur'ān does not elaborate. He was told, however, that God's judgement had been passed and there was no point in his pleading: *"Abraham! Leave off all this [pleading]. Your Lord's judgement must come to pass. They shall be afflicted by an irrevocable torment."* (Verse 76)

Abraham complied and the curtains dropped in order to be raised again on a scene full of activity at Sodom and Gomorrah, Lot's country.

Perversion Brings a Painful Doom

When Our messengers came to Lot he was troubled on their account, for he was powerless to offer them protection. He said: 'This is a woeful day.' (Verse 77)

Lot was aware of the perversity of his people, who preferred to satisfy their sexual desires with men instead of women. In so doing they rebelled against nature, which avails itself of God's wisdom in creating all species in pairs so that procreation and regeneration can take place. Undistorted nature finds true pleasure in conforming to this wisdom, naturally and instinctively.

There are indeed all kinds of perversion. The case of Lot's people, however, is singular. It suggests that psychological disturbances are infectious, like physical illnesses. It is possible that a psychological disorder such as that of the people of Sodom may spread as a result of a disturbance of values in any particular society and the presence of bad examples which produces an unhealthy environment. It is possible that such a psychological disorder spreads despite the fact that it is in conflict with nature which is subject to the same law that governs life itself. This law determines that upright nature finds its pleasure in what meets the requirements of life and ensures its continuity not in what stifles life. Sexual perversion is of the latter sort because it puts the seeds of life in a wicked soil that is not conducive to their growth. For this reason, healthy human nature instinctively, not only morally, finds the practices of Lot's people repulsive. Sound human nature is subject to God's law who grants life and who has made healthy pleasure attendant on what enriches life.

Sometimes, we find pleasure in death for the achievement of a goal which is, to us, more sublime than this life. Such a pleasure, however, is moral, not physical. Besides, such death does not stifle life. On the contrary, it enriches life and elevates it to a sublime standard. There is no comparison between such a pleasure in death and a perversion that stifles life.

Knowing what scandal awaited him in front of his guests, and what ill-treatment awaited these guests from his own people, Lot was troubled on their account and exclaimed, *"this is a woeful day."* The woeful day soon started when his people rushed towards him: *"His people came running towards him, for they had been long keen on abominable practices."* (Verse 78) They were impelled by their desires, rushing like one who has lost self-control. This was the reason for the distress Lot felt on his guests' account.

When Lot looked at his people coming hurriedly towards his home, intent on abusing him and his guests, he tried to arouse their upright nature and direct them to the opposite sex with whom healthy nature finds pleasure. He was even ready to give his daughters in marriage to those frenzied people to satisfy their maddening desires in a clean, pure way. *"He said: 'My people! Here are my daughters: they are purer for you. Have fear of God and do not disgrace me by wronging my guests. Is there not one right-minded man among you?'"* (Verse 78) All the connotations of purity, psychological and physical, are meant here. Lot's daughters would provide a proper, sound and natural way for the satisfaction of sexual desire, arousing healthy feelings as well. It is a situation of complete purity, natural as well as moral and religious. Moreover, they are physically purer. The will of the Creator has provided a clean, pure place for the new emerging life.

Lot also tried to appeal to their fear of God, and their sense of propriety in providing hospitality to one's guests: *"Have fear of God and do not disgrace me by wronging my guests. Is there not any right-minded man among you?"* (Verse 78)

The issue then is one of sensibility or the lack of it, in addition to its being an issue of healthy nature, and propriety behaviour. None of this, however, could counteract their perversity and psychopathic minds. Their frenzy continued in full force. Their reply was even more singular: *"They answered: 'You know we have no need of your daughters; and indeed you well know what we want.'"* (Verse 79) Here is an implicit reminder to Lot that had they had any desire to marry his daughters, they would have done so, because that was their right, and they had a claim to them. But, instead they said: *"Indeed you well know what we want."* A wicked hint to an evil practice!

Lot was confounded. He felt his position was very weak, especially since he was a stranger who had settled among these people, having emigrated from a far-away land. He realized that he had no clan or tribe to support him; he had no strength upon which he could fall back on such a difficult day. Sad and distressed, he put all his feelings in words that were full of sorrow: *"He said: 'Would that with you I had real strength, or that I could lean on some mighty support.'"* (Verse 80) He addressed this to his guests who were angels in the form of young men. Feeling that they were far from strong, he expressed his seemingly unrealistic wish for support from them or from somewhere else. In his difficulty, Lot overlooked the fact that he could indeed lean on the mighty support of God who does not fail His obedient servants.

When the Prophet recited this verse he said: "May God have mercy on my brother Lot. He had indeed the mighty support he was looking for."

When his distress was at its highest and matters had come to a head, the angels informed Lot of the mighty support he had. They informed him of their identity, so that he might be saved along with the good members of his family, with the exception of his wife who belonged to the evil people: *"[The angels] said: 'Lot, we are messengers from your Lord. They shall not touch you. Depart with your household, during the night, and let none of you look back, except for your wife. She shall suffer the same fate which is to befall them. Their appointed time is the morning. Is not the morning near?'"* (Verse 81) We note that the first instruction required that none of the good people who believed in God should delay their departure, or look back because all those who remained in the townships would be destroyed by morning. The rhetorical question about the morning being so near was meant to help Lot relax. Once the morning appeared, God would cause Lot's people to suffer by His own strength what could never have been achieved by the strength Lot wished he had.

The final scene is one of fearful destruction which Lot's people deserved. At the appointed time, *"when Our Judgement came to pass We turned those [towns] upside down, and rained on them stones of clay, ranged one upon another, marked out as from your Lord. Nor is such [punishment] far from the wrongdoers."* (Verses 82–83) It is a scene of total destruction, leaving nothing standing. Note here that turning everything in those towns upside down is akin, in effect, to the perversity of Lot's people which had brought them down from man's high standard to the abject level of animals. Indeed, they were lower than animals because animals are bound by their nature. They do not distort it. The stones showered on them were a fitting means of punishment, because they were stained with mud. The stones were showered heavily *"ranged one upon another."* We also note that these stones were *"marked out as from your Lord,"* the same way as cattle are marked out and left free for breeding. This gives the impression that these stones were left to breed and increase in order to be available at this time of need. It is a fine expression which imparts its own connotations far better than any interpretation could hope to achieve. This is followed by a statement that God's punishment is always available, at any time it is needed, and it will always overwhelm those who deserve it.

The calamity portrayed here sounds similar to some volcanic eruptions which cause subsidence, so that what has been erected on earth is swallowed up, while all this is accompanied with fire, stones, mud and lava. God has much in store for the evil-doers. We do not say this in order to suggest that Lot's people were punished by a volcano erupting at that particular time. Nor do we deny it. All we can say is that this might have happened, but we do not know for certain. We do not like to restrict God's action to any one phenomenon which is familiar to us. But it is probable that God had previously determined to cause a volcanic eruption to bring about the fate of Lot's people as had been predetermined by His knowledge. Such timing is indeed part of the manifestation of His supremacy in the universe, and His conduct of all its affairs. It is also equally possible that what happened to Lot's people occurred as a result of special action determined by God in order to destroy Lot's people in that particular fashion at that particular time. If we understand God's will as it relates to everything in the universe on the lines we have explained in commenting on the fortunes of Abraham's wife, we will have no problem in understanding any event which takes place by God's will.

5

Social Perspective

And to Madyan We sent their brother Shu'ayb. He said: 'My people! Worship God alone. You have no deity other than Him. Do not give short measure and weight. I see you now in a happy state, yet I dread lest suffering befall you on a fateful day which will encompass all. (84)

وَإِلَىٰ مَدْيَنَ أَخَاهُمْ شُعَيْبًا قَالَ يَٰقَوْمِ ٱعْبُدُوا۟ ٱللَّهَ مَا لَكُم مِّنْ إِلَٰهٍ غَيْرُهُۥ وَلَا تَنقُصُوا۟ ٱلْمِكْيَالَ وَٱلْمِيزَانَ إِنِّىٓ أَرَىٰكُم بِخَيْرٍ وَإِنِّىٓ أَخَافُ عَلَيْكُمْ عَذَابَ يَوْمٍ مُّحِيطٍ ۝

My people, always give full measure and weight, in all fairness, and do not deprive people of what is rightfully theirs, and do not spread corruption on earth by wicked actions. (85)

وَيَٰقَوْمِ أَوْفُوا۟ ٱلْمِكْيَالَ وَٱلْمِيزَانَ بِٱلْقِسْطِ وَلَا تَبْخَسُوا۟ ٱلنَّاسَ أَشْيَآءَهُمْ وَلَا تَعْثَوْا۟ فِى ٱلْأَرْضِ مُفْسِدِينَ ۝

That which rests with God is better for you, if you truly believe. I am not your keeper.' (86)

بَقِيَّتُ ٱللَّهِ خَيْرٌ لَّكُمْ إِن كُنتُم مُّؤْمِنِينَ وَمَآ أَنَا۠ عَلَيْكُم بِحَفِيظٍ ۝

They said: 'Shu'ayb, do your prayers compel you to demand of us that we should renounce all that our forefathers worshipped, or that we refrain from doing what we please with our property? You are indeed the one who is clement and right-minded!' (87)

قَالُوا يَٰشُعَيْبُ أَصَلَوٰتُكَ تَأْمُرُكَ أَن نَّتْرُكَ مَا يَعْبُدُ ءَابَآؤُنَآ أَوْ أَن نَّفْعَلَ فِىٓ أَمْوَٰلِنَا مَا نَشَٰٓؤُاْ إِنَّكَ لَأَنتَ ٱلْحَلِيمُ ٱلرَّشِيدُ ۝

He said: 'Think, my people! If I take my stand on a clear evidence from my Lord and He has provided me with goodly sustenance which He alone can give? I have no desire to do, in opposition to you, what I ask you not to do. All that I desire is to set things to rights in so far as it lies within my power. My success depends on God alone. In Him have I placed my trust, and to Him I always turn. (88)

قَالَ يَٰقَوْمِ أَرَءَيْتُمْ إِن كُنتُ عَلَىٰ بَيِّنَةٍ مِّن رَّبِّى وَرَزَقَنِى مِنْهُ رِزْقًا حَسَنًا وَمَآ أُرِيدُ أَنْ أُخَالِفَكُمْ إِلَىٰ مَآ أَنْهَٰكُمْ عَنْهُ إِنْ أُرِيدُ إِلَّا ٱلْإِصْلَٰحَ مَا ٱسْتَطَعْتُ وَمَا تَوْفِيقِىٓ إِلَّا بِٱللَّهِ عَلَيْهِ تَوَكَّلْتُ وَإِلَيْهِ أُنِيبُ ۝

My people, let not your disagreement with me bring upon you a fate similar to those that befell the peoples of Noah, Hūd or Ṣāliḥ; nor were Lot's people far away from you. (89)

وَيَٰقَوْمِ لَا يَجْرِمَنَّكُمْ شِقَاقِىٓ أَن يُصِيبَكُم مِّثْلُ مَآ أَصَابَ قَوْمَ نُوحٍ أَوْ قَوْمَ هُودٍ أَوْ قَوْمَ صَٰلِحٍ وَمَا قَوْمُ لُوطٍ مِّنكُم بِبَعِيدٍ ۝

Hence, pray to your Lord to forgive you your sins, and then turn towards Him in repentance. My Lord is indeed Merciful and All-loving.' (90)

وَٱسْتَغْفِرُواْ رَبَّكُمْ ثُمَّ تُوبُوٓاْ إِلَيْهِ إِنَّ رَبِّى رَحِيمٌ وَدُودٌ ۝

They said: 'Shu'ayb, we cannot understand much of what you say. But we do see clearly how weak you are in our midst. Were it not for your family, we would have stoned you. You do not command a position of great respect among us.' (91)

قَالُوا۟ يَٰشُعَيْبُ مَا نَفْقَهُ كَثِيرًا مِّمَّا تَقُولُ وَإِنَّا لَنَرَىٰكَ فِينَا ضَعِيفًا وَلَوْلَا رَهْطُكَ لَرَجَمْنَٰكَ وَمَا أَنتَ عَلَيْنَا بِعَزِيزٍ ۝

Said he: 'My people, do you hold my family in greater esteem than God? You have turned your backs on Him. My Lord encompasses [with His might] all that you do. (92)

قَالَ يَٰقَوْمِ أَرَهْطِىٓ أَعَزُّ عَلَيْكُم مِّنَ ٱللَّهِ وَٱتَّخَذْتُمُوهُ وَرَآءَكُمْ ظِهْرِيًّا إِنَّ رَبِّى بِمَا تَعْمَلُونَ مُحِيطٌ ۝

Do what you will, my people, and so will I. You shall come to know who shall be visited by suffering that will cover him with ignominy, and who is a liar. Watch, then [for what is coming], and I shall watch with you.' (93)

وَيَٰقَوْمِ ٱعْمَلُوا۟ عَلَىٰ مَكَانَتِكُمْ إِنِّى عَٰمِلٌ سَوْفَ تَعْلَمُونَ مَن يَأْتِيهِ عَذَابٌ يُخْزِيهِ وَمَنْ هُوَ كَٰذِبٌ وَٱرْتَقِبُوٓا۟ إِنِّى مَعَكُمْ رَقِيبٌ ۝

When Our judgement came to pass, by Our grace We saved Shu'ayb and those who shared his faith. The blast overtook the wrongdoers, and when morning came, they lay lifeless on the ground, in their very homes, (94)

وَلَمَّا جَآءَ أَمْرُنَا نَجَّيْنَا شُعَيْبًا وَٱلَّذِينَ ءَامَنُوا۟ مَعَهُۥ بِرَحْمَةٍ مِّنَّا وَأَخَذَتِ ٱلَّذِينَ ظَلَمُوا۟ ٱلصَّيْحَةُ فَأَصْبَحُوا۟ فِى دِيَٰرِهِمْ جَٰثِمِينَ ۝

as though they had never prospered there. Oh, away with the people of Madyan, even as the Thamūd have been done away with! (95)

كَأَن لَّمْ يَغْنَوْا۟ فِيهَآ أَلَا بُعْدًا لِّمَدْيَنَ كَمَا بَعِدَتْ ثَمُودُ ۝

Indeed, We sent Moses with Our signs and a manifest authority, (96)

وَلَقَدۡ أَرۡسَلۡنَا مُوسَىٰ بِـَٔايَٰتِنَا وَسُلۡطَٰنٍ مُّبِينٍ ﴿٩٦﴾

to Pharaoh and his noble men. They, however, followed only Pharaoh's bidding. Pharaoh's bidding led by no means to what is right. (97)

إِلَىٰ فِرۡعَوۡنَ وَمَلَإِيْهِۦ فَٱتَّبَعُوٓاْ أَمۡرَ فِرۡعَوۡنَ وَمَآ أَمۡرُ فِرۡعَوۡنَ بِرَشِيدٍ ﴿٩٧﴾

He will come at the head of his people on the Day of Resurrection, leading them to the fire. Vile was the destination towards which they were led. (98)

يَقۡدُمُ قَوۡمَهُۥ يَوۡمَ ٱلۡقِيَٰمَةِ فَأَوۡرَدَهُمُ ٱلنَّارَ وَبِئۡسَ ٱلۡوِرۡدُ ٱلۡمَوۡرُودُ ﴿٩٨﴾

A curse is made to follow them in this world and on the Day of Resurrection. Vile was the renewable gift which they were given. (99)

وَأُتۡبِعُواْ فِي هَٰذِهِۦ لَعۡنَةً وَيَوۡمَ ٱلۡقِيَٰمَةِ بِئۡسَ ٱلرِّفۡدُ ٱلۡمَرۡفُودُ ﴿٩٩﴾

Preview

This is yet another stage of the same message preaching the same faith. Here we have an account of Shu'ayb and his people, who lived at Madyan. Coupled with the main issue of faith and God's oneness, we also have here the issue of honesty and justice in business transactions. It is an issue closely related to faith in God, submission to Him alone and the implementation of His laws. The people of Madyan, however, were totally astonished at the two issues being linked together. They could not comprehend the relationship between financial transactions and prayer, which is a manifestation of submission to God.

The history given here follows the same lines as the accounts of Hūd with the 'Ād, and Ṣāliḥ with the Thamūd. Its conclusion, and the style and expressions used to portray the final outcome, however, make it more akin to Ṣāliḥ's history. Indeed the two histories portray the same type of suffering, expressed in similar terms, befalling the two peoples.

Faith and Fair Trading

"And to Madyan We sent their brother Shuʿayb. He said: 'My people! Worship God alone. You have no deity other than Him.'" (Verse 84) Submission to God alone is the first article of faith as well as the first rule of life and the first principle of law and human transactions. It is the principle without which faith, worship or human dealings cannot take their proper shape.

"Do not give short measure and weight. I see you now in a happy state, yet I dread lest suffering befall you on a fateful day which will encompass all. My people, always give full measure and weight, in all fairness, and do not deprive people of what is rightfully theirs, and do not spread corruption on earth by wicked actions. That which rests with God is better for you, if you truly believe. I am not your keeper." (Verses 84–86) The main issue here is honesty and justice, which comes second only to the issue of faith and submission to God. In other words, it is the issue of the law which governs business dealings on the basis of faith. The people of Madyan, whose country was an enclave of land lying between Hijaz and Syria, used to give short measure and weight, thus wronging other people in respect of what was rightfully theirs. That is, they used to give other people less than the value of their goods. Their misconduct reflected badly on their integrity and honour and showed that they were far from clean both externally and at heart. Their geographical position meant that they were able to control the trade route of the caravans moving between the north and the south of Arabia. This enabled them to dictate unfair terms on other peoples' trade.

Here we see the link between believing in God's oneness and submission to Him alone on the one hand, and honesty, fair trading, honourable transactions and combating all kinds of cheating and stealing, whether perpetrated by individuals or governments, on the other. This relationship appears to be a safeguard ensuring a better human life, justice and peace among people. It is the only safeguard based on fearing God and seeking His pleasure. Hence, it has a very solid foundation which cannot be influenced by special interests or personal desires.

In the Islamic view, business dealings, and morality generally, must have a solid basis which is not influenced by changeable factors. Thus Islam differs fundamentally with all other social and moral theories devised by human beings and governed by their differing bents of thought and their temporary interest.

When business dealings and morality have such a solid basis, they are not influenced by immediate or material interests or by differing environments with different factors and considerations. Hence, rules of morality and those that govern human dealings are not subject to whether people are nomadic, agrarian or industrialized. Such changeable factors lose their influence on the moral concepts of society or the moral values which govern business transactions when the basis of legislation for all spheres of life is divine law. Then the essential basis of morality is to seek God's pleasure, hoping to win His reward and avoid His punishment. All that is advanced by human-made theories and doctrines about morality being the product of the economic situation and the social conditions prevailing in a particular society become meaningless in the light of Islamic moral theory.

"Do not give short measure and weight. I see you now in a happy state." (Verse 84) God has given you ample provision for your sustenance, so you have no need to indulge in vile practices to add to your riches. You will not become poor if you give full measure and weight and give people what is rightfully theirs. Your happy state is indeed threatened by your cheating practices and your unlawful earnings. *"Yet I dread lest suffering befall you on a fateful day which will encompass all."* (Verse 84) This may come on the Day of Judgement, or it may indeed occur in this life when your cheating practices yield their bitter fruits and rebound on your society and your trade. People will then suffer injustice brought about by some of them against others.

Shu'ayb repeats his advice positively after having expressed it in the form of a prohibition. *"My people, always give full measure and weight, in all fairness.*" (Verse 85) To give full measure and weight is more expressive than not falling short on both of them. It is closer to giving others more than their due. Different forms of expression have different connotations and leave different effects. The effect of giving full measure and full weight is much more kindly than that of not falling short.

"*Do not deprive people of what is rightfully theirs.*" (Verse 85) This is much more general than what is valued according to measure and weight. It stresses the fair evaluation of everything which belongs to others, whether this evaluation is in weight, measure, price or otherwise. It also includes material as well as moral evaluations. It may be said to further encompass actions and personal qualities. The Arabic term used here includes both the material and the abstract.

When people suffer maltreatment in respect of what rightfully belongs to them, this gives rise to bitterness, grudges and despair. Such feelings can only ruin society and destroy social links as they adversely affect consciences and hearts. They leave no room for anything good in life.

"*Do not spread corruption on earth by wicked actions.*" (Verse 85) They must not willingly seek to spread corruption because it rebounds on them. Instead, their hearts should awaken to something far better and far more rewarding than their stained earnings: "*That which rests with God is better for you, if you truly believe.*" (Verse 86) What is with God is far better and lasts much longer. At the outset, Shu'ayb called on his people to worship God alone. He reminds them of this here, when he mentions their lasting reward which they will receive from God if they respond to his call, and follow his advice in their business dealings. After all, his advice is part of that faith.

Having called on them to believe in God alone, he leaves them to Him, declaring that he cannot influence their destiny, and is not their guardian. He is not responsible for preventing them from error and is not answerable for their erroneous practices, should they choose to indulge in them. His task is to convey his message to them, which he has done: "*I am not your keeper.*" (Verse 86) This expression awakens the addressees to the gravity of the matter and to their heavy responsibility. It puts them face to face with what awaits them in the end, when they will have no guardian or intermediary.

Religion and Financial Dealings

The people of Madyan were hardened in their corrupt practices. Their reply was sarcastic. Every word of it smacked of sarcasm. Yet it also indicated their ignorance and mulish obstinacy: *"They said: 'Shu'ayb, do your prayers compel you to demand of us that we should renounce all that our forefathers worshipped, or that we refrain from doing what we please with our property? You are indeed the one who is clement and right-minded!'"* (Verse 87)

They did not realize, nor wanted to realize, that prayers are required by faith, as a manifestation of true submission to God. Faith cannot be established without the recognition of God's oneness and the renunciation of everything else they or their forefathers worshipped. Likewise, it cannot be established unless God's legislation in matters of trade and finance, as well as in all spheres of life, are implemented. All these are a complete whole, and faith cannot be separated from prayers or legislation which caters for all aspects of human life.

The people of Madyan, who had such an ill-conceived idea of the connection between faith and worship, and between the two and business transactions lived a long time ago. But rather than denounce their attitude at length we should remind ourselves that people today stick to certain concepts which are not much different from those of Shu'ayb's people. The world of *jāhiliyyah* which we see around us today is not much better or more intelligent than the earlier one. The sort of ascription of Godhead to other beings alongside God, which was practised by Shu'ayb's people, is still practised today by most of mankind, including those who claim to be Jews, Christians, or Muslims. All try to establish a barrier separating faith and worship on the one hand and law and business transactions on the other. They claim that faith and worship belong to God and should be conducted according to His instructions, while the law and business do not concern Him. These should be conducted according to the bidding of some other authority. This is indeed the essence of attributing partners to God.

We must not forget that the Jews today are the only people who are determined to conduct their transactions according to their faith and religious law, regardless of the distortion that has crept into their faith.

290

The Knesset, Israel's legislative body, once held a stormy session debating the case of an Israeli ship serving its non-Jewish passengers with meals which were not approved by the Jewish religion. The company and the ship concerned were compelled to serve only kosher food, even if it meant that the company would incur financial losses. This incident should serve as a lesson for many of those who today call themselves Muslims.

We find among us today some who claim to be Muslim questioning the validity of any link between faith and morality, especially when they consider financial dealings. Some of our intellectuals who have higher degrees awarded by various universities affect amazement as they wonder: what has Islam got to do with personal affairs? Why should Islam be concerned with how we dress on the beach, or how a woman appears in public, or how we satisfy our sexual urges? Why should Islam concern itself with drinking a glass of wine, or indeed with anything done by those who classify themselves as civilized? Now we ask what is the difference between such questions and those put by the people of Madyan to their Prophet Shu'ayb? *"Do your prayers compel you to demand of us that we should renounce all that our forefathers worshipped, or that we refrain from doing what we please with our property?"* (Verse 87)

The second part of their question implies a very strong objection to religion having anything to do with the economy. To them, business dealings have no connection whatsoever with faith or even with moral values, taken separately from faith. Why should religion be concerned with financial transactions or with devious business methods which evade man-made laws? Indeed these people, living in our midst, arrogantly claim that the economy would collapse if moral values were allowed to interfere with it. They object even to some Western economic theories, such as the moral theory, and label it as confused reactionary thinking.

Let us then not claim for ourselves a standard much higher than that of the people of Madyan in their ancient *jāhiliyyah*, when we live today in an even darker *jāhiliyyah* which boasts of its enlightenment, advanced knowledge and civilization. Our state of *jāhiliyyah* today motivates many among us to accuse those who maintain that there is an important link which groups together faith in God, personal behaviour in all spheres of life and financial dealings, of being reactionary, advocating obsolete ideas.

Faith in God's oneness cannot be rightly and firmly established in people's hearts when God's laws, which regulate individual behaviour and social and financial dealings, are abandoned in favour of man-made laws. It is not possible for faith and unfaith to coexist in the same heart side by side. Unfaith, or the acknowledgement of other gods alongside God, can take different forms such as the ones which prevail in our societies today. This still represents the acknowledgement of other gods, which is a criterion common to all unbelievers throughout history.

The people of Madyan were sarcastic when they addressed their Prophet Shu'ayb, just as certain people today resort to sarcasm when they speak of those who advocate submission to God alone in all affairs. They said to Shu'ayb: "*You are indeed the one who is clement and right-minded!*" (Verse 87) They obviously meant the opposite. To them, wisdom and right meant that they should follow in their fathers' footsteps and worship the same gods they worshipped. It also meant that they should separate worship from business. The same ideas are advocated by present-day intellectuals who do not hide their sarcasm when they speak of the advocates of Islam and describe them as reactionary.

A Kind Prophet's Argument

Shu'ayb, fully confident of the truth of his message, and aware of his people's ignorance and short-sightedness, does not let their sarcasm affect him. On the contrary, he seeks to inform them politely that he takes his stand on clear evidence from his Lord, which he feels in his innermost heart. He explains to them that he is fully confident of the truth of what he advocates because his knowledge far exceeds theirs. When he calls on them to stick to honest dealings, the effects of such honesty also apply to him since he is a businessman. He is after no personal gain which he seeks to realize for himself. He does not intend to do behind their backs what he has forbidden them so that he enjoys a market free from competition. His call is one of reform which includes himself. The path he enjoins them to follow will not cause them any losses, as they mistakenly think.

> He said: 'Think, my people! If I take my stand on a clear evidence from my Lord and He has provided me with goodly sustenance which He alone can give? I have no desire to do, in opposition to you, what I ask you not to do. All that I desire is to set things to rights in so far as it lies within my power. My success depends on God alone. In Him have I placed my trust, and to Him I always turn.' (Verse 88)

Shu'ayb addresses them in a friendly and appealing way, reminding them of his close links with them: *"Think my people! If I take my stand on a clear evidence from my Lord."* I feel His presence beyond any doubt, and I am certain that it is He who bestows revelations on me, and instructs me to convey His message to you. With full confidence and certainty I take my stand, based on this evidence which is to me very real. *"And He has provided me with goodly sustenance which He alone can give..."* Part of this is my own wealth with which I conduct my business.

"I have no desire to do, in opposition to you, what I ask you not to do." (Verse 88) I am after no personal gain which I may realize by so doing. *"All that I desire is to set things right in so far as it lies within my power."* (Verse 88)

It is, then, the general reform of society which Shu'ayb is after. It is a reform which brings benefit to every individual and every community. Some may think that to adhere to moral values and implement the divine law may make them lose some chances which may be open to them, or lose some gain which they would otherwise achieve. But implementing the divine law can only make them lose evil gains and wicked opportunities. It compensates them with goodly gains and lawful provisions. It also establishes a society which is characterized by the co-operation of its individuals. It is a society which is free from grudges, treachery and selfish quarrels.

"My success depends on God alone." (Verse 88) He alone can grant me success, as He knows my intentions and the sincerity of my efforts. *"In Him have I placed my trust."* (Verse 88) I depend on no one other than Him. *"To Him I always turn."* (Verse 88) From Him alone I seek

help to overcome the difficulties that may beset me and to Him alone I submit my work and efforts.

Shu'ayb then tries another way of reminding them of the truth. He reminds them of the doom that befell the peoples of Noah, Hūd, Ṣāliḥ and Lot. This may open their hardened hearts in a way which rational, cool and well-argued reminders may not. "*My people, let not your disagreement with me bring upon you a fate similar to those that befell the peoples of Noah, Hūd or Ṣāliḥ; nor were Lot's people far away from you.*" (Verse 89)

He tells them that they must not let their opposition to him harden their attitude of blind rejection. He says to them plainly that he fears that they may bring upon themselves a doom which is not unlike that which befell earlier communities. He reminds them especially of the people of Lot who lived close by and who had recently been destroyed.

When he has raised this prospect before them he then opens the doors to forgiveness and repentance. He uses the kindest and gentlest terms in order to assure them of God's mercy and compassion: "*Hence, pray to your Lord to forgive you your sins, and then turn towards Him in repentance. My Lord is indeed Merciful and All-loving.*" (Verse 90)

Thus Shu'ayb tries all methods of admonition and remonstration in the hope that his people's hearts will open up and respond to the truth. They, however, are so hardened in their erring ways and in their misconceptions of values and motives that their response remains negative. We have seen an example of their response in their mocking at Shu'ayb and his prayer.

When All Arguments Fail

"*They said: 'Shu'ayb, we cannot understand much of what you say. But we do see clearly how weak you are in our midst. Were it not for your family, we would have stoned you. You do not command a position of great respect among us.*'" (Verse 91) The people of Madyan made it clear to Shu'ayb that they were fed up with him and with his message. They did not want to know anything about the truth he was presenting and did not care for anything which differed with their attitude to life or with their practices. Thus, in their view, only physical strength mattered. Plain truth was of no real significance, regardless of the strength of its argument, if it was not supported by physical power: *"We do see clearly how weak you are in our midst. Were it not for your family, we would have stoned you."* What restrained them from doing so was the fact that they reckoned with the power of Shu'ayb's clan and family who were supposed to come to his defence. They did not reckon with the power of God who would not leave His messenger to the mercy of His enemies. They rudely told Shu'ayb: *"You do not command a position of great respect among us."* They had no respect for him as a noble person, nor for his own strength. They only had to consider what his clan might do if anything happened to him.

When people are devoid of proper faith, sound values and noble ideals, they care nothing for anything beyond their immediate interests or their material well-being. To them, any good cause or apparent truth has no sanctity whatsoever. They do not hesitate to assault the advocates of God's cause if these have no apparent power to protect them.

Shu'ayb was angry with his people for their arrogance towards God. He made it clear that he did not derive his power from his clan or family. He confronted them with their misjudgement of the true powers which can influence things in the universe, and pointed out to them that their insolence would not benefit them with God, aware as He always is of people's actions. Shu'ayb said his last word and parted ways with his people on the basis that there was no common ground of faith between them. He warned them against the suffering that befell all people who adopted their attitude and then left them to their destiny.

> *Said he: 'My people, do you hold my family in greater esteem than God? You have turned your backs on Him. My Lord encompasses [with His might] all that you do.'* (Verse 92)

Any group of people, strong and powerful as they may be, are, after all, human, subject to God's power. Hence, they are weak. How can you then give such a group of human beings more importance than you give to God? How can you fear them more than you fear Him? *"You have turned your backs on Him."* This is an image of physical rejection which heightens the enormity of their error. They turn their backs on God who has created them and who has given them all the goods they enjoy in this life. Their attitude is one of ingratitude and insolence as much as it is one of rejection of faith.

"*My Lord encompasses [with His might] all that you do.*" The Arabic expression used here gives an image of complete and perfect knowledge, as well as complete and overall power. Angry at his people's impudence towards God, Shu'ayb takes the proper attitude of a true believer. He does not find any gratification or reassurance in the fact that his own family and clan enjoyed such respect and power that afforded him protection from possible assault. This is evidence of true faith. A true believer finds no real power or protection other than that given him by God. He is unhappy to have a community to protect him, which is held in awe by others, when God, his Lord, is not held in awe. The true loyalty of a person who submits himself to God is not to his clan or nation; it is to God and to his faith. This is the parting point between the Islamic concept of loyalties and the un-Islamic one.

Shu'ayb's anger and his disavowal of any protection given him by anyone other than God prompt him to challenge his people and then disassociate himself from them totally. "*Do what you will, my people, and so will I. You shall come to know who shall be visited by suffering that will cover him with ignominy, and who is a liar. Watch, then [for what is coming], and I shall watch with you.*" (Verse 93) He challenges them to do what they can, to go along their way to the end. He will work according to his method and programme. Time will tell who will suffer and who will prosper. The way he throws down his challenge and invites them to watch for the outcome tells of his absolute trust in God.

The curtains fall here to open up again when the issue is finally resolved. We see the people of Madyan prostrate, lifeless in their homes, after having been overtaken by a dreadful cry, similar to that which overwhelmed the Thamūd, Ṣāliḥ's people. There is great similarity between what happened to both peoples. In both cases, their houses were no longer inhabited, as if they never lived there: "*When Our judgement came to pass, by Our grace We saved Shu'ayb and those who shared his faith. The blast overtook the wrongdoers, and when morning came, they lay lifeless on the ground, in their very homes, as though they had never prospered there. Oh, away with the people of Madyan, even as the Thamūd have been done away with!"* (Verses 94–95) Another black page of history was turned after God's word came to pass against those who rejected His warnings.

A Double Curse for Pharaoh's People

In the series of historical accounts given in this *sūrah*, the final reference is made to Moses and Pharaoh. We have here only a very brief account with several references to the details of the story, but no specifics are given here. The end which Pharaoh and his people met is recorded, along with a very vivid and real scene of the Day of Resurrection. We also have a statement of a basic Islamic principle whereby individual responsibility cannot be overlooked simply because the individual concerned chooses to follow his master or ruler.

The account given here opens with God's sending Moses to Pharaoh, the great ruler of Egypt, and the chiefs of his government. God gives Moses strength and clear authority. *"We sent Moses with Our signs and a manifest authority to Pharaoh and his noble men."* (Verses 96–97) No details are given before the end is stated. The people simply obeyed Pharaoh and disobeyed God, despite all the stupidity, short-sightedness and excesses which characterized all that Pharaoh had done. *"They, however, followed only Pharaoh's bidding. Pharaoh's bidding led by no means to what is right."* (Verse 97)

The people chose to follow Pharaoh blindly, without stopping to think whether he guided them rightly or not. They degraded themselves and trampled over their own freedom and the will with which God had endowed them. Hence, it was only natural, as the Qur'ān states, that Pharaoh will lead them on the Day of Resurrection, and that they will follow him: *"He will come at the head of his people on the Day of Resurrection."* (Verse 98)

We have so far been listening to a story that happened in the past and to a promise which will be realized in the future. The scene, however, changes here and what was to be the future is now past. Pharaoh has led his people to hell, and the matter is over: *"leading them to the fire."* (Verse 98) He has led them like a shepherd leads his flock. After all, they were sheep moving blindly. They have foregone the very basic essential of humanity, namely, the freedom of choice. He has led them to hell. The Arabic expression used here has the added connotation of aiming to lead them to a fountain where they can drink. What a drink they will have, which satisfies no thirst: *"Vile was the destination towards which they were led."* (Verse 98)

We note here that all this, the leadership of Pharaoh, and their destination to which he has led them took place a long time ago. A comment is made on it, followed by ridicule: *"A curse is made to follow them in this world and on the Day of Resurrection. Vile was the renewable gift which they were given."* (Verse 99)

The curse followed them in this life and will be sure to follow them on the Day of Resurrection. This was the gift Pharaoh gave to his people. He had indeed promised his sorcerers generous gifts. Now everyone realizes what sort of gifts Pharaoh is able to give. What is more is the fact that the gift is always renewable, never ending. *"Vile was the renewable gift which they were given."* (Verse 99)

6

Single Message, Different People

These are some of the accounts of past communities which We relate to you. Some still remain while others are extinct, like a field mown-down. (100)

ذَٰلِكَ مِنْ أَنۢبَآءِ ٱلْقُرَىٰ نَقُصُّهُۥ عَلَيْكَ مِنْهَا قَآئِمٌ وَحَصِيدٌ ﴿١٠٠﴾

No wrong did We do to them, but it was they who wronged themselves. Those deities of theirs which they were keen to invoke instead of God availed them nothing when your Lord's judgement came to pass; they only added to their ruin. (101)

وَمَا ظَلَمْنَٰهُمْ وَلَٰكِن ظَلَمُوٓاْ أَنفُسَهُمْ فَمَآ أَغْنَتْ عَنْهُمْ ءَالِهَتُهُمُ ٱلَّتِى يَدْعُونَ مِن دُونِ ٱللَّهِ مِن شَىْءٍ لَّمَّا جَآءَ أَمْرُ رَبِّكَ وَمَا زَادُوهُمْ غَيْرَ تَتْبِيبٍ ﴿١٠١﴾

Such is your Lord's punishment whenever He takes to task any community which is bent on evil-doing; His punishment is indeed grievous, severe. (102)

وَكَذَٰلِكَ أَخْذُ رَبِّكَ إِذَآ أَخَذَ ٱلْقُرَىٰ وَهِىَ ظَٰلِمَةٌ إِنَّ أَخْذَهُۥٓ أَلِيمٌ شَدِيدٌ ﴿١٠٢﴾

In this there is surely a sign for those who fear the suffering in the life to come. That is a day when all mankind shall be gathered together, and that is a day which will be witnessed [by all]. (103)

إِنَّ فِى ذَٰلِكَ لَءَايَةً لِّمَنْ خَافَ عَذَابَ ٱلْءَاخِرَةِ ذَٰلِكَ يَوْمٌ مَّجْمُوعٌ لَّهُ ٱلنَّاسُ وَذَٰلِكَ يَوْمٌ مَّشْهُودٌ ﴿١٠٣﴾

We shall not delay it beyond an appointed term. (104)

وَمَا نُؤَخِّرُهُۥٓ إِلَّا لِأَجَلٍ مَّعۡدُودٍ ۝

When that day comes, not a soul will speak except by His leave. Some among them will be wretched, and some happy. (105)

يَوۡمَ يَأۡتِ لَا تَكَلَّمُ نَفۡسٌ إِلَّا بِإِذۡنِهِۦ فَمِنۡهُمۡ شَقِيٌّ وَسَعِيدٌ ۝

Those who will have brought wretchedness upon themselves, they will be in the fire where, moaning and sobbing, (106)

فَأَمَّا ٱلَّذِينَ شَقُواْ فَفِي ٱلنَّارِ لَهُمۡ فِيهَا زَفِيرٌ وَشَهِيقٌ ۝

they will abide as long as the heavens and the earth endure, unless your Lord wills it otherwise. Your Lord always does whatever He wills. (107)

خَٰلِدِينَ فِيهَا مَا دَامَتِ ٱلسَّمَٰوَٰتُ وَٱلۡأَرۡضُ إِلَّا مَا شَآءَ رَبُّكَ إِنَّ رَبَّكَ فَعَّالٌ لِّمَا يُرِيدُ ۝

And those who are blessed with happiness will be in Paradise, abiding there as long as the heavens and the earth endure, unless your Lord wills it otherwise: an unceasing gift. (108)

وَأَمَّا ٱلَّذِينَ سُعِدُواْ فَفِي ٱلۡجَنَّةِ خَٰلِدِينَ فِيهَا مَا دَامَتِ ٱلسَّمَٰوَٰتُ وَٱلۡأَرۡضُ إِلَّا مَا شَآءَ رَبُّكَ عَطَآءً غَيۡرَ مَجۡذُوذٍ ۝

So be not in doubt about anything which these people worship. They worship only as their fathers worshipped before them. We shall most certainly give them their full due, without any reduction. (109)

فَلَا تَكُ فِي مِرۡيَةٍ مِّمَّا يَعۡبُدُ هَٰٓؤُلَآءِ مَا يَعۡبُدُونَ إِلَّا كَمَا يَعۡبُدُ ءَابَآؤُهُم مِّن قَبۡلُ وَإِنَّا لَمُوَفُّوهُمۡ نَصِيبَهُمۡ غَيۡرَ مَنقُوصٍ ۝

Indeed, We gave the Scriptures to Moses, and there was strife over them. Had it not been for a decree that had already gone forth from your Lord, judgement would have been passed on them. Yet, they are in grave doubt concerning that. (110)

وَلَقَدْ ءَاتَيْنَا مُوسَى ٱلْكِتَـٰبَ فَٱخْتُلِفَ فِيهِ وَلَوْلَا كَلِمَةٌ سَبَقَتْ مِن رَّبِّكَ لَقُضِىَ بَيْنَهُمْ وَإِنَّهُمْ لَفِى شَكٍّ مِّنْهُ مُرِيبٍ ﴿١١٠﴾

To each and all your Lord will surely give their full due for whatever they may have done. He is indeed aware of all that they do. (111)

وَإِنَّ كُلًّا لَّمَّا لَيُوَفِّيَنَّهُمْ رَبُّكَ أَعْمَـٰلَهُمْ إِنَّهُۥ بِمَا يَعْمَلُونَ خَبِيرٌ ﴿١١١﴾

Follow, then, the right course as you are bidden, together with those who, with you, have turned to Him; and let none of you transgress. Surely, He sees all that you do. (112)

فَٱسْتَقِمْ كَمَا أُمِرْتَ وَمَن تَابَ مَعَكَ وَلَا تَطْغَوْاْ إِنَّهُۥ بِمَا تَعْمَلُونَ بَصِيرٌ ﴿١١٢﴾

Put no trust in those who do wrong, lest the fire touch you. You would, then, have none to protect you from God, nor would you find any help. (113)

وَلَا تَرْكَنُوٓاْ إِلَى ٱلَّذِينَ ظَلَمُواْ فَتَمَسَّكُمُ ٱلنَّارُ وَمَا لَكُم مِّن دُونِ ٱللَّهِ مِنْ أَوْلِيَآءَ ثُمَّ لَا تُنصَرُونَ ﴿١١٣﴾

Attend to your prayers at both ends of the day and in the early watches of the night. Surely, good deeds erase evil ones. This is a reminder for those who are thoughtful. (114)

وَأَقِمِ ٱلصَّلَوٰةَ طَرَفَىِ ٱلنَّهَارِ وَزُلَفًا مِّنَ ٱلَّيْلِ إِنَّ ٱلْحَسَنَـٰتِ يُذْهِبْنَ ٱلسَّيِّـَٔاتِ ذَٰلِكَ ذِكْرَىٰ لِلذَّٰكِرِينَ ﴿١١٤﴾

And be patient in adversity; God does not fail to reward those who do good. (115)

وَٱصْبِرْ فَإِنَّ ٱللَّهَ لَا يُضِيعُ أَجْرَ ٱلْمُحْسِنِينَ ﴿١١٥﴾

If only there had been among the generations that have gone before you some people of virtue to speak out against the spread of corruption on earth, as did the few whom We saved from among them! The wrongdoers pursued what ensured for them a life of comfort and plenty; they were hardened in sin. (116)

فَلَوْلَا كَانَ مِنَ ٱلْقُرُونِ مِن قَبْلِكُمْ أُوْلُواْ بَقِيَّةٍ يَنْهَوْنَ عَنِ ٱلْفَسَادِ فِى ٱلْأَرْضِ إِلَّا قَلِيلًا مِّمَّنْ أَنجَيْنَا مِنْهُمْ وَٱتَّبَعَ ٱلَّذِينَ ظَلَمُواْ مَآ أُتْرِفُواْ فِيهِ وَكَانُواْ مُجْرِمِينَ ﴿١١٦﴾

In truth, your Lord would have not destroyed those cities, without just cause, had their people been righteous. (117)

وَمَا كَانَ رَبُّكَ لِيُهْلِكَ ٱلْقُرَىٰ بِظُلْمٍ وَأَهْلُهَا مُصْلِحُونَ ﴿١١٧﴾

Had your Lord so willed, He would have made all mankind one single community. As it is, they continue to differ, (118)

وَلَوْ شَآءَ رَبُّكَ لَجَعَلَ ٱلنَّاسَ أُمَّةً وَٰحِدَةً وَلَا يَزَالُونَ مُخْتَلِفِينَ ﴿١١٨﴾

except those upon whom your Lord has bestowed His grace. And to this end He created them. The word of your Lord shall be fulfilled: 'I shall certainly fill hell with *jinn* and humans all.' (119)

إِلَّا مَن رَّحِمَ رَبُّكَ وَلِذَٰلِكَ خَلَقَهُمْ وَتَمَّتْ كَلِمَةُ رَبِّكَ لَأَمْلَأَنَّ جَهَنَّمَ مِنَ ٱلْجِنَّةِ وَٱلنَّاسِ أَجْمَعِينَ ﴿١١٩﴾

All that We relate to you of the histories of earlier messengers is a means by which We strengthen your heart. Through these [accounts] there has come to you the truth, as well as an admonition and a reminder for all believers. (120)

وَكُلّاً نَّقُصُّ عَلَيْكَ مِنْ أَنبَآءِ الرُّسُلِ مَا نُثَبِّتُ بِهِۦ فُؤَادَكَ وَجَآءَكَ فِى هَٰذِهِ الْحَقُّ وَمَوْعِظَةٌ وَذِكْرَىٰ لِلْمُؤْمِنِينَ ۝

Say to those who will not believe: 'Do whatever lies within your power, and so shall we. (121)

وَقُل لِّلَّذِينَ لَا يُؤْمِنُونَ اعْمَلُوا عَلَىٰ مَكَانَتِكُمْ إِنَّا عَٰمِلُونَ ۝

Wait if you will; we too are waiting.' (122)

وَانتَظِرُوٓا إِنَّا مُنتَظِرُونَ ۝

God alone knows whatever is hidden in the heavens and the earth. All authority over all matters belongs to Him alone. Worship Him, then, and place your trust in Him alone. Your Lord is not unaware of what you do. (123)

وَلِلَّهِ غَيْبُ السَّمَٰوَٰتِ وَالْأَرْضِ وَإِلَيْهِ يُرْجَعُ الْأَمْرُ كُلُّهُۥ فَاعْبُدْهُ وَتَوَكَّلْ عَلَيْهِ وَمَا رَبُّكَ بِغَٰفِلٍ عَمَّا تَعْمَلُونَ ۝

Preview

This is the concluding passage of the *sūrah*. Its discourse is closely related to what was said in the opening passage and to the historical accounts the *sūrah* provides. The first comment (Verses 100–102) directly relates to the historical accounts, and is followed by one which utilizes the punishment meted out to those early communities as a means of inspiring awe of punishment in the hereafter. This is given in a very awesome scene of the Day of Judgement, which is held out before our eyes. (Verses 103–108)

The following comment takes the fate of those earlier communities and the scene of the Day of Resurrection as its basis. It clarifies that those idolaters who opposed the Prophet Muḥammad put themselves in the same position as those communities with regard to their punishment in this world and the next. It is true that these would not be annihilated *in toto*, but this is due to a decree already made by God Almighty. Hence the punishment of the people of Moses has been deferred although they have disputed endlessly over their Scriptures. Yet both the people of Moses and the Arab idolaters will certainly be given their full reward. Hence, the Prophet and his followers are advised to remain steadfast, persevering with the implementation of what has been revealed to him. They must not incline towards the unbelievers who associate partners with God. They are to attend to their prayers and persevere, knowing that God will never allow the reward of the righteous to be wasted. (Verses 109–115)

The *sūrah* then refers once more to the earlier communities in which those who stood out against corruption were few in number. The large majority continued with their erring ways, thus earning their full punishment. God would never unjustly destroy the people of any community if they did good. (Verses 116–117)

The passage also explains why God has made people with different types of thought and action. He could certainly have made them all of one type, but His will has chosen to give human beings free choice. (Verses 118–119)

The *sūrah* concludes by stating that one reason for providing such historical accounts in the Qur'ān is to strengthen the Prophet's own attitude. The Prophet is instructed to say his final word to the unbelievers, leaving them to the fate they are certain to meet. In turn, he should place his trust in God, worshipping Him alone and let God's judgement be passed on all mankind. (Verses 120–123)

Summing up Past Lessons

These are some of the accounts of past communities which We relate to you. Some still remain while others are extinct, like a field mown-down. No wrong did We do to them, but it was they who wronged themselves. Those deities of theirs which they were keen to invoke instead of God availed them nothing when your Lord's judgement came to pass; they only added to their ruin. Such is your Lord's punishment whenever He takes to task any community which is bent on evil-doing; His punishment is indeed grievous, severe. (Verses 100–102)

So far, the *sūrah* has portrayed the suffering which overwhelmed various ancient nations: some were drowned in floods, some perished in a devastating storm, some by an awful cry, and some found the earth under their feet subside, opening up to swallow them and their dwellings. Then when all these scenes of destruction in this world are visible before our eyes, and when our hearts are deeply touched by what has been related of events and punishments, we have the final comment: *"These are some of the accounts of past communities which We relate to you."* (Verse 100) You, Prophet, had no knowledge of any of this. You came to know of them only through divine revelation. This is indeed one of the objectives of telling such stories in the Qur'ān.

"Some still remain." (Verse 100) Their ruins which still exist testify to the standard of civilization and strength that these communities attained. Of these the ruins of 'Ād at al-Aḥqāf and Thamūd at al-Ḥijr are the best examples. *"Others are extinct, like a field mown-down."* (Verse 100) They were wiped out, without a trace, as in the cases of the peoples of Noah and Lot. After all, what are people? And what is civilization? They are but fields of human beings, similar to agricultural fields. Some plants are good and pleasing, others are foul. Some acquire strength and spread, others wither and die.

"No wrong did We do to them, but it was they who wronged themselves." (Verse 101) They chose to be blind and to stifle their instincts and senses. They turned away from divine guidance, ignored God's signs and greeted His warnings with contempt. Hence, they brought on themselves the suffering they received, wronging themselves while no wrong was done them.

"Those deities of theirs which they were keen to invoke instead of God availed them nothing when your Lord's judgement came to pass; they only added to their ruin." (Verse 101) This verse states another objective behind relating such historical accounts in the Qur'ān. The *sūrah* opened with a warning to all those who submit to deities other than God.

The same warnings were repeated by every messenger and every prophet. They were told that these false deities could not protect them from God. Their destinies confirmed the earlier warnings. When God's judgement came to pass, none of their deities could avail them of anything. None was able to spare them any portion of the suffering which befell them. Indeed, their false gods could only add to their ruin. This because when they relied on false gods, they added venom and contempt to their opposition to God's messengers and His messages. Hence, their punishment was even more severe. This is the meaning of the expression: *"they only added."* Indeed, those deities could do them neither good nor harm. They were, however, the cause of their increased punishment.

"Such is your Lord's punishment whenever He takes to task any community which is bent on evil-doing." (Verse 102) It is only when a community indulges in evil that God takes it to task and brings about its destruction. Punished communities are always bent on evildoing.

They do evil when they ascribe a share of Godhead to anyone other than God. They are unjust to themselves when they spread corruption in the land and turn their backs on calls for upright behaviour and for acknowledgement that God is the only deity in the universe. In such communities, injustice spreads and tyrants rule.

"His punishment is indeed grievous, severe." (Verse 102) God leaves people to enjoy themselves for a while. He tests them and sends them messengers and clear signs. When, however, evil reigns supreme in a community, and the advocates of truth are only a minority unable to influence the majority, bent on evil-doing; when the small community of believers disassociate themselves from the rest of their people, who are persistent in error, and consider themselves to be a separate community with their own religion, leadership and loyalties; when they make all this plain to the rest of their people and leave them to their destiny, as determined by God, then God brings about His punishment of the evil-doers which is *"grievous, severe"*.

Grievous and severe as the punishment in this world is, it is only an indication of the suffering in the hereafter. This is only fully appreciated by those who dread such punishment. These are they who are farsighted enough to realize that the One who punishes evil-doing communities in this life will hold them answerable for their sins in the life to come.

Hence, they fear such future-life punishment, and do righteous deeds in this life to spare themselves.

At this point, the *sūrah* portrays scenes from the Day of Judgement, in the familiar Qur'ānic style which relates such scenes to scenes of this world with no gap evident between the two.

> *In this there is surely a sign for those who fear the suffering in the life to come. That is a day when all mankind shall be gathered together, and that is a day which will be witnessed [by all]. We shall not delay it beyond an appointed term. When that day comes, not a soul will speak except by His leave. Some among them will be wretched, and some happy. Those who will have brought wretchedness upon themselves, they will be in the fire where, moaning and sobbing, they will abide as long as the heavens and the earth endure, unless your Lord wills it otherwise. Your Lord always does whatever He wills. And those who are blessed with happiness will be in Paradise, abiding there as long as the heavens and the earth endure, unless your Lord wills it otherwise: an unceasing gift.* (Verses 103–108)

"*In this there is surely a sign for those who fear the suffering in the life to come.*" (Verse 103) The severe punishment meted out in this world bears some similarity to the suffering of the hereafter. Hence, it serves as a reminder of that future suffering. Such reminders, however, are appreciated only by those who fear the punishment in the hereafter. Their fear of God awakens their hearts and opens their eyes. On the other hand, those who are heedless of the hereafter do not respond to any sign. They are blind. They do not appreciate the purpose of creation and re-creation. They only see their immediate situation in this life. Indeed, they do not learn from the lessons presented in this life.

The *sūrah* then proceeds to describe the Day of Judgement: "*that is a day when all mankind shall be gathered together, and that is a day which will be witnessed [by all].*" (Verse 103) We have here a scene of all mankind being gathered together, leaving them no choice in the matter. They are led to the gathering place. All come forward, and everyone awaits the outcome.

"When that day comes, not a soul will speak except by His leave."
(Verse 105) A deadly silence continues without interruption. It is a
scene full of awe, which overwhelms all. No one dares ask permission
to speak. Permission, however, is given by God to whomever He
chooses. At this point people are divided into two groups: *"Some among
them will be wretched, and some happy."* (Verse 105)

As we read on we visualize the wretched in their misery in the fire,
where they moan, sigh and sob. The air there is too hot, too suffocating.
We also see *"those who are blessed with happiness"* in Paradise, where
they receive their reward which continues uninterrupted. Both groups
remain in their respective abodes *"as long as the heavens and the earth
endure."* This is an expression which imparts a feeling of permanence,
which is indeed the intended connotation here.

That continuity is qualified in both cases by God's choice. Indeed,
every situation and every law is subject to God's will. It is His will
which determines the law but is yet not subject to it. His is a free-will
which can change any law whenever He chooses: *"your Lord always
does whatever He wills."* (Verse 107)

In the case of the happy group, however, the *sūrah* reassures them
that it is God's will that their reward will not cease, even if it is ever
assumed that they would change abode and leave Paradise to go
somewhere else. Such an eventuality is only supposed here to emphasize
that God's will is completely free.

The Safe Path to Follow

Having spoken about the punishment of the hereafter, and its
similarities with what can be meted out in this life, the *sūrah* draws
some lessons for the Prophet and his few followers in Makkah,
reassuring them that they follow the truth. It also warns those who
deny God's message against what will befall them in the hereafter. It
firstly reassures the Prophet and tells him not to entertain any doubt
with regard to the fallacy of the religion the pagan Arabs were following.
Like earlier communities mentioned in the *sūrah*, those Arabs were
only worshipping what their forefathers before them had worshipped.
Hence, they will inevitably have their befitting requital. If such

punishment is deferred, as was the case with Moses' people, both will have their due reward at the right time.

> *So be not in doubt about anything which these people worship. They worship only as their fathers worshipped before them. We shall most certainly give them their full due, without any reduction. Indeed, We gave the Scriptures to Moses, and there was strife over them. Had it not been for a decree that had already gone forth from your Lord, judgement would have been passed on them. Yet, they are in grave doubt concerning that. To each and all your Lord will surely give their full due for whatever they may have done. He is indeed aware of all that they do.* (Verses 109–111)

You must not entertain any doubt about the falsehood those people followed. This address is made to the Prophet, but the warnings are given to his people. This approach is perhaps more effective because it implies that the whole matter is something explained objectively by God to His Prophet. There is no argument with anyone. Those who offer such false worship are not directly addressed because they do not deserve to be given attention. Thus, the objective truth, in the manner it is stated, may by itself arouse their interest more than if they were to be addressed directly. *"So be not in doubt about anything which these people worship. They worship only as their fathers worshipped before them."* (Verse 109) Hence, the same suffering awaits them. It is, however, implied here: *"We shall most certainly give them their full due."* (Verse 109) What is due to them is known from what befell other people before them. The *sūrah* has portrayed some examples of this.

It is possible that they may not be destroyed, just as Moses' people were not totally destroyed, despite the divisions and strife that arose between them over their faith and worship. *"Indeed, We gave the Scriptures to Moses, and there was strife over them."* (Verse 110) God has decreed that they will be held answerable for all their deeds on the Day of Judgement: *"Had it not been for a decree that had already gone forth from your Lord, judgement would have been passed on them."* (Verse 110)

There is a certain wisdom behind this decree. They were not totally destroyed because they had Scriptures. All those who received

Scriptures, through any Prophet, will not be punished until the Day of Judgement. The Scriptures are clear pointers to the right path, and succeeding generations can study them and follow them, just as the generation which was first addressed by them. This cannot apply to physical miracles which are witnessed only by those who are present at the time they happen. Those who witness such miracles either believe as a result of what they see and thus save themselves, or continue to reject the faith and are punished in consequence. Both the Torah and the Gospel are full books, available to succeeding generations, until the final Scriptures are given, confirming both the Torah and the Gospel, and replacing them as guidance for all mankind. All people will be questioned on the basis of this final revelation, including the followers of the Torah and the Gospel. *"Yet, they are"* – meaning Moses' people, *"in grave doubt concerning that."* (Verse 110) That is, concerning Moses' Scriptures which were not written until much later, when its reports suffered much confusion. Hence, its followers are not fully certain of it.

Since judgement has been deferred, everyone will receive the reward due for his actions, whether good or bad, from God, who is aware of all actions. *"To each and all your Lord will surely give their full due for whatever they may have done. He is indeed aware of all that they do."* (Verse 111) The Arabic expression employed here contains multiple emphasis, so that the delay of accountability and reward should not induce anyone to doubt their inevitability. Such varied emphasis also serves to assert that the beliefs of those people are totally false and that they are akin to the false beliefs of past communities.

Such strong emphasis was also necessary considering the tough phase the Islamic movement was going through at the time. The unbelievers had adopted an attitude of stubborn hostility to the Prophet and his few followers. Islam was making little headway in Makkah. Severe punishment was inflicted on the few believers, while the enemies of Islam went about their city completely secure. God's threatened punishment was delayed to its appointed time. It was, then, a critical period, when some people could not help being shaken. Indeed, even the strongest of believers can feel lonely and isolated. They need to be reassured. Nothing can reassure believers better than knowing that their enemies are God's enemies, and that they undoubtedly hold false beliefs. Again, believers are reassured when they realize God's wisdom in leaving the unbelievers alone for a while, and postponing their punishment to the day which will certainly overwhelm them.

Thus, we see how the Qur'ānic revelations set the necessary requirements for moving forward in advocating Islam. We also see how the Qur'ān sets landmarks for the Muslim community as they wage their fight against the enemies of Islam.

A Needed Reminder

The assurance is thus given that God's laws will not fail, whether they relate to His creation, the religion He has revealed, or to His promises and warnings. Believers and advocates of Islam must, therefore, follow it strictly without deviation or change. *"Follow, then, the right course as you are bidden, together with those who, with you, have turned to Him; and let none of you transgress. Surely, He sees all that you do. Put no trust in those who do wrong, lest the fire touch you. You would, then, have none to protect you from God, nor would you find any help. Attend to your prayers at both ends of the day and in the early watches of the night. Surely, good deeds erase evil ones. This is a reminder for those who are thoughtful. And be patient in adversity; God does not fail to reward those who do good."* (Verses 112–115)

These instructions are given to the Prophet and to those with him who have turned to God in repentance. *"Follow, then, the right course as you are bidden."* (Verse 112) The Prophet felt the power behind the order detailing these tasks and how awesome a responsibility it was. He is reported to have said: "This *sūrah*, Hūd, has made me grow grey." Here, he is commanded to follow the right path without any deviation. This requires him to always be alert, careful, watchful, and aware of his path. He was to be in full control of his feelings, for these can lead to deviation, major or otherwise.

It is worth noting here that this order to keep to the right course is followed by a negative injunction. The Prophet and his followers are not warned against complacency or slackening, but are warned against excess and transgression.

This is because the order to follow the right course may cause people to be over-alert and may lead to exaggeration, which, in turn, transforms this naturally easy religion into one that is difficult to follow. God wants the religion He has revealed to remain as it is. He wants the believers to follow the right path without exaggeration or excessive rigidity.

"*Surely, He sees all that you do.*" (Verse 112) The use of the verb 'see' is very apt here, where good and sound judgement are called into action.

"*Put no trust in those who do wrong, lest the fire touch you. You would, then, have none to protect you from God, nor would you find any help.*" (Verse 113) Do not incline towards or have any trust in tyrants who oppress and subjugate others by their sheer force, making them submit to false gods. If you trust them, or incline towards them, you are endorsing the great evil they practise, and you become party to it. Such deviation would bring about the punishment of hell and leave you without God's support or protection.

Following the right path during such times may be very hard. Indeed, believers may need to have something to comfort them. God, therefore, guides His Messenger and the believers to what gives them the greatest comfort: "*Attend to your prayers at both ends of the day and in the early watches of the night.*" (Verse 114) God knows that this is the source of comfort when every other source fails.

Prayers strengthen the believer's spirit, and sustain his heart and will to fulfil difficult duties. They also establish a bond between the hearts of afflicted believers and their merciful Lord, who is near and who responds to prayers. Prayers help to overcome loneliness and isolation in the face of a powerful, tyrannical society.

The verse here mentions the two ends of the day, meaning the morning and the evening, and some watches of the night. These times cover all the obligatory prayers, without specifying their number. The number and the exact timing are specified by the traditions of the Prophet.

The order to attend to prayers is followed by the statement that good does away with evil. This is a general statement which includes all good deeds. Prayer is one of the best deeds any person can do, hence it is one of the best actions for erasing sin and error. "*This is a reminder for those who are thoughtful.*" (Verse 114) Prayer is, in essence, a method of remembering God, and being thoughtful of Him. Hence, this comment is very apt here.

To follow the right course and to maintain it requires patience. Similarly, awaiting the time God has set for the fulfilment of His promises and warnings requires patience. Hence, these orders are followed by another one: *"And be patient in adversity; God does not fail to reward those who do good."* (Verse 115) To follow the right course is to do good; and to pray at the appointed times is to do good. Moreover, to be patient and to persevere against the unbelievers' schemes is to do good. God will certainly reward those who do good.

What Saves Erring Communities

As the *sūrah* draws to its end, it finishes its comment on the destruction of earlier communities which turned their backs on God's messengers. It says rather indirectly that had there been among them groups of good people who tried to earn for themselves a good position with God by speaking out loud against corruption and injustice, God would not have exterminated them as He did. God does not punish any community for its injustice if its people are righteous; that is, if the righteous among its people have enough power to resist injustice and corruption. There were in each of those lands only a handful of believers who had no influence on their community and wielded no power. God saved those believers, and destroyed the rest, including both the powerful, wealthy masters and their weak and poor followers who accepted their commands without question.

> *If only there had been among the generations that have gone before you some people of virtue to speak out against the spread of corruption on earth, as did the few whom We saved from among them! The wrongdoers pursued what ensured for them a life of comfort and plenty; they were hardened in sin. In truth, your Lord would have not destroyed those cities, without just cause, had their people been righteous.* (Verses 116–117)

This explains the divine law which applies to all nations and communities. If corruption, that is, any form of subjugating people to any authority other than that of God, spreads in any community, that community will not be destroyed by God, provided that a section of its people rises to stop such corruption. On the other hand, if injustice and corruption go unchecked, or if those who speak out against them have little influence on the continued spread of these evils, then the divine law operates against these communities and they are either destroyed immediately or by gradual weakening and imbalance.

Hence, those who call on their communities to submit to God alone, and work against all other forms of submission to other authorities provide a safety net for their nations and communities. In this light, we can appreciate the value of the struggle by the advocates of Islam who resist all forms of evil, injustice and corruption and who try to establish this religion, which is based on submission to God alone. By their struggle, they not only discharge their own responsibility towards God and towards their various nations, but they also ensure that their nations are spared God's immediate punishment which brings about their total destruction.

Why Let Differences Occur

Then follows a comment on the fact that people have different inclinations and follow different ways. "*Had your Lord so willed, He would have made all mankind one single community. As it is, they continue to differ, except those upon whom your Lord has bestowed His grace. And to this end He created them. The word of your Lord shall be fulfilled: 'I shall certainly fill hell with* jinn *and humans all.'*" (Verses 118–119)

God could have created all mankind in the same form and with the same aptitude. He could have made them copies of one original. This is, however, not the nature of the life God has chosen for this earth. He has willed to make man, to whom He has assigned the task of building the earth, a creature of varying inclinations and ways. It is God's will that man should have the freedom to choose his own line, views, and his own way of life and to be responsible for the choices he makes. It is also God's will that man should be rewarded for the choice he makes between good and evil. Whatever choice they make, people operate within the law God has set for His creation and according to His will that man should be able to choose freely.

It is, then, God's will that mankind are not made of a single community. Hence, they are bound to differ. Their differences go as far as the basics of faith. Only those who are able to stick to the truth, which is one, by definition, are spared such differences. They, however, differ with the rest of mankind who have lost sight of the truth.

"The word of your Lord shall be fulfilled: 'I shall certainly fill hell with jinn *and humans all.'"* (Verse 119) From this statement, we deduce that those who stick to the truth enjoy God's grace and have a different end. Heaven will be full of them, in the same way as hell will be full of those who preferred error to the truth.

The *sūrah* concludes with an address to the Prophet, explaining the reason behind relating to him such accounts of the histories of earlier communities. It is to strengthen his heart and to provide a reminder for all believers. To those who reject the faith, he should say his final word, indicating the parting of his way from theirs and leaving them to wait for whatever fate God decides for them: *"All that We relate to you of the histories of earlier messengers is a means by which We strengthen your heart. Through these [accounts] there has come to you the truth, as well as an admonition and a reminder for all believers. Say to those who will not believe: 'Do whatever lies within your power, and so shall we. Wait if you will; we too are waiting.' God alone knows whatever is hidden in the heavens and the earth. All authority over all matters belongs to Him alone. Worship Him, then, and place your trust in Him alone. Your Lord is not unaware of what you do."* (Verses 120–123)

It is clear from these verses that the Prophet faced so much trouble from his people and their rejection of his call, and had to shoulder such a heavy burden in conveying his message particularly in respect of the unbelievers' rejection of his call. Hence he needed to be comforted by God, despite his inexhaustible treasure of patience, perseverance and confidence in the truth.

"Through these [accounts] there has come to you the truth;" that is, in this *sūrah*. Whatever has been outlined in the *sūrah* of the nature of the Islamic faith and the histories of earlier prophets and messengers, and the operation of the divine laws, especially as they relate to the fulfilment of God's promises and warnings, is true beyond any shadow of a doubt. *"As well as an admonition and reminder for all believers."* (Verse 120) In such histories, the believers are warned against what

befell earlier nations. They are reminded of God's commandments and His laws.

However, those who are bent on rejecting the truth and do not believe can benefit nothing from such an admonition. There is only one attitude to take towards them, and that is a firm one indicating that there is no common ground between them and the believers. The Prophet is instructed to say to them what one of his prophet brothers, whose story is related in this *sūrah* said to his people before leaving them to their destiny: *"Say to those who will not believe: 'Do whatever lies within your power, and so shall we. Wait if you will; we too are waiting.'"* (Verses 121–122) What they are waiting for is known only to God:

"God alone knows whatever is hidden in the heavens and the earth. All authority over all matters belongs to Him alone." (Verse 123) Everything is in His hands, including the destiny of the Prophet, the believers and the unbelievers. All power and all authority belong to Him alone. He is, then, the One who deserves to be worshipped: *"Worship Him, then, and place your trust in Him alone."* (Verse 123) He is the protector of His obedient servants and He alone can give them victory. Moreover, He is aware of everything that every person does, whether good or bad. To each and all He gives their just rewards: *"Your Lord is not unaware of what you do."* (Verse 123)

Thus the *sūrah* concludes. It opened with the call to worship God alone, and to turn to Him in repentance, and concludes with the same message of submission. Worship God alone, seek His guidance and follow His instructions. In between, the *sūrah* dwelt at length on matters which relate to the universe, the human soul and the history of nations.

All, however, relate to one simple message. Thus the artistic co-ordination of the opening and the conclusion and the harmony between the stories related in the *sūrah* and the flow of its style, are coupled with the presence of an overall theme and a simple message which pervades the whole *sūrah*. We need only consider this to realize that the harmony which the Qur'ān exhibits is unparalleled. Had it been the word of someone other than God, this would not be a characteristic of the Qur'ān. Indeed, it would have suffered from a great deal of confusion.

The Central Theme

Looking at the *surah* in total, and indeed at the entire part of the Qur'ān revealed in the Makkan period, we find that it always reverts to the central theme of faith, outlining Islamic beliefs. Therefore, we need to reflect a little on how this central theme is addressed in the *surah*. We may need to repeat some of what we have already said so as to make these final comments more coherent.

The fundamental issue emphasized in the *surah* as a whole is the divine order to worship God alone, prohibiting the worship of anyone or anything else, making it clear that this is the sum of religion and faith. At the outset, the *surah* provides an outline of the Qur'ān, God's book revealed to Muḥammad, His last Messenger. This issue is addressed in this outline, while the historical accounts give a glimpse of the progress of faith in human history, and the final passage directs the Prophet on how to address the unbelievers. The *surah* also makes clear that all promises and warnings, reckoning, reward and punishment in the hereafter are all based on this basic principle.

We find that addressing all worship solely to God is expressed in two different ways:

1. *My people! Worship God alone; you have no deity other than Him.* (Verse 50)

2. *Worship none but God. I come to you from Him as a warner and a bearer of glad tidings.* (Verse 2)

It is clear that the two ways differ in the fact that one gives an order and the other states a prohibition. Do they, however, contain the same meaning? The first gives an order to worship God, making it clear that He is the only deity worthy of worship. The second prohibits the worship of anyone else. Needless to say, the second meaning is the correlate of the first, but the first verse states the first meaning in words leaving the second implied. Since this is the central issue, God in His wisdom determined not to leave the prohibition of worshipping other deities implicit. He wanted it stated separately, even though it is clearly implied in the first order. This gives us a clear sense of the seriousness Islam attaches to this issue.

The express statement of both aspects of this fundamental issue tells us that people need both to be categorically emphasized. It is not sufficient to state that there is no deity to be worshipped other than God, relying on the implicit correlate of prohibiting the worship of anyone or anything else. There have been times in human history when people did not deny God or abandon worshipping Him, but they also worshipped other beings beside Him. If this were to happen again, people would be guilty of idolatry, worshipping false deities alongside God while thinking they were Muslims who worship God alone. Hence, the Qur'ān states the concept of God's oneness as it should be manifested in peoples' lives, stating both the commandment and the prohibition so that each endorses and confirms the other, leaving no loophole for polytheism to manipulate. This dual emphasis is often repeated in the Qur'ān, in verses such as the following:

> Alif. Lām. Rā. *This is a book, with verses which have been perfected and distinctly spelled out, bestowed on you by One who is Wise, All-aware. Worship none but God. I come to you from Him as a warner and a bearer of glad tidings.* (Verses 1–2)

> *We sent forth Noah to his people: 'I have come to you with a plain warning. Worship none but God. I certainly fear that suffering should befall you on a grievous day.'* (Verses 25–26)

> *To 'Ād, We sent their brother Hūd. He said: 'My people! Worship God alone; you have no deity other than Him. You are indeed inventors of falsehood.'* (Verse 50)

> *God has said: 'Do not take [for worship] two deities, for He is but One God. Hence, of Me alone stand in awe.'* (16: 51)

> *Abraham was neither a Jew nor a Christian; but he was wholly devoted to God, having surrendered himself to Him. He was not of those who associate partners with God.* (3: 67)

> *I have turned my face with pure and complete devotion to Him who brought the heavens and the earth into being. I am not one of those who associate partners with God.* (6: 79)

There is then a consistent mode of expression throughout the Qur'ān. It is certainly significant in driving home the concept of God's oneness with both its aspects. It also shows God's prior knowledge that to preserve this concept free of confusion requires such repeated and lucid emphasis. God certainly knows His creation and what suits them. His knowledge is perfect and admits no defects.

The Concept of God's Worship

We need also to reflect on the term 'worship' and how it is used in this *sūrah*, and in the Qur'ān in general. This will give us an idea of what lies beyond this unequivocal statement ordering the worship of God alone and the prohibition of any gesture of worship to anyone else.

The *Fiqh* terms 'worship', denoting dealings between a person and God, and 'transactions', referring to people's dealings with one another, were not used in the very early period of Islam, when the Qur'ān was being revealed. Their use started later. We wrote elsewhere on the history of such usage as follows:

> The division of human activities into 'worship' and 'transactions' began sometime after scholars started to write books on Islamic law, or *Fiqh*. At the beginning, the division was typically academic in nature, but regrettably, it had some negative effects in people's minds. These were later to affect Islamic life in general. People started to think that the concept of worship applied only to the first type of activity addressed in its special section in books on Islamic law. Gradually, this concept was seen to have less and less to do with the aspect addressed in the section on 'transactions' in legal works. This represents a deviation from the holistic Islamic approach which is inevitably followed by a deviation in Islamic life in general.

> Under Islam, there is no human activity to which the concept of worship does not apply. The Islamic code of living aims to implement this concept in all aspects of life. All Islamic legislation, whether it relates to government, economy, criminal, civil and family law, or indeed any other aspect of life, has no objective other than the implementation of the concept of worship in human life. Human activity cannot be described in such terms,

so as to serve this objective which the Qur'ān describes as the aim of human existence, unless it is undertaken in accordance with the divine way of life. That is, to attribute Godhead to God alone and to address all worship to Him only. Otherwise, human activity would be in conflict with the aim of human existence, or in other words, be deviant from the divine faith.

When we consider the types of human activity *Fiqh* scholars describe as 'worship' in the light of the Qur'ān, we are bound to realize that they are not addressed separately from the other type of activity such scholars call 'transactions'. Indeed, both are interlinked in the Qur'ān and its directives. Both belong to the concept of worship which puts into effect the principle of man's servitude to the One God who has no partners.

As time passed, some people began to think that they could be Muslims when their worship activity was in accordance with Islamic rules, while their transactions were conducted according to some other system produced by some other deities which legislate for them without God's authority. But this is a great myth. Islam is a complete whole. Anyone who tries to divide it into two parts undermines its unity; or, to use a different expression, abandons Islam altogether.

This is a fundamental issue that needs to be carefully considered by every Muslim who wishes to implement the true meaning of Islam and serve the goal of human existence.[1]

We may add here what we have already stated in this volume:

The Arabs who were first addressed by the Qur'ān did not confine the import of the term *'abada* to mere worship rituals. Indeed, when the Arabs were first addressed by this term in Makkah, no worship rituals had then been assigned to them. They understood it to mean that they were required to submit themselves to God alone in all their life affairs and to renounce submission to anyone else. The Prophet defined 'worship' in one of his pronouncements

---

1. S. Quṭb, *Khaṣā'iṣ al-Taṣawwur al-Islāmī wa Muqawwimātuh*, Dār al-Shurūq, Cairo, pp. 129–130.

as meaning 'compliance,' not as offering worship rituals. He was answering 'Adī ibn Ḥātim's question about the Jews and the Christians and their treatment of their rabbis and monks as gods. He said: "Yes, indeed. They (meaning the rabbis and monks) made lawful to them what God has forbidden, and forbade them what God has made lawful, and they complied. This is how they worshipped them."

The term 'worship' has come to signify worship rituals since these are one form of showing submission to God. This form does not by any means, however, encompass the full meaning of 'worship'.[2]

Indeed, had the true essence of worship been the mere offering of worship rituals, it would not have warranted the sending of all God's messengers. It would not have warranted the great efforts exerted by those Prophets (peace be upon them all) and the hard suffering to which the advocates of Islam have been subjected throughout the ages. Saving mankind, however, from submission to creatures of all sorts and returning them to submission to God in all matters is indeed worth that heavy price.

The establishment of the oneness of God, the only God, Lord and Sustainer in the universe, and the only source of legislation in all matters, and the establishment of the only way of life acceptable to God are all aims which merit the sending of God's messengers. They also merit the exertion of great efforts by the messengers as well as the endurance of all the suffering the advocates of Islam have endured throughout history. This is not because God needs to achieve these aims: He is in need of nothing and no one. They are worthy aims simply because human life cannot be put right, reformed, elevated and become worthy of man without the establishment of the faith based on God's oneness.[3]

We need now to add some further elaboration to these final comments on the *sūrah*. We should first look at the impact the truth of God's oneness produces on man's existence, natural needs and

---

2. In this volume, Chapter 3, p. 260.
3. Ibid., p. 262

constitution; and how it influences his concept of life, which in turn influences his whole entity.

This holistic concept of life addresses people, their aspirations, needs and desires, setting them all to deal with One Being from whom everything may be requested and to whom all things are addressed. It is this One Being who is loved and feared; whose pleasure is sought and whose anger must be avoided, because He is the One who creates, owns and conducts everything.

At the same time, this concept refers mankind to a single source from which to derive all concepts, standards, values and laws. He is the One who has the right answer to every question that man may need to ask as he goes about his life.

Bearing all this in mind, man's whole entity is perfectly integrated, in feeling and action, faith and practice, ability and perception, life and death, health and sustenance, this present life and the life to come. This integration spares man much confusion that he would otherwise suffer.

When man is so integrated, he is in his best situation, which is a situation of unity. We should remember that unity applies to God, the Creator, and also applies to the universe despite its limitless aspects and situations, and to all living creatures with their endless variety and abilities. Unity also applies to the objective of human life, namely worship, in all its aspects and forms. This is certain to be the result whenever man searches for the truth in this world.

When man is in a position that perfectly fits with all aspects of the truth, he finds himself at the highest level of his own strength, and in full harmony with the world in which he lives, and with everything that he has a mutual impact on. This harmony allows man to play his best role in life and achieve maximum results for all his efforts.

When this truth achieved its fullness with the first Muslim community, it was able to play a great role with far-reaching effects on mankind and human history. When this happens again, as it inevitably will by God's leave, God will let it accomplish great results, no matter what impediments it may have to face. The very presence of this truth in its fullness initiates an irresistible force, because it is part of the universal power that works in harmony with the Creator's own power.

The importance of this truth is not merely to correct our concept of faith, which is an extremely important objective; it also adds to the proper and coherent appreciation of life. The value of human life is greatly enriched when it becomes, in totality, an aspect of worship, with every activity, major or minor, a part or a symbol of such worship. Needless to say, this is true only when we look at the implied significance in such activity, which is acknowledging God as the only deity to whom all worship should be addressed. This is the highest position to which man may aspire, and through which he achieves his ultimate perfection. It is the position which the Prophet achieved when he ascended to his highest rank, as a recipient of God's revelation, and when he went on his night journey: "*Blessed is He who from on high has bestowed upon His servant the standard by which to discern the true from the false.*" (25: 1) "*Limitless in His glory is He who transported His servant by night from the Sacred Mosque [in Makkah] to the Aqṣā Mosque [in Jerusalem] – the environs of which We have blessed – so that We might show him some of Our signs. Indeed He alone is the One who hears all and sees all.*"[4] (17: 1)

True Freedom

The unity of worship, in the sense of submission to God alone, has a profound impact on human life because it liberates people from submission to anyone else. Thus man ensures his true dignity and freedom which cannot be guaranteed under any system where people are subjugated by others, in one form or another. Such subjugation can be manifested in beliefs, rituals or laws, but their effects are the same, in the sense of submission to beings other than God.

People cannot live without self-surrender to one thing or another. Those who do not submit to God soon find themselves in the worst type of submission to others. They lose out to their desires which spiral out of control. Hence, they lose their very humanity: "*The unbelievers may enjoy their life in this world and eat like animals eat, but the fire is their ultimate abode.*" (47: 12) The greatest loss man can suffer is the

---

4. S. Quṭb, ibid., pp. 126–131.

loss of his own humanity. Moreover, they fall into different aspects of submission to other creatures, such as submission to rulers who always try to tighten their grip on power, pursuing their own self interest.

Submission to other creatures can also take subtle forms, which may even be more domineering and cruel than the political form. One example is submission to fashion houses. We ask: what power do these have over a very large section of humanity, which claims to be civilized? When a fashion deity prescribes a certain style in clothes, cars, buildings, parties, etc. people slavishly toe the line. No one even contemplates dissidence. If people submitted themselves to God in an even smaller measure than they do to fashion lords, they would be truly devout. How can submission be practically demonstrated if not in the form people follow with fashion? What is the meaning of Lordship and sovereignty if they are different from those exercised by fashion makers?

The poor woman who feels she must wear something too revealing, despite its being unsuitable for her figure, and wear make-up that leaves her subject to ridicule, simply cannot stand up to the lords of fashion with their immense power. What woman can resist such humiliation when she sees the whole of society around her toeing the line? If this is not submission to lordship, what is? Yet this is only one form of humiliating submission which people endure when they turn their backs on submission to God alone. Repugnant dictatorship is not limited to the political sphere and government.

How important is the unity of worship and submission to the preservation of people's lives, honour and property? All these become vulnerable when people submit to other human beings, whether in legal affairs, traditions or beliefs.

In the sphere of beliefs and concepts, submission to anyone other than God means falling prey to endless myths, legends and superstitions, examples of which are easily found in both pagan societies and popular myth. Pledges and sacrifices are often offered under such false beliefs. Such sacrifices may not be limited to money and property, but may also include the sacrifice of children. People live in fear of false deities, priests who claim to be in touch with deities, sorcerers who claim to have contact with the *jinn*, saints and holy men who claim to possess powerful secrets, etc. Under the influence of such fears, and similarly false hopes, people waste their talents and energy.

We have cited the example of fashion houses which human beings submit themselves to within a social context. However, we may also ask what the financial costs involved in such submission are.

An average family spends half its income on perfume, make-up, hairstyles, clothing, shoes and jewellery, etc. Similarly, an average family spends half its efforts on being up to date with such changing tastes. What is more is that most of the fashion houses are financed by Jews who make the greatest profits from the fashion industries. Men and women never stop meeting the demands of such submission, sacrificing in the process effort, money, honour and morality.

False idols are set up, such as the motherland, nation, race, class, production, etc. Their honour is celebrated in spectacular forms, and people are urged to come forward with their offerings. Anyone who shows a reluctance to so come forward is accused of treason and made to endure humiliation. If personal honour runs against the requirements of submission to such false deities, honour is slain and the media never tires of describing such a travesty in superlative terms of praise.

Islam makes *jihād* obligatory. Its purpose is to ensure that only God is worshipped by man, and that mankind liberates itself from submission to tyrants and idols. Thus, it is the means by which humanity rises to the sublime level God wants it to achieve. Undoubtedly *jihād* requires sacrifices, but those who submit to beings other than God have to make even greater sacrifices. People who refrain from *jihād* for fear of having to make sacrifices should reckon how much submission to others costs them in terms of their lives, children and money, in addition to sacrificing morality and honour. Never does *jihād* against all worldly forces equal the heavy cost of submission to others.

Loss Compounded

Dedicating worship and submission to God alone, to the exclusion of all else, pays great returns in directing all human efforts to the task of building and improving human life. Elsewhere in this volume we identified that anyone who sets himself up in a position of a deity demanding worship, i.e. complete obedience, needs to devote all national resources for his own protection, and also for establishing himself as a deity. He also needs to have a machinery and media to sing his praises, and to blow up his image to that of a superior person fit to be worshipped. These cannot stop their praises for a moment. On the contrary, they always try to make the masses share in such worship rituals. The reason being that whenever the great praise exercise slackens even a little, the tyrant's image reverts back to that of a small powerless creature. Hence, the exercise is constantly renewed to endorse his image once again. If a portion of such efforts and funds are dedicated to ensure real progress in human life, all people in society would share in its fruits. But such energy, funds, and at times life and honour, are not spent for human benefit as long as people do not submit to God alone.

Such losses are not incurred in only one particular system. They are common to all systems, even though situations differ and types of the sacrifice required also differ.

> What happened with those who rebelled against submission to God alone, allowing some of their numbers to rule over them implementing a law other than God's law, is that they ended up enduring the misery of submission to others. Such submission, however, squanders away their dignity and freedom, regardless of the type of government, even though they may think that some forms of government ensures such dignity and freedom.

> When Europe rebelled against a Church that tyrannized under the false guise of religion, it tried to run away from God. People in Europe thought that they could best preserve their freedom, dignity and humanity under democratic government. They pinned their hopes on the guarantees provided by democratic constitutions, parliamentary systems, a free press, judicial and legal checks, majority rule, and similar ideals. But what happened in practice? Capitalism managed to exercise tyrannical power reducing all checks and institutions into little more than slogans or myths. The great majority of the people became subservient to the powerful minority that owned the capital which enabled it to control the parliamentary majority, the constitution, the press and all other checks and balances that people imagined would guarantee their freedom and other rights.

Certain groups turned away from individualistic or democratic systems which usher in a tyranny of capital or class and established 'collective' systems. But what has this meant in practice? They simply replaced subservience to the capitalist class with subservience to the working class. Or we may say, they replaced subservience to capitalists and big companies with subservience to the state which controlled capital and enjoyed total power. This made the tyranny of the state an even worse tyranny.

In every situation or regime where some people are subservient to others, a heavy tax is paid to different deities, in cash and kind. Submission is inevitable. If it is not made to God, then it is made to others. When submission is purely to God, it sets people free, and preserves their dignity and honour. By contrast, submission to other beings destroys people's humanity, dignity, freedom and all their good qualities, wastes their money and ruins their material interests.

Hence, the central issue of Godhead and people's relation with Him is given such careful and detailed attention in all divine messages and Scriptures. This *sūrah* is an example of this care. The basic issue here is not concerned with the worship of statues in the ignorant societies of the ancient past; its concerns are man throughout all generations, and all forms of *jāhiliyyah*, past and present. Indeed, all *jāhiliyyah* systems are based on making people subservient to others.[5]

To sum up, what is clear in the Qur'ān is that the issue of submission, obedience and sovereignty, all of which are in this *sūrah* included under worship, is an issue of faith and belief, not one of a legal or political system. The question is whether faith and belief are truly established in human life or not. If it is, then we have the question of outlining a code for daily living which takes the form of a system of government, legal provisions and a community that implements them.

---

5. This is a quotation from the Prologue to *Sūrah* 10, Jonah, in the present volume, pp. 21–22.

Moreover, worship is not a question of rituals to be offered, but one of submission, obedience, a political system, a legal code, provisions and practicalities. Hence, it deserves all the attention it receives in the divine system represented by Islam. It deserves that all God's messengers were sent with their messages, as well as all the sacrifices that were made by the advocates of Islam.

Past and Present

We also need to have a brief look at the order of the historical accounts given in the *sūrah* and what this signifies in terms of the progress of the faith based on submission to God alone.

In our discussion of the history of the Prophet Noah, we made clear that the first religion known to humanity was the one based on submission to God alone, i.e. islam. It was the one preached by Adam, the father of the human race, then by Noah, its second father, and then by all God's messengers. In its broad sense, Islam means belief in God's absolute oneness, offering all worship to Him alone, and belief that He is the Lord whom people must obey and submit themselves to, which means that He is the Sovereign who has the sole authority to legislate for human life.

We also explained that deviation into *jāhiliyyah*, in either beliefs and worship rituals, or submission and obedience, or in all of these, was a subsequent development, after mankind had known the true faith of islam, as explained by God's messengers (peace be upon them all). Human beliefs, and human life generally became corrupted as a result of people's submission to deities other than God. Such submission, in any form, indicates deviation from the faith based on God's oneness.

The chronological order given in the *sūrah* clearly shows the fundamental flaw in the methodology of comparative religion, which has led to erroneous conclusions. The basic flaw in this methodology is that it traces the line of successive forms of *jāhiliyyah* in human history, and ignores the line of belief in God's oneness as preached by His messengers. Even as scholars of comparative religion trace their preferred line, they refer only to what is derived from the periods of *jāhiliyyah* in human society, which correspond to those highlighted in history. We should remember that historical studies record, merely on the basis of probability, only a tiny portion of human history. What is worse is that when such scholars find some heritage of the worship of the One God, as preached by divine messengers, surviving in a distorted form in an ancient *jāhiliyyah,* as in the case of Ekhnaton in ancient Egypt, they deliberately ignore its reference to God's messages. Ekhnaton ruled Egypt after the Prophet Joseph preached the message of God's oneness. An example of his preaching is related in the Qur'ān, in his discourse with his two fellow prisoners: "*I have left the faith of people who do not believe in God, and who deny the truth of the life to come. I follow the faith of my forefathers, Abraham, Isaac and Jacob. It is not for us to associate any partners with God. This is part of God's grace which He has bestowed on us and on all mankind, but most people do not give thanks. My two prison companions! Which is better: [to believe] in diverse lords, or to believe in God, the One who holds sway over all that exists? Those you worship instead of Him are nothing but names you and your fathers have invented, and for which God has given no sanction from on high. All judgement rests with God alone. He has ordained that you should worship none but Him. This is the true faith, but most people do not know it.*" (12: 37–40)

Comparative religion's approach and methodology is hostile to the religious approach. This is due to the historical hostility between the Church and scientific and academic research. Hence the methodology was devised in such a way as to ensure that its conclusions would undermine the Church and what it advocates. It is, thus, a discredited methodology because it sets its conclusions at the outset. Even when hostility to the Church weakened after its tyrannical grip on scientific research, politics and the economy was broken, the same methodology and approach continued because academics could not rid themselves of their founding principles. Flawed conclusions are inevitable when the methodology is basically flawed.

That said, we should be clear that whatever the approach, methodology and conclusions are, the outcome is basically at variance with what God has stated in the Qur'ān. If a non-Muslim researcher is free to accept conclusions that are clearly inconsistent with the Qur'ān, it is not permissible for a self-confessed Muslim researcher to do so. The Qur'ānic statements on Islam and *jāhiliyyah,* the fact that islam, in the broad sense, existed in human society long before *jāhiliyyah,* and also that belief in God's oneness was very much in people's minds long before polytheism and dualism are absolutely clear, admitting no ambiguity whatsoever. This comes under what is 'essentially known' of our faith. Anyone who wishes to adopt the conclusions of present-day research in comparative religion should make his choice: he either accepts God's statements or those of comparative religion's academics. In other words, he should choose between Islam and non-Islam, because God's word on this issue is clear and definitive; it is not implied or inferred.

Historical Progress

But this is not our main point of discussion here. We want to look at the line of progress pure faith took in human history. The faith of submission to God alone, i.e. islam in its broader sense, and *jāhiliyyah* compete for human minds. Satan tries to exploit man's weaknesses and nature as a creature with a dual susceptibility to good and evil. He tries to turn people away from the pure faith in order to sink them into *jāhiliyyah.* When people have sunk deep into *jāhiliyyah,* God sends a messenger to turn them back to the pure faith. The first thing he purges from their minds is submission to anyone other than God in any aspect of their life, not merely in worship rituals or beliefs. With this clear in our minds, we can understand humanity's situation today and determine the nature of Islamic advocacy.

Humanity as a whole reflects a return to the *jāhiliyyah* from which the Prophet Muḥammad saved it during his lifetime. This *jāhiliyyah* takes different forms. In some communities, it is reflected in the clear denial of God's very existence, which means that it pertains to faith and beliefs. The clearest example of this type is that of the Communists. In others, we see a confused recognition of God's existence and a clear deviation in worship rituals and in submission and obedience. This is the case of idol worshippers like the Hindus, and also the case of the Christians and Jews. In other communities we find a clear admission of God's existence and a proper performance of worship rituals, coupled with serious deviation in people's concept of the meaning of the declaration that there is no deity other than God and that Muḥammad is God's Messenger. There is also utter confusion about the question of submission and obedience. This is the type of *jāhiliyyah* practised by people who claim to be Muslims. They imagine that simply by pronouncing the basic declaration and offering acts of worship they have become Muslims entitled to all that is due to believers in Islam, despite their flawed understanding of the meaning of this declaration and their submission to other creatures. But all these are forms of *jāhiliyyah*, which means that they are either disbelief like the first type, or association of partners with Him like all others.

This view of present-day human reality confirms that another cycle has passed and that humanity is back in *jāhiliyyah*, which defines the basic role of the advocates of Islamic revival, their basic task in rescuing humanity and their starting point. These advocates must begin by calling on people to embrace Islam anew and to abandon the miserable state of *jāhiliyyah* into which they have sunk. They must also define the basic meaning of Islam, which is: belief that all Godhead belongs to God, offering all worship to Him alone, submitting themselves to Him and obeying Him in all their affairs. Unless all these elements are met, then people have not embraced the faith of Islam and cannot be considered Muslims, enjoying the rights and privileges which Islam guarantees for them, with regard to their lives and property. If any of these elements is breached, it is a breach of all of them, taking the person concerned out of Islam into *jāhiliyyah*, and branding him as unbeliever, or idolater, or both.

Humanity is today at a point when *jāhiliyyah* has the upper hand, and this can only be met with a turn to Islam, so as to return people to the worship of God alone. The issues must be absolutely clear in the minds of the advocates of Islam. Without such decisive clarity, they will fail to discharge their duty in this critical period of human history. They will vacillate when they confront *jāhiliyyah* society, thinking it to be Muslim. They will not be able to define their objectives, since they cannot define their starting point. They must start at the point where humanity actually is, not where it claims to be. The gulf between the reality and the claim is wide indeed.

Different Messengers, One Attitude

Every messenger was sent to his own community. At the start of his message, the messenger would be a member of his community, addressing them as a brother, desiring for them all the goodness a brother desires for his siblings. He wanted them to have all the goodness he had found in God's guidance, and for which he found clear evidence granted by his Lord. This was the attitude of every single messenger at the beginning; but it was not the same with any of them at the end.

A group from among every community responded to the message. They began to worship God alone. Thus, they surrendered themselves totally to God, forming together a community of believers, or a Muslim community, in the broader sense of the term. Another group rejected the message, denying its truth and continuing to submit to deities other than God. They remained in *jāhiliyyah*. Thus, they became a community of unbelievers.

This means that by their different attitudes towards God's messenger and his message, the same people became two communities: one Muslim and the other idolater. They were no longer one community, despite being of the same race and origin. Ties of race, land and common interests could no longer unite them and govern their relations. With the divine message a new bond came into being, uniting or dividing the same people. This is the bond of faith, with the type of submission it requires and the code of living it lays down.

What the advocates of Islamic revival today must clearly understand is that God never set the believers apart from the unbelievers until the believers themselves split away from the rest of their people. In so doing they declared their rejection of idolatry, submitted to God alone, and refused to obey any tyrannical authority. They also refused to participate in the social life of the community ruled by an authority implementing laws different from those of God.

God did not act to destroy the wrongdoers until the believers had separated themselves from them. This means that the believers must declare to the rest of their people that they are a community apart, with a distinctive faith, way of life and line of action. This is essential before God acts to fulfil His promise of granting victory to the believers and inflicting His punishment on the unbelievers.

It is particularly important that advocates of Islamic revival should understand this constant rule so as to plan their method of operation. The first step is to call on people to submit themselves to God alone, and to no one else. The same people will eventually split into two groups. The believers then separate themselves from the rest. When all this takes place, God's promise to grant victory to the believers becomes due for fulfilment, as consistently happened throughout history.

The period of advocacy and calling on people to believe may be prolonged before the separation occurs in practical terms. However, mental separation should start right at the beginning. Separating the two communities may be delayed, while one generation or more of believers provide sacrifices and endure hardship and torture. The believers must, nevertheless, remain convinced that God's promise is more true than the apparent reality. It will not fail to come at the appropriate time. God never fails to honour His promises.

Who Understands the Qur'ān?

These observations about the historical accounts given in the *sūrah* reveal to us the nature of the Islamic approach, as outlined in the Qur'ān. It is a practical approach in the face of human realities. These histories were related to the Prophet when he was in Makkah. The small number of believers were confined to their city, and the message practically besieged within it. The road ahead must have seemed to those believers to be long, arduous and without an end in sight. These histories showed them the end and outlined the different stages ahead. The Qur'ān thus took the believers by the hand, helped them on the road that had become a continuation of the march that started at the beginning of human history advocating the true faith of self-surrender to God alone. Thus, they no longer felt that their road was deserted. They felt themselves to be a new group in a continuous procession walking along a well charted road. They moved from the starting point to the finishing line according to a well defined plan.

Thus did the Qur'ān act with the Muslim community, moving it in safe and measured steps. Thus it can do today and in future with the advocates of Islamic revival, moving them along the same way. These advocates need the Qur'ān as a guiding light, marking its movement and outlining its stages.

When the Qur'ān plays this role, it is no longer treated as mere words recited for blessing. It comes alive as if it is being bestowed now from on high to guide the Muslim community which implements its directives and hopes for the fulfilment of God's promise which it clearly states.

This is what we mean when we say that this Qur'ān reveals its secrets only to the Muslim group which moves according to its guidance, to put its message into practice. It does not reveal these secrets to those who only read it for blessings, artistic or scientific study, or to appreciate its artistic beauty and fine style. None of these will truly appreciate much of the Qur'ān, because the Qur'ān was not bestowed from on high for such purposes. It was rather revealed to act as a practical guide providing directives for implementation.

Those who face up to *jāhiliyyah* with the message of Islam, and who endeavour to return erring humanity to the faith based on submission to God alone, and who strive against tyranny in order to liberate mankind from servitude to others, are the ones who truly understand the Qur'ān. They are the ones who live in an environment similar to that which prevailed when the Qur'ān was revealed. They make the same attempt made by those who were the first to be addressed by the Qur'ān. As they make their endeavours, they appreciate the meaning of its verses, because they see how such meaning applies to events and practical situations. This by itself is compensation for all the pain they have to endure and the sacrifice they have to make.

What am I saying? Is it compensation? Certainly not. It is a great blessing from God. "*Say: 'In God's bounty and grace, in this let them rejoice; for this is better than all that they may amass.'*" (10: 58)

All praise is due to God Almighty for His endless blessings.

334

Index

335